DATSUN

510, 610, 710
1968-1977
SHOP MANUAL

By
ALAN AHLSTRAND

ERIC JORGENSEN
Editor

JEFF ROBINSON
Publisher

CLYMER PUBLICATIONS

World's largest publisher of books
devoted exclusively to automobiles and motorcycles

12860 MUSCATINE STREET · P.O. BOX 20 · ARLETA, CALIFORNIA 91331

FIRST EDITION
Published June, 1972

SECOND EDITION
Revised by Alan Ahlstrand to cover 1973-1974 models
Published September, 1975

THIRD EDITION
Revised by Alan Ahlstrand to cover 1975-1976 models
Published January, 1978

FOURTH EDITION
Revised by Alan Ahlstrand to cover 1977 models
First Printing September, 1978
Second Printing June, 1979
Third Printing May, 1981
Fourth Printing August, 1982

Printed in U.S.A.

ISBN: 0-89287-281-0

•

COVER
Photos and illustrations courtesy of Nissan Motor Corporation in U.S.A.

CONTENTS

QUICK REFERENCE DATA

TUNE-UP SPECIFICATIONS

Valve Clearance	
Engine cold	
Intake	0.008 in. (0.20mm)
Exhaust	0.010 in. (0.25mm)
Engine hot	
Intake	0.010 in. (0.25mm)
Exhaust	0.012 in. (0.30mm)
Spark Plug Gap	
1968-1972	0.031-0.035 in. (0.8-0.9mm)
1973-1974	0.028-0.031 in. (0.7-0.8mm)
1975-1976 610	0.039-0.043 in. (1.0-1.1mm)
1975 and later 710	
Breaker point ignition	0.031-0.035 in. (0.8-0.9mm)
Breakerless ignition	0.039-0.043 in. (1.0-1.1mm)
Points Gap	0.018-0.022 in. (0.45-0.55mm)
Dwell Angle	49-55°
Reluctor Air Gap	0.008-0.016 in. (0.2-0.4mm)
Ignition Timing	
L16, 1968-1969	5° ATDC
L16, 1970-1971 (advanced)	10° BTDC
L16, 1970-1971 (retarded)	0°
L16, 1972 (advanced)	7° BTDC
L16, 1972 (retarded)	0°
L16, 1973 (advanced)	12° BTDC
L16, 1973 (retarded)	
Cars through chassis No. PL510-429350	5° BTDC
Cars from chassis No. PL510-429351	8° BTDC
Trucks through chassis No. PL620-141296	5° BTDC
Trucks from chassis No. PL620-141297	8° BTDC
L18, 1973 (advanced)	12° BTDC
L18, 1973 (retarded)	
Through chassis No. PL610-815989	5° BTDC
From chassis No. PL610-815990	8° BTDC
L18 and L20B, 1974-on	12° BTDC

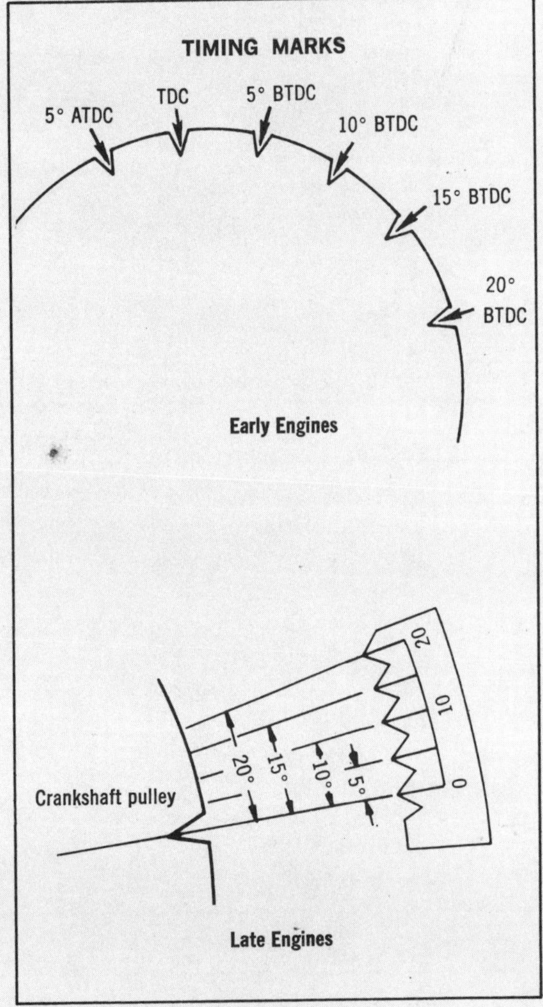

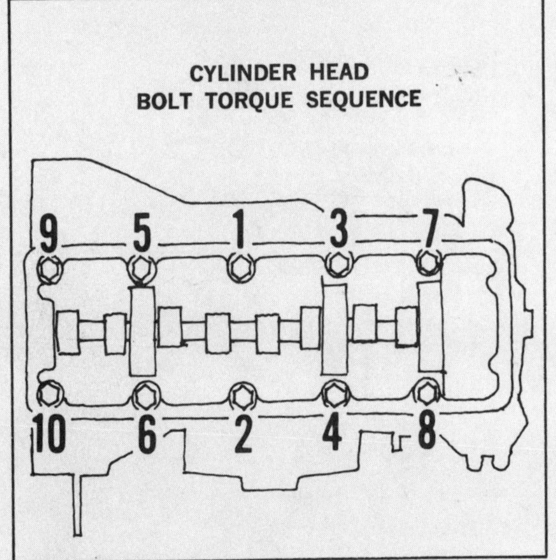

APPROXIMATE REFILL CAPACITY

Engine oil	
510 & 610; 1975 and later 710	
With filter change	4½ quarts
Without filter change	4 quarts
1974 710	
With filter change	4⅜ quarts
Without filter change	3⅞ quarts
Transmission oil (manual)	2⅛ quarts
Transmission fluid (automatic)	5⅞ quarts
Differential oil	
510, 610, independent rear suspension	1¾ pints
510, 710, rigid axle	2¾ pints
610, rigid axle	
1973-1975*	2¾ pints
1976	2⅛ pints

*2 pints for 1974 station wagon with automatic transmission.

LUBRICANT VISCOSITY

Engine oil, multiviscosity	
+32°F (0°C) and below	SAE 5W-30
−10°F (−23°C) and over	SAE 10W-30, 10W-40
+10°F (−12°C) and over	SAE 20W-40
Engine oil, single viscosity	
−10° to +32°F (−23° to 0°C)	SAE 10W
+10° to 60°F (−12° to +16°C)	SAE 10W-20
+32° to 90°F (0° to 32°C)	SAE 30
+60°F (+16°C) and over	SAE 40
Gear oil	
+86°F (30°C) and below	SAE 80
+32° to 104°F (0° to 40°C)	SAE 90
+50°F (10°C) and over	SAE 140

TIRE PRESSURES

Year	Model	Tire Size	Load	Pressure (psi) Front	Rear
1968-1973	510	5.60-13	Up to 600 lb.*	24	28
			600-750 lb.	28	32
1968-1973	510	165SR-13	All	28	28
1973-1974	610, 710	6.45-13	Up to 600 lb.*	24	28
			600-750 lb.	28	32
1973-1974	610, 710	165SR-13	All	28	28
1975 and later	610, 710	6.45-13	Up to 600 lb.**	26	28
			600-750 lb.	28	32
1975 and later	610, 710	165R-13	All	28	28***

*Add 4 psi for speeds over 70 mph
**Add 2 psi to front and 4 psi to rear for speeds over 70 mph
***Add 2 psi to rear for speeds over 70 mph

HEAD BOLT TORQUES

	Ft.-lb.	Mkg
Early L16 (through engine L16 203415)	43-51	5.9-7.0
Late L16 (from engine L16 203416), all L18, all L20B	47-61	6.5-8.5

DATSUN

SERVICE • REPAIR HANDBOOK

510, 610, AND 710 • 1968-1977

CHAPTER ONE

GENERAL INFORMATION

This manual provides tune-up, maintenance, and repair information for the following Datsuns:

510 (1968-1973)

610 (1973-1976)

710 (1974-1977)

Changes applying to 1977 Datsun 710's are covered in a supplement at the back of the book.

All models use 4-cylinder versions of the L-series engine, an inline, overhead cam design. A 4-speed manual transmission is standard on all models, with a 3-speed automatic optional.

The vehicle identification number is stamped on the firewall (**Figure 1**). The number is also stamped on a plate riveted to the instrument panel and visible from outside the car (**Figure 2**).

The body plate (**Figure 3**) is riveted to the firewall. The plate lists vehicle type, engine size, maximum horsepower, wheelbase, vehicle number, and engine number. The engine number on all models is also stamped on the right-hand side of the cylinder block.

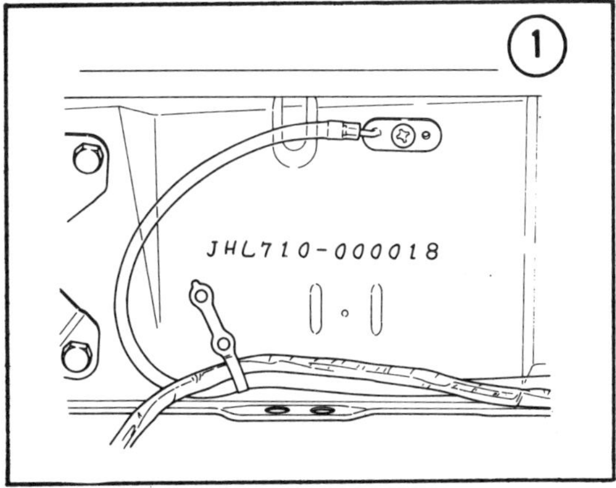

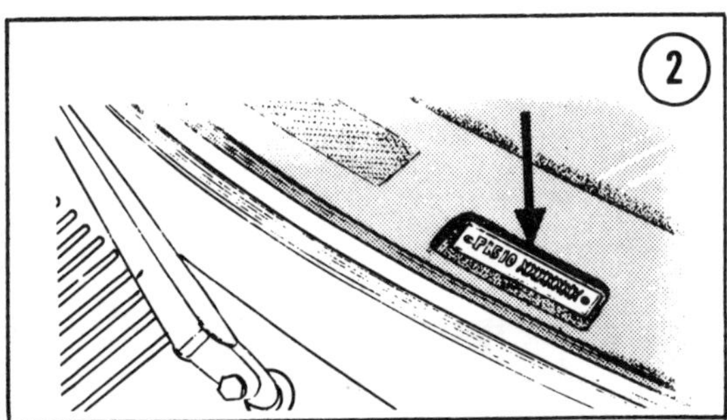

SERVICE HINTS

Observing the following practices will save time, effort, and frustration, as well as prevent possible injury.

1. Throughout this manual, with 2 exceptions, the word "front" refers to the front of the vehicle. The front end of any part is the end nearest the front of the vehicle when the part is installed.

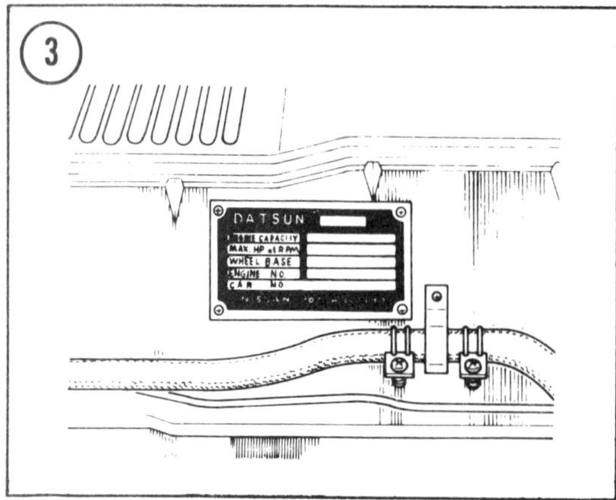

The 2 exceptions are the steering wheel and the instrument panel. The front of these 2 parts is the side which faces the driver.

2. The position of the driver also determines "left" and "right." For example, the steering wheel is on the left side.

3. When working under a vehicle, do not trust a hydraulic or mechanical jack to hold the vehicle up by itself. Always use jackstands. When raising a front end, position the stands as shown in **Figure 4**. On cars with independent rear suspension, position the stands beneath the areas indicated in **Figure 5**. On rigid-axle vehicles, place the jackstands beneath the axle housing (**Figure 6**).

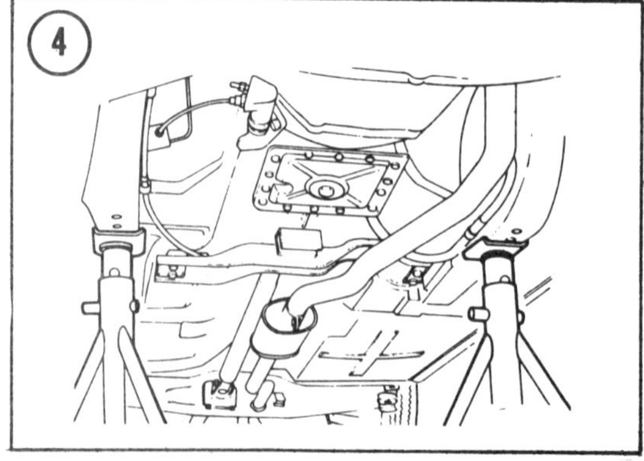

4. Disconnect the battery ground cable before working near electrical connections and before disconnecting wires.

5. Avoid flames or sparks when working near a charging battery or flammable liquids such as gasoline.

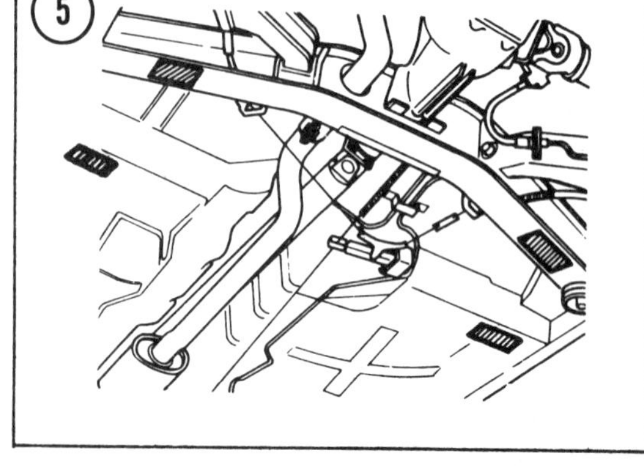

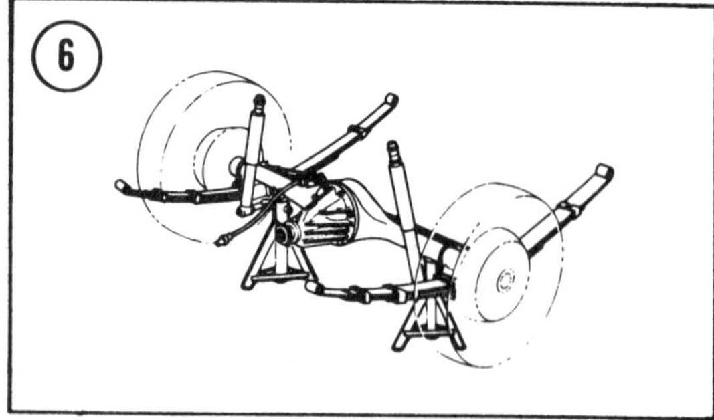

6. Tag all similar internal parts for location, and mark all mating parts for position. Record number and thickness of any shims as they are removed. Small parts such as bolts can be identified by placing them in plastic sandwich bags, sealed and labeled with masking tape.

7. Protect finished surfaces from physical damage or corrosion. Keep gasoline and brake fluid off painted surfaces.

8. Frozen or very tight bolts and screws can often be loosened by soaking with penetrating oil, then striking the bolt head a few times with a hammer and punch (or screwdriver for screws). Heat is to be avoided unless absolutely necessary, since it may melt, warp, or remove the temper from many parts.

9. No parts, except those assembled with a press fit, require unusual force during assembly. If a part is hard to remove or install, find out why before proceeding.

10. Cover all openings after removing parts to keep dirt, small tools, etc., from falling in.

11. When assembling 2 parts, start all fasteners, then tighten them evenly.

12. When buying replacement parts, always take the old part to the parts store, if possible, for comparison to the new part.

13. Dimensions and capacities are expressed in inch units familiar to U.S. mechanics, as well as in metric units. *Metric tools are required* to work on Datsuns.

MANUAL ORGANIZATION

This chapter provides general information for the models covered by this book.

Chapter Two explains all periodic lubrication and routine maintenance necessary to keep your Datsun running well. Chapter Two also includes recommended tune-up procedures, eliminating the need constantly to consult chapters on the various subassemblies.

Chapter Three provides methods and suggestions for quick and accurate diagnosis and repair of problems. Troubleshooting procedures discuss typical symptoms and logical methods to pinpoint the trouble. It also describes equipment useful for both preventive maintenance and troubleshooting.

Subsequent chapters describe specific symptoms such as the engine, transmission, and electrical system. Each chapter provides disassembly, repair, and assembly procedures in simple step-by-step form. If a repair is impractical for the home mechanic, it is so indicated. It is usually faster and less expensive to take such repairs to a Datsun dealer or other competent repair shop.

Some of the procedures in this manual call for special tools. In all such cases, the tool is illustrated, either in actual use or alone. These tools are available from Datsun dealers on a special order basis. A well-equipped mechanic may find he can substitute other similar tools already on hand, or can fabricate his own. Also, when a procedure requires a special tool, a great deal of time and expense can be saved by having a dealer or repair shop perform only the step which requires the special tool, but doing the rest of the work yourself.

The terms NOTE, CAUTION, and WARNING have specific meanings in this book. A NOTE provides additional information to make a step or procedure easier or clearer. Disregarding a NOTE could cause inconvenience, but would not cause damage or personal injury.

A CAUTION emphasizes areas where equipment damage could occur. Disregarding a CAUTION could cause permanent mechanical damage; however, personal injury is unlikely.

A WARNING emphasizes areas where personal injury or even death could result from negligence. Mechanical damage could also occur. WARNINGS are to be taken seriously. In some cases serious injury or death has been caused by mechanics disregarding similar warnings.

CHAPTER TWO

LUBRICATION, MAINTENANCE, AND TUNE-UP

This chapter deals with the normal maintenance necessary to keep your Datsun running properly. It includes summaries of service intervals in table form (**Tables 1, 2, 3, and 4**). All items in Tables 2, 3, and 4 are numbered to correspond with the number in the boldface headings under *Periodic Checks and Maintenance.*

Table 1 FUEL STOP CHECKS

Item	Procedure
Engine oil	Check level
Coolant	Check level
Battery electrolyte	Check level
Windshield washers	Check container level
Brake fluid	Check level
Clutch fluid	Check level
Tire pressures	Check

ROUTINE CHECKS

The following checks should be done at each stop for gas.

1. Check engine oil level (**Figure 1**). Top up to "H" mark on dipstick if necessary, using a grade recommended in **Tables 5 and 6**.
2. Check coolant level (**Figure 2**). It should be one inch below the filler cap.

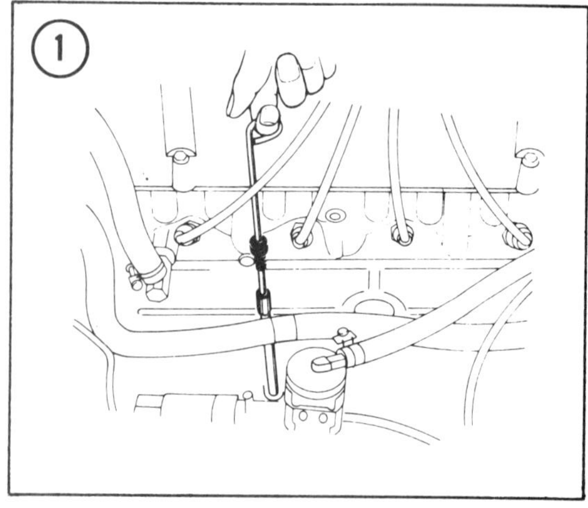

WARNING

Do not remove the radiator cap quickly when the engine is hot. Cover the cap with a rag and turn it ¼ turn counterclockwise. After cooling system pressure has been released, press the cap down, turn counterclockwise, and remove.

3. Remove the battery filler caps and check electrolyte level (**Figure 3**). It should be approximately ¼ in. above the plates inside the battery. If low, top up with distilled water. Do not overfill.
4. Check the level of the windshield washer container. It should be kept full.

Table 2 SCHEDULED MAINTENANCE, 1968-1973

Paragraph in Text	Service	Months or Thousands of Miles 3	6	12	24	30	36
1	Engine oil	X					
2	Manual transmission oil	X					
3	Automatic transmission fluid	X					
4	Differential oil	X					
5	Hydraulic systems	X					
6	Fuel lines	X					
7	Spark plugs	X		X			
8	Distributor points	X		X			
9	Ignition timing	X					
10	Carburetor	X					
11	Valve clearances		X				
12	Engine leak inspection		X				
13	Drive belts		X				
14	Throttle linkage		X				
15	Automatic choke		X				
16	Steering linkage, suspension		X				
17	Hinges, latches, locks		X				
18	PCV system			X			
20	Evaporative emission control system			X			
21	Cooling system			X			
22	Vacuum lines			X			
23	ATC air cleaner			X			
24	Fuel filter			X			
25	Spark timing control system			X			
26	Boost controlled deceleration device			X			
27	Brake fluid			X			
28	Brake booster (power brakes)			X	X		
29	Battery			X			
30	Brake inspection	X		X			
31	Shock absorbers			X			
32	Drive shaft			X			
33	Wheel alignment			X			
34	Pedals			X			
35	Engine compression				X		
36	Coolant				X		
37	Air cleaner element				X		
38	Air injection system				X		
39	Proportioning valve				X		
40	Steering linkage, suspension ball-joints					X	
41	Wheel bearings					X	
42	Manual transmission						X
43	Differential						X
44	Rear axle shafts (IRS)						X
45	Headlights						X
46	Drive shaft						X
47	Tune-up			X			

Table 3 SCHEDULED MAINTENANCE, 1974

Paragraph in Text	Service	Months or Thousands of Miles 4	8	12	24	36
1	Engine oil	X				
2	Manual transmission oil	X				
3	Automatic transmission fluid	X				
4	Differential oil	X				
5	Hydraulic systems	X				
6	Fuel lines	X				
7	Spark plugs			X		
8	Distributor points			X		
11	Valve clearances			X		
12	Engine leak inspection	X				
13	Drive belts			X		
14	Throttle linkage		X			
15	Automatic choke			X		
16	Steering gear	X				
17	Hinges, latches, locks		X			
18	PCV system			X		
19	EGR system			X		
20	Evaporative emission control system			X		
21	Cooling system			X		
22	Vacuum lines			X		
23	ATC air cleaner			X		
24	Fuel filter				X	
25	Spark timing control system			X		
26	Boost controlled deceleration device			X		
27	Brake fluid			X		
28	Brake booster			X		
29	Battery		X			
30	Brake inspection	X		X		
31	Shock absorbers			X		
32	Drive shaft			X		
33	Wheel alignment		X			
34	Pedals			X		
35	Engine compression			X		
36	Coolant				X	
37	Air cleaner element				X	
38	Air injection system				X	
39	Proportioning valve				X	
40	Steering linkage, suspension ball-joints				X	
41	Wheel bearings				X	
42	Manual transmission					X
43	Differential					X
44	Rear axle shafts (IRS)					X
45	Drive shaft					X
46	Headlights					X
47	Tune-up			X		

Table 4 SCHEDULED MAINTENANCE, 1975-76

Paragraph in Text	Service	Thousands of Miles (Months) 6.25 (6)	12.5 (12)	25 (24)
1	Engine oil	X		
2	Manual transmission oil	X		
3	Automatic transmission fluid	X		
4	Differential oil	X		
5	Hydraulic systems	X		
6	Fuel lines			X
13	Drive belts		X	
15	Automatic choke		X	
16	Steering gear		X	
17	Hinges, latches, locks	X		
18	PCV system			X
19	EGR system		X	
20	Evaporative emission control system		X	
21	Cooling system		X	
22	Vacuum lines		X	
23	ATC air cleaner		X	
24	Fuel filter			X
25	Spark timing control system			X
26	Boost controlled deceleration device		X	
27	Brake fluid		X	
28	Brake booster	X	X	
30	Brake inspection	X	X	
33	Wheel alignment		X	
36	Coolant		X	
37	Air cleaner element		X	
39	Proportioning valve	X		
40	Steering linkage, suspension ball-joints			X
41	Wheel bearings			X
42	Manual transmission			X
43	Differential			X
47	Tune-up		X	

Table 5 LUBRICANT VISCOSITY

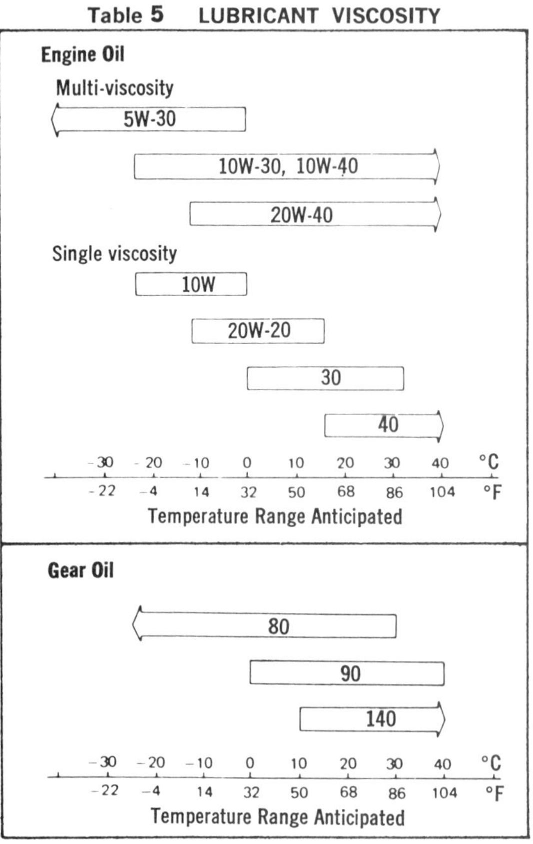

Table 6 RECOMMENDED LUBRICANTS

Engine	API Service SD or SE
Manual transmission	API GL-4
Automatic transmission	Dexron
Differential	API GL-5
Brake and clutch fluid	DOT 3

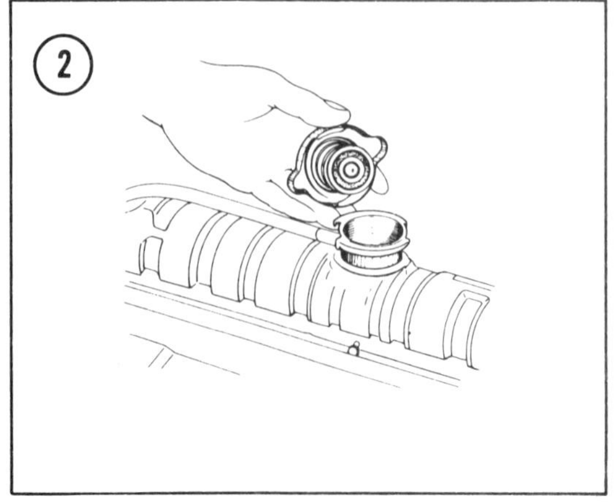

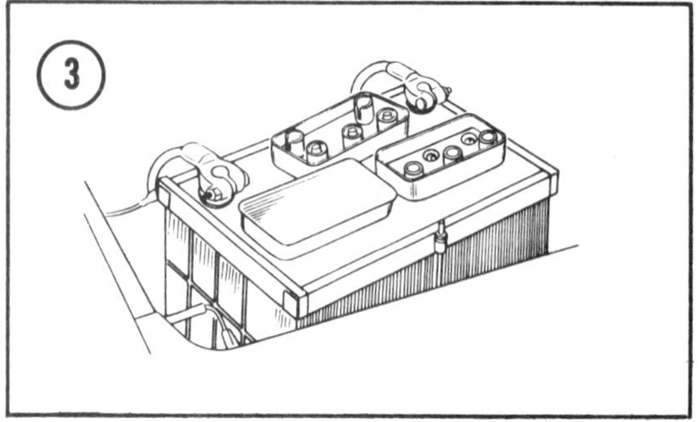

CAUTION

Do not use radiator anti-freeze in the windshield washer container. The run-off may damage the vehicle's paint.

5. Check fluid level in the brake and clutch master cylinders (**Figure 4**). Since the reservoirs are translucent, this can be done at a glance. Fluid should be between the lines on the reservoirs. If low, top up with brake fluid marked DOT 3. The same fluid is used for clutch and for the brakes.

CAUTION

Do not remove reservoir caps unless topping up fluid. Clean the area around the caps before removing.

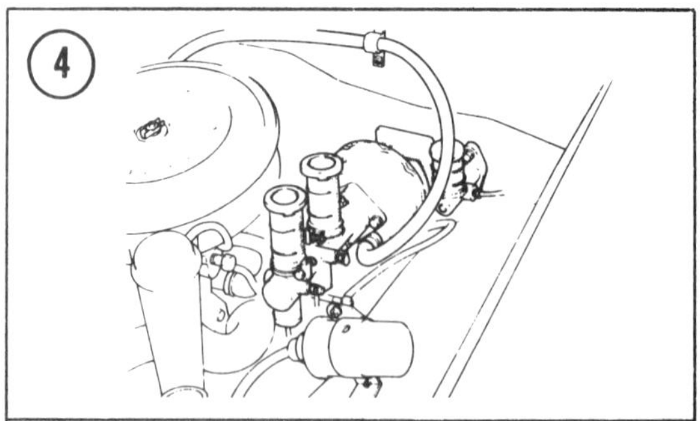

6. Check tire pressures. This should be done when the tires are cold. Recommended pressures are listed in **Table 7**.

PERIODIC CHECKS AND MAINTENANCE

The following procedures are done at specified intervals of miles or time. The service schedule for 1968-73 autos is based on intervals of 3,000 miles or 3 months. The schedule

2

Table 7 TIRE PRESSURES

Vehicle	Front (psi)	Rear (psi)
1968-1973 510, 5.60-13 tires		
Up to 600 lb. load*	24	28
600-750 lb. load	28	32
1968-1974 510, 610, 710, 165SR-13 tires	28	28
1973-1974 610 and 710, 6.45-13 tires		
Up to 600 lb. load*	24	28
600-750 lb. load	28	32
1975 and later 610 and 710, 6.45-13 tires		
Up to 600 lb. load**	26	28
600-750 lb. load	28	32
1975 and later 610 and 710, 165R-13 tires***	28	28

*Add 4 psi for speeds over 70 mph.
**Add 2 psi to front and 4 psi to rear for speeds over 70 mph.
***Add 2 psi to rear for speeds over 70 mph.

Table 8 APPROXIMATE REFILL CAPACITIES

Engine Oil	
510, 610, 1975 and later 710	
With filter change	4½ quarts
Without filter change	4 quarts
1974 710	
With filter change	4⅜ quarts
Without filter change	3⅞ quarts
Transmission Oil (Manual)	2⅛ quarts
Transmission Fluid (Automatic)	5⅞ quarts
Differential Oil	
510, 610, independent rear suspension	1¾ pints
510, 710, rigid axle	2¾ pints
610, rigid axle	
1973-75*	2¾ pints
1976	2⅛ pints

*2 pints for 1974 station wagon with automatic transmission.

for 1974 autos is based on intervals of 4,000 miles or 4 months. The 1975-1976 schedule is based on intervals of 6,250 miles or 6 months.

These service schedules are intended for cars given normal use. More frequent service is required under the following conditions:

a. Stop-and-go driving

b. Constant high-speed driving

c. Severe dust

d. Rough or salted roads

e. Very hot, very cold, or rainy weather

Some maintenance procedures are included in the *Tune-up* section at the end of the chapter, and detailed instructions will be found there. Other steps are explained in various chapters. Chapter references are included with these steps.

1. Engine Oil

Use an oil recommended in Tables 5 and 6. To drain the oil, first drive the vehicle until the engine warms up. This allows oil to drain freely.

Place a container under the oil pan and remove the drain plug. Let the oil drain completely (10-15 minutes). Then check the drain plug gasket and reinstall the plug.

Remove the filler cap on the valve rocker cover and fill with the recommended oil. Capacity is listed in **Table 8**.

Wait several minutes after filling, then check the dipstick to be sure oil level is correct. Oil used must be rated "For API Service SD or SE."

On 1968-74 cars, the oil filter is replaced at alternate oil changes. On 1975-76 models, the filter is replaced at each oil change.

To remove the old filter, unscrew it by hand or use a filter wrench (**Figure 5**). Clean the gasket contact point on the engine with a lint-free cloth. Coat the gasket on the new filter with clean oil and screw it in until it stops. Tighten ⅓ turn further by hand. Do not overtighten. Do not use a filter wrench.

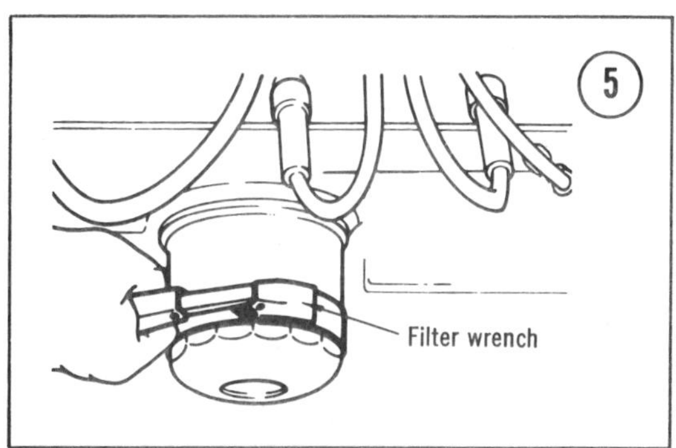

2. Manual Transmission Oil Level

To check, remove the filler plug from the right-hand side of the transmission. Make sure the oil level is within ¼ in. of the bottom of the filter plug threads. Top up with an oil recommended in Tables 5 and 6 if it is low.

3. Automatic Transmission Fluid Level

Check fluid level as described in *Automatic Transmission Checking* procedures, Chapter Nine.

4. Differential Oil Level

To check, remove the filler plug from the back of the differential (independent rear suspension) or from the axle housing (rigid axle). Oil level should be within ¼ in. of the bottom of the filler plug threads. If necessary, top up with an oil recommended in Tables 5 and 6.

5. Hydraulic Systems

Check for leaks. Inspect the brake master cylinder, calipers (disc brakes), and wheel cylinders for wetness. Do the same for the clutch master and operating cylinders, and for all hydraulic line connections.

6. Fuel Lines

Inspect the fuel lines. Start at the gas tank and work forward, checking all connections for wetness. Make sure the lines are securely in their clips.

7. Spark Plugs

Remove the plugs and compare their condition to **Figure 6**. Clean the plugs. File both electrodes flat. A rounded electrode increases the amount of voltage necessary to fire the plug. Regap the plugs to specifications (**Table 9**, end of chapter) if necessary.

8. Distributor Points

Clean the points using fine emery paper or a file made for the purpose. Do not attempt to remove all roughness while cleaning. Check the point gap as described in the *Tune-up* section, and adjust if needed.

9. Ignition Timing

Check the timing and adjust if needed, following the procedure outline in the *Tune-up* section.

10. Carburetor

Check idle speed and fuel mixture as described in the *Tune-up* section.

11. Valve Clearance Adjustment

The recommended service intervals are 6,000 miles (1968-73) or 12,000 miles (1974). On 1974 vehicles, more frequent adjustment may be necessary if the valves are noisy or the idle becomes rough. Valve adjustment procedures are described in the *Tune-up* section of this chapter.

12. Engine Inspection

The engine should be checked visually for leaks. Check the oil pan drain plug, oil pan gasket, oil filter, front cover, and oil pump. Greasy looking dirt at these points may indicate an oil leak. Inspect the radiator and hose connections for coolant residue or rust. Check the fuel connections (fuel filter, fuel pump, carburetor) for wetness that may indicate gasoline leakage.

13. Drive Belts

Figure 7 shows the drive belts used on a car with air conditioning and an air injection system. Cars without this equipment use only the alternator belt. Measure tension by pressing down on the belt halfway between pulleys. Apply about 22 lb. (10 kg) pressure. Play between the water pump and alternator pulleys should be about ½ in. Play between the idler pulley and compressor clutch should be ¼-⅓ in. Play between the air pump pulley and compressor clutch should be about ½ in.

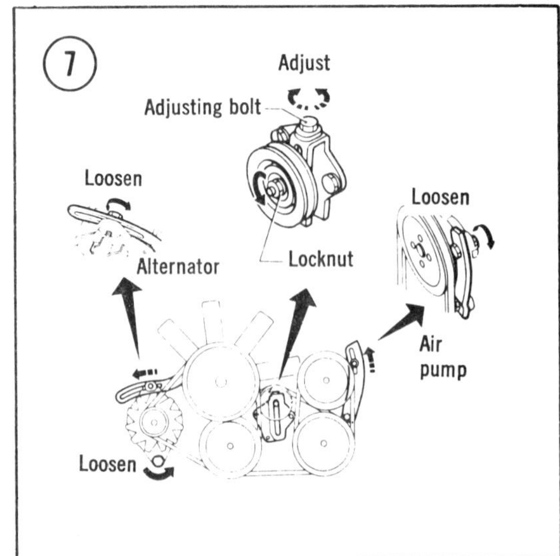

14. Throttle Linkage

All models use a rod and bellcrank throttle linkage. Check for binding and lubricate as needed.

SPARK PLUG CONDITION

6

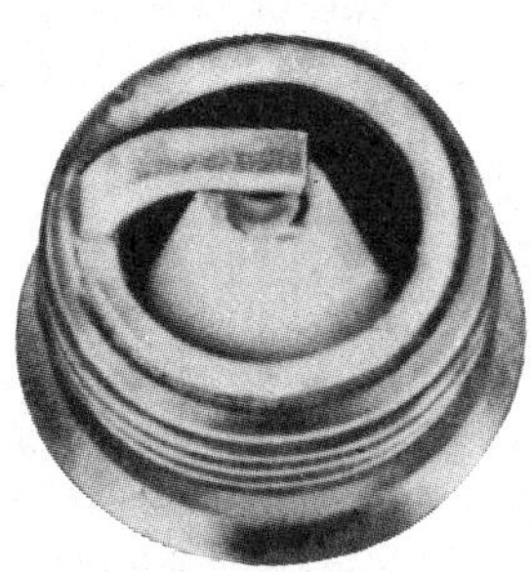

NORMAL

• Identified by light tan or gray deposits on the firing tip.
• Can be cleaned.

GAP BRIDGED

• Identified by deposit buildup closing gap between electrodes.
• Caused by oil or carbon fouling. If deposits are not excessive, the plug can be cleaned.

OIL FOULED

• Identified by wet black deposits on the insulator shell bore electrodes.
• Caused by excessive oil entering combustion chamber through worn rings and pistons, excessive clearance between valve guides and stems, or worn or loose bearings. Can be cleaned. If engine is not repaired, use a hotter plug.

CARBON FOULED

• Identified by black, dry fluffy carbon deposits on insulator tips, exposed shell surfaces and electrodes.
• Caused by too cold a plug, weak ignition, dirty air cleaner, defective fuel pump, too rich a fuel mixture, improperly operating heat riser, or excessive idling. Can be cleaned.

LEAD FOULED

• Identified by dark gray, black, yellow, or tan deposits or a fused glazed coating on the insulator tip.
• Caused by highly leaded gasoline. Can be cleaned.

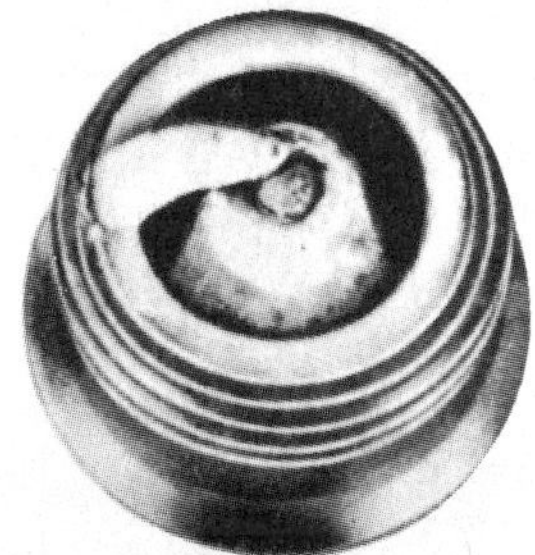

WORN

• Identified by severely eroded or worn electrodes.
• Caused by normal wear. Should be replaced.

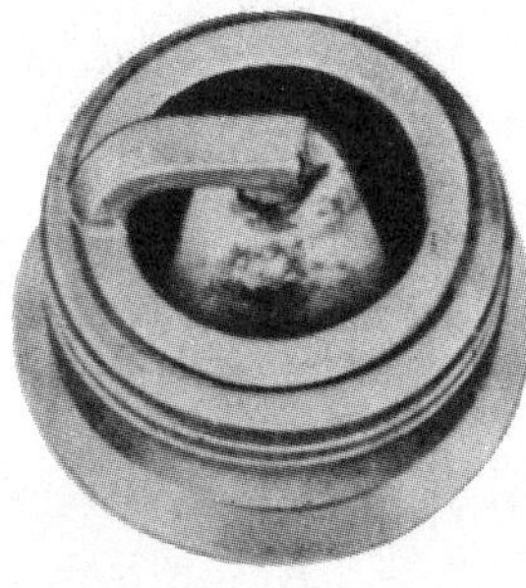

FUSED SPOT DEPOSIT

• Identified by melted or spotty deposits resembling bubbles or blisters.
• Caused by sudden acceleration. Can be cleaned.

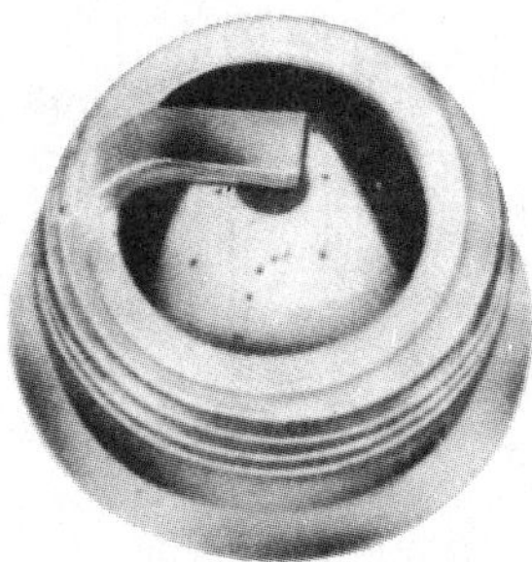

OVERHEATING

• Identified by a white or light gray insulator with small black or gray brown spots and with bluish-burnt appearance of electrodes.
• Caused by engine overheating, wrong type of fuel, loose spark plugs, too hot a plug, low fuel pump pressure, or incorrect ignition timing. Replace the plug.

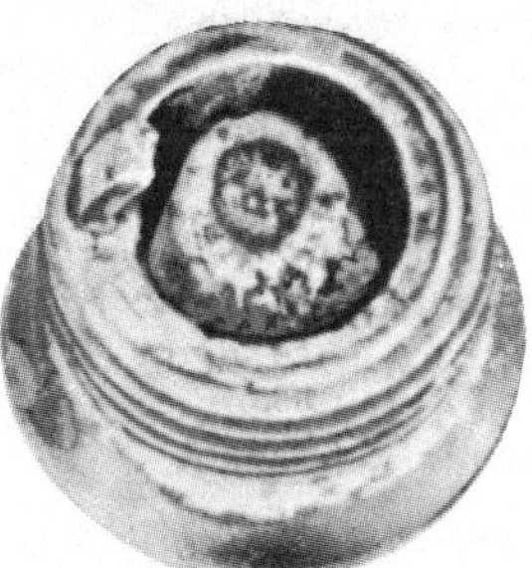

PREIGNITION

• Identified by melted electrodes and possibly blistered insulator. Metallic deposits on insulator indicate engine damage.
• Caused by wrong type of fuel, incorrect ignition timing or advance, too hot a plug, burned valves, or engine overheating. Replace the plug.

15. Automatic Choke (1972-1976)

Operate the choke valve by hand. Make sure the valve and linkage move smoothly. Lubricate as needed.

16. Steering Linkage, Suspension

Remove the steering gear filler plug (1, **Figure 8**). If necessary, top up with gear oil recommended in Tables 5 and 6.

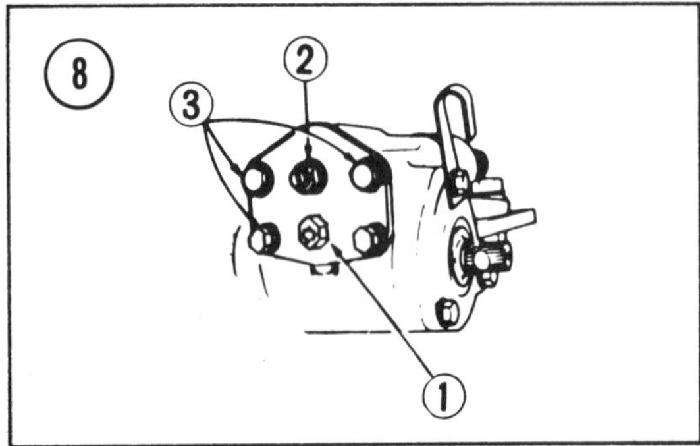

1. Filler plug
2. Adjusting screw
3. Cover bolts

Check the steering linkage and steering gear mounting bolts for looseness. See Chapter Twelve for details of the steering system.

Check all fasteners in the front and rear suspensions for looseness. See Chapters Eleven and Twelve for tightening torques.

17. Hinges, Latches, Locks

Lightly grease the hood latch and trunk or tailgate lock with molybdenum disulphide grease. Apply 1-2 drops of oil to hinges on doors, hood, and tailgate or trunk. Lubricate striker plates with a non-staining stick lube such as Door Ease. Lubricate lock tumblers by applying a thin coat of Lubriplate, lock oil, or graphite to the key. Insert and work the lock several times. Wipe the key clean.

18. PCV System

The positive crankcase ventilation (PCV) system is designed to route crankcase emissions into the combustion chambers for burning.

a. Replace the PCV valve (**Figure 9**).

b. Referring to Figure 9, check the PCV hoses for leaks and loose connections. Disconnect the hoses and blow them out with compressed air. Replace any hoses which cannot be unplugged.

19. EGR System (1974-1976)

Test the exhaust gas recirculation system as described in Chapter Five.

20. Evaporative Emission Control System

Inspect fuel vapor lines, starting at the fuel tank and working forward. Tighten loose connections and replace damaged lines. Make sure the lines are secure in their clips and do not rub against any part of the car. On 1975-76 cars, remove the carbon canister filter (**Figure 10**) from the bottom of the canister. Then install a new filter. The canister is located at the left front corner of the engine compartment.

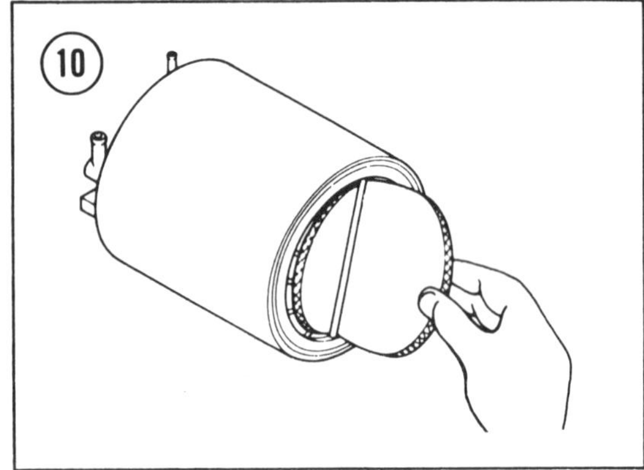

21. Cooling System

Inspect all coolant hoses and connections. Replace hoses that are cracked, deteriorated, or extremely soft. Make sure all clamps are tight.

22. Vacuum Lines

Check vacuum lines for cracks or deterioration. **Figure 11** shows the lines used on 1974 610's. The 1974 710's do not use the air injection hose. The 1973 and earlier cars do not use the exhaust gas recirculation hose. **Figure 12** shows the 1975-76 California car vacuum lines. **Figure 13** shows the lines used on 1975-76 non-California cars.

23. ATC Air Cleaner

The automatic temperature control air cleaner is used on 1972 and later models. It should be tested as described in Chapter Five.

24. Fuel Filter Replacement

Figure 14 shows a typical Datsun fuel filter. To replace, disconnect the inlet line and plug

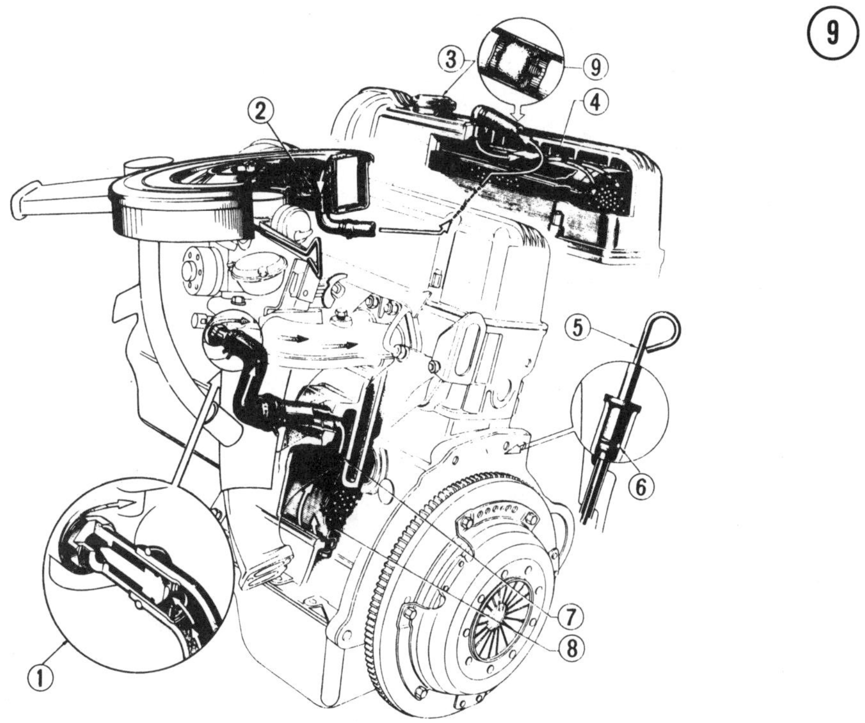

(9)

CRANKCASE EMISSION CONTROL

1. PCV valve
2. Flame arrester
3. Sealed filler cap
4. Baffle plate
5. Oil level gauge
6. O-ring
7. Oil separator
8. Baffle plate
9. Flame arrester

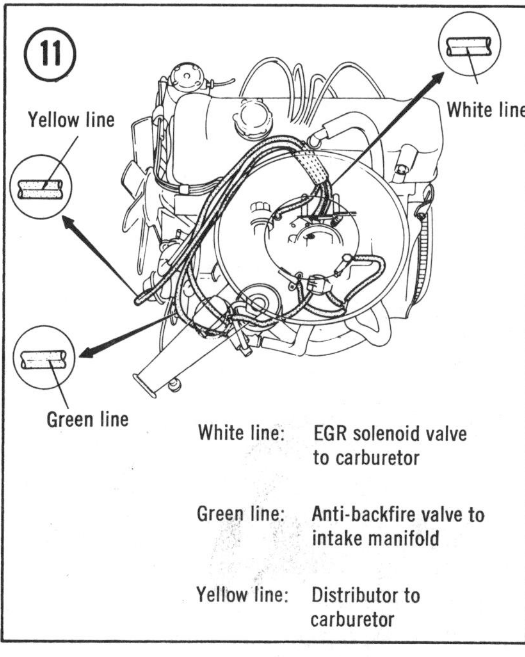

it. Then disconnect the outlet line and pull the filter out of its clip. Install a new filter in the reverse order.

25. Spark Timing Control System

Test system as described in Chapter Seven.

26. Boost Controlled Deceleration Device

Although the boost controlled deceleration device does not usually require adjustment, it should be tested regularly. With the transmission in neutral, hold engine speed at 3,000-3,500 rpm, then release the throttle quickly. The engine should slow to specified idle speed within a few seconds. If it does not, have the BCDD tested by a Datsun dealer.

27. Brake Fluid

The brake fluid should be drained and replaced. Fill the hydraulic system with fluid

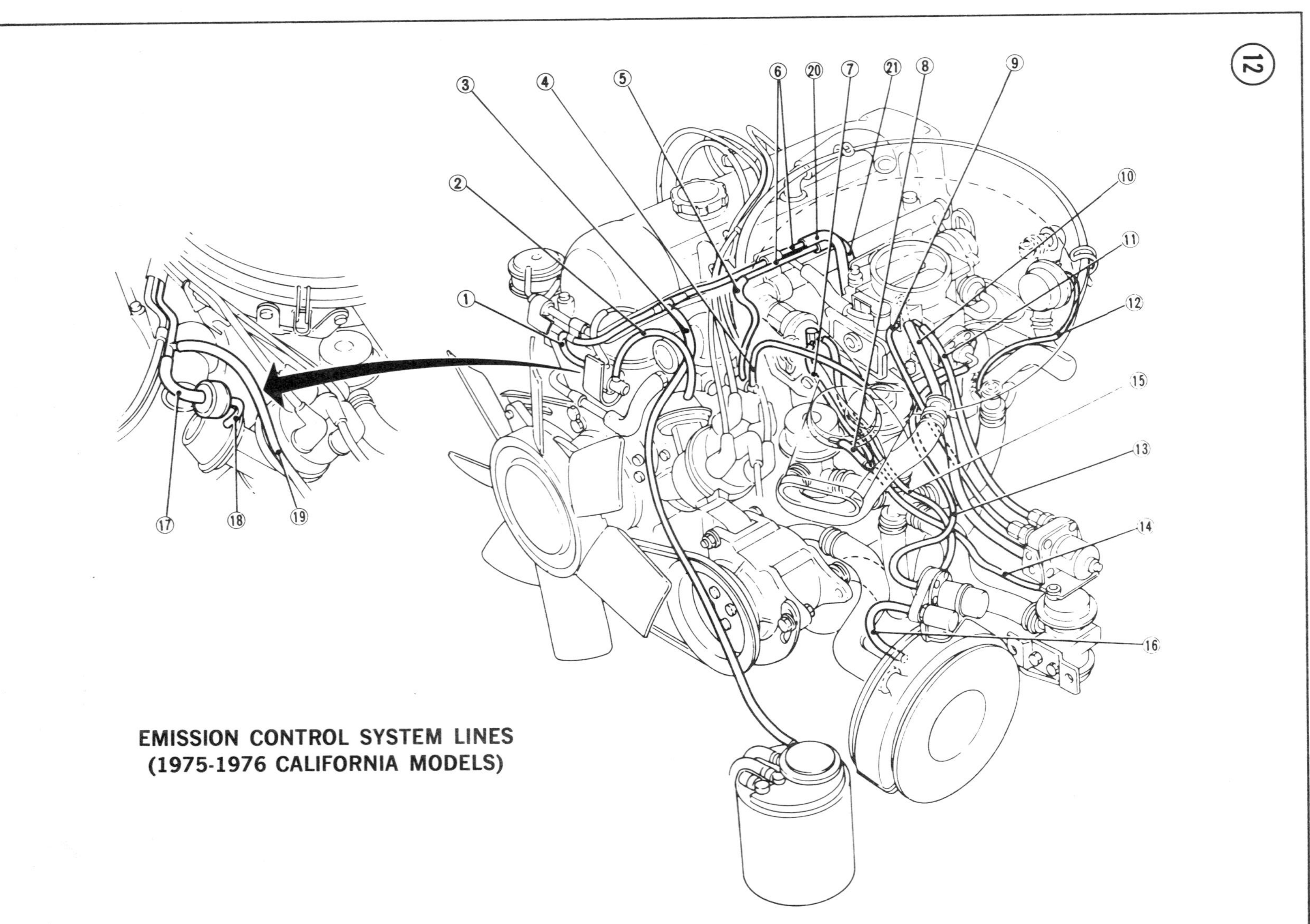

EMISSION CONTROL SYSTEM LINES
(1975-1976 CALIFORNIA MODELS)

1. Vacuum switching valve to vacuum tube (yellow)
2. Vacuum switching valve to distributor (yellow)
3. Vacuum tube to carbon canister (yellow)
4. Thermal vacuum valve to EGR control valve (white)
5. Vacuum tube to thermal vacuum valve (white)
6. Vacuum tube
7. Vacuum hose connector to intake manifold (green)
8. Air control valve to vacuum hose connector (green)
9. Carburetor to altitude compensator (secondary, green) (optional)
10. Air cleaner to altitude compensator (air hose, white) (optional)
11. Carburetor to altitude compensator (primary, red) (optional)
12. AB valve to intake manifold (green)
13. BCDD to control valve (white)
14. Vacuum hose connector to EAR control valve (green)
15. BCDD control vanve to intake manifold (green)
16. Control valve to air pump air cleaner
17. Vacuum tube to SDV valve (yellow)
18. SDV valve to distributor (yelow)
19. Vacuum tube to carbon canister (yellow)
20. Vacuum tube to carburetor (yellow)
21. Vacuum tube to carburetor (white)

marked DOT 3, then bleed the brakes as described in Chapter Ten.

28. Brake Booster (Power Brakes)

Test the brake booster, check valve, and vacuum hose as described in Chapter Ten.

2

29. Battery

Inspect and test the battery as described in Chapter Seven.

30. Brake Inspection

Every 3,000 miles (1968-1974), 4,000 miles (1974), or 6,250 miles (1975-1976), inspect front brake pads. At alternate inspections, check rear brake drums and shoes. Inspection procedures are described in Chapter Ten.

31. Shock Absorbers

Check the shock absorbers for signs of fluid leakage. The front shock absorbers are built into the suspension struts.

Push the vehicle down firmly and let it up quickly. If it bounces more than once, replace the shock absorbers as described in Chapters Eleven and Twelve.

32. Drive Shaft

Check the drive shaft for wear. The easiest way to do this is to shake the drive shaft while watching the universal joints. If play can be detected in the U-joints, disassemble and repair them as described in Chapter Twelve. After checking for U-joint wear, tighten the bolts attaching the drive shaft to the differential flange (and to the transmission flange on early pickups).

33. Wheel Alignment

Have wheel alignment checked and adjusted if necessary by a dealer or front-end specialist.

34. Pedal Lubrication

Using multipurpose grease, lubricate brake and clutch pedals at their pivot points. Also lubricate the pivot points (in the pedals) of the brake and clutch master cylinder pushrods.

35. Engine Compression

Test as described in Chapter Three.

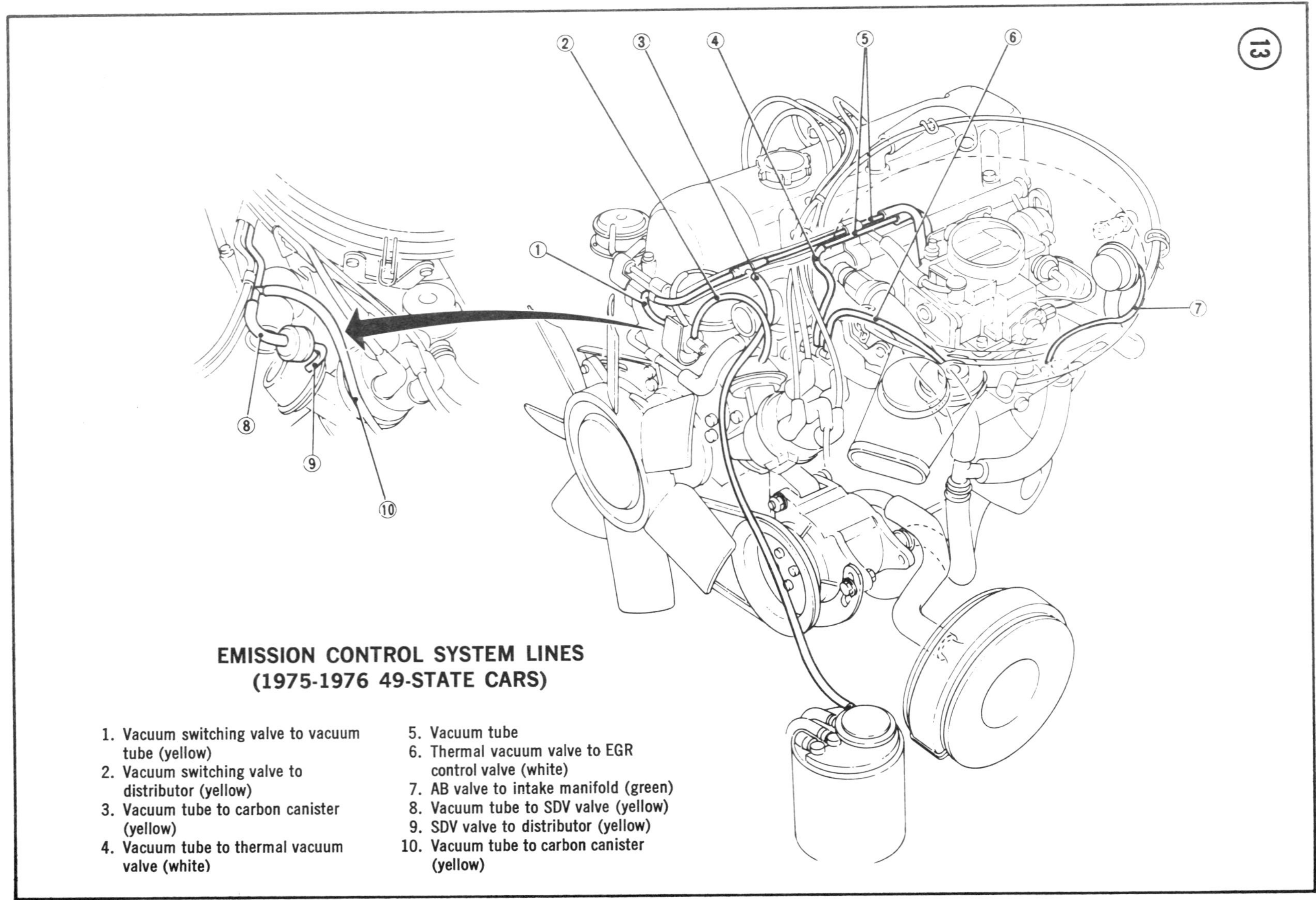

EMISSION CONTROL SYSTEM LINES (1975-1976 49-STATE CARS)

1. Vacuum switching valve to vacuum tube (yellow)
2. Vacuum switching valve to distributor (yellow)
3. Vacuum tube to carbon canister (yellow)
4. Vacuum tube to thermal vacuum valve (white)
5. Vacuum tube
6. Thermal vacuum valve to EGR control valve (white)
7. AB valve to intake manifold (green)
8. Vacuum tube to SDV valve (yellow)
9. SDV valve to distributor (yellow)
10. Vacuum tube to carbon canister (yellow)

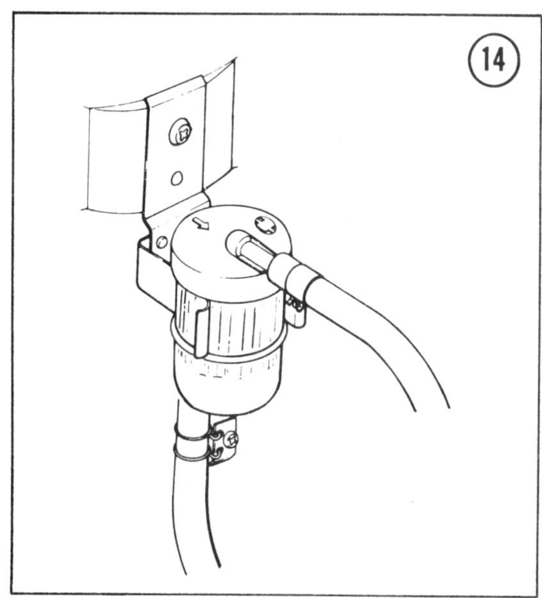

36. Coolant

Flush, drain, and refill the cooling system as described in Chapter Six.

37. Air Cleaner Element

Replace as described in Chapter Five.

38. Air Injection System

Air injection systems are used on 1968-71 510's, 1974 610's, and all 1975-76 models. Inspect the system as described in Chapter Five. On 1975-76 cars, replace the air pump air filter (**Figure 15**). This is located on the left side of the engine compartment.

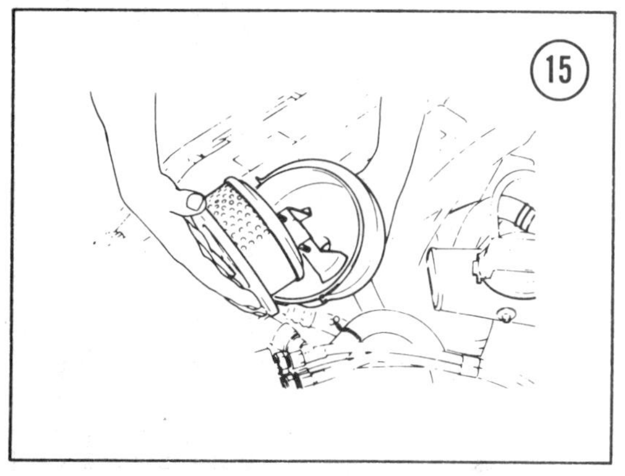

39. Proportioning Valve

Test the proportioning valve as described in Chapter Ten.

40. Steering Linkage, Suspension Ball-joints

Lubricate as described under *Steering Linkage*, Chapter Twelve.

41. Wheel Bearings

Clean, repack, and adjust as described in Chapter Twelve.

42. Manual Transmission Oil Change

To change the oil, first warm it up by driving a short distance. Then remove the filler and drain plugs and drain the oil. Reinstall the drain plug and fill with an oil recommended in Tables 5 and 6. The easiest way to fill the transmission is to run a long tube from the engine compartment, along the right-hand side of the engine and transmission, and into the filler hole.

Capacity is listed in Table 8. When the transmission is full, reinstall the filler plug.

> NOTE: *Check the old transmission oil for such signs of damage as gear teeth and pieces of brass from synchronizers.*

43. Differential Oil Change

This procedure is much like that used to change the transmission oil. First drive the car a short distance to warm the oil. Then remove the filler and drain plugs from the differential or axle housing. When the oil has drained, reinstall the drain plug and fill with gear oil recommended in Tables 5 and 6. Capacity is given in Table 8. Reinstall the filler plug after filling.

44. Rear Axle Shafts (IRS)

Independent rear suspension (IRS) is used on 510 and 610 sedans and hardtops. On these autos, disassemble, clean, and lubricate the axle shafts as described in Chapter Eleven.

45. Headlights

Have the aim of the headlights checked by a Datsun dealer or certified lamp adjusting station.

46. Drive Shaft

Disassemble, clean, and lubricate the universal joints as described in Chapter Eleven.

TUNE-UP

Under normal conditions, a complete tune-up should be done every 12,000 miles on 1968-74 cars, and every 12,500 miles on 1975-76 models. More frequent tune-ups may be required if the car is used under the severe conditions described earlier in this chapter. Tune-up specifications are given in Table 9 at the end of this chapter.

Since different engine systems interact, procedures should be done in the following order:

a. Tighten cylinder head bolts
b. Adjust valve clearances
c. Work on ignition system
d. Adjust carburetor

Cylinder Head Bolts

Tighten early L16 head bolts (through engine No. L16 203415) to 43-51 ft.-lb. Tighten late L16 (from engine No. L16 203416), all L18, and all L20B head bolts to 47-61 ft.-lb. Late head bolts have a circle stamped in the top of the bolt, around the hexagonal hole. Early head bolts do not have a circle. When tightening, follow the sequence shown in **Figure 16**. The engine must be cool when tightening.

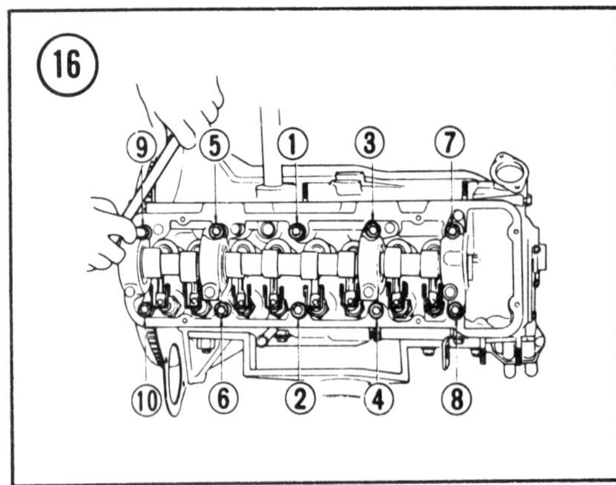

Valve Adjustment

The valves are adjusted first with the engine cold, then at operating temperature. Adjustment is made with the engine turned off in both cases. Unlike conventional overhead valve engines, where valve clearances are measured between rocker arm and valve stem, Datsun L-series valve clearances are measured between the camshaft lobes and a friction surface on the center of each rocker arm. Adjust as follows.

1. Remove the valve rocker cover and spark plugs. Removing the plugs makes it easier to turn the engine by hand.
2. Rotate the engine by hand until No. 1 piston is at top dead center on its compression stroke. This is evident when the 0° timing mark at the front of the engine aligns with the pointer (or crankshaft pulley notch). In addition, the distributor rotor will point to No. 1 terminal in the distributor cap. Be sure to check rotor position, because the timing marks also line up when No. 4 cylinder is at TDC on its compression stroke.
3. Referring to **Figure 17**, loosen the locknut on the rocker arm pivot. If the 17mm crow's foot wrench shown in Figure 17 is not available, an open-end wrench can be used. However, the crow's foot wrench is needed to torque the locknut accurately. Insert a feeler gauge between the rocker arm and camshaft lobe. Turn the pivot adjusting nut with a second wrench. Set intake valve clearances at 0.008 in. (0.20 mm) and exhaust valve clearances at 0.010 in. (0.25mm). Tighten the pivot locking nut to 36-43 ft.-lb. and recheck the clearance.

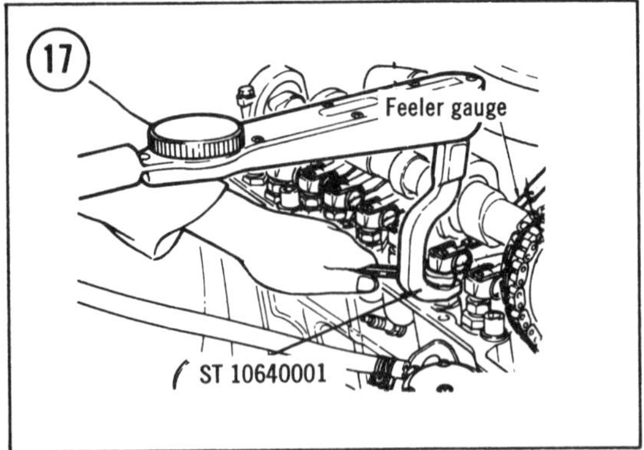

4. Valves for the remaining cylinders are adjusted in the same manner as No. 1 cylinder. Each cylinder is at top dead center on its compression stroke when the distributor rotor points to the distributor cap terminal for that cylinder, and both valves for that cylinder are closed. If there is any doubt, place a finger on the spark plug hole while the engine is being turned. If the piston is on the compression stroke, pressure buildup will be felt. Adjust the valves for No. 3 cylinder, then No. 4, then No. 2.

5. After adjusting valve clearances with the engine cold, run the engine until it warms to normal operating temperature. Recheck the clearances. Intake valves should now be 0.010 in. (0.25mm) and exhaust valves 0.012 in. (0.30mm). Readjust the valve clearances if necessary.

Spark Plugs

Examine the plugs and compare their condition to Figure 6. Then discard the plugs. Their condition is an indicator of engine condition, and can warn of developing trouble. Check the gap on the new plugs and compare to Table 9. Adjust the gap if needed, then install the plugs.

Distributor Cap and Rotor

Pry back the distributor cap clips and remove the cap. Label the spark plug and coil wires so they can be reconnected properly, then pull them out of the cap. Remove dirt and corrosion from the wire terminals and the terminals inside the cap. If the cap and rotor are damaged or excessively worn, replace them. Replace the wires if insulation is melted, brittle, or cracked.

Breaker Points, Condenser

Breaker point ignition is used on all models except 1975-76 California cars.

1. Loosen the screw on the primary lead terminal(s). See **Figure 18** (single-point distributors) or **Figure 19** (dual-point distributors). Slide the points lead wire(s) off the terminal(s).

2. Remove 2 screws securing the points (2 screws from each points set on dual-point distributors). Carefully note how the points are positioned, then lift them out of the distributor. Install new points exactly as the old ones were.

3. Apply a *small* amount of distributor cam lubricant to the distributor cam lobes.

4. Remove the condenser and install a new one.

5. Using a crayon or felt pen, make alignment marks on the distributor body and engine. Then loosen the distributor fixing bolt and carefully turn the distributor by hand until a cam lobe opens the points to the maximum gap. Insert a feeler gauge in the gap (**Figure 20**) and adjust by turning the eccentric adjusting screw. On dual-point distributors, adjust both points sets in this manner.

6. After setting points gap, rotate the distributor back to its original position and tighten the fixing bolt.

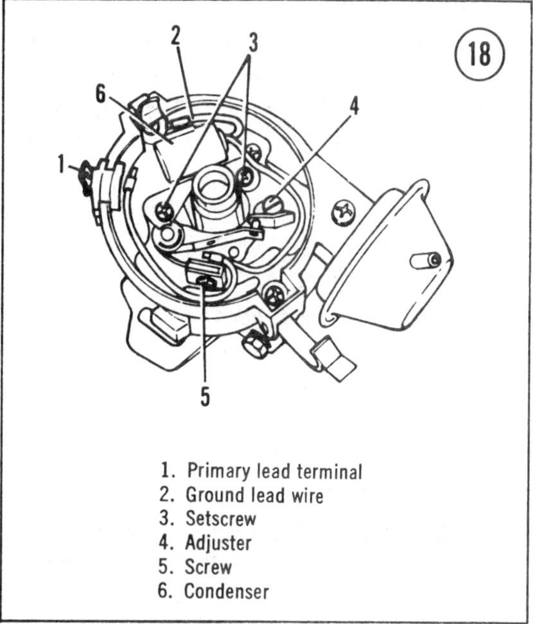

1. Primary lead terminal
2. Ground lead wire
3. Setscrew
4. Adjuster
5. Screw
6. Condenser

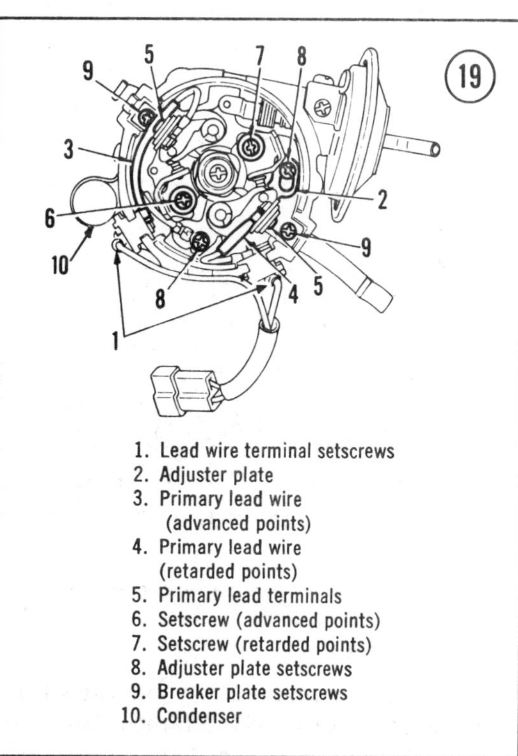

1. Lead wire terminal setscrews
2. Adjuster plate
3. Primary lead wire (advanced points)
4. Primary lead wire (retarded points)
5. Primary lead terminals
6. Setscrew (advanced points)
7. Setscrew (retarded points)
8. Adjuster plate setscrews
9. Breaker plate setscrews
10. Condenser

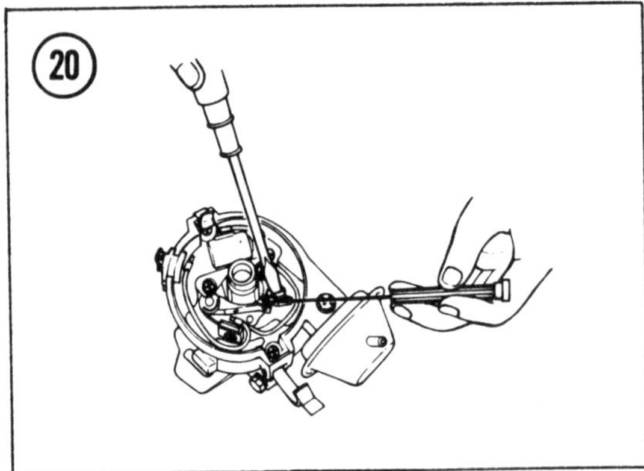

7. Install the distributor rotor and cap. Be sure the spark plug and coil wires are connected properly.

Reluctor, Pickup Coil

The reluctor and pickup coil are part of the transistor ignition system used on 1975-1976 California autos. The gap between these parts should be checked at each tune-up. To measure, insert a feeler gauge as shown in **Figure 21**. Adjustment may be unnecessary, since there is no friction between reluctor and pickup coil. To adjust, loosen the pickup coil screw and pivot the coil in or out as needed.

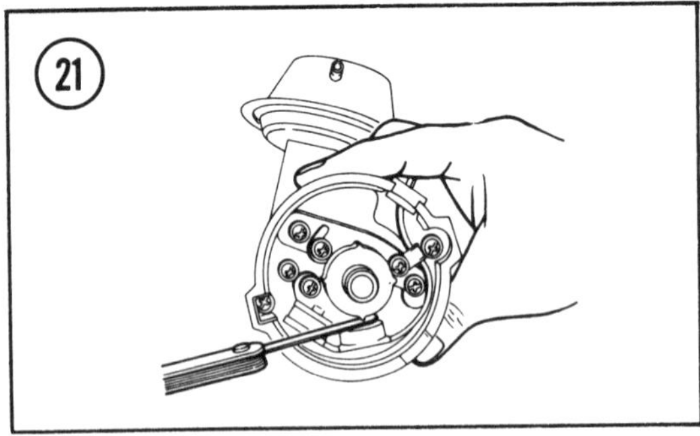

Ignition Timing (Single-point and Breakerless Distributors)

Ignition timing requires a stroboscopic timing light of the type described in Chapter Three. Connect the light according to manufacturer's instructions.

1. Clean the crankshaft pulley and timing marks. Early L-series engines have timing marks on the crankshaft pulley and a pointer on the engine front cover (**Figure 22**). Late L-series

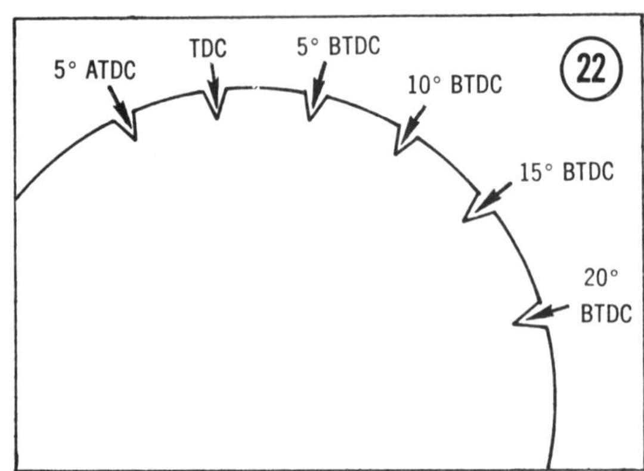

engines have timing marks on the front cover and an indicator notch in the front pulley (**Figure 23**).

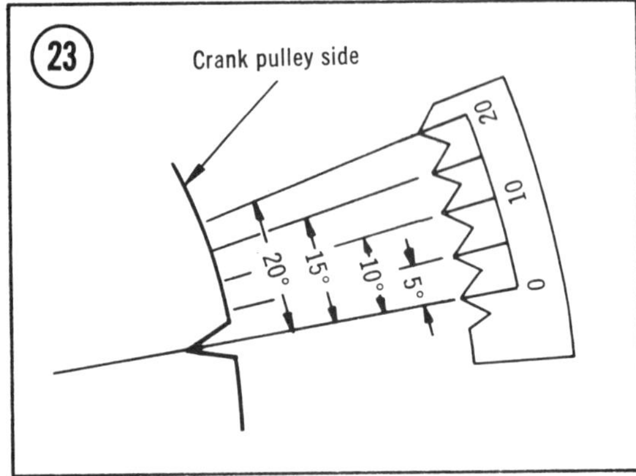

2. Find the correct timing setting in Table 9. Apply white chalk to the mark and to the pointer or crankshaft pulley notch.
3. Disconnect the vacuum line from the distributor. Plug the line with tape.
4. Start the engine. If necessary, adjust idle speed to specifications (Table 9). Loosen the distributor fixing bolt and turn the distributor until the correct timing mark aligns with the timing pointer. Tighten the fixing bolt, shut the engine off, and reconnect the vacuum line.

Ignition Timing (Dual-point Distributors)

1. Clean the crankshaft pulley and timing marks. Early L-series engines have timing marks on the crankshaft pulley and a timing pointer on the front cover (Figure 22). Late L-series engines have timing marks on the front cover and

an indicator notch in the crankshaft pulley (Figure 23).

2. Find the correct advanced and retarded timing settings in Table 9. Apply chalk or paint to the corresponding timing marks. Use different colors so the marks can be told apart under the timing light.

3. Disconnect the vacuum line from the distributor. Plug the line with tape.

4. Start the engine. Compare idle speed with Table 9 and adjust if necessary.

5. On 1970-1972 models, advanced points should function when engine is warm and idling. To check this, detach wire from retarded points terminal. The terminal, on the side of the distributor, is farther from the vertically mounted condenser than the advanced points terminal.

If the engine keeps running, the advanced points are functioning. If it dies, test the spark advance control system. See Chapter Seven.

6. On 1973 models, the retarded points normally function with the engine warm and idling. To set timing, however, the advanced points must be made to function. To do this, disconnect the wiring connector from the distributor harness. Connect a jumper wire as shown in **Figure 24**.

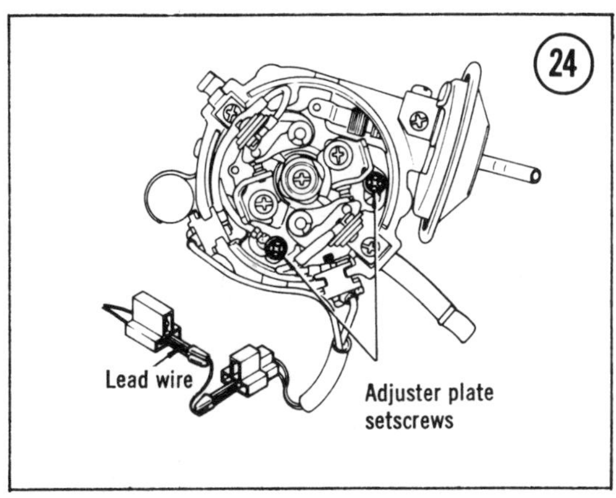

7. Point the timing light at the crankshaft pulley and check the advanced timing setting. If necessary, loosen the distributor fixing bolt and rotate the distributor to change timing. Then tighten the setscrew.

8. On 1970-1972 models, disconnect the wire from the advance points terminal on the side of the distributor. This is the terminal closest to the vertically mounted condenser. Connect a jumper wire from the disconnected wire to the retarded points terminal (farthest from the condenser). This will cause retarded points to function. Engine speed should drop 100-150 rpm.

9. On 1973 models, disconnect the jumper wire (Figure 24) from the *distributor* side of the wiring connector. Connect the jumper wire to the other terminal in distributor side of connector. This causes the retarded points to function.

10. Point the timing light at the crankshaft pulley. Timing should be at the retarded setting specified in Table 9. If it is, no further steps are necessary.

11. If retarded timing is incorrect, adjust the position of the retarded breaker points.

> NOTE: *Adjust the point position, not point gap.*

To adjust, loosen the adjuster plate setscrews. Figure 24 shows the screws on a 1973 distributor; earlier models are the same. Insert a screwdriver in the adjusting slot (**Figure 25**) and twist it to change phase difference (the difference between advanced and retarded settings). Twisting the screwdriver clockwise increases phase difference (retards retarded timing). Twisting it counterclockwise decreases phase difference (advances retarded timing).

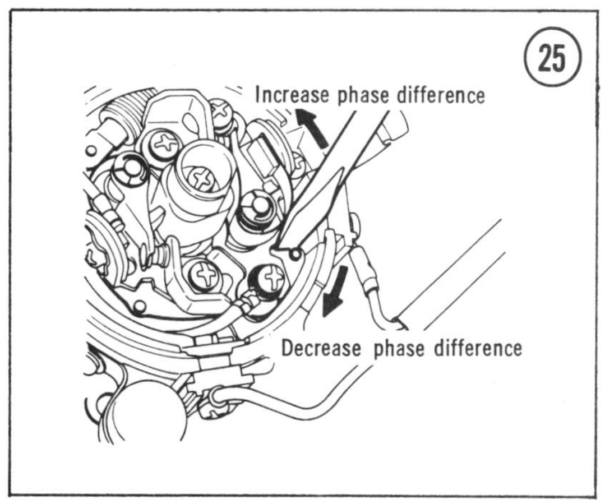

To gauge the adjustment, refer to the graduations on the breaker plate (**Figure 26**). Each graduation represents a 4° change in ignition timing (measured at the crankshaft pulley).

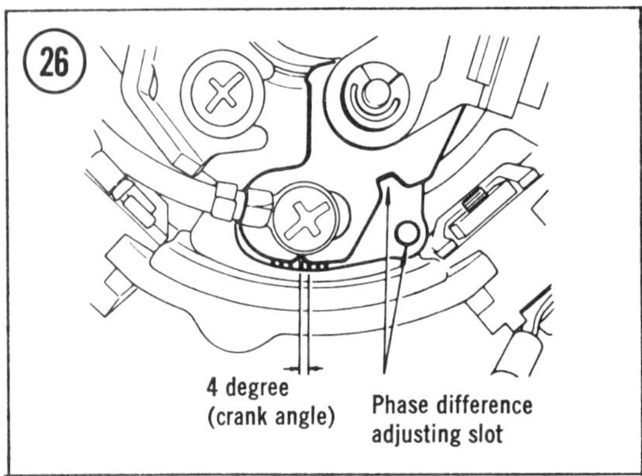

12. Once the retarded timing is set properly, recheck advanced timing as described in Steps 4-7. If it is incorrect, repeat Steps 8-11.

Carburetor Adjustment (1968-1972)

1. Remove the air cleaner. Connect an accurate tune-up tachometer to the engine.

2. Warm the engine to normal operating temperature. Run it at 2,000 rpm for 15 seconds, then let it idle for one minute.

3. Set idle speed at 750 rpm (manual transmission) or 770 rpm (automatic). **Figure 27** shows the idle speed and mixture screws on an automatic choke carburetor. The screws are the same on manual choke carburetors.

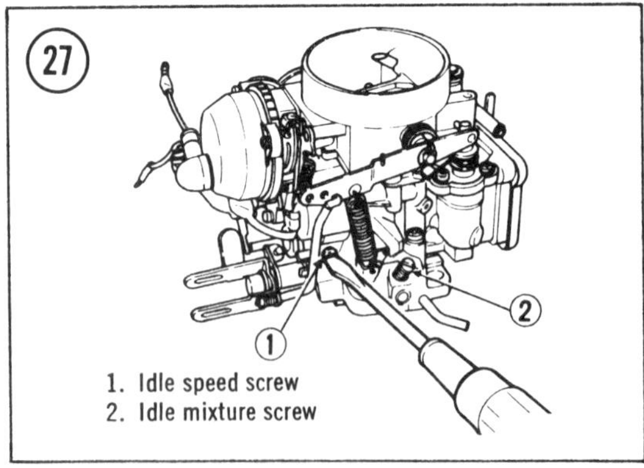

4. Adjust the idle mixture screw to obtain the smoothest possible idle. If necessary, reset idle speed to 750 rpm (manual) or 770 rpm (automatic).

5. Turn the idle mixture screw clockwise (for a leaner mixture) until idle speed drops to 700 rpm (manual transmission) or 720 rpm (automatic).

6. Place automatic transmission in DRIVE. The rpm should drop to 650 (1968-1969); 575 (1970-1971); or 600 (1972).

Carburetor Adjustment (1973-1974)

Datsun recommends using a CO meter to adjust the idle on 1973-1974 engines. Although it is possible to adjust the carburetor without the CO meter, the instrument is necessary to ensure that exhaust emissions are within legal limits.

1. Remove the air cleaner and connect an accurate tune-up tachometer to the engine.

2. Warm the engine to normal operating temperature, then let it idle for one minute.

3. Set engine speed at 800 rpm (L16 and L18 engines) or 750 rpm (L20B engine). Figure 27 shows the idle speed and mixture screws.

4. On 1974 610's, disconnect the hose from the air injection check valve (**Figure 28**).

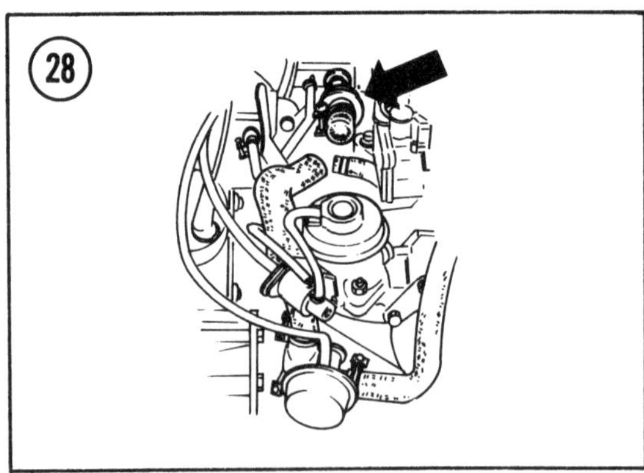

5. Place automatic transmission in DRIVE.

6. Using the idle mixture screw, set CO percentage at 1.5 per cent (L16 and L18 engines) or 3 per cent (L20B). If a CO meter is not available, turn the mixture screw as far clockwise (lean) as possible without roughening the idle. This method should not be used unless absolutely necessary, and results should be checked on a CO meter as soon as possible.

7. Check engine speed. It should be 800 rpm in neutral (L16 and L18 engines) or 750 rpm in neutral (L20B engines). If necessary, readjust with the idle speed screw.

8. After adjustment, idle speed should be 800 rpm in neutral (L16 and L18 engines) or 750 rpm in neutral (L20B engines). With automatic transmissions, engine speed should drop to 650 rpm when shifted to DRIVE.

Carburetor Adjustment (1975-1976)

Datsun recommends use of a CO meter to set idle mixture. While mixture can be set without a CO meter, the instrument is necessary to ensure that exhaust emissions are within legal limits.

1. Disconnect the air hose from the check valve (Figure 28).
2. Warm the engine to normal operating temperature, then connect a tune-up tachometer.
3. Race engine 2 or 3 times at 1,500-2,000 rpm.
4. On automatic transmissions, block the wheels so the car cannot roll forward, then shift to DRIVE.
5. Set idle speed at 750 rpm (manual transmission) or 650 rpm (automatic). **Figure 29** shows the idle speed adjusting screw.
6. If a CO meter is available, set CO percentage at 1-3 per cent. Do this by turning the idle mixture screw (Figure 29). If this adjustment changes idle speed, reset it with the idle speed screw. Then race the engine 2 or 3 times at 1,500-2,000 rpm and recheck CO percentage.

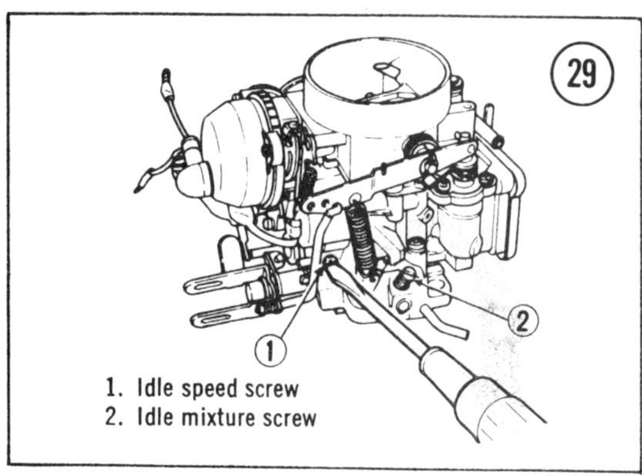

1. Idle speed screw
2. Idle mixture screw

7. If a CO meter is not available, set idle speed at 815 rpm (manual transmission) or 670 rpm (automatic). Adjust with the idle speed screw (Figure 29). Then turn the idle mixture screw (Figure 29) to obtain the fastest smooth idle. Reset idle speed to 815 rpm (manual) or 670 rpm (automatic) with the idle speed screw. Then turn the idle *mixture* screw clockwise until engine speed drops 60-70 rpm (manual) or 15-25 rpm (automatic).
8. Reconnect the air hose to the check valve. If engine speed increases, reset it with the idle speed screw.

Table 9 TUNE-UP SPECIFICATIONS

Valve Clearance	
Engine cold	
Intake	0.008 in. (0.20mm)
Exhaust	0.010 in. (0.25mm)
Engine hot	
Intake	0.010 in. (0.25mm)
Exhaust	0.012 in. (0.30mm)
Spark Plug Gap	
1968-1972	0.031-0.035 in. (0.8-0.9mm)
1973-1974	0.028-0031 in. (0.7-0.8mm)
1975-1976 610	0.039-0.043 in. (1.0-1.1mm)
1975 and later 710	
Breaker point ignition	0.031-0.035 in. (0.8-0.9mm)
Breakerless ignition	0.039-0.043 in. (1.0-1.1mm)
Points Gap	0.018-0.022 in. (0.45-0.55mm)
Dwell Angle	49-55°
Reluctor Air Gap	0.008-0.016 in. (0.2-0.4mm)
Ignition Timing	
L16, 1968-69	5° ATDC
L16, 1970-71 (advanced)	10° BTDC
L16, 1970-71 (retarded)	0°
L16, 1972 (advanced)	7° BTDC
L16, 1972 (retarded)	0°
L16, 1973 (advanced)	12° BTDC
L16, 1973 (retarded)	
Cars through chassis No. PL510-429350	5° BTDC
Cars from chassis No. PL510-429351	8° BTDC
Trucks through chassis No. PL620-141296	5° BTDC
Trucks from chassis No. PL620-141297	8° BTDC
L18, 1973 (advanced)	12° BTDC
L18, 1973 (retarded)	
Through chassis No. PL610-815989	5° BTDC
From chassis No. PL610-815990	8° BTDC
L18 and L20B, 1974 and later	12° BTDC

CHAPTER THREE

TROUBLESHOOTING

Troubleshooting the Datsun can be relatively easy if done in a logical, orderly manner. The first step in any troubleshooting procedure must be defining the symptoms as closely as possible. After the symptoms are defined, areas which could cause the problems are tested and analyzed. Guessing at the cause of a problem may provide the solution, but it can easily lead to frustration, wasted time, and a series of expensive, unnecessary parts replacements.

The troubleshooting procedures in this chapter analyze typical symptoms, and show logical methods of isolating causes. These are not the only methods. There may be several ways to solve a problem, but only a systematic, methodical approach can guarantee success.

TROUBLESHOOTING INSTRUMENTS

The following equipment is necessary to troubleshoot any engine properly:

a. Voltmeter, ammeter, and ohmmeter
b. Hydrometer
c. Compression tester
d. Vacuum gauge
e. Fuel pressure gauge
f. Dwell meter
g. Tachometer
h. Strobe timing light
i. Exhaust gas analyzer

Items a-f are basic for any car. Items g-i are necessary for exhaust emission control compliance. The following is a brief description of each instrument. Consult a basic auto repair manual for more detailed information.

Voltmeter, Ammeter, and Ohmmeter

For testing the ignition and electrical systems, a good voltmeter is needed. A voltmeter covering 0-20 volts is satisfactory. It should have an accuracy of about ±½ volt, which excludes the type found in car instrument panels.

An ohmmeter measures electrical resistance. It is useful for checking continuity (open and short circuits) and testing fuses and lights.

The ammeter measures electrical current. Ammeters for automotive use should cover 0-10 amperes and 0-100 amperes. These are useful for checking battery starting and charging current.

Some inexpensive volt-ohm-milliammeters combine all 3 instruments into one. See **Figure 1**. The ammeter ranges are usually too small for automotive work, though.

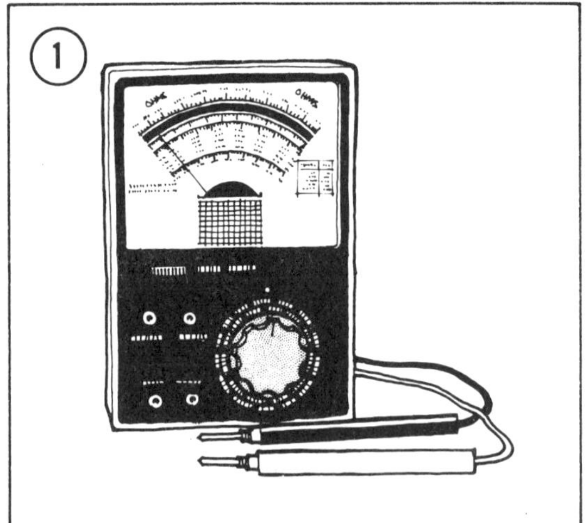

Hydrometer

The hydrometer gives a useful indication of battery condition and charge by measuring the specific gravity of the electrolyte in each cell. See **Figure 2**. Complete details on use and interpretation of readings are given in Chapter Seven.

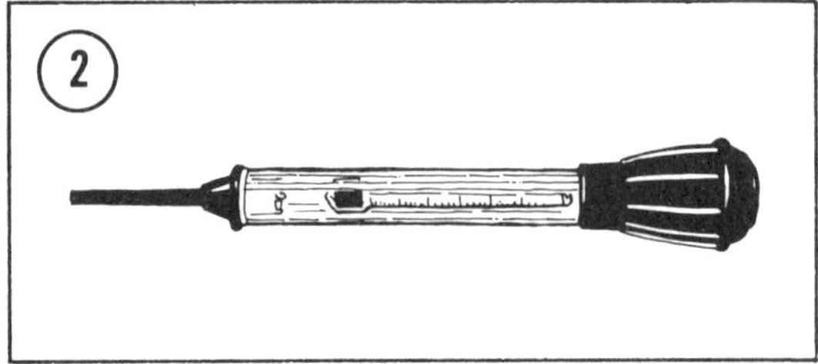

Compression Tester

The compression tester measures the compression pressure built up in each cylinder. Interpretation of compression test results can indicate general cylinder and valve condition. **Figure 3** shows a compression tester in use.

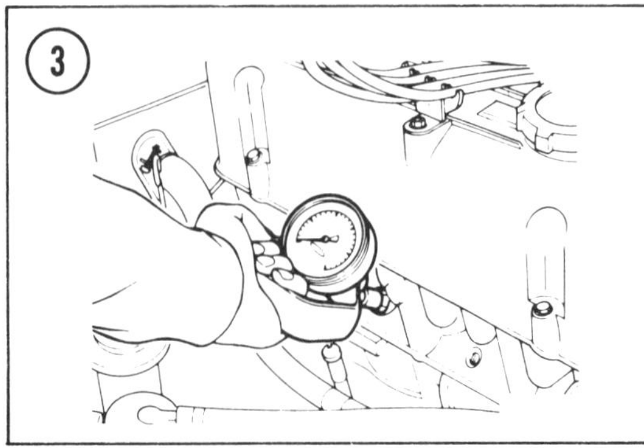

There are 2 types of compression tests: "wet" and "dry." These tests are interpreted together to isolate problems in cylinder and valves. The dry compression test is done first. To test:

1. Warm the engine to normal operating temperature. Make sure choke is completely open.
2. Remove the spark plugs.
3. Connect the compression tester to one cylinder following manufacturer's instructions.
4. Have an assistant crank the engine over until there is no further increase in compression. Hold the accelerator to the floor while cranking.
5. Remove the tester and record the compression reading.
6. Repeat Steps 3-5 for each cylinder. On 1968-1972 autos, compression should be 163-171 psi (11.5-12.0 kg/cm^2). On 1973-1976 cars, compression should be 128-171 psi (9-12 kg/cm^2).

When interpreting the results, actual readings are not as important as the difference in readings. Low readings, although they may be even, are a sign of wear. Low readings in 2 adjacent cylinders may indicate a defective head gasket. No cylinder should test at less than 80 per cent of the highest cylinder. A greater difference indicates worn or broken rings, leaky or sticking valves, a defective head gasket, or a combination of all.

If the dry compression test indicates a problem, isolate the cause with a wet compression test. This is done in the same way as the dry compression test, except that about one tablespoon of oil is poured down the spark plug hole before performing Steps 3-5. If the wet compression readings are much greater than the dry compression readings, the trouble is probably due to worn or broken rings. If there is little difference between wet and dry readings, the trouble is probably due to leaky or sticking valves. If 2 adjacent cylinders are low, and the wet and dry readings are close, the head gasket may be damaged.

Vacuum Gauge

The vacuum gauge (**Figure 4**) is used to test emission control components and power brakes. The gauge is connected to a vacuum line or component. Vacuum is then measured under

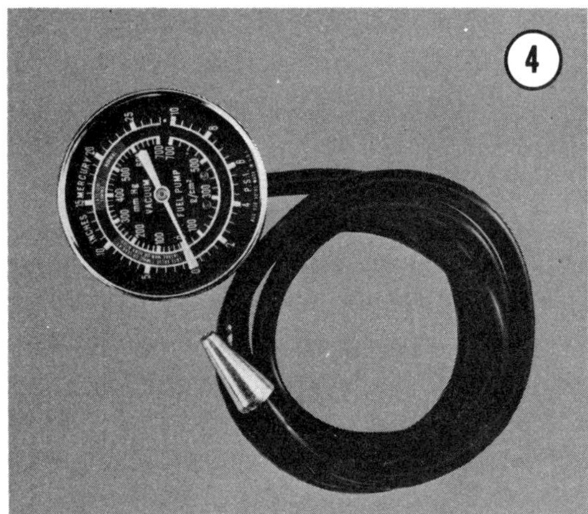

4

specified engine conditions to determine whether a part is defective.

Fuel Pressure Gauge

This instrument is necessary to test fuel pump performance. Fuel pressure gauges are usually combined with vacuum gauges. See Figure 4.

Dwell Meter

A dwell meter measures how many degrees of cam rotation that the distributor points remain closed when the engine is running. Since this angle is determined by breaker point gap, it is an accurate indication of point gap. Many tachometers intended for testing and tuning include a dwell meter (**Figure 5**). Follow the instrument manufacturer's instructions to measure dwell.

Tachometer

A tachometer is necessary for setting ignition timing and adjusting the carburetor. The best instrument for this purpose is one with a range of 0-2,000 rpm. Tachometers with an extended range (0-6,000 or 0-8,000 rpm) may lack accuracy at lower speeds. The tachometer should be able to detect changes of 25 rpm.

Strobe Timing Light

This instrument (**Figure 6**) is necessary for tuning and emission control adjustments. It permits very accurate ignition timing. The light

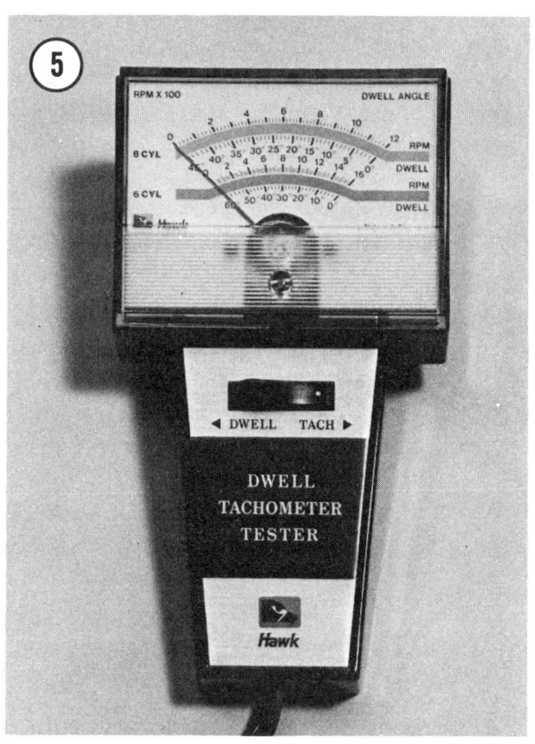

5

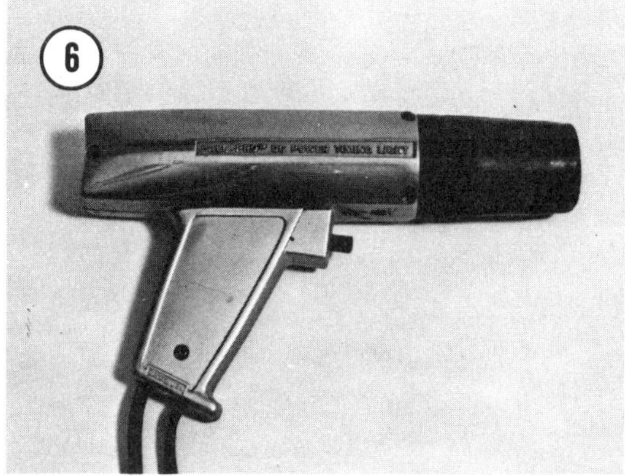

6

flashes precisely at the same instant that No. 1 cylinder fires, so the position of the crankshaft pulley at that instant can be seen. Marks on the crankshaft pulley and engine front cover are lined up to set timing.

Suitable lights range from inexpensive neon bulb types to powerful xenon strobes. Neon timing lights are difficult to see and must be used in dimly lit areas. Xenon strobe timing lights can be used outside in bright sunlight. Timing lights should be connected according to manufacturer's instructions.

Exhaust Analyzer

This instrument is necessary to check emission control adjustments accurately. It samples the exhaust gases from the tailpipe and indicates the amount of carbon monoxide (percentage) and unburned hydrocarbons (parts per million) in the exhaust. Exhaust analyzers are relatively expensive to buy, but some large rent-all dealers have them available at a modest price.

STARTER

Starter system troubles are relatively easy to isolate. The following are common symptoms and causes.

1. *Engine cranks very slowly or not at all*—Turn on the headlights. If the lights are very dim, the battery or connecting wires are probably the cause. Check the battery as described in Chapter Seven. Check the wiring for breaks, shorts, and dirty connections.

If the battery and connecting wires are not at fault, turn the headlights on and try to crank the engine. If the lights dim drastically, the starter is probably shorted to ground. Have it tested or install a rebuilt unit.

If the lights remain bright or dim only slightly while trying to start the engine, the trouble may be in the starter, solenoid, or wiring. To isolate the trouble, short the 2 large solenoid terminals together (*not* to ground). If the starter cranks normally, check the solenoid and wiring up to the ignition switch. If the starter still fails to crank properly, inspect brushes as described in Chapter Seven. If the brushes are good, have the starter tested or install a rebuilt unit.

2. *Starter turns, but does not engage with engine*—This problem is usually caused by a sticking solenoid, but occasionally the pinion can jam on the flywheel. With manual transmissions, the pinion can be temporarily freed by rocking the car in high gear. With automatic transmissions, this is not possible; the starter must be removed.

3. *Loud grinding noises when starter runs*—This may mean the teeth on pinion and flywheel are not meshing properly, or it may mean the overrunning clutch is broken. In the first case, remove the starter and examine the ring gear. In the latter case, replace the starter with a rebuilt unit.

CHARGING SYSTEM

Charging system troubles may be in the battery, alternator, voltage regulator, and fan belt. The following symptoms are typical.

1. *Alternator warning light does not come on when ignition is turned on*—This may indicate a defective ignition switch, battery, voltage regulator, or light. First, try to start the car. If it does not start, check the ignition switch and battery. If the car starts, find the voltage regulator and disconnect the wire from terminal "L"; this is the lamp wire. Ground the wire. If the light comes on, the voltage regulator is defective, not properly grounded, or the alternator brushes are not making contact. See Chapter Seven for brush checking and replacement, and voltage regulator replacement. If the light does not come on when the wire is grounded, the bulb is probably burned out; replace it.

2. *Alternator warning light comes on and stays on*—This usually indicates that no charging is taking place. First check fan belt tension as described in Chapter Two. Then check battery condition with a hydrometer, and check all electrical connections in the charging system. If this does not locate the trouble, check the alternator as described in Chapter Seven. If the alternator is working properly, have the voltage regulator tested.

3. *Alternator warning light flashes erratically*—This usually indicates the charging system is working intermittently. Check fan belt tension, and check all electrical conections in the charging system. Check the alternator.

4. *Battery requires frequent additions of water, or lamps require frequent replacement*—The alternator is probably overcharging the battery. The voltage regulator is probably at fault. Have it tested by a Datsun dealer or competent electrical shop.

5. *Excessive noise from alternator*—Check for loose alternator mountings or pulley. The problem may also be worn alternator bearings or

improperly seated brushes. Remove the alternator and repair (Chapter Seven).

ENGINE

These procedures are to be used when the starter cranks the engine over normally. If not, refer to *Starter* section in this chapter.

1. *Engine will not start*—This problem could be caused by the ignition system or the fuel system. First find out if there is high voltage to the spark plugs. To do this, disconnect one of the spark plug wires. Hold the wire about ¼-½ in. from ground (any bare metal in the engine compartment) with an insulated screwdriver. Crank the engine over. If sparks do not jump to ground, or the sparks are very weak, the problem may be in the ignition system. See the *Ignition System* section of this chapter for further details. If good sparks occur, the trouble may be in the fuel system. See the *Fuel System* section of this chapter.

2. *Engine misses steadily*—Disconnect one spark plug wire at a time and ground the wire. If engine miss increases, that cylinder was working properly. Reconnect the wire and check the others. When a wire is disconnected and the miss remains the same, that cylinder is not firing. Check spark as described in Step 1. If no spark occurs for one cylinder only, check the distributor cap, wire, and spark plug. If spark occurs on the non-firing cylinder, check compression to isolate the trouble.

3. *Engine misses erratically at all speeds*—There are several possible causes, which may be difficult to find. The problem could be in the ignition system, exhaust system (exhaust restriction), or fuel system. Follow troubleshooting procedures for these systems carefully to isolate the trouble.

4. *Engine misses at idle only*—Trouble could exist anywhere in the ignition system. Follow ignition troubleshooting procedures carefully. The problem could also be in the carburetor idle adjustment. On 1974 vehicles, the exhaust gas recirculation system may be at fault. See Chapter Five. If one cylinder misses *and* has a low compression reading, the cause could be broken or worn rings or defective valves.

5. *Engine misses at high speed only*—Problems could exist in the ignition system or fuel system. Check the fuel system as described in *Fuel System Troubleshooting*. Also check spark plugs and wires. See *Ignition System Troubleshooting*.

6. *Low performance at all speeds, poor acceleration*—Trouble usually exists in ignition system or fuel system. Check both systems with appropriate procedures.

7. *Excessive fuel consumption*—This can be caused by many factors seemingly unrelated to fuel consumption. Check for clutch slippage, brake drag, defective wheel bearings, and poor front end alignment. Check ignition system and fuel system as described later.

8. *Engine "diesels" (keeps on running) after ignition is switched off*—Check anti-dieseling solenoid (if so equipped). Check idle mixture, idle speed, and float level. See Chapter Five. Check ignition timing (Chapter Seven). Be sure spark plugs are of correct heat range. Check for engine overheating. Check valve clearance. Remove and decarbonize cylinder head.

9. *Oil pressure light does not come on when ignition is switched on*—Check the alternator warning light. If it is not on either, go to Step 1, *Charging System Troubleshooting*. If only the oil pressure light is off, open the hood and locate the oil pressure sender by the oil filter. The sender uses a single yellow/black wire. Make sure the wire is connected to the sender and making good contact. Pull the wire off and ground it. If the light comes on, the sender is defective or improperly grounded to the engine. If the sender is grounded properly, replace it. If the light does not come on when the wire is grounded, the bulb is probably bad. Replace it.

10. *Oil pressure light comes on or flickers while the engine is running*—This indicates low oil pressure or no pressure at all. *Stop the engine immediately;* coast to a stop with the clutch disengaged (manual transmission) or shift to neutral (automatic transmission). The cause may be merely a low oil level or overheating engine. Check the oil level (Chapter Two) and the engine temperature. Check for a shorted oil pressure sender with an ohmmeter or other continuity tester. Inspect oil pump as described in

Chapter Four. Listen for unusual noises from the engine, indicating bad bearings, etc. Do not start the engine until you know why the light went on and the problem has been corrected.

IGNITION SYSTEM

These procedures assume the battery is in good enough condition to crank the engine at a normal rate.

1. *No spark to one plug*—On breaker point ignition systems (all except 1975-1976 California cars), the only possible causes are a defective distributor cap or spark plug wire. On 1975-1976 California cars (transistor ignition system), the reluctor may be damaged, although this is highly unlikely. Ensure that the wire is making good contact with the distributor cap. Check the cap for moisture, dirt, cracks, carbon tracking between the contacts, or other visible defects.

2. *No spark to any plugs*—This could be caused by trouble in the primary or secondary circuits. First remove the coil wire from the center of the distributor cap. Hold the end of the wire about ¼ in. from ground with an insulated screwdriver. Crank the engine. If sparks occur, the trouble is in the rotor or distributor cap. Remove the cap and check for burns, moisture, dirt, carbon tracking, cracks, etc. Check the rotor for excessive burning, pitting, wear, or cracks. Replace if necessary.

If the coil does not produce any spark, examine the secondary wire (thick wire running from coil to distributor). If the wire shows signs of age or wear, it may be broken. Replace it and test for spark again.

> NOTE: *The next steps do not apply to 1975-76 California cars. Testing the transistor ignition system used on these cars requires special equipment, and the system can easily be damaged. If the preceding steps have not located the problem, have the system tested by a Datsun dealer or competent ignition specialist.*

If the wire is good, crank the engine so the breaker points are open. Examine them for excessive gap, burning, pitting, and looseness. Replace or adjust them if necessary. With the points open, check voltage from the negative terminal on the coil (the one with the black wire) to ground with a voltmeter or test light.

If voltage is present, the coil is probably bad. Have it checked or substitute a coil known to be good. If voltage is not present, check wire connections to coil and distributor. Temporarily disconnect the wire from the coil negative terminal and measure voltage from the terminal to ground. If voltage is present, the distributor is shorted. Examine breaker points and connecting wires carefully. If voltage is still not present, measure voltage from the coil positive terminal to ground. Voltage on the positive terminal, but not on the negative, indicates a defective coil. No voltage on the positive terminal indicates an open wire between the positive terminal and the battery.

3. *Weak spark*—If the spark is so small that it cannot jump ¼-½ in. to ground, check battery condition as described in Chapter Seven. Other causes are bad breaker points, bad condenser, incorrect point gap, dirty or loose connections in the primary circuit, or dirty or burned rotor or distributor cap. Also, distributor cam lobes should be checked for wear.

4. *Spark plug missing*—This is usually caused by fouled or damaged plugs, plugs of the wrong heat range, or incorrect plug gap. Clean and regap the spark plugs. This trouble can also be caused by weak spark (symptom 3) or incorrect ignition timing.

FUEL SYSTEM

Fuel system problems must be isolated at the carburetor, fuel pump, or fuel lines. These procedures assume the ignition system has been checked and properly adjusted.

1. *Engine will not start*—First make sure fuel is being delivered to the carburetor. Remove the air cleaner, look into the carburetor throat, and operate the throttle linkage several times. There should be a stream of fuel from the accelerator pump discharge tube each time the throttle is opened. If not, check the fuel pump delivery (described later), float valve, and float adjustment (Chapter Five).

If fuel is delivered and the engine still will not start, check the manual choke (1968-1971 vehicles) to make sure it opens and closes properly when the control knob is moved. On 1972 and later vehicles, check the automatic choke for sticking or damage. If necessary, rebuild or replace the carburetor.

2. *Engine runs at fast idle*—Check the choke setting, idle mixture, and idle speed adjustments. See Chapter Five.

3. *Rough idle or engine miss with frequent stalling*—Check idle mixture and idle speed adjustments. On all 1974-1976 vehicles, check the exhaust gas recirculation system (Chapter Five).

4. *Stumbling when accelerating from idle*—Check idle speed and mixture adjustments. Check the accelerator pump. Examine the carburetor for dirt and other foreign material that could be clogging the jets and passages. See Chapter Five.

5. *Engine misses at high speed or lacks power*—This indicates possible fuel starvation. Check fuel pump pressure and capacity. Clean main jet and float needle valve. Check for a clogged fuel filter or air cleaner element.

6. *Black exhaust smoke*—This indicates a badly overrich mixture. Check idle mixture and idle speed adjustment. Make sure the choke is fully open when the engine is warm. Check for excessive fuel pump pressure, leaky float, or worn needle valve.

7. *Excessive fuel consumption*—Check for overrich mixture. Make sure the choke is fully open when the engine is warm. Check idle mixture and idle speed. Check for excessive fuel pump pressure, leaky float, or worn needle valve.

Fuel Pump Pressure Testing

1. Install a T-fitting in the fuel line close to the carburetor.

2. Connect a fuel pressure gauge to the fitting with a short tube.

3. Start the engine and run it at varying speeds. Compare fuel pressure with **Table 1**. If pressure is appreciably lower than specified, the cause could be a worn fuel pump, ruptured diaphragm, worn, warped, sticky, or dirty valves and seats, or a weak diaphragm return spring. Excessive pressure indicates the diaphragm is too tight. Replace it.

Table 1 FUEL PUMP SPECIFICATIONS

Engine	Pressure	Volume per minute
L-series through 1973	2.5-3.4 psi	2.1 pints (1,000cc)
L-series, 1974-76	3.0-3.8 psi	2.1 pints (1,000cc)

Fuel Pump Capacity Testing

1. Disconnect the fuel line from the carburetor.

2. Place a graduated container of about 2 quarts capacity at the end of the fuel line.

3. Start the engine and run it at 1,000 rpm for one minute. There is enough fuel in the float chamber for this.

4. Stop the engine. Compare the amount of fuel delivered with Table 1. If no fuel, or only a very small amount, flows from the pump, the fuel filter or lines may be clogged. Inspect the filter and replace if necessary. Repeat the test with a source of fuel other than the gas tank. If fuel flow increases, a line may be clogged. On vehicles with evaporative emission control, the relief valve in the fuel filler cap may be clogged. Try sucking air through the cap. If this is not possible, replace the cap.

If fuel flow is insufficient when using a fuel source other than the gas tank, the pump is probably defective. Repair or replace it.

CLUTCH

All clutch problems, except adjustments or hydraulic system repairs, require removal of the engine or transmission to identify the cause and make repairs.

1. *Slippage*—This condition is most noticeable when accelerating in high gear at relatively low speed. To check slippage, drive at a steady speed in second or third gear. Without letting up the accelerator, push in the clutch long enough to let engine speed increase (one or two seconds). Then let the clutch out rapidly. If the clutch is good, engine speed will drop suddenly or the car will jump forward. If the clutch is slipping, engine speed will drop slowly and the car will not jump forward.

Slippage results from insufficient clutch pedal free play, oil or grease on the disc, worn pressure plate, or a weak diaphragm spring. Riding the clutch pedal can cause the disc surfaces to become glazed, resulting in slippage. Also check the withdrawal lever to make sure it is not binding and preventing full engagement.

2. *Drag or failure to release*—This trouble usually causes difficult shifting and gear clash especially when downshifting. The cause may be excessive clutch pedal free play, warped or bent pressure plate or clutch disc, air in the clutch hydraulic system, or defective clutch master and operating cylinders. Also check condition of the transmission main drive gear splines.

3. *Chatter or grabbing*—There are several possible causes. Check the clutch hydraulic system for air or worn parts. Bleed if necessary as described in Chapter Eight. Check tightness of transmission-to-frame and engine-to-transmission mounting bolts. Check for worn or misaligned pressure plate and clutch disc.

4. *Other noises*—Noise usually indicates a dry or defective release bearing. Check the bearing and replace if necessary. Also check parts for misalignment or uneven wear.

MANUAL TRANSMISSION

Transmission problems are usually indicated by one or more of the following symptoms:

a. Difficulty shifting gears
b. Gear clash when downshifting
c. Excessive noise in neutral
d. Excessive noise in gear
e. Jumping out of gear
f. Oil leaks

Transmission symptoms are sometimes difficult to distinguish from clutch symptoms. Be sure the clutch is not causing the trouble before working on the transmission. Transmission procedures are described in Chapter Nine.

AUTOMATIC TRANSMISSION

Automatic transmission procedures are described in Chapter Nine.

BRAKES

1. *Brake pedal goes to floor*—There are numerous causes for this, including excessively worn linings, air in the hydraulic system, leaky brake lines, leaky wheel cylinders and disc brake calipers, or leaky or worn master cylinder. Check for leaks and thin brake linings. Bleed and adjust the brakes. If the problem still exists, rebuild the wheel cylinders and calipers and/or master cylinder.

2. *Spongy pedal*—Normally caused by air in the system; bleed and adjust the brakes.

3. *Brakes pull*—Check brake adjustment. Also check for wet or greasy brake linings (from leaks), leaky wheel cylinders and calipers, loose calipers, frozen or seized pistons, and restricted brake lines or hoses. Check front end alignment, and look for suspension damage. Tires also affect braking; check tire pressure and condition.

4. *Brake squeal or chatter*—Check brake lining thickness and brake drum roundness. Check discs for excessive runout. Make sure the shoes are not loose. Clean away all dirt on shoes, drums, discs, and pads.

5. *Dragging brakes*—Check brake adjustment, including handbrake. Check for broken or weak shoe return springs, worn piston seals (disc brakes), swollen rubber parts due to improper brake fluid or contamination. Clean or replace defective parts.

6. *Hard pedal*—Check brake linings for contamination. Also check for restricted brake lines and hoses. If equipped with power brakes, test the brake booster (Chapter Ten).

7. *High speed fade*—Check for distorted or out-of-round brake discs or drums. Be sure recommended brake fluid is installed. Drain entire system and refill if in doubt.

8. *Pulsating pedal*—Check for distorted or out-of-round brake drums. On cars, check for excessive brake disc runout.

STEERING AND SUSPENSION

The following symptoms indicate steering or suspension trouble.

a. Steering is hard

b. Car pulls to one side
c. Car wanders or front wheels wobble
d. Steering has excessive play
e. Tire wear is abnormal

Unusual steering, pulling, or wandering is usually caused by bent or otherwise misaligned suspension parts. This is difficult to check without proper alignment equipment. See Chapter Twelve for repairs that you can perform, and those that must be left to a dealer or front end specialist.

If the trouble seems to be excessive play, check wheel bearing adjustment first. Next check steering free play. Check suspension and tie rod ball-joints. Check pitman arm nut and idler arm nut for looseness. See Chapter Twelve.

Tire wear may be caused by suspension troubles, but it may have many other causes. See *Tire Wear Analysis* in this chapter.

TIRE WEAR ANALYSIS

Abnormal tire wear should always be analyzed to determine its cause, which should then be corrected. The most common factors are:

a. Incorrect tire pressure
b. Improper driving
c. Overloading
d. Bad road surfaces
e. Incorrect wheel alignment

Figure 7 identifies wear patterns and indicates the most probable causes.

WHEEL BALANCING

All 4 wheels and tires must be in balance along 2 axes. To be in static balance (**Figure 8**), weight must be distributed evenly around the axis of rotation. (A) shows a statically unbalanced wheel; (B) shows the result—wheel tramp or hopping; (C) shows proper static balance.

To be in dynamic balance (**Figure 9**), the centerline of the weight must coincide with the centerline of the wheel. (A) shows a dynamically unbalanced wheel; (B) shows the result—wheel wobble or shimmy; (C) shows proper dynamic balance.

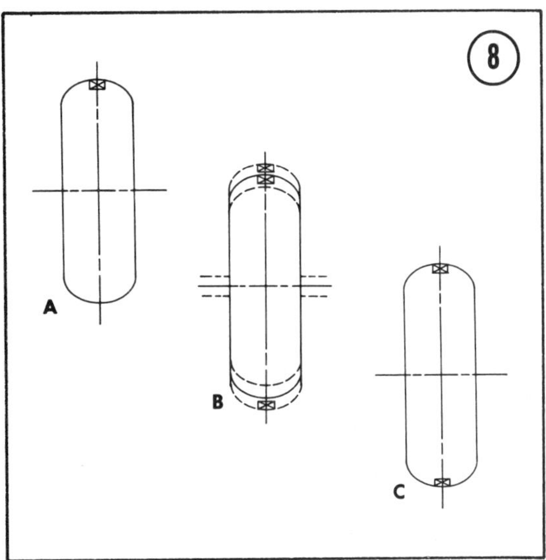

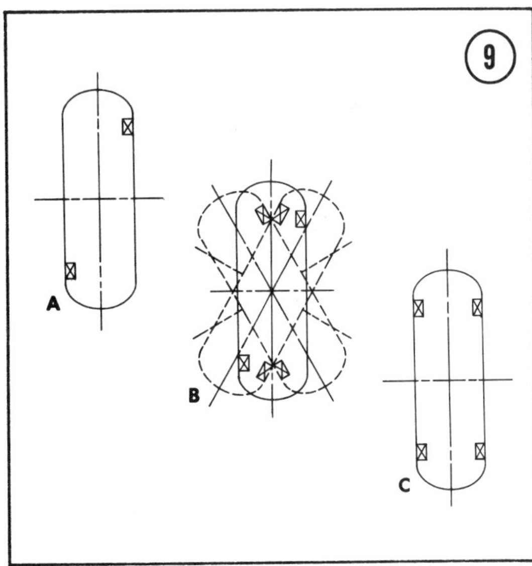

3

7

Underinflation—Worn more on sides than in center.

Wheel Alignment—Worn more on one side than the other. Edges of tread feathered.

Wheel Balance – Scalloped edges indicate wheel wobble or tramp due to wheel unbalance.

Road Abrasion—Rough wear on entire tire or in patches.

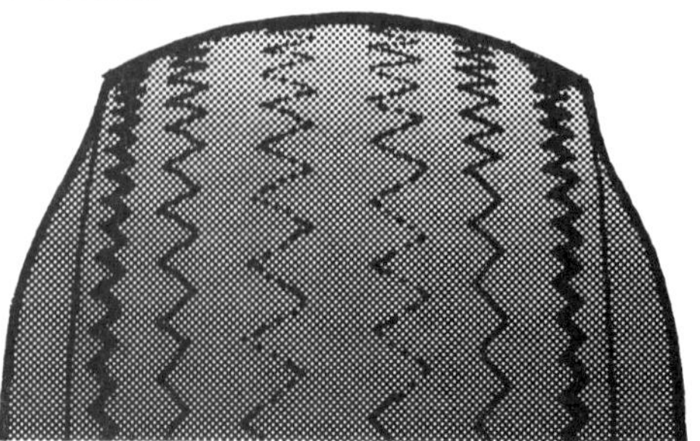

Overinflation—Worn more in center than on sides.

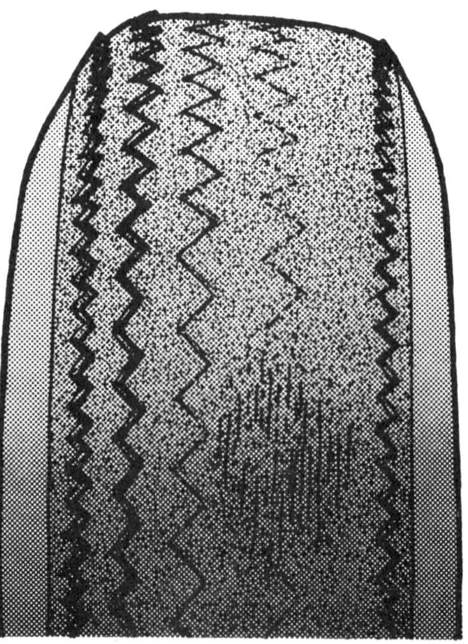

Combination—Most tires exhibit a combination of the above. This tire was overinflated (center worn) and the toe-in was incorrect (feathering). The driver cornered hard at high speed (feathering, rounded shoulders) and braked rapidly (worn spots). The scaly roughness indicates a rough road surface.

CHAPTER FOUR

4

ENGINE

All models use 4-cylinder versions of Datsun's L-series engine. Six-cylinder versions of the same engine are used in the 240-260-280 Z sports cars.

The overhead camshaft, mounted in 4 brackets on top of the cylinder head, operates the valves through finger rockers. The crankshaft, supported by 5 main bearings, drives the camshaft through a double-row chain and 2 sprockets. The lubrication system consists of an external oil pump and full-flow filter.

The L16 engine, used in 510's, displaces 97.3 cu. in. (1595cc). The L18, used in 1973 610's and 1974 710's, displaces 108 cu. in. (1770cc). The L20B, used in 1974 610's and all 1975-76 models, displaces 119.1 cu. in. (1952cc). Specifications and tightening torques (**Tables 1 and 2**) are at the end of the chapter.

ENGINE REMOVAL

Although it is possible to remove the engine separately from the transmission, it is much easier to remove engine and transmission as a unit and then separate them. Remove as follows.

1. Using a soft-lead pencil, scribe alignment marks around the hood hinges onto the hood. Remove the hood. The marks will ease hood installation.
2. Disconnect negative cable from battery.
3. Completely drain the cooling system, then remove the radiator (Chapter Six).
4. Remove the air cleaner (Chapter Five). On 1970-72 cars, connect the thin hoses (large arrows, **Figure 1**), running from the flow guide valve to the air cleaner and engine. The flow guide valve is part of the evaporative emission control system.

5. Disconnect the inlet line from the fuel pump. Plug the line so it won't siphon gas from tank.
6. Disconnect the heater hoses at engine or firewall, whichever you find more convenient. **Figure 2** shows a typical firewall connection.

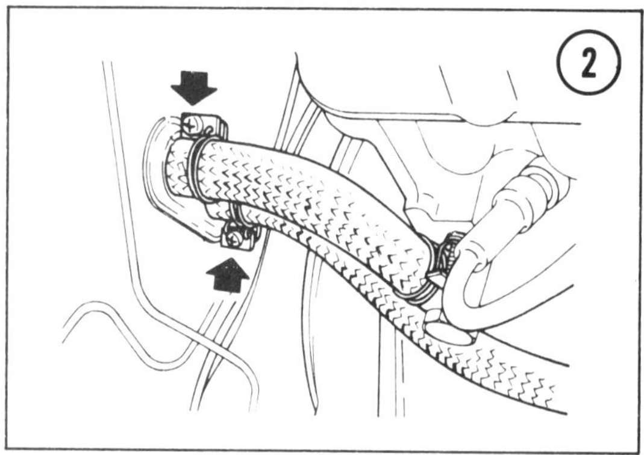

7. Remove throttle linkage return spring (1, **Figure 3**) and disconnect the joint (2). Detach and remove the torsion shaft (3).

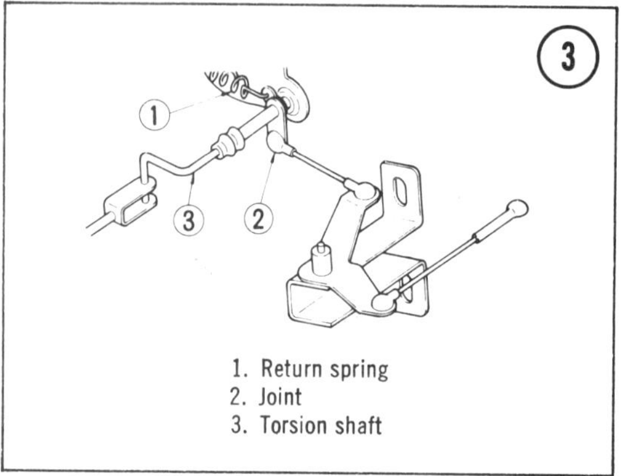

1. Return spring
2. Joint
3. Torsion shaft

8. On manual chokes, disconnect the choke cable. On automatic chokes, disconnect the choke electrical wire.

9. Disconnect the wires from starter, alternator, ignition coil, oil pressure switch, and water temperature sender(s). On 1975-76 cars, disconnect the wiring connectors. One is above the right-hand motor mount (**Figure 4**); the other is beneath the ignition coil (**Figure 5**).

10. Disconnect the engine ground cable.

11. On manual transmission cars, remove the shift lever (**Figure 6**). Remove the clutch operating cylinder (Chapter Eight). Disconnect the speedometer cable. Disconnect the wires from the electrical switches on the right-hand side of the transmission.

12. On automatic transmissions, disconnect the fluid cooler lines from the bottom of the radiator (**Figure 7**). Disconnect the inhibitor switch wires from the right-hand side of the transmission.

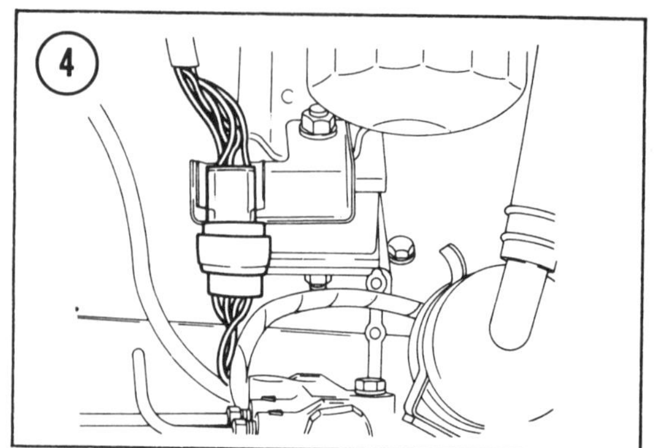

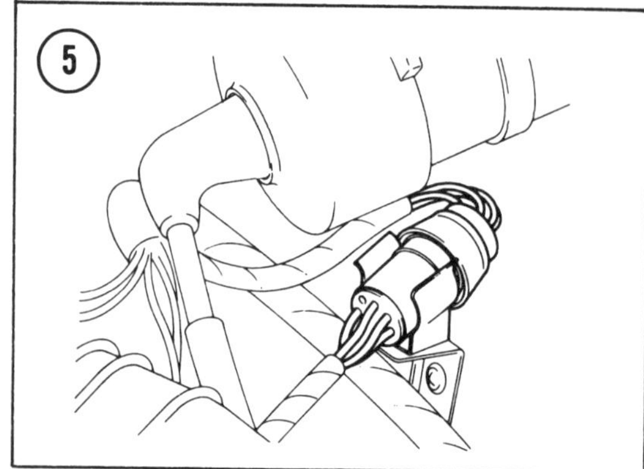

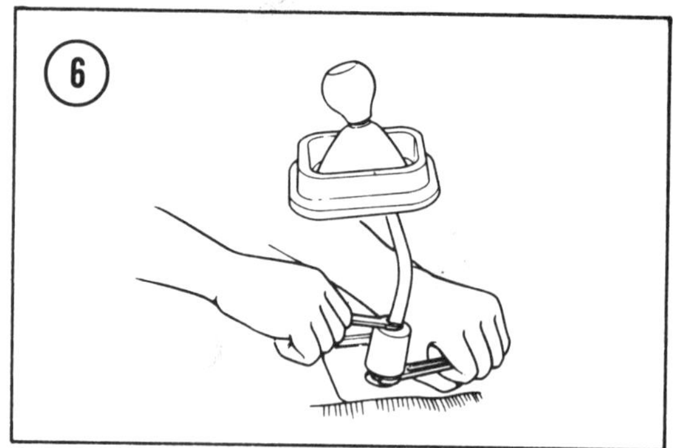

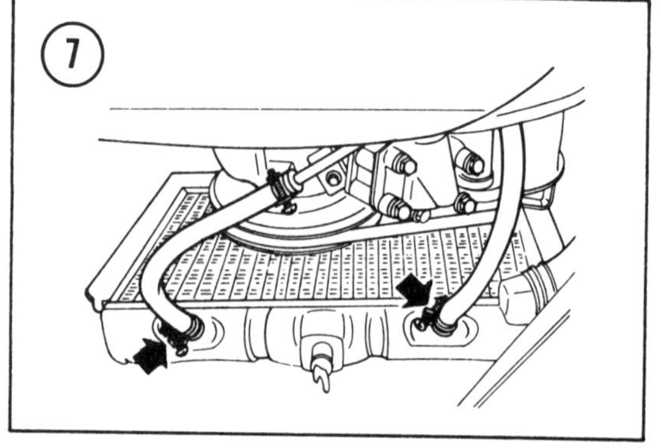

Disconnect the downshift solenoid wire and vacuum line from the left side. Disconnect the speedometer cable.

13. On 1974-76 610's and 1975-76 710's with automatic transmission, disconnect the control rod from the bottom end of the selector lever (**Figure 8**). On all others, disconnect the range selector lever from the manual shaft (**Figure 9**).

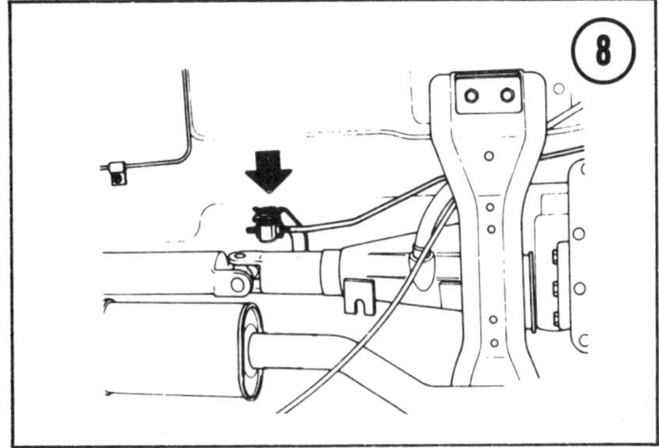

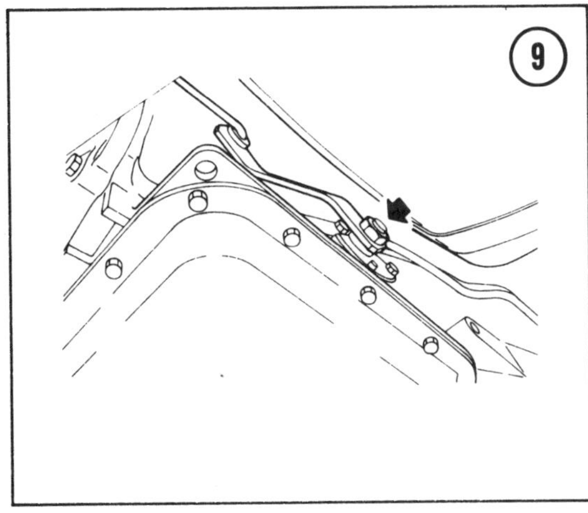

14. Remove the drive shaft (Chapter Eleven).

15. Disconnect the front exhaust tube from the manifold. On 1975-76 California cars, disconnect the front exhaust tube from the catalytic converter as well.

16. If equipped with power brakes, disconnect the booster vacuum line from intake manifold.

17. Place a jack beneath the transmission. Detach the transmission mounting bracket from the transmission, then from the vehicle.

18. Unbolt the engine mounting brackets from the rubber insulators.

NOTE: *At this point, there should be no wires, hoses, or linkages attaching the engine or transmission to the vehicle. Recheck this to be sure nothing will hamper engine removal.*

19. Attach a hoist to the engine slinger brackets at front and rear ends of the engine. Gradually lower the jack beneath the transmission while raising the engine. Remove the jack from beneath the transmission. Continue raising the engine, tilting as necessary, until it is clear of the vehicle.

CAUTION

Do not let the engine strike equipment installed on the engine compartment walls during removal.

20. Once the engine and transmission are clear of the car, lower them to a suitable support or stand and disconnect the hoist.

21. Remove the bolts attaching the transmission to the engine.

22. Check the rubber mounting insulators for wear or damage. Replace as needed.

ENGINE INSTALLATION

Engine installation is simply the reverse of removal. Fasten the engine securely to its mounts before tightening anything else. See Table 2 (end of chapter) for tightening torques. Bleed and adjust the clutch as described in Chapter Eight. Fill the engine and transmission with oils recommended in Chapter Two. Fill the cooling system with a 50/50 mixture of antifreeze and water.

DISASSEMBLY SEQUENCES

The following 3 sequences are basic outlines that tell how much of the engine to remove and disassemble to perform a specific type of service. They are designed to keep engine disassembly to a minimum, thus avoiding unnecessary work. The major assemblies mentioned in these sequences are covered in detail under their own headings in this chapter, unless otherwise noted.

To use these sequences, first determine what type of service you plan to do (a valve job, for example). Then turn to the sequence for that type of service. To perform a step within a sequence, turn to the section covering the major assembly mentioned in that step, and perform the removal and inspection procedures. Do the same for each step until all necessary disassembly has been completed. To reassemble, reverse the sequences, performing the installation procedure for each major assembly mentioned.

Decarbonizing or Valve Service

1. Remove the exhaust and intake manifolds (Chapter Five).
2. Remove the rocker arms and camshaft.
3. Remove the cylinder head.
4. Remove and inspect valves. Inspect valve guides and seats, repairing or replacing as necessary.
5. Assemble by reversing Steps 1-4.

Valve and Ring Service

1. Perform Steps 1-4 for valve service.
2. Remove the oil pan.
3. Remove the pistons together with the connecting rods.
4. Remove the piston rings. It is not necessary to separate the pistons from the connecting rods unless a piston, connecting rod, or piston pin needs repair or replacement.
5. Assemble by reversing Steps 1-4.

General Overhaul

1. Remove the engine and transmission and separate them. Remove the clutch (Chapter Eight) from manual transmission vehicles.
2. Remove the oil filter, dipstick, and oil pressure sender from the right-hand side of the cylinder block.
3. Remove the motor mounts.
4. Remove the fuel pump, carburetor, and manifolds. If equipped with an air pump, remove it also. See Chapter Five.
5. Remove the fan, water pump, and thermostat (Chapter Six). Remove the thermostat housing from the cylinder head.
6. Remove the alternator and the distributor (Chapter Seven).
7. Remove the rocker arms and camshaft.
8. Remove the cylinder head.
9. Remove the flywheel.
10. Remove the oil pan, strainer, oil pump, and pump driving spindle.
11. Remove the engine front cover. Remove the timing chain and related parts.
12. Remove piston-connecting rod assemblies.
13. Remove the crankshaft.
14. Inspect the cylinder block.
15. Assembly is the reverse of these steps.

CAMSHAFT AND ROCKER ARMS

Figure 10 shows the camshaft. **Figure 11** shows rocker arm and valve parts.

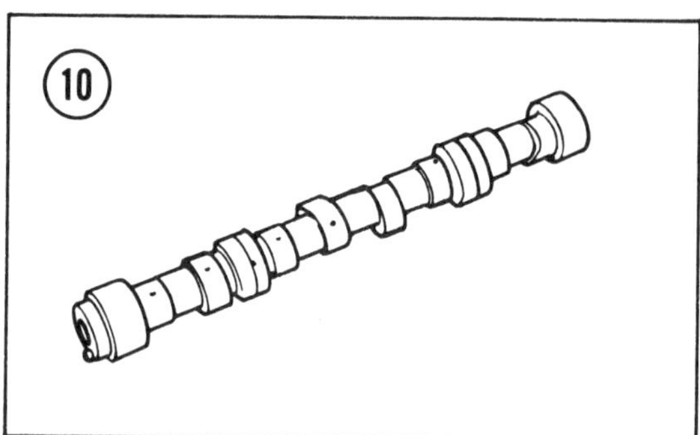

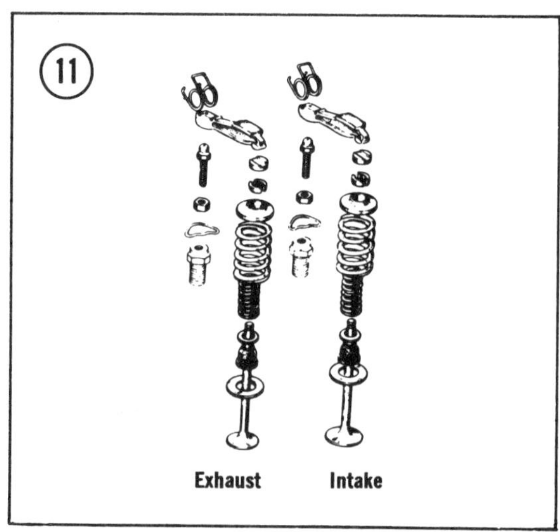

Rocker Arm Removal

1. Remove the rocker arm cover.
2. Remove the springs looped over the tops of the rocker arms.

3. Loosen the locknut on the rocker arm pivot. Compress the valve spring by using a heavy-bladed screwdriver as a lever and the camshaft as a fulcrum. See **Figure 12**.

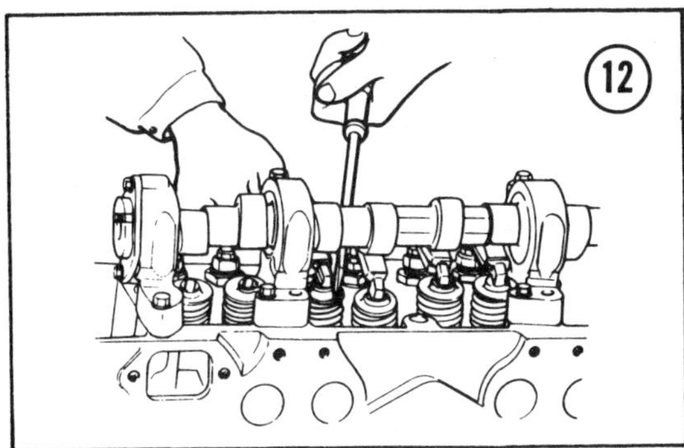

4. Withdraw the rocker arm while holding the valve springs down with the screwdriver. Be careful not to lose the rocker arm guide located between the rocker arm and the top of the valve stem.

5. If the rocker pivot is visibly worn, unscrew it from the cylinder head, together with its locknut.

6. Install by reversing Steps 1-5.

Rocker Arm Inspection

Examine the rocker arm for visible wear on its cam contact surface, pivot contact surface, and valve contact surface. If wear or any defects can be seen, replace the rocker arm. If the rocker arm pivot is visibly worn, both the pivot and its corresponding rocker arm must be replaced.

Camshaft Removal

1. Remove the rocker arm cover.
2. Remove the fuel pump (Chapter Five).
3. Check camshaft end play. Position a dial gauge as shown in **Figure 13**. Slide the camshaft back and forth against the dial gauge pointer. The reading on the gauge is camshaft end play. It should range from 0.003-0.015 in. (0.08-0.38mm). Replace the camshaft locate plate if end play is not within specifications.
4. Turn the engine over by hand until the timing marks on camshaft and timing chain are aligned. See **Figure 14**. This will enable you to position the camshaft correctly during installation.

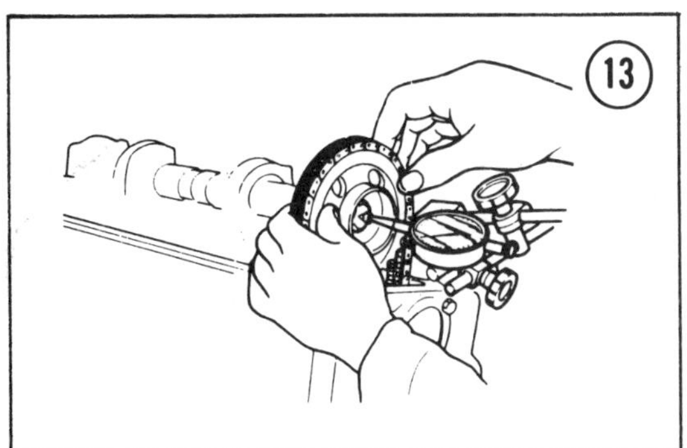

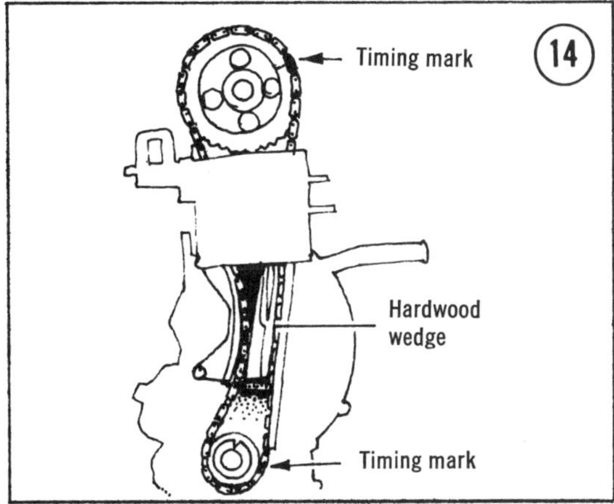

5. Remove all rocker arms as described earlier.
6. Insert a hardwood wedge, such as Datsun tool No. ST 17420001, between the sides of the chain. Figure 14 shows the tool in place; **Figure 15** shows it alone. This tool keeps the timing marks on crankshaft sprocket and chain aligned. It also prevents the chain tensioner piston from popping out. If the chain slips off the sprocket or the piston falls out, the front cover and oil pan must be removed to reinstall it.

> NOTE: *If you make your own tool, use a piece of hardwood about one inch thick. Do not use plywood, since this may leave fragments in the engine. Drill a hole in the top of the tool so it can be pulled out.*

7. Remove the bolt from the front end of the camshaft. Remove the fuel pump cam and camshaft sprocket. Take the sprocket out of the chain, and drape the chain out of the way.
8. Remove 2 bolts and take the camshaft locate plate off the front camshaft bracket.

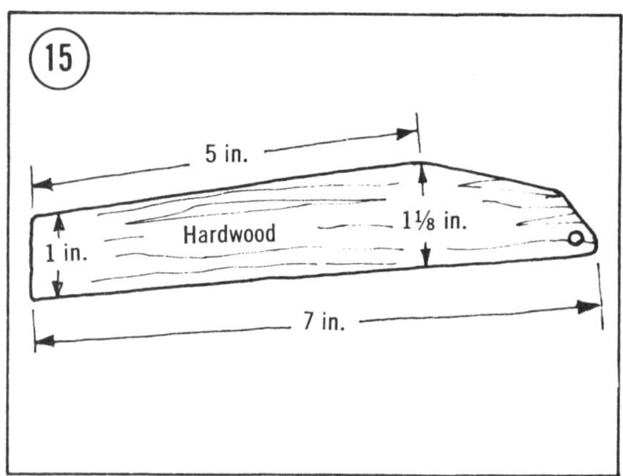

9. Carefully withdraw the camshaft toward the front of the engine. Rotate the camshaft slowly while removing. Be careful not to scratch the camshaft bearing surfaces.

CAUTION

Never remove camshaft brackets from the cylinder head, even though removal looks easy. If the brackets are removed, it will be extremely difficult if not impossible to realign the bearing centers.

Camshaft Inspection

1. Measure the inner diameter of the camshaft bearings (**Figure 16**). This figure must be between 1.8898-1.8904 in. (48.00-48.016mm). If any bearings are worn beyond the maximum, replace the entire cylinder head.

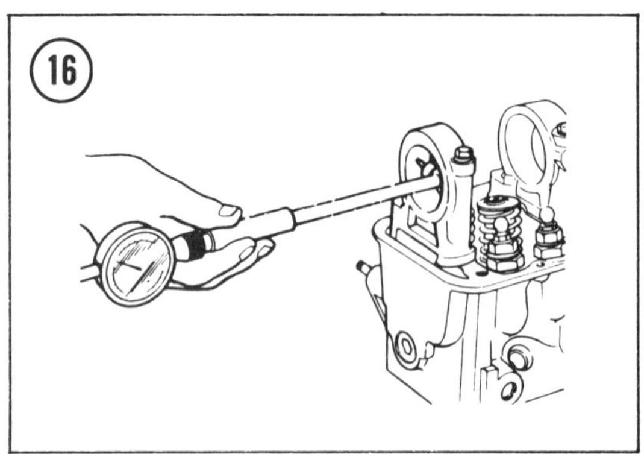

2. Measure the outer diameter of the camshaft journals. Subtract these figures from the bearing inner diameters to determine oil clearance. Normal oil clearance is 0.0015-0.0026 in. (0.038-0.076mm). If the bearings were within specifications in Step 1, and oil clearance exceeds 0.004 in. (0.1mm), the camshaft must be replaced.

3. Measure camshaft bend. Rotate the camshaft between accurate centers (such as V-blocks or a lathe) with a dial indicator contacting the second and third journals. See **Figure 17**. Actual bend is half the reading shown on the gauge when the camshaft is rotated one full turn. Normal bend is 0.0008 in. (0.02mm) or less. Replace the camshaft if bend exceeds 0.002 in. (0.05mm).

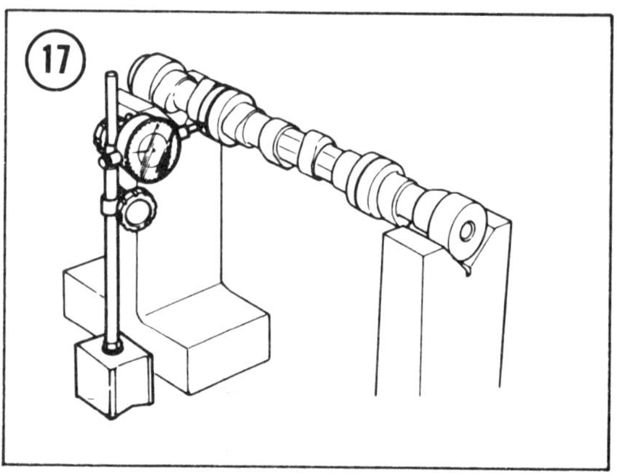

4. Check the camshaft sprocket for runout. Measure with the sprocket installed on the camshaft, as shown in **Figure 18**. Replace sprocket if runout exceeds 0.004 in. (0.1mm).

Camshaft Installation

1. Coat the camshaft journals and bearing surfaces with clean engine oil.

2. Carefully install the camshaft in the brackets. Rotate the camshaft slowly while inserting to ease installation.

3. Install the camshaft locate plate and secure it with 2 bolts. The small groove in the locating plate goes on top and faces the front.

4. Install the rocker arms as described earlier.

5. Lift up the timing chain and remove the support tool. Place the camshaft sprocket in the chain, making sure the timing marks on sprocket and chain are aligned.

6. Slide the sprocket onto the camshaft. Use the sprocket locating hole that was used before removal. Install the fuel pump cam, then the sprocket bolt and lockwasher. Tighten to 87-116 ft.-lb. (12-16 mkg).

7. Install the fuel pump (Chapter Five) and rocker arm cover.

OIL PAN AND PUMP

Oil Pan Removal/Installation

1. Set the handbrake and place the transmission in gear. Jack up the front end of the vehicle and place it on jackstands.

2. Remove the splash pan from under the front end (if so equipped).

3. Remove the suspension crossmember and stabilizer (Chapter Twelve). Crossmember removal requires that the engine be supported by a hoist.

4. Unbolt the oil pan from the engine. Lower it clear and take it out from under the vehicle.

5. Clean the oil pan thoroughly. If it is difficult to clean, have the pan boiled out by a machine shop. Check for cracks, dents, bent gasket surfaces, and damaged drain hole threads. Replace the oil pan if damage is severe.

6. Check for a clogged oil strainer. Remove the strainer and clean it if necessary.

7. Installation is the reverse of these steps. Remove all traces of old gasket and sealer from the oil pan and cylinder block. Use new gaskets, coated on both sides with gasket sealer. Tighten the oil pan bolts evenly, a little at a time, to prevent warping the oil pan.

Oil Pump Removal/Installation

1. Turn the engine over until No. 1 piston is at top dead center (TDC) on the compression stroke. When this occurs, the timing pointer will point to the 0° mark on the crankshaft pulley and the distributor rotor will point to No. 1 spark plug's wire terminal in the distributor cap.

2. Remove the distributor (Chapter Seven).

3. Dain the engine oil.

4. Remove the splash pan from under the front of the car (if so equipped).

5. Remove 4 pump mounting bolts. Take out the pump and its driving spindle. See **Figure 19**.

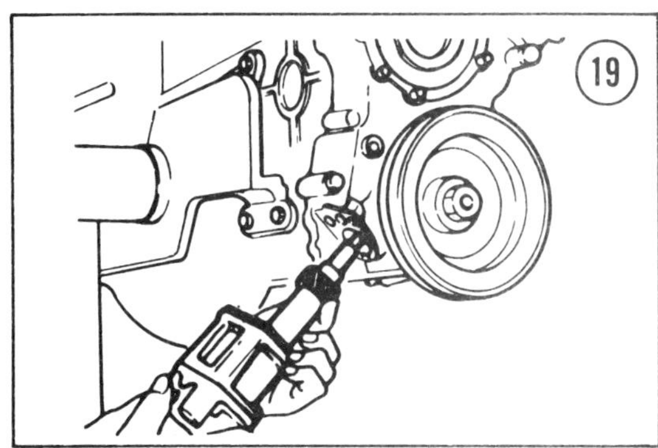

6. Installation is the reverse of these steps. Make sure the punched mark on the distributor driving spindle lines up with the hole in the oil pump (**Figure 20**). Install the distributor as described in Chapter Seven. Fill the engine with an oil recommended in Chapter Two.

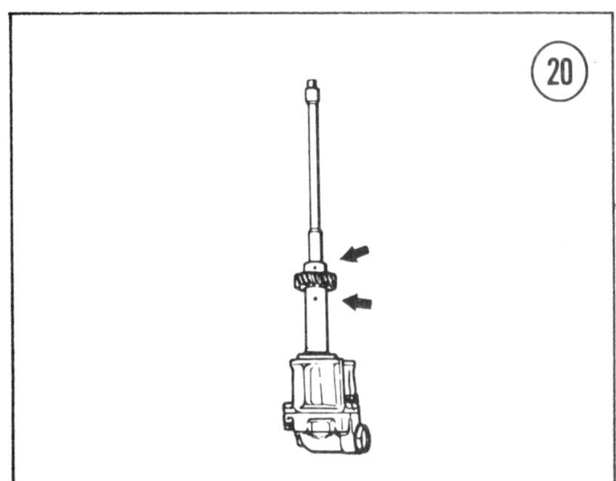

Disassembly/Inspection/Assembly

1. Remove the oil pump cover and gasket. See **Figure 21**.

2. Lift out the inner and outer pump rotors. Remove the regulator valve parts.

4

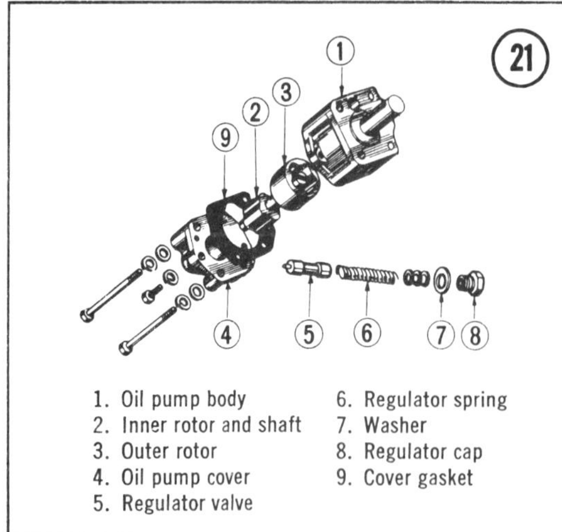

1. Oil pump body
2. Inner rotor and shaft
3. Outer rotor
4. Oil pump cover
5. Regulator valve
6. Regulator spring
7. Washer
8. Regulator cap
9. Cover gasket

3. Clean all parts in solvent. Check the distributor driving spindle and pump rotors for wear, scoring, or visible damage. Check oil pump clearances (**Figure 22**) and compare with specifications at the end of the chapter. Replace the pump if any clearances are excessive.

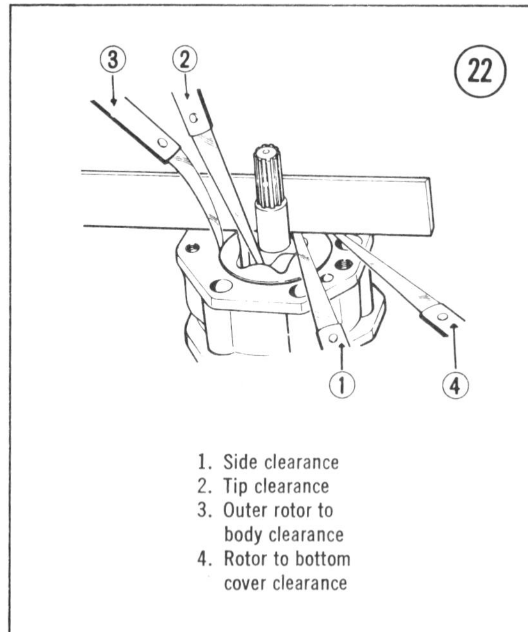

1. Side clearance
2. Tip clearance
3. Outer rotor to body clearance
4. Rotor to bottom cover clearance

4. Measure the regulator valve spring free length. Compare with specifications (end of chapter). Replace the spring if it is too long or too short.

5. Install the regulator valve parts. Tighten the valve cap to 29-36 ft.-lb. (4-5 mkg).

6. Install the inner rotor in the pump. Place the outer rotor over it. Install a new cover gasket, coated lightly on both sides with gasket sealer. Install the pump cover. Take care not to fold the cover gasket.

FRONT COVER, TIMING CHAIN, AND SPROCKETS

Front Cover Removal

1. Remove the radiator and fan (Chapter Six). Remove the air pump belt (if so equipped).
2. Remove the distributor (Chapter Seven).
3. Remove the oil pan, oil pump, and pump driving spindle as described earlier in this chapter.
4. Remove the crankshaft pulley.
5. Remove bolts attaching the front cover to cylinder head and block. See **Figure 23**.

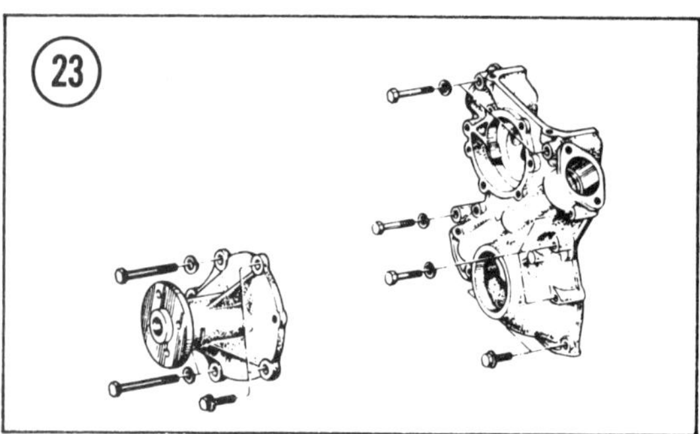

6. Withdraw the front cover forward and down, together with the water pump.

Front Cover Installation

Front cover installation is the reverse of removal, plus the following.

1. Use new left and right cover gaskets, coated on both sides with gasket sealer. Apply small amounts of sealer to the corners of the front cover. See **Figure 24**.
2. Install a new front cover oil seal as described in the next procedure. This should be done whenever the front cover is removed.
3. Take care not to bend the front portion of the head gasket when installing the cover. Be sure to install the cylinder head-to-cover bolts.
4. Fill the engine with oil and the radiator with coolant.

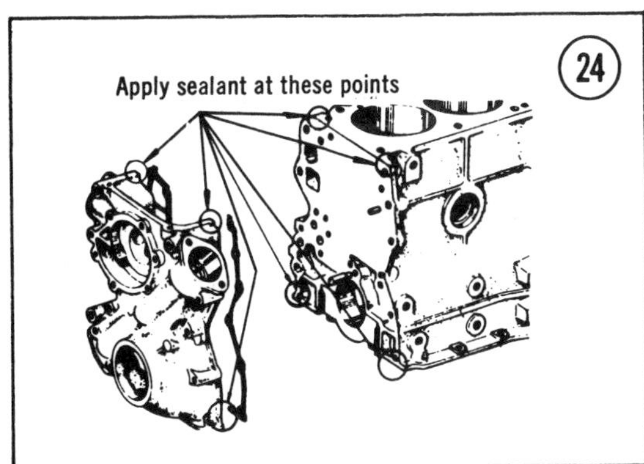

Front Oil Seal Replacement

1. Remove the front cover as described earlier.
2. Carefully pry out the old oil seal. Do not gouge the aluminum front cover.
3. Tap in a new oil seal. Coat the seal lip with multipurpose grease.
4. Install the front cover as described earlier.

Sprocket and Chain Removal

1. Remove the valve rocker cover.
2. Remove the fuel pump (Chapter Five).
3. Remove the oil pan, oil pump, and pump driving spindle as described earlier in this chapter.
4. Remove the front cover as described earlier.
5. Install the crankshaft pulley bolt in the crankshaft. Put a wrench on the bolt and turn the engine over by hand until the timing marks in chain and sprockets are aligned (**Figure 25**).

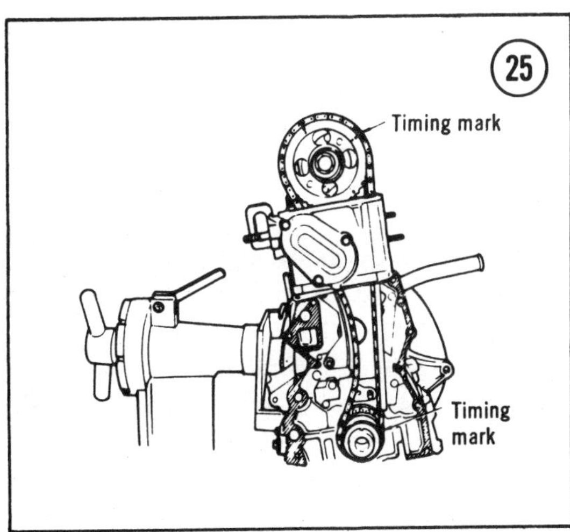

6. Referring to **Figure 26**, remove 2 bolts and lockwashers that attach the chain tensioner to the block.

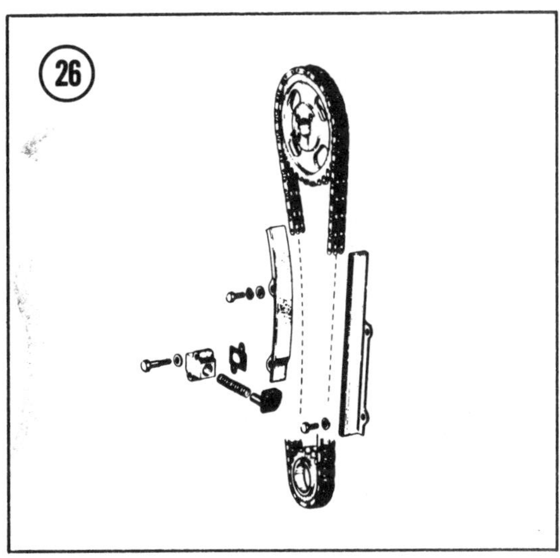

7. Remove 4 bolts and lockwashers holding the left and right chain guides to the block. Remove the guides.
8. Remove the camshaft sprocket and fuel pump from the front of the camshaft.
9. Remove the timing chain from the crankshaft sprocket.
10. Remove the crankshaft sprocket, distributor drive gear, and oil thrower with a puller as shown in **Figure 27**.

CAUTION

Do not rotate the crankshaft and camshaft separately, or the valves may strike the piston tops.

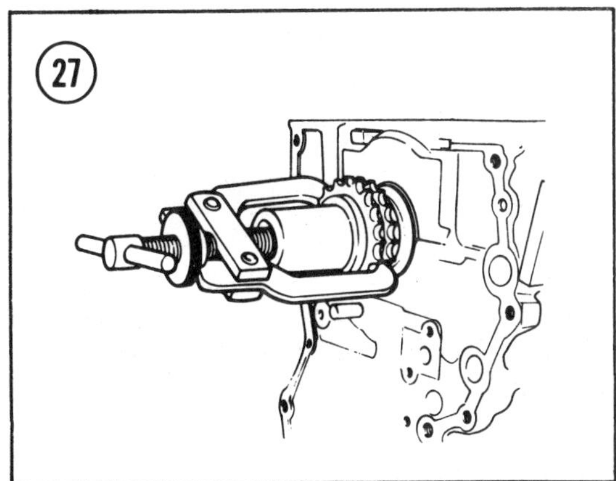

Inspection

1. Thoroughly clean all parts in solvent before inspection.

2. Check the chain tensioner assembly and chain guides for wear or damage. Replace if these are evident.

3. Inspect the sprockets, distributor drive gear, and oil thrower for wear or damage. Replace as needed.

4. Check the chain for wear, damage, or stretching of the roller links. Replace the chain if visibly defective. Check again for stretching as described in the next procedure.

Installation and Chain Inspection

1. Install the Woodruff keys in the crankshaft keyways if they have been removed.

2. Install the crankshaft sprocket, distributor drive gear, and oil thrower. See **Figure 28**.

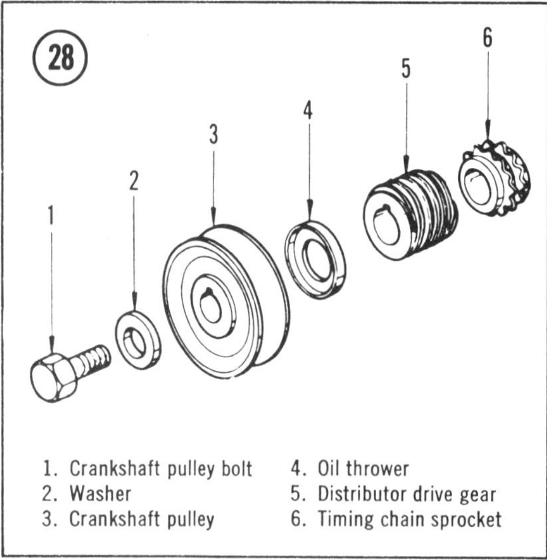

1. Crankshaft pulley bolt
2. Washer
3. Crankshaft pulley
4. Oil thrower
5. Distributor drive gear
6. Timing chain sprocket

3. Install the timing chain over the crankshaft and camshaft sprockets. Make sure the timing marks on the chain are aligned with the timing marks on the sprockets. See Figure 14.

4. Slide the camshaft sprocket onto the camshaft. Make sure the Woodruff keys on the crankshaft point straight up.

5. Bolt the chain guides to the cylinder block.

6. Install the chain tensioner. Push the tensioner spindle as far into the tensioner body as it will go.

7. Make sure that No. 1 piston is still at top dead center on its compression stroke.

8. Refer to **Figures 29 and 30** for this step. Figure 29 shows the camshaft locate plate; Figure 30 shows the camshaft sprocket. Note that there are 3 location holes in the sprocket, each with its own location notch and timing mark. Face the engine from the front. Note the relative positions of the location notch in the sprocket and the oblong groove in the camshaft locate plate. If the notch is completely to the left of the groove (as shown in top drawing, Figure 30), the timing chain is stretched excessively. Perform Steps 9-11 to adjust it. If the notch is not completely to the left (counterclockwise) of the groove, the timing chain is satisfactory and Steps 9-11 may be skipped.

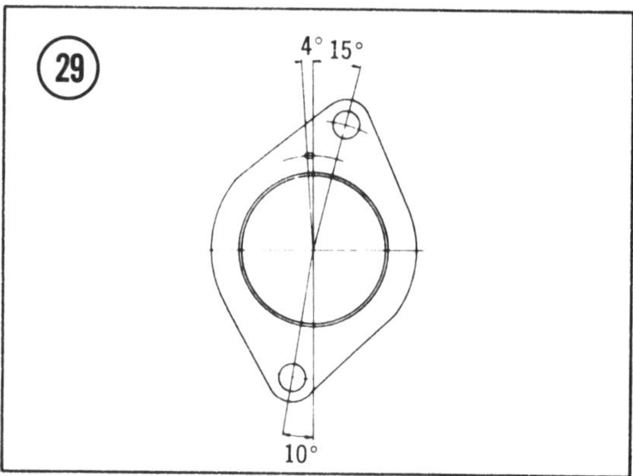

9. Remove the camshaft sprocket and reinstall it, using No. 2 location hole. No. 2 notch should now be at the right (clockwise) end of the oblong groove.

10. If the location notch position still is not correct, remove the camshaft sprocket again and reinstall it, this time using No. 3 location hole. No. 3 hole should now be at the right end of the oblong groove.

11. If the hole still is not in the correct position, the timing chain is stretched beyond use and must be replaced. Install the new chain as described in Steps 3 and 4, using No. 1 location hole in the camshaft sprocket.

12. Install the front cover as described earlier.

13. Install the oil pan and pump as described earlier in this chapter.

14. Install the distributor (Chapter Seven).

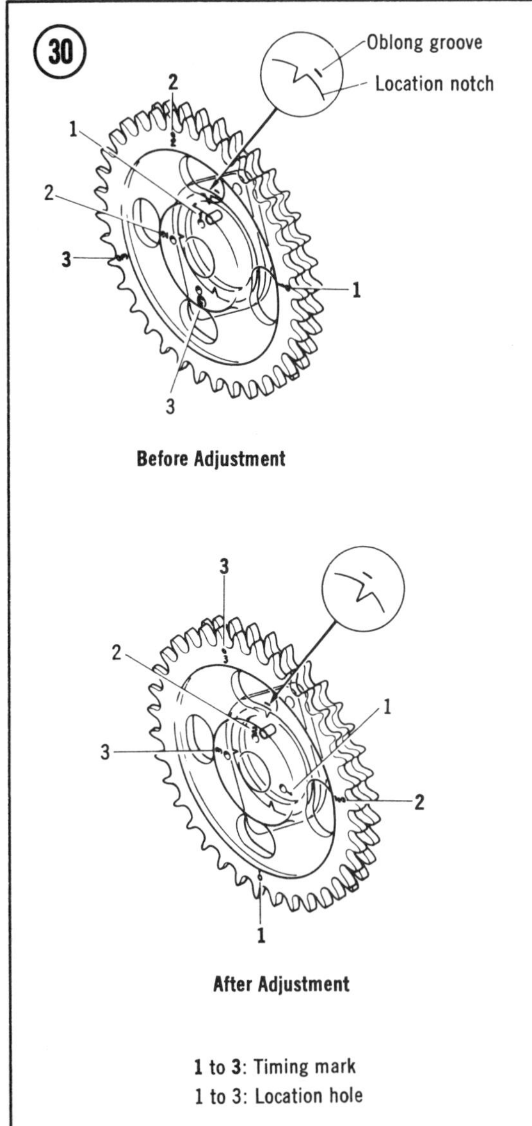

15. Install the fuel pump (Chapter Five).
16. Install the rocker arm cover.
17. Install the fan and radiator (Chapter Six).
18. Fill the engine with oil and the radiator with coolant.

CYLINDER HEAD

Some of the following procedures must be done by a dealer or machine shop, since they require special knowledge and expensive machine tools. Others, while possible for the home mechanic, are difficult or time-consuming. A general practice among those who do their own service is to remove the cylinder head, perform all disassembly except valve removal, and take the head to a machine shop for inspection and service. Since the cost is low in relation to the required effort and equipment, this is usually the best approach, even for more experienced owners.

Cylinder Head Removal

1. Completely drain the cooling system.
2. Remove all spark plugs.
3. Remove the air cleaner (Chapter Five).
4. Remove the rocker arm cover.
5. Remove the intake manifold, exhaust manifold, and fuel pump (Chapter Five).
6. Detach heater hoses from cylinder head.
7. Remove the thermostat housing and water outlet elbow from the left front of cylinder head.
8. Turn the camshaft so its sprocket locating pin is straight up. This provides a reference point for later installation.
9. Remove the camshaft sprocket as described under *Camshaft Removal* earlier in this chapter.
10. Remove 2 bolts attaching the cylinder head to the engine front cover.
11. Remove the 10 cylinder head bolts with a 10mm Allen socket (**Figure 31**). To prevent warping the cylinder head, loosen the bolts in several stages, following the order given in **Figure 32**.

NOTE: *There are different lengths of cylinder head bolts. Tag them as they are removed so they can be reinstalled in the same holes later.*

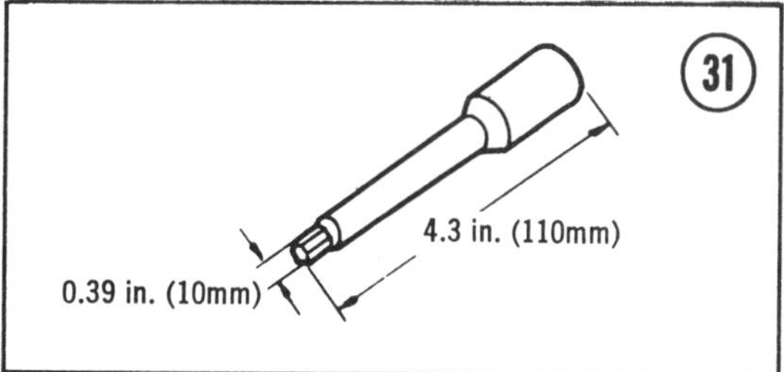

12. Once the head bolts are removed, lift the cylinder head off the engine. If the head is difficult to remove, tap it gently with a rubber mallet. If that does not work, try reinstalling the spark

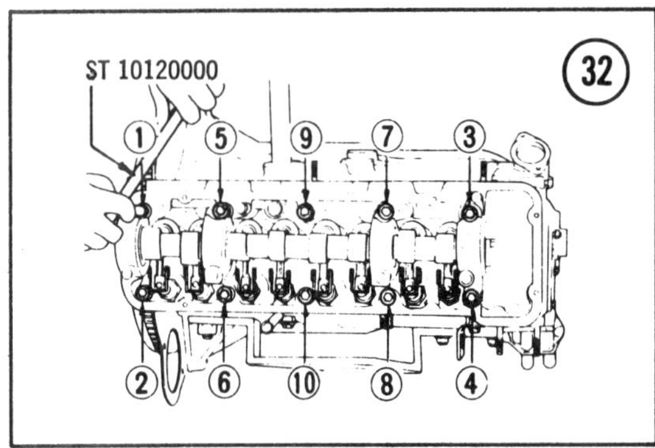

plugs and turning the engine over by hand. The compression should force the head loose.

CAUTION

Never remove the camshaft brackets from the cylinder head, even though removal appears easy. If the brackets are removed, it will be extremely difficult if not impossible to realign the bearing centers.

Cylinder Head Inspection

1. Check the cylinder head for water leaks before cleaning.
2. Clean the cylinder head thoroughly in solvent. While cleaning, check for cracks or other visible damage. Look for corrosion or foreign material in oil or water passages. Clean the passages with a stiff spiral wire brush, then blow them out with compressed air.
3. Check the cylinder head bottom (block mating) surface for flatness. Place an accurate straightedge along the surface. If there is any gap between the straightedge and cylinder head surface, measure it with a feeler gauge. Have the cylinder head resurfaced by a machine shop if the gap exceeds 0.004 in. (0.1mm).
4. Check studs in the cylinder head for general condition. Replace damaged studs.

Decarbonizing

1. Without removing valves, remove all deposits from the combustion chambers, intake ports, and exhaust ports. Use a wire brush dipped in solvent, or make a scraper out of hardwood. Be careful not to scratch or gouge the combustion chambers.
2. After all carbon is removed from the combustion chambers and ports, clean the entire head in solvent.
3. Clean away all carbon on the piston tops. Do not remove the carbon ridge at the top of the cylinder bore.

Cylinder Head Installation

1. Be sure the cylinder head, block, and cylinder bores are clean. Check all visible oil passages for cleanliness.
2. Install the camshaft and rocker arms in the cylinder head. Turn the camshaft so its sprocket locating pin is straight up. This must be done before the cylinder head is installed to prevent the valves from striking the piston tops.
3. Install a new cylinder head gasket. Never reuse an old head gasket. Do *not* use gasket sealer on the head gasket.
4. Position cylinder head on block. On early engines, install bolts according to labels made during disassembly. On late engines, install the 4 long bolts in the "A" holes (**Figure 33**). Install the 6 short bolts in the "B" holes.

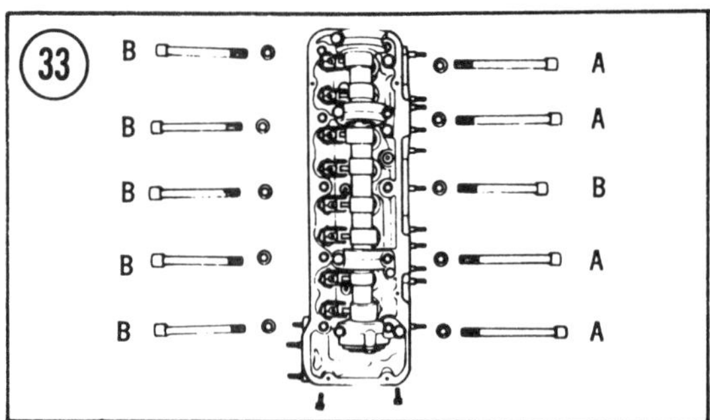

NOTE: *When positioning the cylinder head, look at the valves and make sure none are open far enough to strike the piston tops.*

5. With engine cool, tighten head bolts in order given in **Figure 34**. Tighten in 3 stages: first to 29 ft.-lb. (4 mkg); then to 43 ft.-lb. (6 mkg); then to the final torque specified in Table 2.
6. Install the timing chain, camshaft sprocket, and fuel pump cam as described under *Camshaft Installation* earlier in this chapter.
7. Install the thermostat housing and water outlet elbow on the left front of the cylinder head.

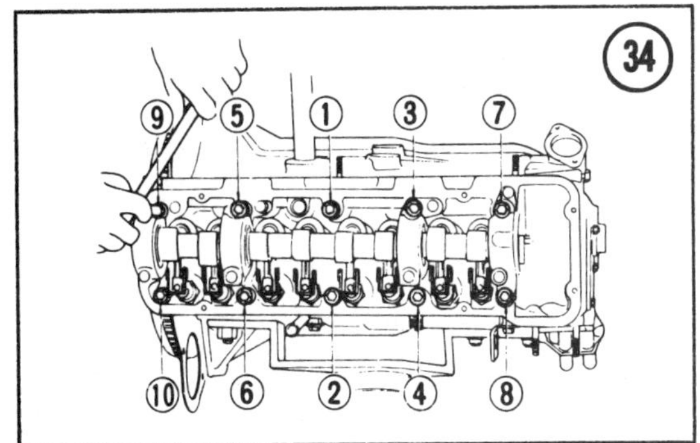

8. Install the manifolds, carburetor, and fuel pump (Chapter Five).

9. Attach the heater hoses to the right rear of the cylinder head.

10. Install spark plugs and rocker arm cover.

11. Install the air cleaner (Chapter Five).

12. Fill the cooling system with a 50/50 mixture of anti-freeze and water. Check the oil level and top up if necessary with a grade recommended in Chapter Two.

13. Run the engine for several minutes, let it cool, then recheck head bolt tightness.

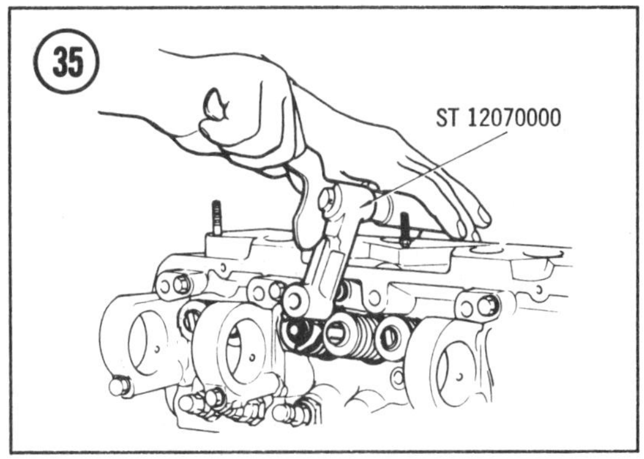

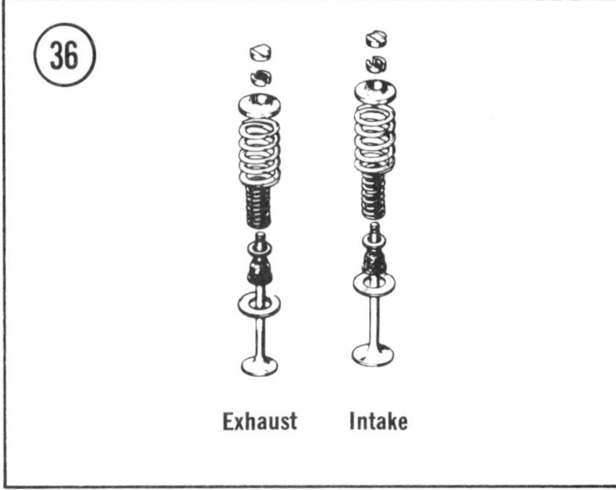

VALVES AND VALVE SEATS

Valve Removal

1. Remove cylinder head as described earlier. Remove camshaft from the head.

2. Compress each valve spring with a compressor like the one shown in **Figure 35**. Remove the valve locking collets (valve keepers) and release the spring tension. Remove the spring washer, oil seal(s), inner and outer valve springs, and spring seat. **Figure 36** shows valve and related parts.

CAUTION
Remove any burrs from valve stem grooves before removing valves. Otherwise the valve guides will be damaged.

Valve and Valve Guide Inspection

1. Clean the valves with a wire brush and solvent. Discard cracked, warped, or burned valves.

2. Measure the valve stems at the bottom, center, and top for wear, using a micrometer. A machine shop can do this when the valves are ground. Also measure the length of each valve, and the diameter of each valve head.

3. The valve faces and stem ends should be refaced when the valves are ground. No more than 0.020 in. (0.5mm) may be removed from valve stem ends. Valve faces may not be ground thinner than 0.020 in. (0.5mm).

4. Remove all carbon and varnish from valve guides with a stiff spiral wire brush.

NOTE: *The next step assumes that all valve stems have been measured and are within specifications. Replace any valves with worn stems before performing this step.*

5. Insert each valve into the guide from which it was removed. Hold the valve just slightly off its seat and rock it back and forth in a direction parallel with the rocker arms. This is the direction in which the greatest wear normally occurs. If the valve stem rocks more than approximately 0.008 in. (0.2mm), the valve guide is probably worn.

6. If there is any doubt about valve guide condition after performing Step 5, measure the valve guide at top, bottom, and center with a bore gauge. Compare with specifications (end of chapter). Have worn guides replaced.

7. Measure valve spring free length and compare with specifications. Replace springs that are too long or too short. Measure spring bend with a square. Replace springs that are bent more than 0.063 in. (1.6mm).

8. Have the valve springs tested under load on a spring tester. Replace weak springs.

9. Inspect valve seat inserts. If worn or burned, they must be reconditioned. This should be done by a dealer or machine shop, although the procedure is described later in this section.

Valve Guide Replacement

This procedure requires a press and reaming tools. If you do not have the necessary equipment, take the job to a dealer or machine shop.

1. Remove worn guides with a press and suitable drift. This can be done at room temperature. Removal will be easier if the cylinder head is heated first.

2. Ream the guide holes in the cylinder head to specifications (end of chapter).

3. Heat the cylinder head to 302-392°F (150-200°C).

4. Press the guides into place from the top of the cylinder head. The guides should protrude 0.4173 in. (10.6mm) from the top of the cylinder head (**Figure 37**).

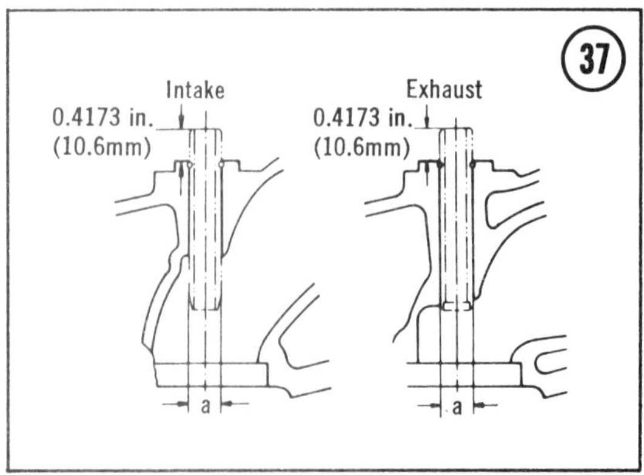

5. Measure valve guide bores. Ream to specifications (**Figure 38**).

Valve Seat Inserts

The valve seats are cut into inserts. Intake valve seats are aluminum/bronze alloy; exhaust valve seats are heat-resistant steel. Replacement requires precision machine tools and special skills. Take the job to a Datsun dealer or machine shop.

1. Remove the old valve seat by boring it out until it collapses. Be sure not to cut the cylinder head during boring.

2. Select a valve seat insert and check its outside diameter. Compare with specifications (end of chapter).

3. Machine the cylinder head recess diameter to fit the valve seat insert, using the valve guide as an axis.

4. Heat the cylinder head to 302-392°F (150-200°C).

5. Press the valve seat insert into place. Be sure it beds securely on the cylinder head. Stake the insert at 5 or more places.

6. Grind the valve seats as described in the following procedure.

Valve Seat Reconditioning

1. Cut the valve seats to specified dimensions, using a cutter (**Figure 39**) or a special stone. **Figure 40** shows valve seat dimensions for early L16 engines. **Figure 41** shows intake valve seat for all 1972-1976 L-series engines. **Figure 42** shows the 1972-1973 L16 exhaust valve seat. **Figure 43** shows the 1973-1976 L18 and L20B exhaust valve seat.

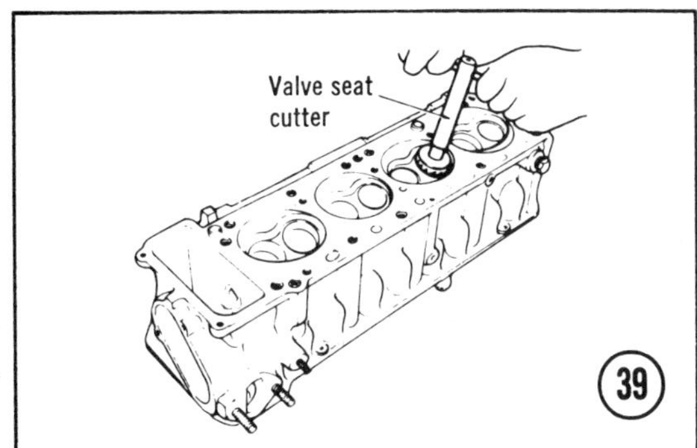

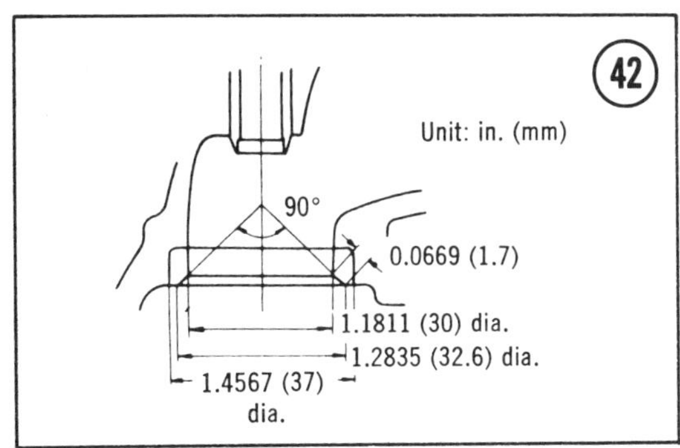

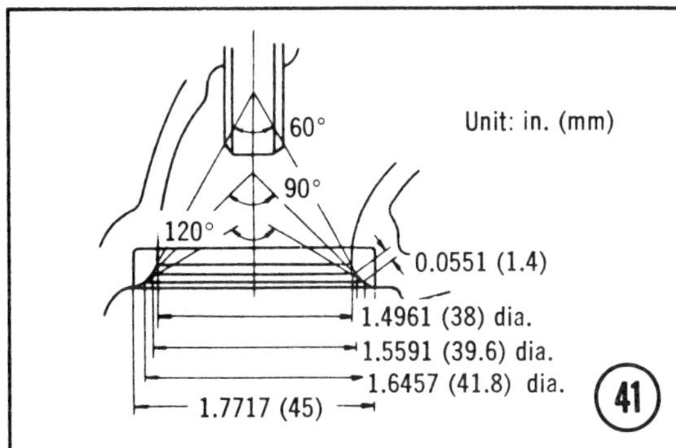

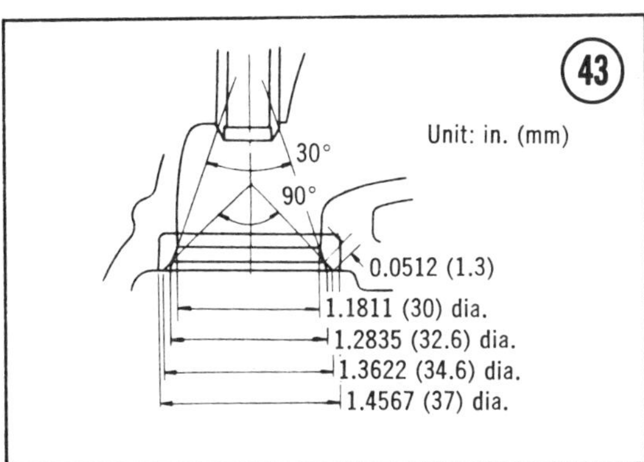

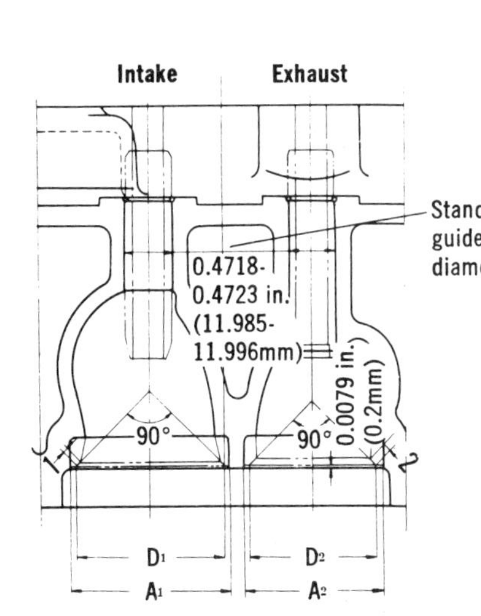

40

VALVE SEAT DIMENSIONS (EARLY L16 ENGINES)

Dimension	Inches	mm
A_1	1.6141-1.6148	41.0-41.016
A_2	1.4566-1.4573	37.0-37.016
D_1	1.4803-1.4881	37.6-37.8
D_2	1.2755-1.2834	32.4-32.6
1	0.0551-0.0708	1.4-1.8
2	0.0629-0.0787	1.6-2.0

2. Coat the corresponding valve face with Prussian blue.
3. Insert the valve into the valve guide.
4. Rotate the valve under light pressure approximately ¼ turn.
5. Lift the valve out. If it seats properly, the dye will transfer evenly to the valve face.

Valve Installation

1. Coat the valves with oil and insert them in the cylinder head.
2. Install the valve spring seats, oil seals, springs, and spring washers. Compress the valve springs and install the keepers.

PISTON/CONNECTING ROD ASSEMBLY

Figure 44 shows the piston and connecting rod components.

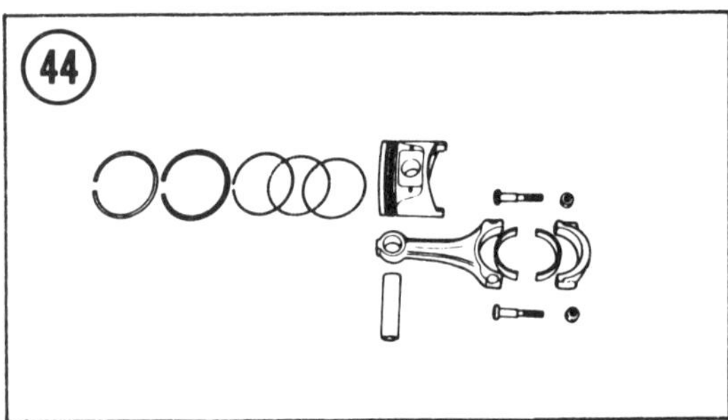
44

Piston Removal

1. Remove the cylinder head and oil pan as described earlier.
2. Remove the carbon ridge at the top of the cylinder bores with a ridge reamer.
3. Rotate the crankshaft so the connecting rod is centered in the bore.
4. Remove the nuts securing the connecting rod cap. Lift off the cap, together with the lower bearing half.
5. Push the piston and connecting rod out of the bore with a wooden hammer handle (**Figure 45**).

> NOTE: *Check for cylinder numbers stamped on connecting rod and cap. Make your own number marks if they are not present.*

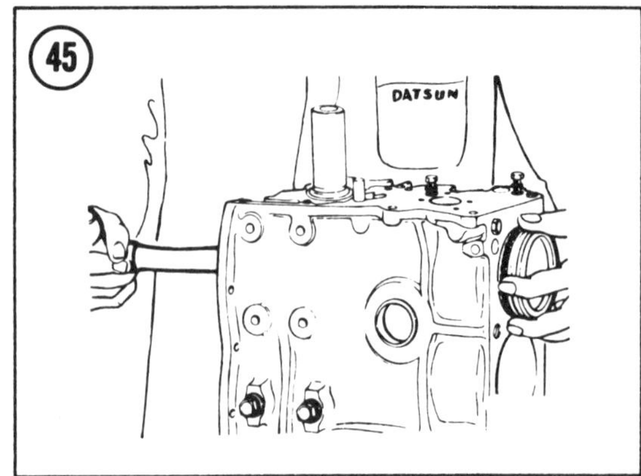

45

6. Remove the piston rings with a ring remover (**Figure 46**).

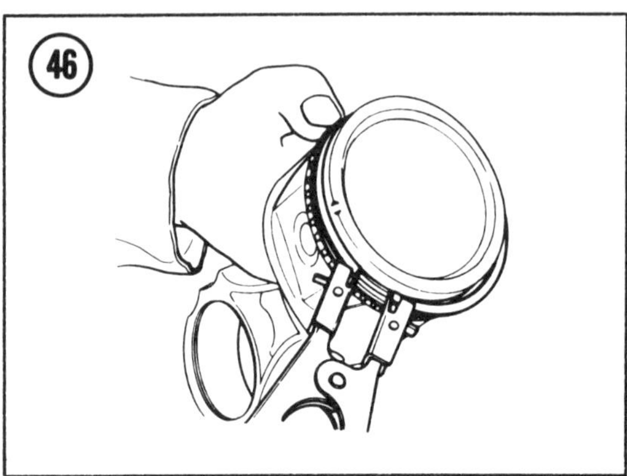
46

Piston Pin Removal/Installation

The pistons are press-fitted to the connecting rods and hand-fitted to the pistons. Removal requires a press and support stand. This is a job for a dealer or machine shop, which is equipped to fit the pistons to the pins, ream the pin bushings to the correct diameter, and install the pistons on the connecting rods.

Piston Clearance Check

This procedure should be done at room temperature. Cylinder walls must be clean and dry.

1. Referring to **Figure 47**, insert the piston without rings upside down in the cylinder bore. Insert a 0.0016 in. (0.04mm) feeler gauge between piston and cylinder wall and attach a spring scale as shown.
2. Pull on the spring scale. Note the amount of force required to pull the feeler gauge out of the

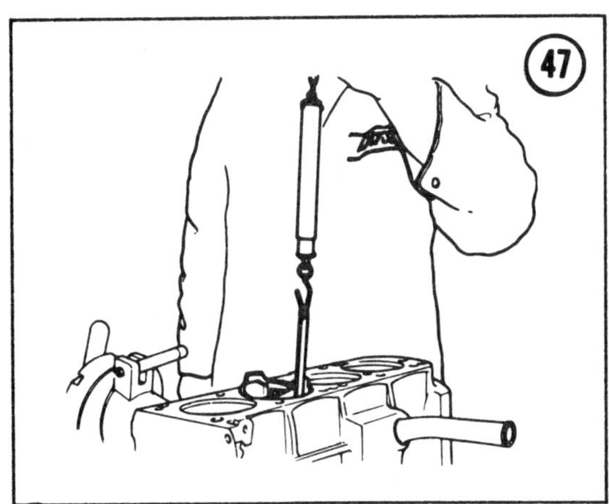

cylinder. The pull should range from 0.44-3.30 lb. (0.2-1.5 kg). If the required pull is greater than specified, piston clearance is less than it should be. If the pull is less, piston clearance is greater.

3. Repeat the procedure for all 4 cylinders and pistons.

Piston Ring Fit/Installation

1. Check the ring gap of each piston ring. To do this, position the ring at the top or bottom of the ring travel area and square it by tapping gently with an inverted piston.

> NOTE: *If the cylinders have not been rebored, check the gap at the bottom of the ring travel, where the cylinder is least worn.*

2. Measure ring gap with a feeler gauge as shown in **Figure 48**. Compare with specifications at the end of the chapter.

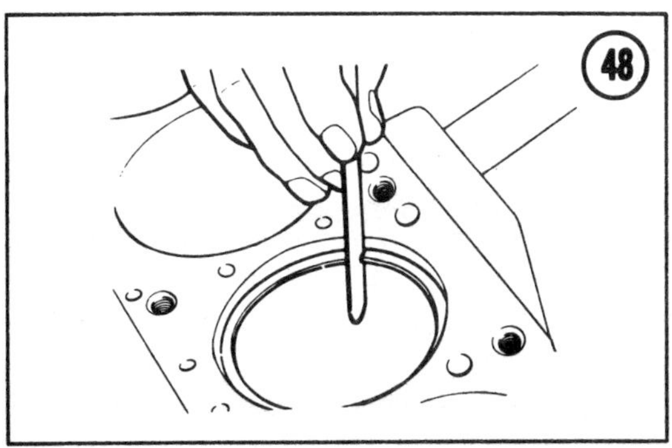

3. Check side clearance of the rings as shown in **Figure 49**. Place the feeler gauge alongside the ring all the way into the groove. Specifications are given at the end of the chapter.

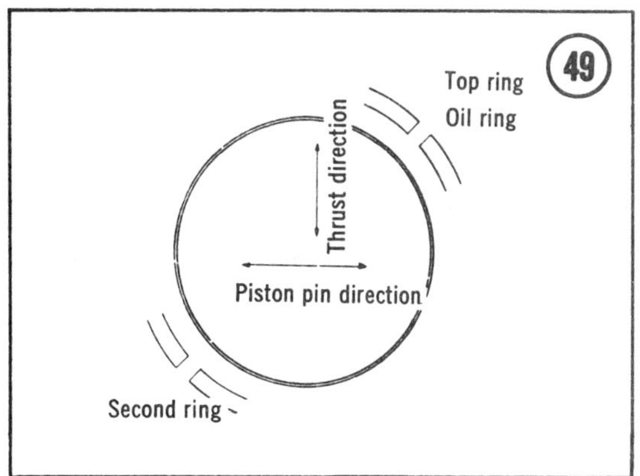

4. Using a ring expander tool, carefully install the oil control ring, then the compression rings. Early L16 engines use one-piece oil rings; all other models use 3-piece oil rings. The wavy segment goes between the flat segments to act as a spacer. Top compression rings have a chrome plated friction surface. Second compression rings are tapered. The flat segments of 3-piece oil rings are interchangeable. See **Figure 50**.

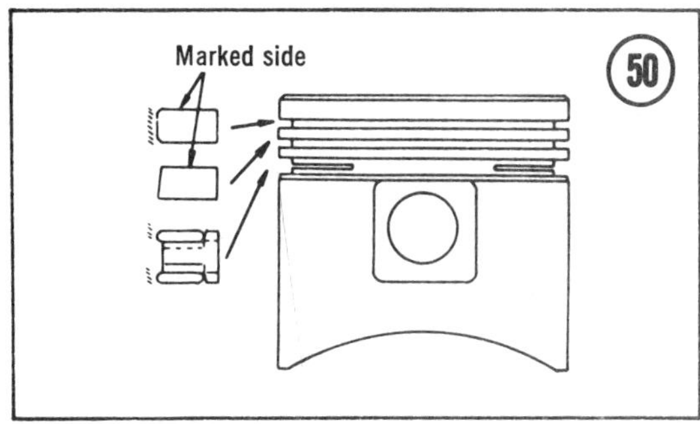

5. Turn the ring gaps 180° from each other. Turn the gaps so they are not in the front-rear or side-to-side directions of an installed piston.

Connecting Rod Inspection

1. Have connecting rod straightness checked by a dealer or machine shop. Maximum permissible bend or twist is 0.002 in. (0.05mm) per 3.94 in. (100mm) of connecting rod length.

2. Install the connecting rods and bearings on the crankshaft. Insert a feeler gauge between the connecting rod big end and crankshaft and measure the clearance (**Figure 51**). Replace the connecting rod if clearance exceeds specifications (end of chapter).

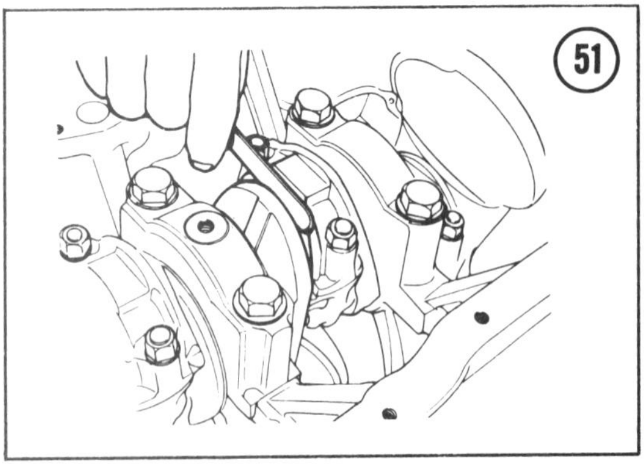

3. If any connecting rods are replaced, make sure new ones are within 0.25 ounce (7 grams) of the old ones.

Measuring Bearing Clearance

1. Place connecting rods and upper bearing halves on the proper crankpins (connecting rod journals).

2. Cut a piece of Plastigage (**Figure 52**) the width of the bearing. Place the Plastigage on the crankpin, then install the lower bearing half and cap.

NOTE: *Do not place Plastigage over the crankpin oil hole.*

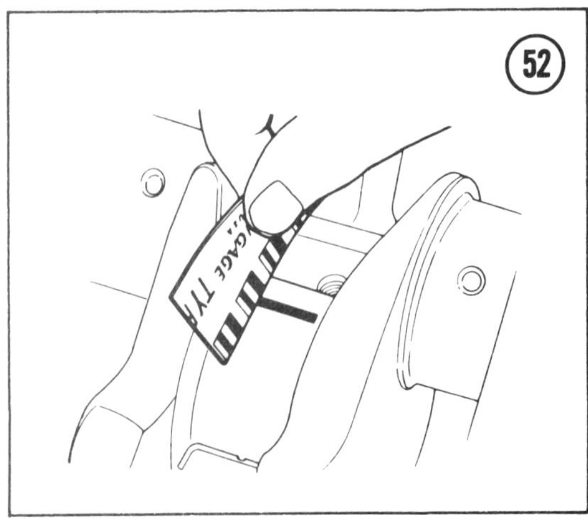

3. Tighten the connecting rod cap to specifications (end of chapter). Do not rotate the crankshaft while the Plastigage is in place.

4. Remove the connecting rod cap. Bearing clearance is determined by comparing the width of the flattened Plastigage to the markings on the envelope (**Figure 53**). If clearance is excessive, the crankshaft must be reground and undersize bearings installed.

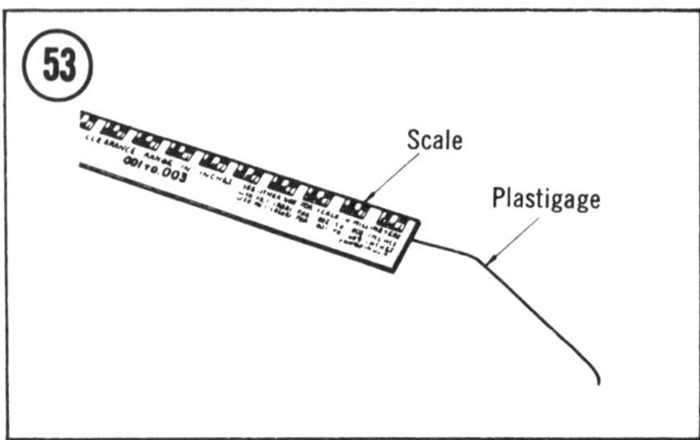

Installing Piston/Connecting Rod Assembly

Refer to Figure 44.

1. Make sure the pistons are correctly installed on the connecting rods. The notch in the piston goes toward the front of the engine. The oil hole in the connecting rod big end goes toward the right-hand side of the engine.

2. When installing new bearings, measure bearing crush. Secure one end of the bearing as shown in **Figure 54**. Push the bearing firmly into its seat and measure the protrusion of the free end (dimension "H"). This should be 0.0006-0.0018 in. (0.015-0.045mm).

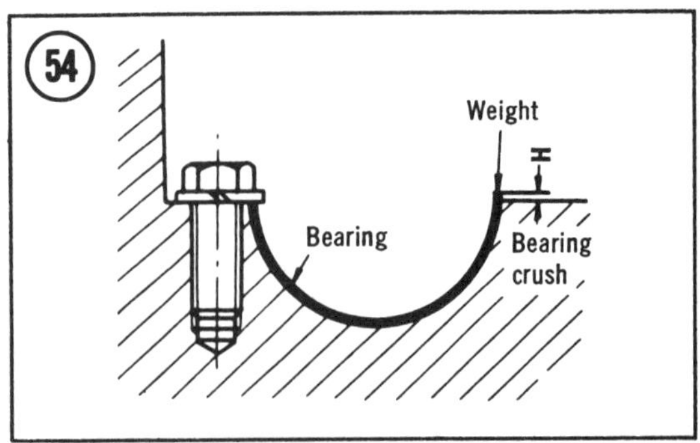

3. Be sure that the ring gaps are positioned correctly.

4. Immerse the entire piston in clean engine oil. Coat the cylinder wall with oil.

5. Slide a ring compressor over the rings. Compress the rings into the grooves.

6. Install the piston/connecting rod assembly in its cylinder as shown in **Figure 55**. Tap lightly with a wooden hammer handle to insert the piston. Be sure the connecting rod number (or punch mark) on the connecting rod corresponds with the cylinder number (counting from the front of the engine).

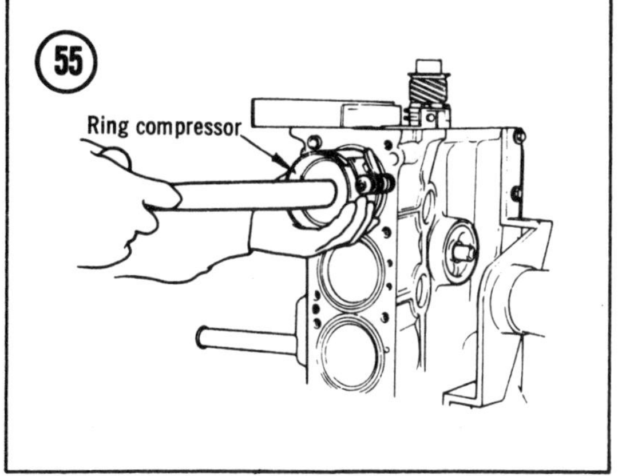

CAUTION

Use extreme care not to let the connecting rod nick crankshaft journal.

7. Clean the connecting rod bearings carefully, including the back sides. Coat the crankpins and bearings with clean engine oil. Place the bearings in the connecting rod and cap.

8. Install the connecting rod cap. Make sure the cylinder number on the rod and cap are on the same side. Tighten the cap nuts to specifications (end of chapter).

9. Recheck connecting rod big end play as described under *Connecting Rod Inspection*, Step 2.

CRANKSHAFT

Removal

1. Unbolt the main bearing caps. Place the caps in order on a bench. A puller may be necessary to remove the center and rear caps. If you do not have such a tool, take the engine to a Datsun dealer for cap removal.

2. Remove 2 side oil seals, then take the rear oil seal off the crankshaft (**Figure 56**).

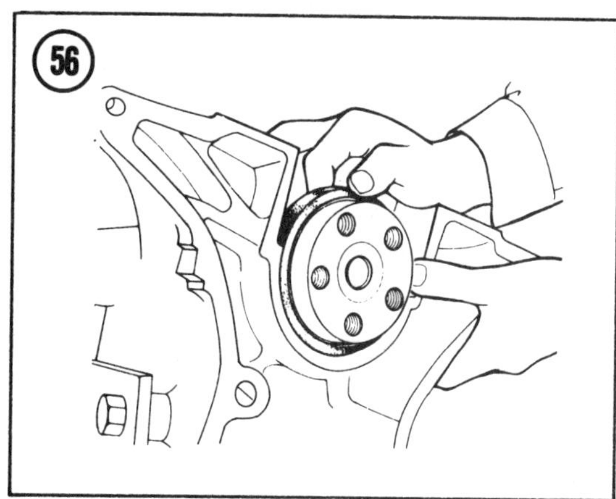

3. Lift the crankshaft out of the engine. Lay the crankshaft, main bearings, and bearing caps in order on a clean surface.

Inspection

1. Clean the crankshaft thoroughly in solvent. Blow out the oil passages with compressed air.

NOTE: *If you don't have precision measuring equipment, have a machine shop perform Steps 2 and 3.*

2. Examine crankpins and main bearing journals for wear, scoring, and cracks. Check all journals against specifications (end of chapter) for out-of-roundness, taper, and wear. If necessary, have the crankshaft reground.

3. Check the crankshaft for bending. Mount the crankshaft between accurate centers (such as V-blocks or a lathe) and rotate it one full turn with a dial gauge contacting the center journal. See **Figure 57**. Actual bend is half the reading shown on the gauge. The crankshaft must be reground if bent beyond specifications.

4. Measure crankshaft end play. Install the crankshaft in the block. Insert a feeler gauge between the crankshaft and the center bearing flange. See **Figure 58**. Replace center bearing or thrust washers if end play exceeds specifications.

Measuring Main Bearing Clearance

Main bearing clearance is measured in the same manner as connecting rod bearing clear-

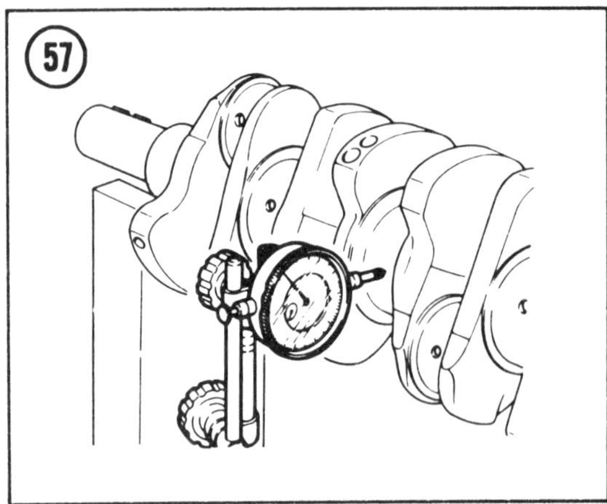

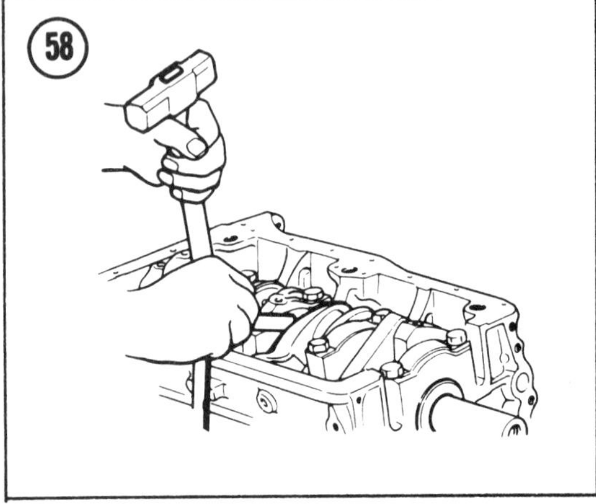

ance, described earlier in this chapter. Excessive clearance requires that the bearings be replaced, the crankshaft be reground, or both.

Installation

1. Thoroughly clean bearings, including the back sides.
2. Install the bearings in the cylinder block and bearing caps. The center bearing is flanged. Nos. 2 and 4 bearings are interchangeable. Nos. 1 and 5 bearings look alike, but No. 1 has an oil hole and No. 5 does not. On 1968-1973 models, all upper and lower bearing halves are interchangeable except No. 1. On 1974-1976 engines, all upper and lower bearings are interchangeable.
3. Make sure the bearing locating tangs are correctly positioned in the cylinder block and bearing cap grooves.
4. Coat the bearings freely with clean engine oil. Lay the crankshaft in the block. Coat the crankshaft journals with engine oil.
5. Install the bearing caps and tighten the cap bolts slightly. Make sure the arrow marks on the caps face the front of the engine.

> NOTE: *Apply small amounts of gasket sealer to rear bearing cap (***Figure 59***).*

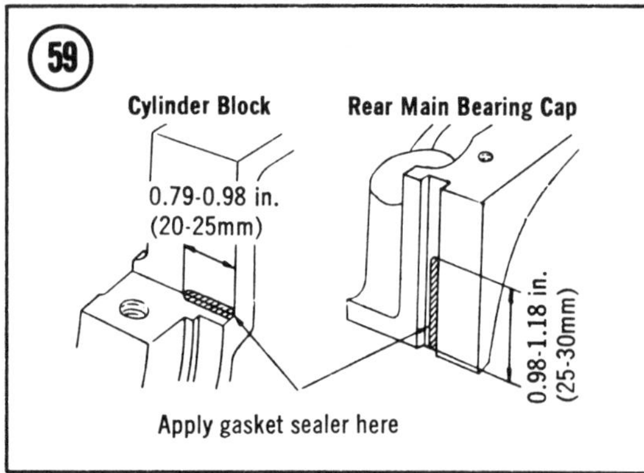

6. Gently push the crankshaft toward the front and rear of the engine to verify that the bearings and caps are properly aligned and seated.
7. Tighten the cap bolts to specifications (end of chapter). Tighten gradually in 2 or 3 separate stages, starting with the center cap and working outward. Rotate the crankshaft during tightening to make sure it is not binding. If the crankshaft is difficult to turn, stop and find out why before tightening further. Check for foreign material on bearings and journals. Make absolutely certain that bearings are the correct size, especially if the crankshaft has been reground. Never use undersize bearings if the crankshaft has not been reground.
8. Recheck crankshaft end play (Figure 58).
9. Tap the rear side seals into place (**Figure 60**). Install the rear seal with a drift such as ST 15310000 (**Figure 61**). Use a piece of 2 in. pipe if the drift is not available.

Pilot Bushing

The pilot bushing, located inside the rear end of the crankshaft, supports the transmission input shaft on manual transmission vehicles. Inspect the bushing for visible wear and dam-

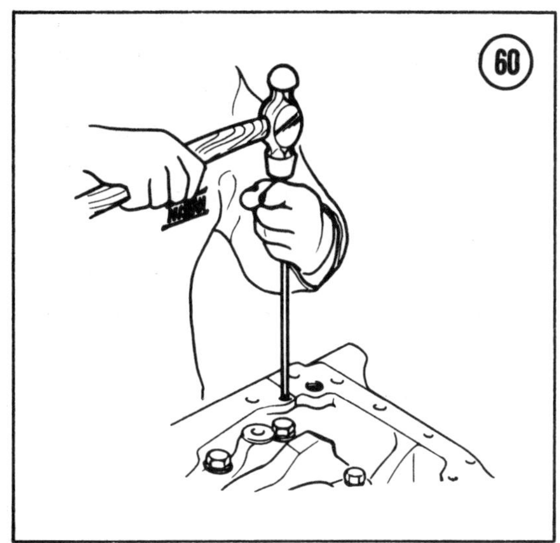

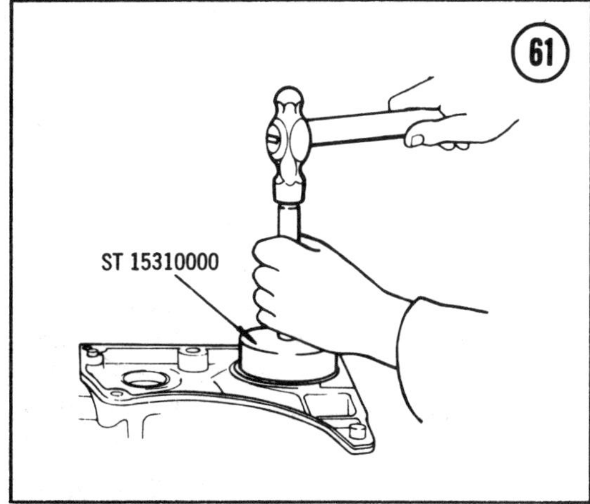

age. Have it replaced by a Datsun dealer or machine shop if defects are apparent.

CYLINDER BLOCK INSPECTION

1. Remove the crankcase oil separator prior to inspection. See **Figure 62**.

2. Clean the block thoroughly with solvent and check all freeze plugs for leaks. Replace any freeze plugs that are suspect. It is a good idea to replace all of them. While cleaning, check oil and water passages for dirt, sludge, and corrosion. If the passages are very dirty, the block should be boiled out by a dealer or machine shop.

> NOTE: *Block boiling necessitates replacement of all freeze plugs. However, a block dirty enough to need boiling almost certainly needs to have these parts replaced anyway.*

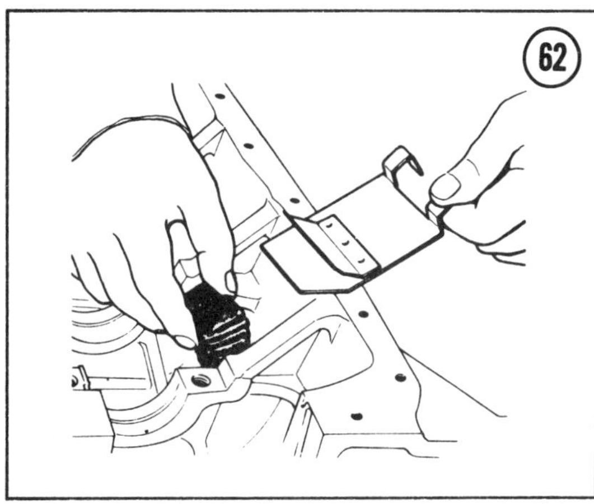

3. Examine the block for cracks.

4. Check flatness of the cylinder block's top surface. Use an accurate straightedge as shown in **Figure 63**. Have the block resurfaced if it is warped more than 0.004 in. (0.1mm).

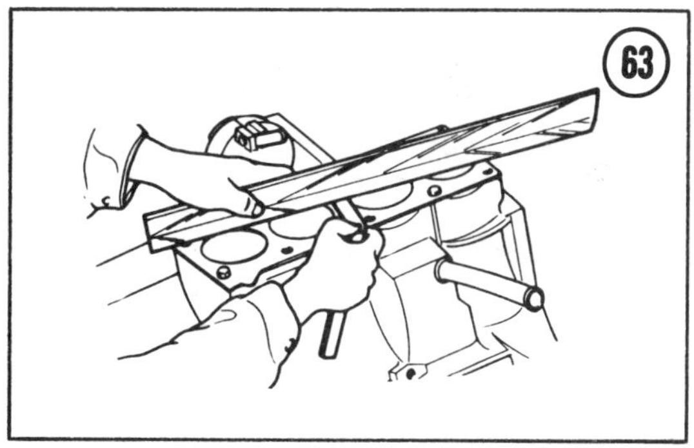

5. Measure the cylinder bores for out-of-roundess or excessive wear with a bore gauge (**Figure 64**). Measure the bores at top, center, and bottom, in front-rear and side-to-side directions. Compare measurements to specifications at the end of the chapter. If the cylinders exceed maximum tolerances, they must be rebored. Reboring is also necessary if the cylinder walls are badly scuffed or scored.

> NOTE: *If one cylinder is bored out, all cylinders must be bored to the same diameter. Cylinders must be bored in the following order: 2-4-1-3.*

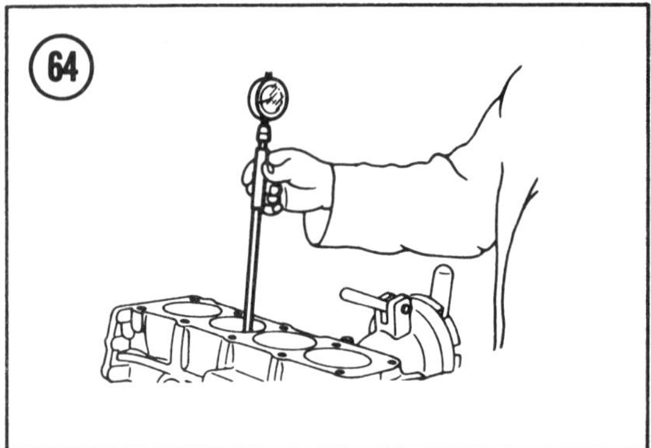

FLYWHEEL

Removal/Installation

1. Remove the engine. Separate the engine and transmission.
2. Remove the clutch from the flywheel. See Chapter Eight.
3. Unbolt the flywheel from the crankshaft (**Figure 65**).

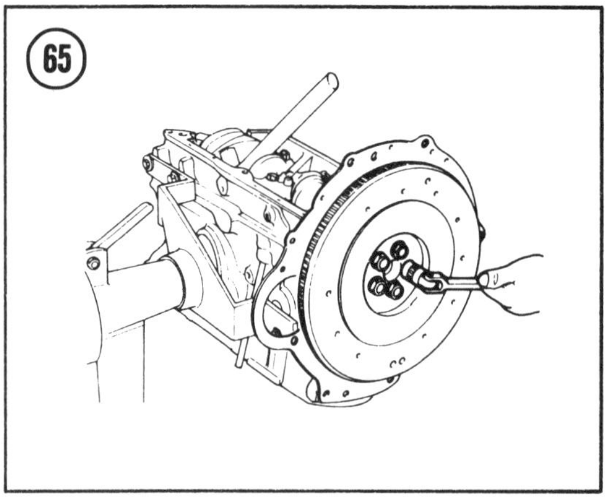

4. Install by reversing Steps 1-3. Tighten flywheel bolts to specifications (end of chapter). Tighten the bolts gradually in a diagonal pattern.

Inspection

1. Check the flywheel for scoring and wear. If the surface is glazed or slightly scratched, have it resurfaced by a machine shop. Replace the flywheel if damage is severe.
2. Measure flywheel runout with a dial gauge (**Figure 66**). Replace or resurface the flywheel if runout is excessive.

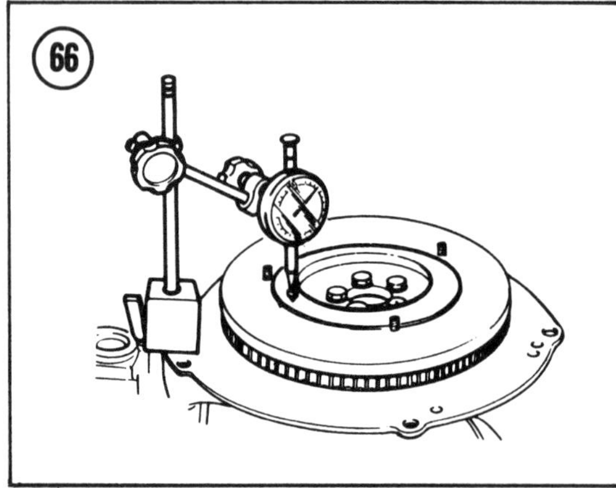

3. Inspect the flywheel ring gear teeth. If the teeth are chipped, broken, or excessively worn, have a new starter ring shrunk onto the flywheel by a dealer or machine shop.

TORQUE CONVERTER DRIVE PLATE

The torque converter drive plate is bolted to the crankshaft in the same manner as the flywheel. The drive plate bolts are torqued to 101-116 ft.-lb. (14-16 mkg).

Drive plate runout is measured in the same manner as flywheel runout. Replace the drive plate if runout exceeds 0.020 in. (0.5mm). The drive plate must also be replaced if the ring gear is damaged or worn excessively.

Table 1 ENGINE SPECIFICATIONS

Valves		
Head diameter, intake	Early L16	1.50 in. (38mm)
	Late L16, L18	1.654 in. (42mm)
	1973-75 L20B	1.650-1.657 in. (41.9-42.1mm)
	1976 L20B	1.654-1.661 in. (42.0-42.2mm)
Head diameter, exhaust	L16	1.299 in. (33mm)
	L18	1.378 in. (35mm)
	L20B	1.378-1.386 in. (35.0-35.2mm)
Stem diameter, intake	Early L16	0.315 in. (8mm)
	Late L16, L18, L20B	0.3136-0.3142 in. (7.965-7.980mm)
Stem diameter, exhaust	Early L16	0.315 in. (8mm)
	Late L16, L18, L20B	0.3128-0.3134 in. (7.945-7.960mm)
Valve length, intake	Early L16	4.56 in. (115.9mm)
	Late L16, L18, L20B	4.524-4.535 in. (114.9-115.2mm)
Valve length, exhaust	Early L16	4.567 in. (116mm)
	Late L16, L18, L20B	4.555-4.567 in. (115.7-116.0mm)
Valve spring free length, outer	Early L16	2.05 in. (52mm)
	Late L16, L18, L20B	1.968 in. (49.98mm)
Valve spring free length, inner	All L-series	1.766 in. (44.85mm)
Valve spring loaded length	Early L16 outer	1.21 in. @ 105 lb. (30.7mm @ 47.8 kg)
	Late L16, L18, L20B outer	1.161 in. @ 108 lb. (29.5mm @ 49.0 kg)
	All inner	0.965 in. @ 56.2 lb. 24.5mm @ 25.5 kg)
Valve Guides		
Stem-to-guide clearance, standard		
Early L16 intake		0.0006 - 0.0018 in. (0.015 - 0.045mm)
Late L16, L18, L20B intake		0.0008 - 0.0021 in. (0.020 - 0.053mm)
All exhaust		0.0016 - 0.0029 in. (0.040 - 0.073mm)
Stem-to-guide clearance, maximum		0.004 in. (0.1mm)
Guide inner diameter		0.3150 - 0.3157 in. (8.000 - 8.018mm)
Guide hole diameter		
For standard guide		0.4718 - 0.4723 in. (11.985 - 11.996mm)
For oversize guide		0.4797 - 0.4802 in. (12.185 - 12.196mm)
Oil Pump		
Outer rotor to body clearance	Standard	0.006 - 0.008 in. (0.15 - 0.21mm)
	Maximum	0.020 in. (0.5mm)
Tip clearance	Standard	Less than 0.005 in. (0.12mm)
	Maximum	0.008 in. (0.2mm)
Side clearance	Standard	0.0016 - 0.0031 in. (0.040 - 0.078mm)
	Maximum	0.008 in. (0.2mm)
Rotor to bottom cover clearance	Standard	0.001 - 0.005 in. (0.03 - 0.13mm)
	Maximum	0.008 in. (0.2mm)
Regulator valve spring length		2.067 in. (52.5mm)
Camshaft		
End-play		0.003 - 0.015 in. (0.08 - 0.38mm)
Lobe lift	Early L16	0.261 in. (6.65mm)
	Late L16, L18, L20B	0.276 in. (7mm)

(continued)

Table 1 SPECIFICATIONS, L-SERIES ENGINES (continued)

Connecting Rods		
Big end play		0.008 - 0.012 in. (0.2 - 0.3mm)
Bearing clearance, normal		0.0010 - 0.0022 in. (0.025 - 0.055mm)
Bearing clearance, maximum		0.005 in. (0.12mm)
Pistons		
Ring gap, early L16	Top ring	0.009 - 0.015 in. (0.23 - 0.38mm)
	Second and oil rings	0.006 - 0.012 in. (0.15 - 0.30mm)
Ring gap, late L16	Top ring	0.010 - 0.016 in. (0.25 - 0.50mm)
	Second ring	0.006 - 0.012 in. (0.15 - 0.30mm)
	Oil ring	0.012 - 0.036 in. (0.30 - 0.90mm)
Ring gap, L18	Top ring	0.014 - 0.022 in. (0.35 - 0.55mm)
	Second ring	0.012 - 0.020 in. (0.30 - 0.50mm)
	Oil ring	0.012 - 0.036 in. (0.30 - 0.90mm)
Ring gap, L20B	Top ring	0.010 - 0.016 in. (0.25 - 0.40mm)
	Second ring	0.012 - 0.020 in. (0.30 - 0.50mm)
	Oil ring	0.012 - 0.036 in. (0.30 - 0.90mm)
Ring side clearance, L16	Top ring	0.0016 - 0.0031 in. (0.04 - 0.08mm)
	Second ring	0.0012 - 0.0028 in. (0.03 - 0.07mm)
	Oil ring*	0.0010 - 0.0025 in. (0.025 - 0.063mm)
Ring side clearance, L18	Top ring	0.0018 - 0.0031 in. (0.045 - 0.080mm)
	Second ring	0.0012 - 0.0028 in. (0.03 - 0.07mm)
Ring side clearance, L20B	Top ring	0.0016 - 0.0029 in. (0.040 - 0.073mm)
	Second ring	0.0012 - 0.0028 in. (0.03 - 0.07mm)
Maximum gap, all rings		0.039 in. (1mm)
Maximum side clearance, all		0.004 in. (0.1mm)
Piston pin clearance		0.0001 - 0.0006 in. (0.003 - 0.015mm)
Crankshaft		
Main bearing clearance	Standard	0.0008 - 0.0024 in. (0.020 - 0.062mm)
	Maximum	0.005 in. (0.12mm)
Journal diameter, L16 and L18		2.1631 - 2.1636 in. (54.942 - 54.955mm)
Journal diameter, L20B		2.3599 - 2.3604 in. (59.942 - 59.955mm)
Journal out-of-round and taper	Standard	Less than 0.0004 in. (0.01mm)
	Maximum	0.001 in. (0.025mm)
Crankpin diameter (all)		1.9670 - 1.9675 in. (49.961 - 49.974mm)
Crankpin out-of-round and taper		Less than 0.0004 in. (0.01mm)
Crankshaft end-play	Standard	0.002 - 0.007 in. (0.05 - 0.18mm)
	Maximum	0.012 in. (0.3mm)
Crankshaft bend		0.002 in. (0.05mm)
Cylinders		
Bore diameter, L16		3.2677 - 3.2679 in. (83.000 - 83.050mm)
Bore diameter, L18 and L20B		3.3465 - 3.3484 in. (85.000 - 85.050mm)
Out-of-round and taper		0.0006 in. (0.015mm)
Maximum wear		0.008 in. (0.2mm)
Maximum difference between bores		0.008 in. (0.2mm)
Flywheel		
Runout		0.006 in. (0.15mm)

*Ring side clearance is measured on one-piece oil rings only.

Table 2 TIGHTENING TORQUES, L-SERIES ENGINES

	Foot-pounds	Mkg
Camshaft locate plate bolts	4½ - 6½	0.6 - 0.9
Camshaft sprocket bolt	87 - 116	12 - 16
Carburetor nuts	4 - 7	0.5 - 1.0
Connecting rod nuts		
8mm rod bolt shaft diameter	23 - 27	3.2 - 3.8
9mm rod shaft diameter	33 - 40	4.5 - 5.5
Crankshaft pulley bolt	87 - 116	12 - 16
Cylinder head bolts*		
Through engine No. L16-203415	43 - 51	6 - 7
From engine No. L16-203416	47 - 62	6.5 - 8.5
Flywheel bolts		
Early (separate lockwasher)	69 - 76	9.5 - 10.5
Late (integral washer)	101 - 116	14 - 16
Front cover bolts		
M6 (small) bolts	3 - 4	0.4 - 0.6
M8 (large) bolts	7 - 9	1.0 - 1.2
Fuel pump nuts	9 - 13	1.2 - 1.8
Main bearing cap bolts	33 - 40	4.5 - 5.5
Motor mounts (510)		
Bracket to cylinder block	19 - 23	2.6 - 3.2
Bracket to rubber insulator	19 - 23	2.6 - 3.2
Insulator to crossmember	9½ - 12	1.3 - 1.7
Motor mounts (1973-74 610)		
Bracket to cylinder block	18 - 25	2.5 - 3.5
Bracket to rubber insulator	18 - 25	2.5 - 3.5
Insulator to crossmember	10 - 13	1.4 - 1.8
Motor mounts (1975-76 610, all 710)		
Bracket to cylinder block	14 - 19	1.9 - 2.6
Bracket to insulator	14 - 19	1.9 - 2.6
Insulator to crossmember	7 - 9	0.9 - 1.2
Oil pan bolts	4½ - 6½	0.6 - 0.9
Oil pan drain plug	14 - 22	2 - 3
Oil pump bolts	8 - 11	1.1 - 1.5
Rocker pivot locknuts	36 - 43	5 - 6

*Late type head bolts are identified by a circular groove stamped in the top surface of the bolt head.

CHAPTER FIVE

FUEL AND EXHAUST SYSTEMS

This chapter includes service procedures for the air cleaner, carburetor, fuel pump, exhaust system, and fuel system-related emission controls.

AIR CLEANER

All models use a viscous paper air cleaner element. The element should be replaced at intervals specified in Chapter Two. The 1972-1974 autos use an automatic temperature control (ATC) air cleaner. When the engine compartment is cold, a vacuum motor shuts off the normal air intake, and the air cleaner draws warm air from around the exhaust manifold.

Air Cleaner Removal/Installation

1. Remove the cover nut or clips, lift off the cover, and lift the element out.
2. Unbolt the air cleaner from its side bracket. Unscrew the band bolt at the base of the air cleaner.
3. Disconnect the hot air tube from the underside of the air cleaner intake nozzle (if so equipped).
4. On 1975-1976 autos, disconnect the fresh air tube from the end of the air cleaner intake nozzle.
5. Lift the air cleaner up. Carefully note all connections, then disconnect the hoses from its underside. The air cleaner can then be lifted off.
6. Install in the reverse order.

ATC Inspection

The most likely cause of ATC (air temperature control) trouble is that the inlet valve is stuck open. This is not apparent in warm weather, but in cold weather, it results in slow acceleration, engine hesitation, or stalling. The inlet valve may also be stuck shut, which causes extremely high fuel consumption and loss of power. **Figure 1** identifies system components.

1. Make sure the vacuum hoses are installed correctly. **Figure 2** shows the 1973 hoses. All other years are basically the same.
2. Check the hoses for cracks, leaks, or plugging.

Valve and Vacuum Motor Check

1. With the engine off, hold a mirror up to the air inlet and see if the valve is open. If it is closed, check the valve linkage for binding.
2. Disconnect the tube from the vacuum motor inlet on top of the air cleaner nozzle. Apply

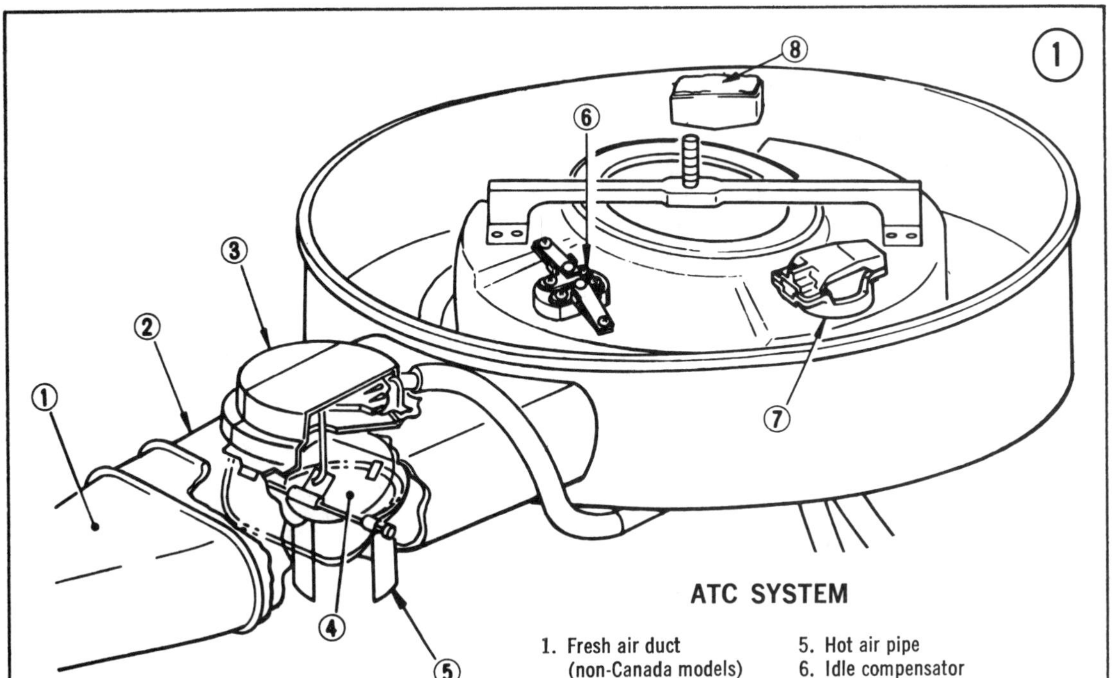

ATC SYSTEM

1. Fresh air duct (non-Canada models)
2. Air inlet pipe
3. Vacuum motor assembly
4. Air control valve
5. Hot air pipe
6. Idle compensator
7. Temperature sensor assembly
8. Blow-by gas filter

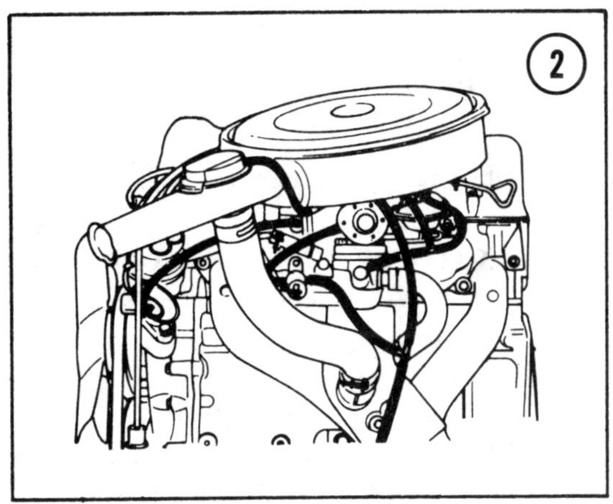

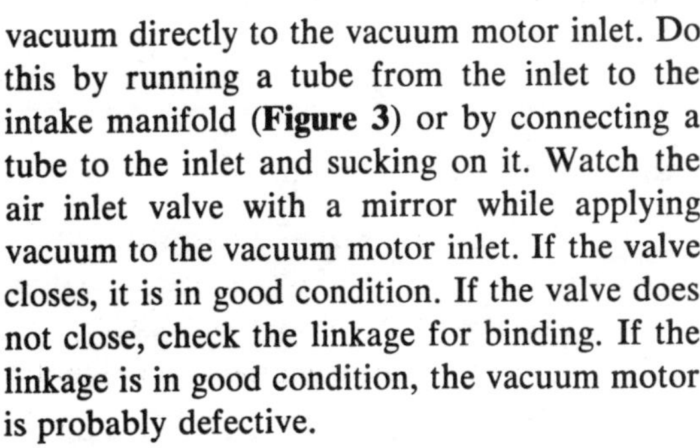

vacuum directly to the vacuum motor inlet. Do this by running a tube from the inlet to the intake manifold (**Figure 3**) or by connecting a tube to the inlet and sucking on it. Watch the air inlet valve with a mirror while applying vacuum to the vacuum motor inlet. If the valve closes, it is in good condition. If the valve does not close, check the linkage for binding. If the linkage is in good condition, the vacuum motor is probably defective.

Sensor Check

Perform this test with the engine cold. The temperature around the sensor must be below 86°F.

1. Check the air inlet valve with a mirror. Make sure it is open.

2. Start the engine and let it idle. If the air inlet valve closes immediately after starting the engine, the valve is in good condition.

3. Let the engine idle until it warms up. Watch the air inlet with a mirror as the engine warms. It should open gradually.

> NOTE: *If this test is conducted at ambient temperatures near 30°F, the valve will take considerable time to open, and may open only partially. This does not indicate a defective sensor.*

If the valves does not work properly, or you are in doubt about it, perform the next 2 steps.

4. Remove the air cleaner cover and tape a thermistor or small thermometer as close to the sensor (3, Figure 1) as possible. Put the air cleaner cover back on.

5. Start the engine and let it idle for several minutes, until the valve is partially open. Remove the air cleaner cover and note the thermometer reading. It should range from 86-126°F. If the reading is obviously outside this range, replace the sensor.

IDLE COMPENSATOR (1973-1976)

The idle compensator (6, Figure 1) is a thermostatic valve operated by underhood temperature. It prevents overrich fuel mixture during hot idle conditions by admitting air to the intake manifold. Air conditioned 1974 610's, and all 1975-1976 autos, use an extra idle compensator, located next to the one shown in Figure 1.

Removal and Testing

1. Remove the top cover from the air cleaner.
2. Remove 2 idle compensator securing screws. Detach the air hose and take the idle compensator out.
3. Connect a tube to the bottom of the idle compensator and suck on it. It should be extremely difficult or impossible to suck air through the tube at temperatures below those specified in **Table 1**.

> NOTE: *When testing a double idle compensator, close off one side with a finger (***Figure 4***).*

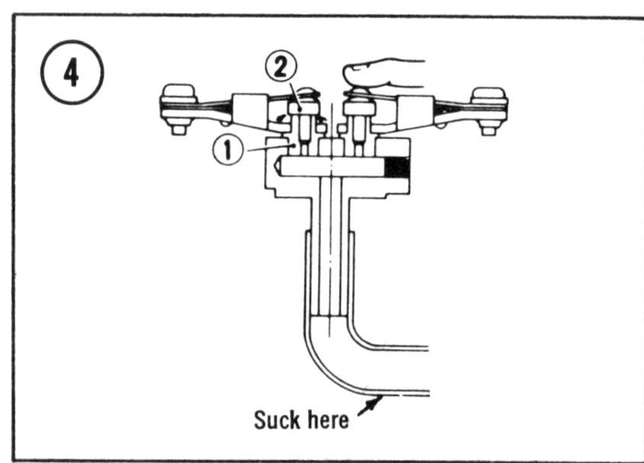

4. Place the idle compensator in water with a thermometer (**Figure 5**). Note valve opening and closing temperatures and compare with Table 1. Replace the idle compensator if it opens at the wrong temperature or fails to open.
5. Install by reversing Steps 1 and 2.

ALTITUDE COMPENSATOR

This device, optional on 1975-1976 California cars, corrects overrich fuel mixture at high altitudes by admitting more air to the carburetor. Compensator operation below the specified altitude of 1,968 feet (600 meters) may

Table 1 IDLE COMPENSATOR OPENING TEMPERATURES

Vehicle	Begins to open	Fully open
1974 610		
Air conditioned	176°F (80°C)	197°F (90°C)
Non-air conditioned	140°F (60°C)	167°F (75°C)
1975-76 (all models)		
No. 1 valve	140°F (60°C)	158°F (70°C)
No. 2 valve	158°F (70°C)	197°F (90°C)

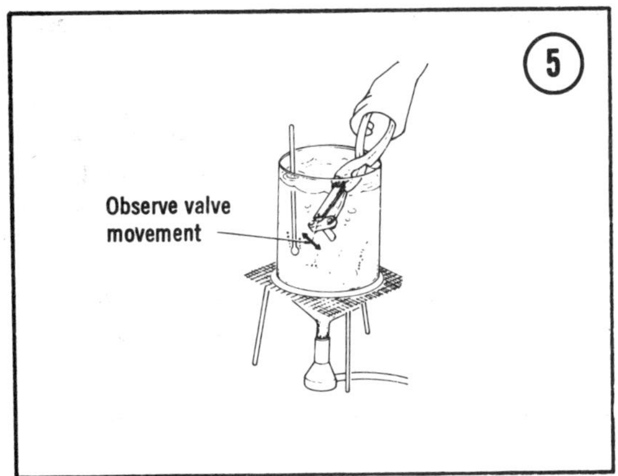

cause hesitation, stumbling, and surge while cruising at approximately 50 mph (80 kph). Failure to operate at high altitudes may cause hesitation, stumbling, and poor throttle response.

To test, try to blow air into the carburetor lines (**Figure 6**). This should be impossible below the specified altitude, and possible above it. If not, replace the altitude compensator.

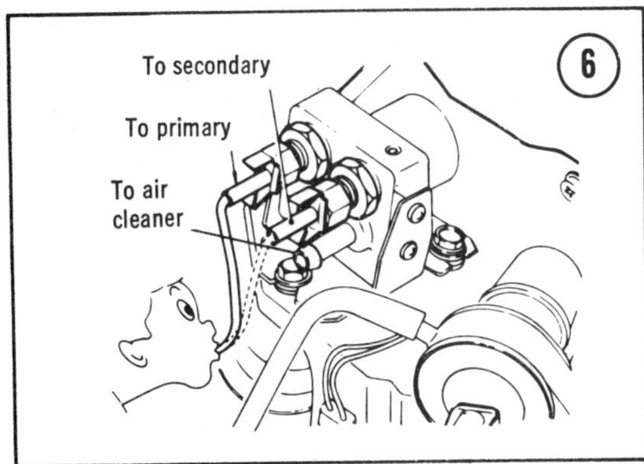

CARBURETOR

All models use Hitachi downdraft, 2-barrel carburetors. The 1968-1971 autos used a manual choke; all other models use an automatic choke. The automatic choke is heated by an electric element.

Removal/Installation

1. Remove the air cleaner as described earlier in this chapter.
2. On early 510's, label and disconnect the fuel inlet and return lines. On all other models, disconnect the inlet line. Plug the inlet line so it will not siphon gas from the tank.
3. Disconnect the choke cable (1968-1971) or choke electrical wire (1972-1976).
4. On 1972-1976 autos, disconnect the wires and vacuum line from the boost controlled deceleration device.
5. On 1973-1976 autos, disconnect the wire from the anti-dieseling solenoid.
6. On 1974-1976 autos, disconnect the exhaust gas recirculation vacuum lines from carburetor.
7. On 1975-1976 autos, disconnect the spark timing control system vacuum line from the carburetor. If equipped with an altitude compensator (optional in California), disconnect its inlet lines also.
8. Disconnect the throttle linkage rod.
9. Remove 4 nuts and lift the carburetor off. Discard the old gasket.
10. Install in reverse order. Use a new gasket.

5

Disassembly

Figure 7 shows the manual choke carburetor used on early models. **Figure 8** shows the automatic choke version used on 1975-1976 autos. The 1972-1974 carburetors are basically the same as the 1975-1976 design. Differences are illustrated as they occur.

1. Remove the throttle return spring. See Figure 7 (1968-1971), Figure 8 (1975-1976), or **Figure 9** (1972-1974).

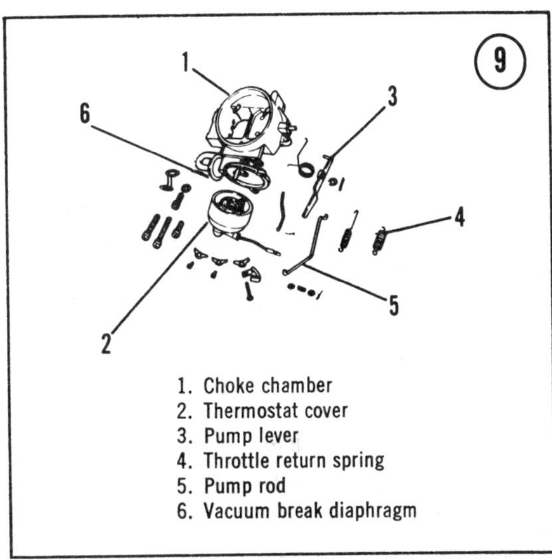

1. Choke chamber
2. Thermostat cover
3. Pump lever
4. Throttle return spring
5. Pump rod
6. Vacuum break diaphragm

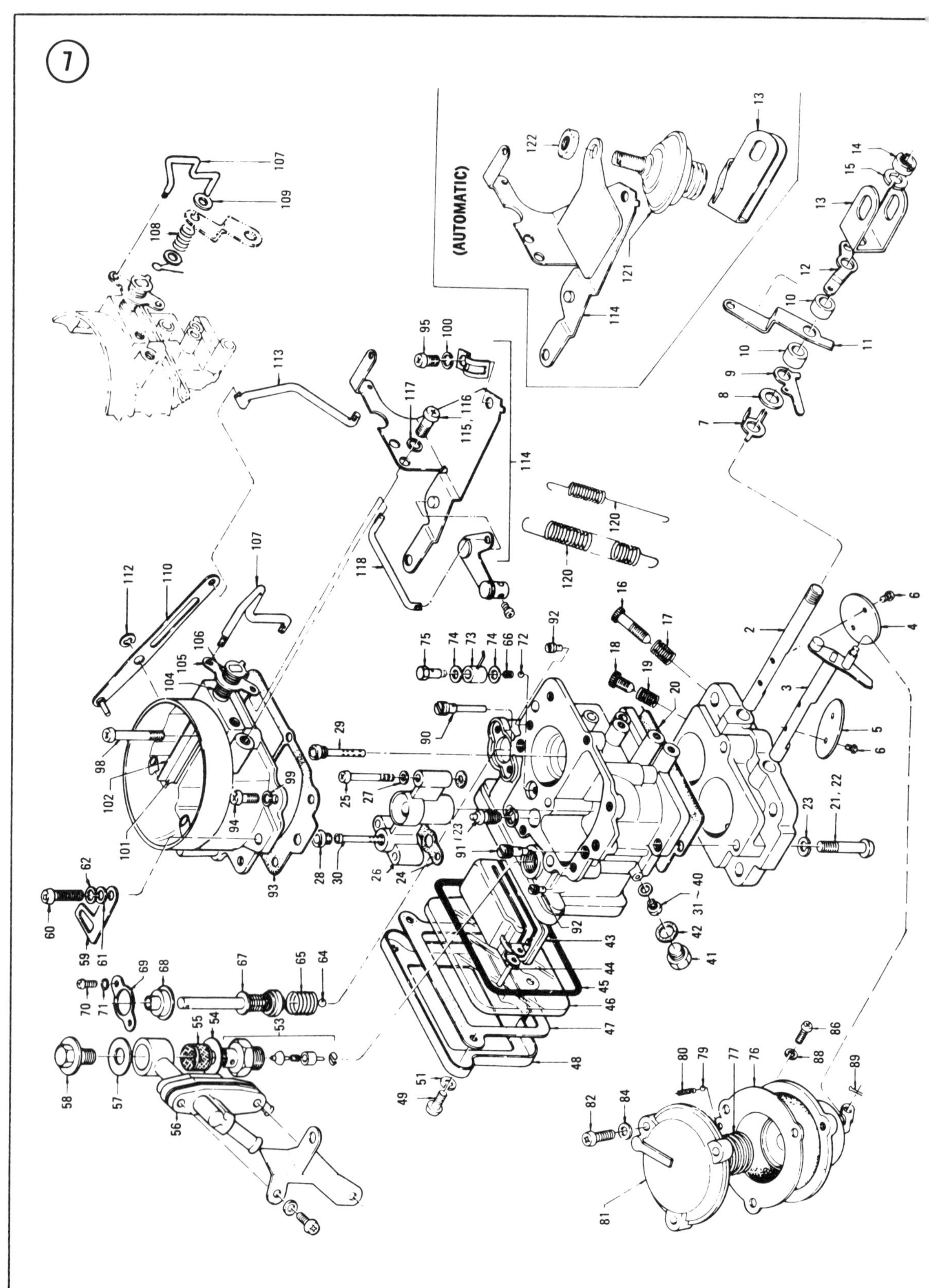
7
(AUTOMATIC)

CARBURETOR — 1968-1971

1. Carburetor assembly
2. Primary throttle shaft
3. Secondary throttle shaft
4. Primary throttle valve
5. Secondary throttle valve
6. Screw
7. Throttle adjustment lever
8. Washer
9. Return plate
10. Sleeve
11. Connecting lever
12. Throttle lever
13. Throttle lever
14. Nut
15. Spring washer
16. Throttle adjustment screw
17. Throttle adjustment spring
18. Idle adjustment screw
19. Adjustment screw spring
20. Throttle chamber gasket
21. Screw
22. Screw
23. Spring washer
24. Venturi gasket
25. Screw
26. Secondary venturi
27. Spring washer
28. Main air bleed
29. Main air bleed
30. Secondary emulsion tube
31. Primary main jet

32-40. Secondary main jet

41. Drain plug
42. Packing
43. Float assembly
44. Collar
45. Rubber seal
46. Float chamber glass
47. Float cover gasket
48. Glass frame
49. Screw
51. Spring washer
53. Needle valve assembly
54. Washer
55. Filter
56. Fuel vapor discharge connector
57. Washer
58. Inlet bolt
59. Fuel return clamp
60. Screw
61. Plain washer
62. Lockwasher
64. Ball
65. Piston return spring
66. Pump injector spring
67. Piston
68. Pump cover
69. Cylinder plate
70. Screw
71. Spring washer
72. Ball
73. Pump nozzle
74. Washer
75. Nozzle setscrew
76. Diaphragm assembly
77. Diaphragm spring
79. Ball
80. Valve spring
81. Diaphragm cover
82. Screw
84. Spring washer
86. Screw
88. Spring washer
89. Stopper pin
90. Slow jet
91. Slow jet
92. Slow air bleed
94. Screw
95. Screw
98. Screw
99. Spring washer
100. Spring washer
101. Choke shaft
102. Choke valve
104. Choke lever spring
105. Choke lever
106. Choke valve spring
107. Fast idle rod
108. Pump spring rod
109. Choke rod washer
110. Pump lever
112. Ring
113. Pump rod
114. Throttle return spring bracket
115. Screw
116. Screw
117. Spring washer
118. Choke rod
120. Throttle return spring
121. Dash pot assembly
122. Nut
123. Power valve

5

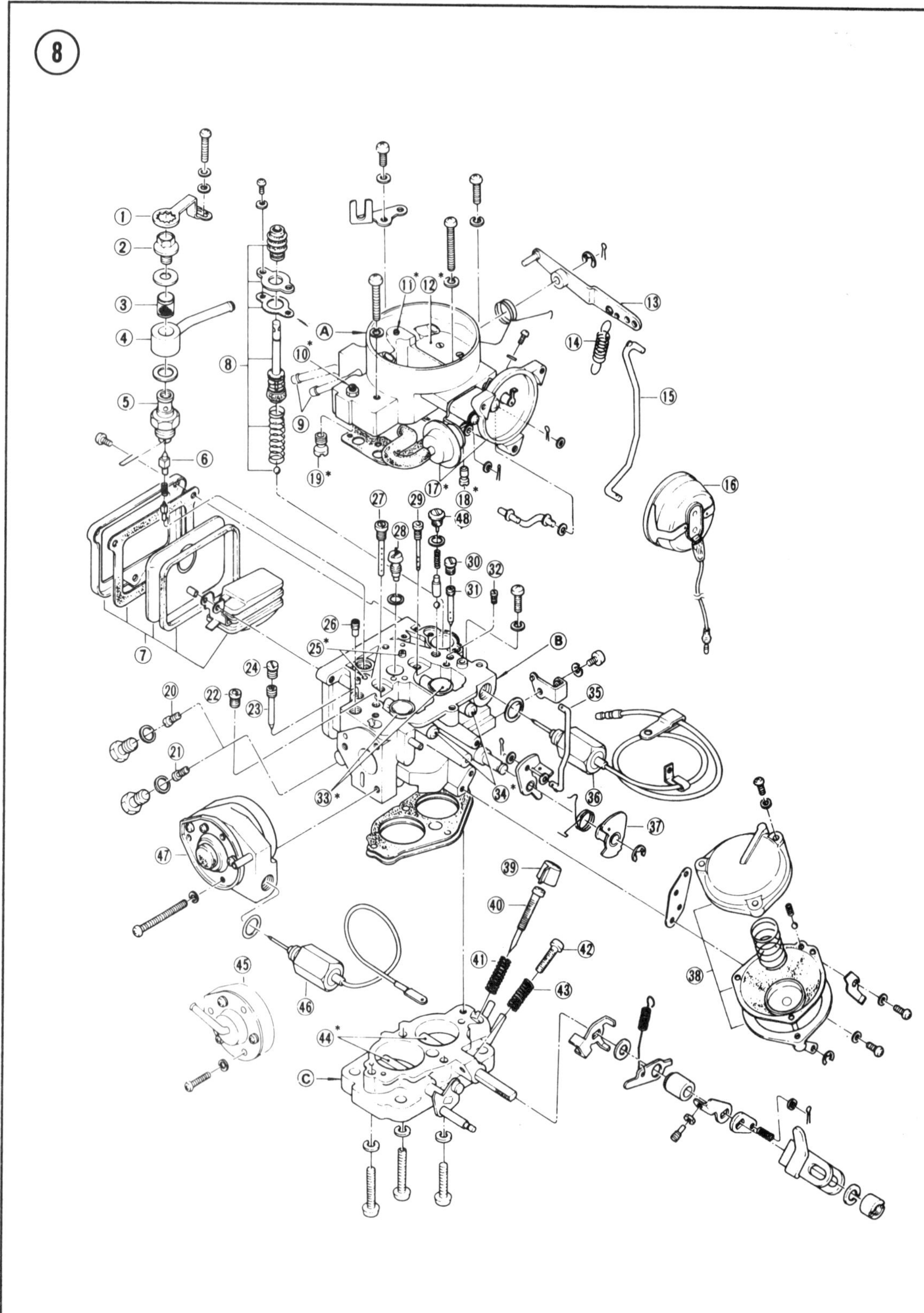
8
1
2
3
4
5
6
7
8
9
10*
11*
12*
13
14
15
16
17*
18*
19*
20
21
22
23
24
25*
26
27
28
29
30
31
32
33*
34*
35
36
37
38
39
40
41
42
43
44*
45
46
47
48
A
B
C

CARBURETOR — 1975-1976 (1972-1974 SIMILAR)

1. Lock lever
2. Filter set screw
3. Fuel filter
4. Fuel nipple
5. Needle valve body
6. Needle valve
7. Fuel chamber parts
8. Accelerating pump parts
9. Altitude compensator pipe (California models)
10. Coasting air bleed adjusting screw*
11. High speed enricher air bleed*
12. Choke valve*
13. Accelerating pump lever
14. Throttle return spring
15. Accelerating pump rod
16. Automatic choke cover
17. Automatic choke body and diaphragm chamber*
18. Richer jet*
19. Coasting air bleed*
20. Primary main jet
21. Secondary main jet
22. Secondary slow air bleed
23. Secondary slow jet
24. Plug
25. Safe orifice*
26. Coasting jet
27. Secondary main air bleed
28. Power valve
29. Primary main air bleed
30. Plug
31. Primary slow jet
32. No. 2 primary slow air bleed
33. Primary and secondary small venturi*
34. Venturi stopper screw*
35. Choke connecting rod
36. Anti-dieseling solenoid valve
37. Fast idle cam
38. Diaphragm chamber parts
39. Idle limiter cap
40. Idle adjust screw
41. Idle adjust screw spring
42. Throttle adjust screw
43. Throttle adjust screw spring
44. Primary and secondary throttle valve*
45. BCDD (California models)
46. Vacuum control solenoid valve
47. BCD (non-California models)
48. Accelerator pump discharge valve

Note: Do not remove the parts marked with an asterisk (*).

2. Disconnect the accelerator pump rod from the pump lever.

3. Remove the snap ring from the pump lever and slide it off its pivot.

4. On manual chokes, disconnect the fast idle and choke rods (107 and 118, Figure 7) from the choke lever (105). Remove the throttle return spring bracket (114).

5. On automatic chokes, disconnect the choke connecting rod, then remove the choke cover. See Figure 8 (1975-76) or Figure 9 (1972-74).

6. Remove 4 screws securing the choke chamber, then lift it off.

7. Remove 4 screws attaching the carburetor body to the throttle chamber, then lift it off.

8. Remove 3 screws securing the float chamber glass. Remove the glass frame, gasket, glass, and seal.

9. Slide the float off its pivot.

10. Remove the secondary throttle diaphragm. On automatic chokes, remove the fast idle cam.

11. Remove the fuel inlet filter assembly. See Figure 7 (1968-1971), Figure 8 (1975-1976), or **Figure 10** (1972-1974).

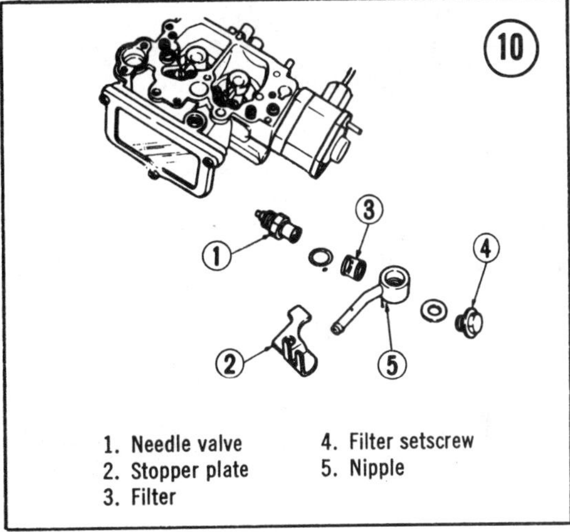

1. Needle valve
2. Stopper plate
3. Filter
4. Filter setscrew
5. Nipple

12. Remove the accelerator pump piston (67, Figure 7, or 8, Figure 8). Turn the carburetor upside down and dump the check ball into your hand.

13. Remove the accelerator pump discharge nozzle (73, Figure 7) or discharge valve (48, Figure 8).

5

14. Unscrew the main air bleeds (28 and 29, Figure 7, or 27 and 29, Figure 8). Take out the emulsion tubes, located under the air bleeds.

> NOTE: *Main air bleeds and emulsion tubes are not interchangeable, but they will fit into the wrong holes. Write down the number stamped in each air bleed, together with its location. Keep each emulsion tube with its air bleed, and keep the air bleeds away from each other.*

15. Unscrew the slow jets (90 and 91, Figure 7, or 23 and 31, Figure 8). On late models, the secondary slow jet (31, Figure 8) is located under a plug (30).

16. On early carburetors, unscrew one slow air bleed (92, Figure 7). On late models, unscrew both air bleeds (22 and 32, Figure 8).

17. Remove the main jet plugs from beneath the float chamber. Unscrew the main jets (31-40, Figure 7, or 20 and 21, Figure 8).

> NOTE: *Write down the number stamped in each main jet, together with its location. The main jets must be reinstalled in the holes from which they were removed.*

18. Unscrew the power valve (123, Figure 7, or 28, Figure 8).

19. On early carburetors, remove 3 screws and take off the coasting enricher solenoid. On later models, remove 3 screws (1, **Figure 11**) and take off the boost controlled deceleration device. Do not remove the 3 screws that hold the device together (2, Figure 11).

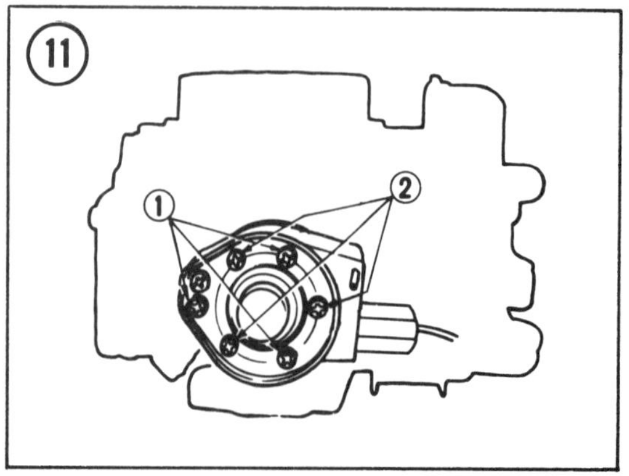

20. On automatic transmission autos, remove the anti-stall dashpot and bracket. Figure 7 shows the early design. All other models are basically the same.

21. On 1973-1976 cars, remove the anti-dieseling solenoid (36, Figure 8). Unscrew round solenoid with Vise Grips; unscrew hexagonal solenoids with an ordinary wrench. Be careful not to damage the solenoid.

22. On early carburetors, remove the secondary venturi (26, Figure 7). On 1972-1974 models, remove both venturis (**Figure 12**). On 1975-76 autos, do *not* remove the venturis.

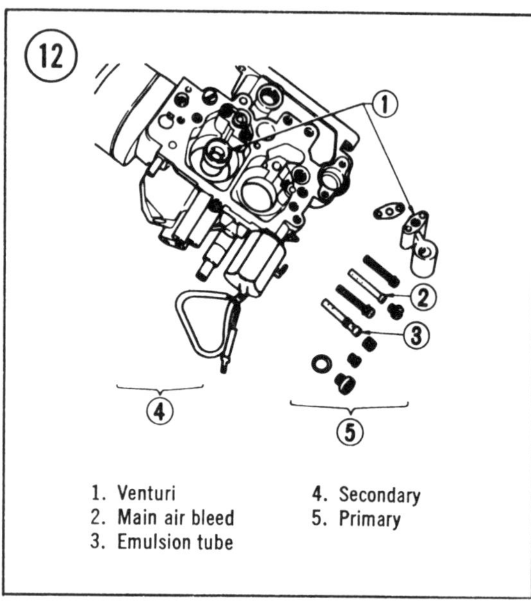

1. Venturi
2. Main air bleed
3. Emulsion tube
4. Secondary
5. Primary

23. If necessary, disassemble the carburetor linkage, referring to Figure 7 (1968-1971) or Figure 8 (1972-1976). Linkage disassembly is not necessary for normal carburetor overhaul, and should be avoided unless parts are bent or otherwise damaged. Do not remove the throttle plates or shaft under any circumstances.

Inspection

1. Clean all parts in solvent, *except* the following: secondary throttle diaphragm; accelerator pump piston assembly; vacuum break diaphragm (automatic chokes); coasting enricher solenoid (early carburetors); boost controlled deceleration device (late carburetors); anti-dieseling solenoid (1973-1976 carburetors).

CAUTION

Do not insert objects such as drill bits or pieces of wire into jets or passages while cleaning. These openings are carefully calibrated, and scratching them may seriously affect carburetor performance.

2. Remove the small wire clip from the needle valve. Pull out the needle and check the needle and seat for wear. Replace the needle valve if wear is detected.

NOTE: *Due to the extremely small size of the needle valve parts, it is a good idea to reassemble the valve immediately after inspection, if it is to be reused.*

3. Check the fuel inlet wire screen for clogging.
4. Check the carburetor bores for wear and out-of-roundness.
5. Check the idle mixture screw for wear at the tip. Replace the screw if wear is detected.
6. Check the venturis for damage. Replace if necessary.
7. Check all jets and passages for clogging and damage. Clean or replace as needed.
8. Check the accelerator pump piston seal and cover for wear, damage, or deterioration. Replace as needed.
9. On automatic chokes, check the bimetal coil and heating coil for damage. Inspect the vacuum break diaphragm (17, Figure 8). To do this, hold the choke valve shut and suck on the diaphragm's vacuum tube. There should be a strong pull on the choke valve.
10. On carburetors with solenoids, connect a 12-volt battery between the solenoid wires (or the solenoid wire and carburetor body). The solenoid plunger should move when current is applied.

Assembly

Assembly is the reverse of disassembly, plus the following.

1. Use new gaskets and seals.
2. If equipped with an anti-dieseling solenoid, use Loctite Stud Lock or equivalent on the threads when installing.
3. Be sure main jets and main air bleeds are installed in the correct holes. Refer to the numbers written down during disassembly.
4. On automatic chokes, align choke cover index mark with center mark on the choke body.
5. After assembly, adjust the float level, fast idle (automatic choke), anti-stall dashpot (automatic transmission), and boost-controlled deceleration device (1972-1976 models).

Fast Idle Adjustment (Automatic Chokes)

Fast idle is the speed at which the engine idles when it is cold and the choke is operating. As the engine warms up, idle speed automatically returns to normal.

1. Place the fast idle screw on the second step of the fast idle cam. See **Figure 13**.
2. Turn the screw until dimension "A" (primary throttle plate to bore clearance) is as specified in **Table 2**.

Anti-stall Dashpot Adjustment (Automatic Transmissions)

1. Warm the engine to normal operating temperature. Make sure the idle speed and mixture are adjusted properly.

Table 2 FAST IDLE CAM CLEARANCE

Vehicle	Inches	mm
1972 manual transmission	0.047	1.19
1972 automatic transmission	0.055	1.39
1973-74 manual transmission	0.035-0.039	0.89-0.99
1973-74 automatic transmission	0.044-0.048	1.11-1.21
1975-76 manual transmission	0.048-0.052	1.23-1.33
1975-76 automatic transmission	0.040-0.048	1.01-1.21

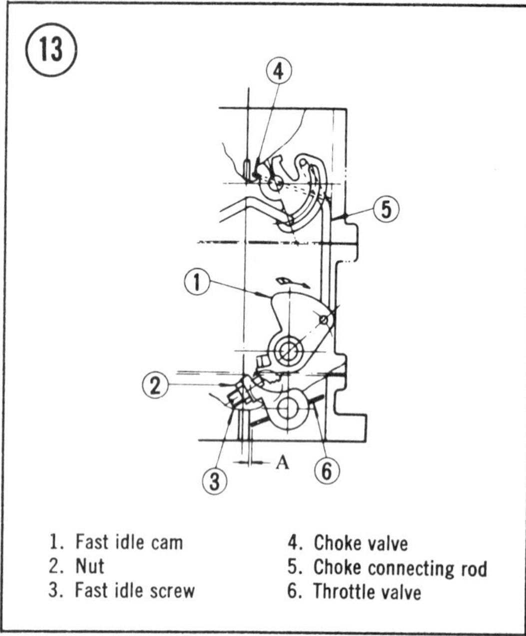

1. Fast idle cam
2. Nut
3. Fast idle screw
4. Choke valve
5. Choke connecting rod
6. Throttle valve

2. Move the throttle by hand until the dashpot just touches the stopper lever. At that point engine speed should be 1,600-1,800 rpm (1972-1974); 1,900-2,100 rpm (1975-1976 manual transmission); or 1,650-1,850 rpm (1975-1976 automatic transmission).
3. If necessary, loosen the lock nut (**Figure 14**) and turn the dashpot until engine speed is correct. Then tighten the locknut.

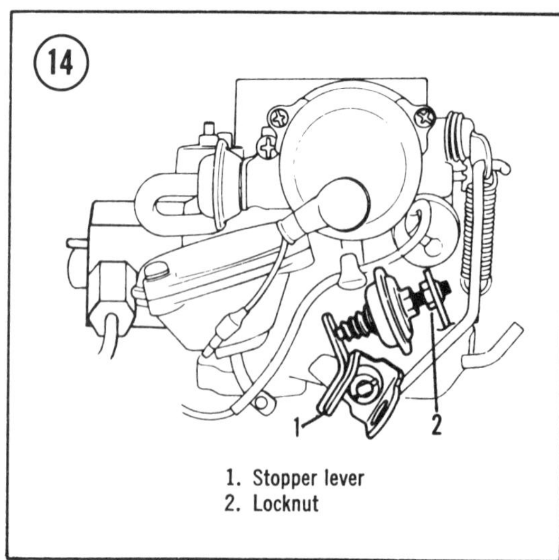

1. Stopper lever
2. Locknut

4. Make sure engine speed drops from 2,000 rpm to 1,000 rpm in about 3 seconds.

Float Level Adjustment

If float level is correct (1968-74 cars), fuel level will be even with the line on the float chamber glass when the engine is idling. On 1975-76 cars, the level will be at the center of the glass, 0.91 in. (23mm) below the top of the float chamber (dimension "H," **Figure 15**).

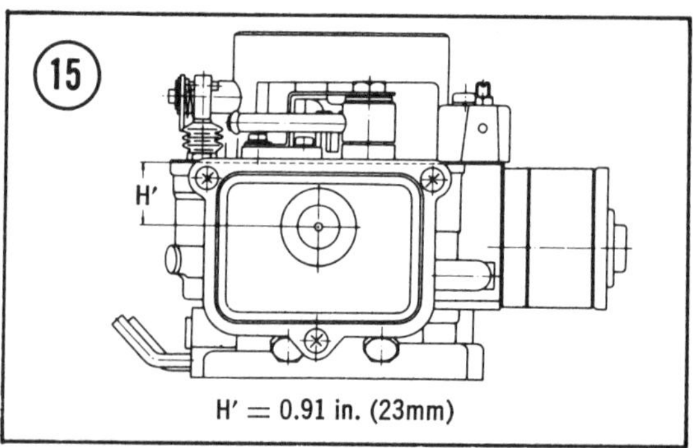

H′ = 0.91 in. (23mm)

To adjust, remove the float chamber glass and slide the float off its pivot. Bend the float seat (1, **Figure 16**) as needed to give a needle valve stroke of 0.059 in. (1.5mm) on 1968-74 cars; 0.051-0.067 in. (1.3-1.7mm) on 1975-76 models.

Boost Controlled Deceleration Device (1972-1976)

The boost controlled deceleration device (Figure 11) admits additional fuel mixture to the engine during deceleration, when there is normally not enough fuel in the combustion chambers to burn. The extra fuel mixture allows combustion to continue, reducing the amount of unburned hydrocarbons in the exhaust.

An improperly adjusted BCDD can cause an abnormally fast or rough idle. To check, remove the adjusting screw cover (attached to the center of the BCDD by 2 screws). Carefully note position of the adjusting screw, then turn it clockwise. If the idle improves, the BCDD requires adjustment. If it does not improve, return the adjusting screw to its original position and reinstall the cover.

If adjustment is necessary, take the job to a Datsun dealer. Although no special tools are required, the procedure is complicated. Improper adjustment can cause poor performance or excessive exhaust emissions.

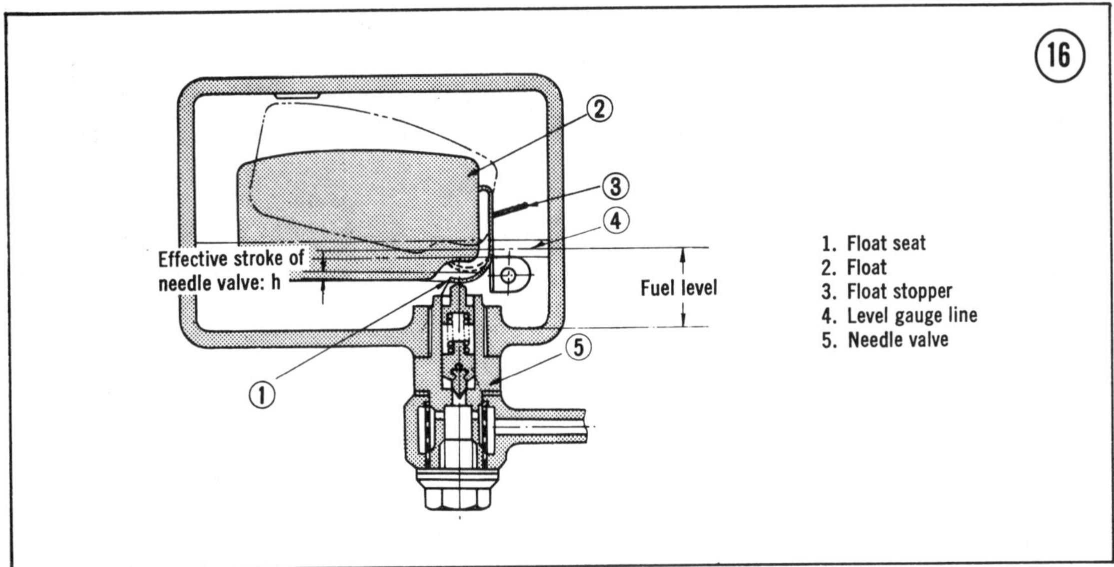

FUEL PUMP

All models use a mechanical fuel pump driven by an eccentric lobe on the camshaft and mounted at the right front corner of the cylinder head. Fuel pump testing is covered in Chapter Three, under *Fuel System Troubleshooting*. This section covers fuel pump removal, inspection, repair, and installation.

Removal/Installation

To remove, disconnect the fuel inlet and outlet lines from the pump. Then remove 2 nuts securing the fuel pump and take it off. **Figure 17** shows the pump being removed.

Disassembly

Figure 18 shows the disassembled pump components.

1. Remove 6 screws and separate the upper and lower body.
2. Remove 5 screws and take the top cover off the upper body.
3. Unscrew the fuel line fittings.
4. Remove both valve retainer screws, then remove the valves.
5. Unhook the diaphragm. To do this, push the diaphragm downward and tilt it until the diaphragm rod slips off the pump operating rod. The diaphragm can then be lifted out.
6. Tap the pivot pin out of the operating lever with a hammer and pin punch.

Inspection

1. Clean all parts in solvent before inspection. Discard all gaskets.
2. Check the valves and springs for wear and damage. Blow through the valves. If they are good, air will travel only one way through them. If air can be blown through both sides of a valve, replace it.
3. Check the diaphragm for small holes, cracks, and wear.
4. Examine the pump operating lever for wear on its camshaft contact surface.
5. Check the pivot pin in the operating lever for wear. A worn pin can cause an oil leak.

5

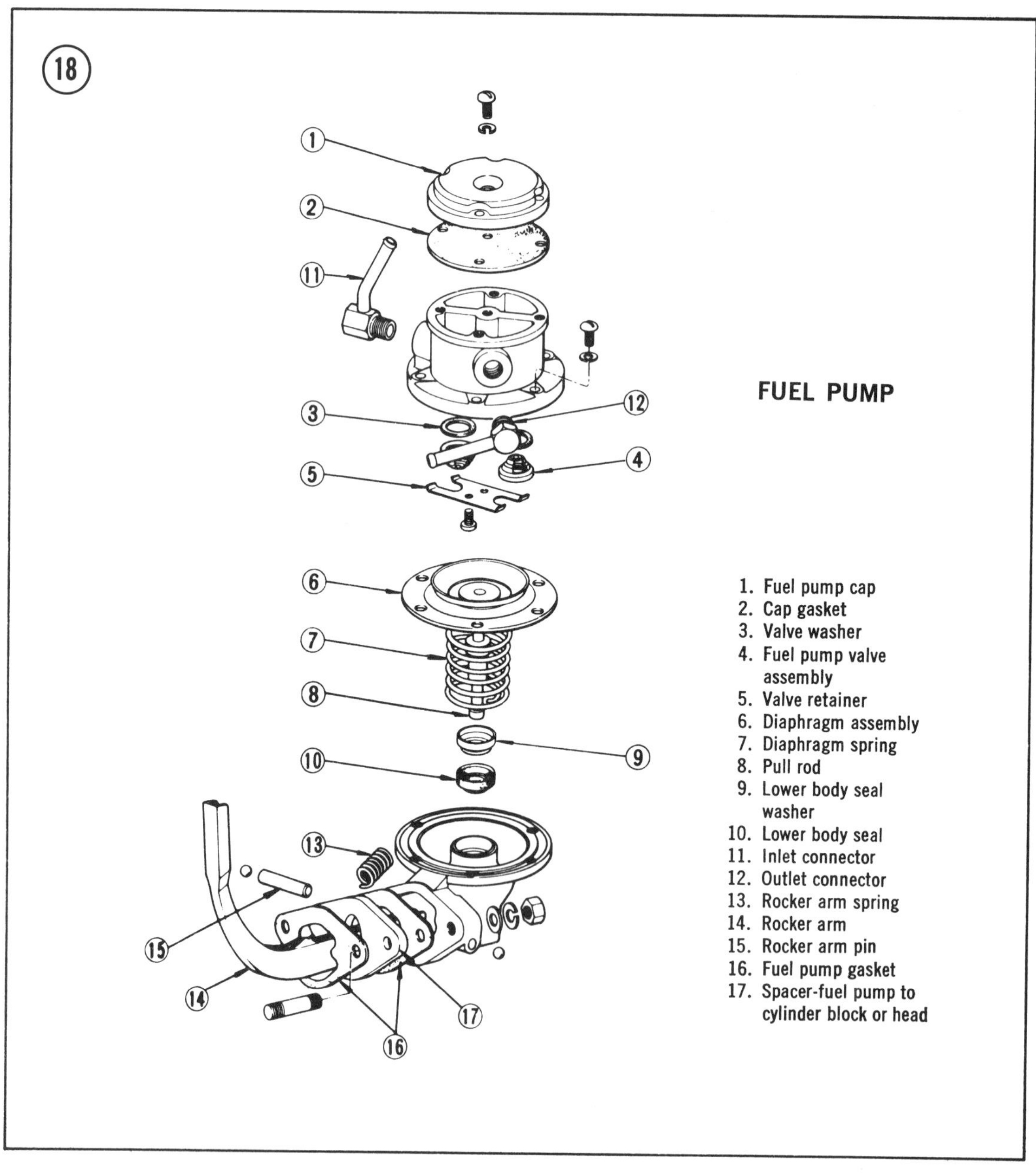

Assembly

Assembly is the reverse of the disassembly procedure, plus the following.

1. Be sure to use new gaskets.
2. Lubricate the operating lever, its pivot pin, and the diaphragm pull rod before assembly.
3. Test the pump before installation. Hold the pump about 3 feet higher than the top of the gas tank (with the fuel inlet line connected) and work the operating lever by hand. Fuel should be pumped after several strokes of the operating lever.

INTAKE AND EXHAUST MANIFOLDS

Figure 19 shows the manifolds used on 1973 engines. Other years are similar. Coolant is routed through the intake manifold to control the temperature of the incoming fuel mixture.

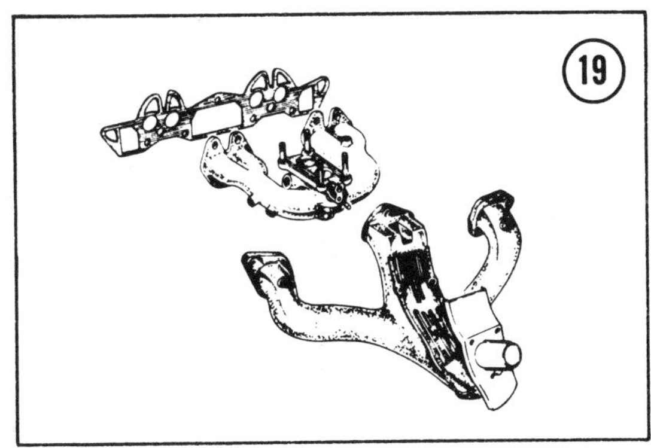

Some models also use an exhaust manifold heat rise (**Figure 20**).

Removal/Installation

1. Perform Steps 1-8, *Carburetor Removal/Installation.*

2. Drain the cooling system by opening the radiator drain tap or disconnecting the lower hose. If the anti-freeze is good, drain it into a clean container and reuse it.

3. Detach the crankcase ventilation hose from the intake manifold.

4. On 1974-76 models, detach the vacuum tube from the exhaust gas recirculation solenoid. Detach the exhaust gas tube running from the exhaust manifold to the exhaust gas recirculation valve.

5. Remove the manifold securing nuts. Take the manifold(s) off the engine.

6. Install in the reverse order.

AIR INJECTION SYSTEM

An air injection system is used with 1968-1971 L16 engines, as well as the L20B engine used on 1974 610's and all 1975-76 cars. The system is designed to pump fresh air into each exhaust port, so combustion can continue for a longer time and reduce emissions. **Figure 21** shows the 1974 system. The 1968-71 version is basically the same. **Figure 22** shows the system used on 1975-76 California cars. The 49-states version is the same, but does not use the air control valve and emergency air relief valve. These 2 valves are designed to prevent excessively high catalytic converter temperatures.

Air pump repair requires special tools, and should be left to a Datsun dealer or other competent mechanic. None of the other components is repairable.

5

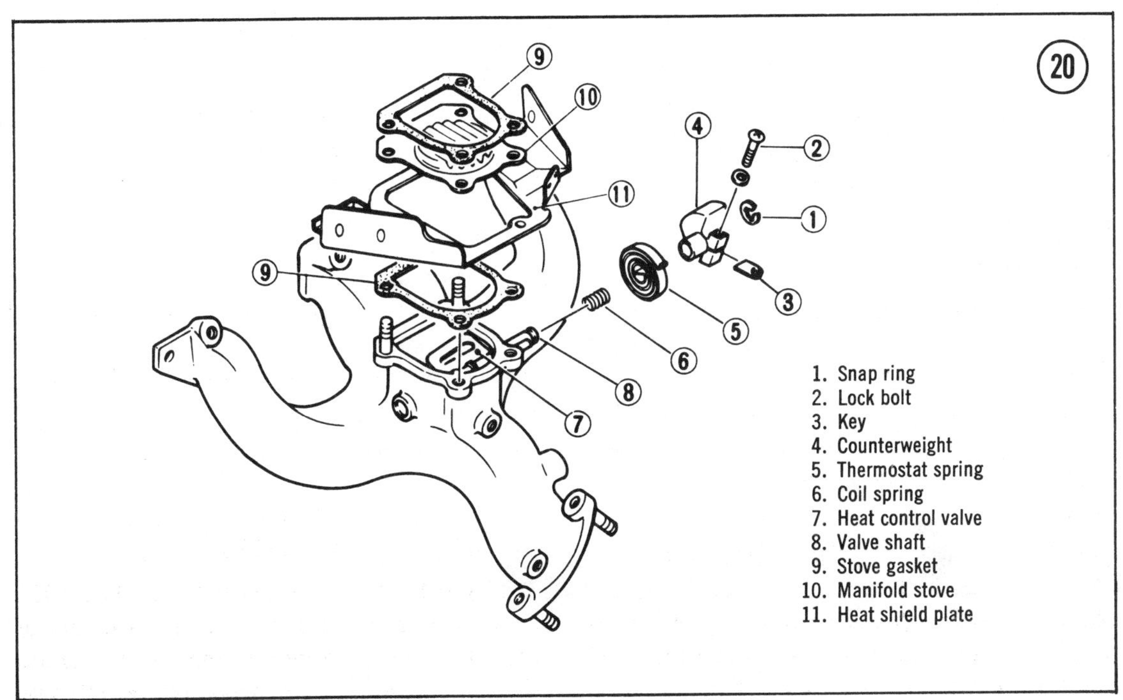

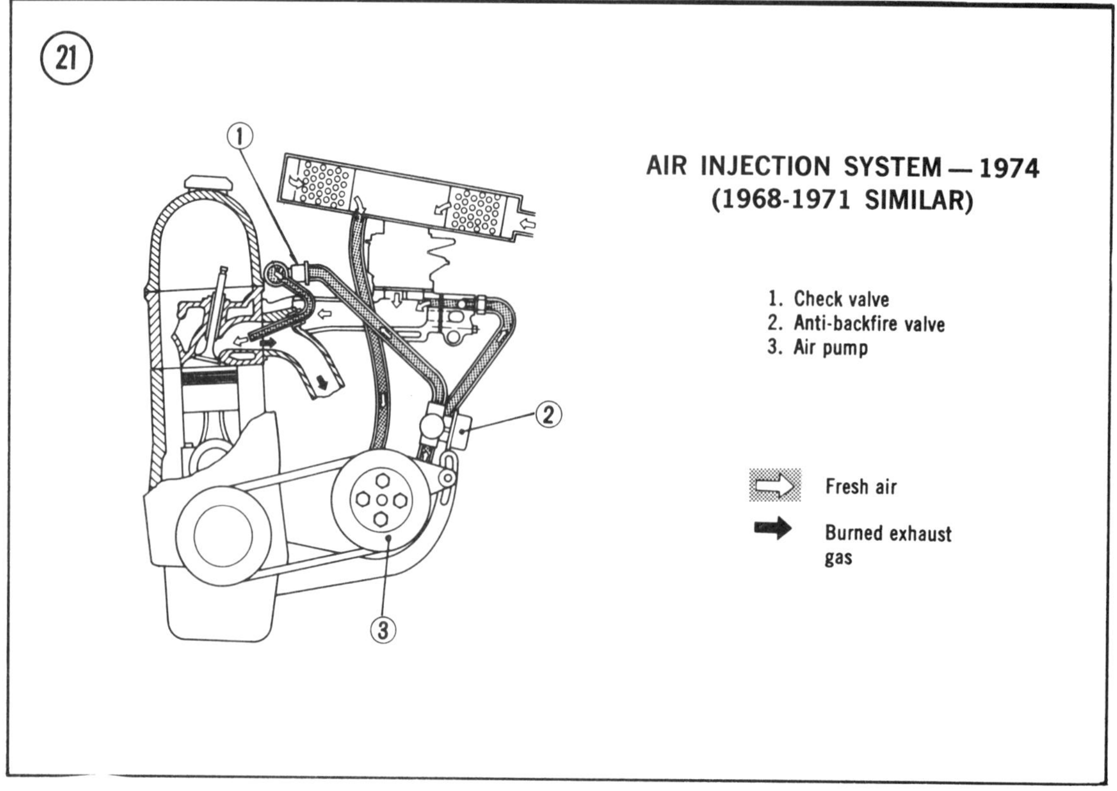

Air Pump Removal/Installation

1. Disconnect the hoses from the air pump.
2. Remove the nut attaching the air pump to its adjusting bracket.
3. Remove the bolt attaching the air pump to its mounting bracket. Remove the air pump belt, then lift the air pump off.
4. Install in the reverse order.

Anti-backfire Valve Test (Through 1974)

1. Warm the engine to normal operating temperature.
2. Check all air injection hoses for leaks. Replace as needed.
3. Disconnect the hose running from the anti-backfire valve to intake manifold. Plug the hose so it is airtight.
4. Working the throttle linkage by hand, open and close the throttle rapidly. Air should flow from the valve for 1-2 seconds. No air flow or continuous air flow indicates a defective valve. Replace it.

Anti-backfire Valve Test (1975-1976)

1. Disconnect the anti-backfire valve hose from the air cleaner.
2. Run the engine at 3,000 rpm, then release the throttle quickly. Suction should be felt at the disconnected hose end. If not, replace the anti-backfire valve.

Check Valve Test

1. Warm the engine to normal operating temperature.
2. Check air injection hoses for leaks. Replace as needed.
3. Disconnect the long hose from the check valve. Look inside the valve. The valve plate should be against its seat (toward you, away from the engine). Push the valve plate in. It should return to its seat without binding.
4. With the hose disconnected, start the engine and watch the valve plate. Plate vibration at idle is permissible. Raise engine speed to 1,500-2,000 rpm. There should be no exhaust gas

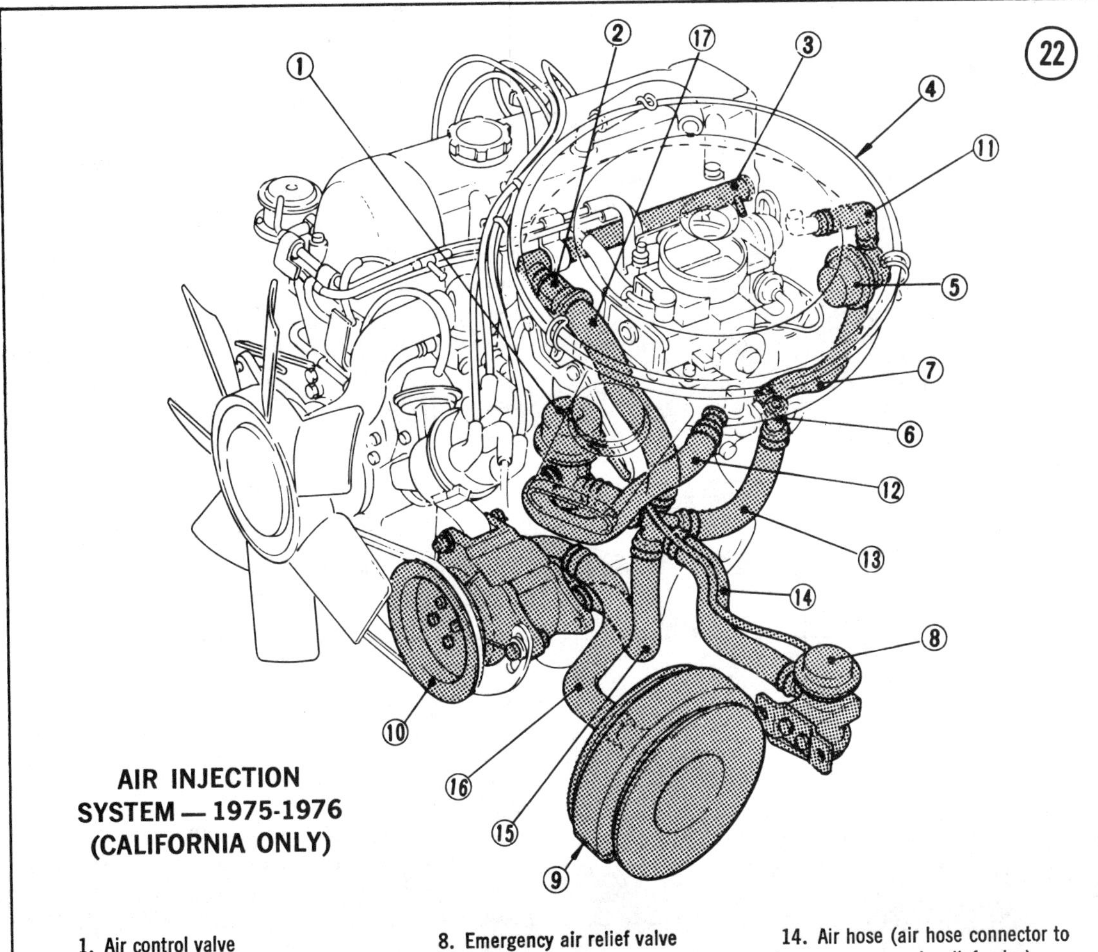

AIR INJECTION SYSTEM — 1975-1976 (CALIFORNIA ONLY)

1. Air control valve
2. Check valve
3. Air gallery pipe
4. Automatic temperature control air cleaner
5. Anti-backfire valve (AB valve)
6. Air relief valve
7. Air hose (AB valve to intake manifold)
8. Emergency air relief valve
9. Air pump air cleaner
10. Air pump
11. Air hose (carburetor air cleaner to AB valve)
12. Air hose (carburetor air cleaner to air control valve)
13. Air hose (air relief valve to air hose connector)
14. Air hose (air hose connector to emergency air relief valve)
15. Air hose (air hose connector to air pump)
16. Air hose (air pump to air pump air cleaner)
17. Air hose (check valve to air hose connector)

leakage past the plate. If there is, replace the check valve.

Emergency Air Relief Valve (1975-1976 California Cars)

1. Warm the engine to normal operating temperature.
2. Check all hoses for leaks or damage. Tighten or replace as needed.
3. Run the engine at 2,000 rpm. Place a hand over the air outlet at the top of the EAR valve. No air should be felt.
4. Disconnect the vacuum (thin) hose from the EAR valve. There should now be air flow from the valve outlet at 2,000 rpm. If not, replace the valve.

Air Control Valve

(1975-1976 California Cars)

1. Warm the engine to normal operating temperature.
2. Check all hoses for leaks or damage. Tighten or replace as needed.

3. With the engine idling, disconnect the valve's outlet hose (**Figure 23**). If there is no air flow from the hose, replace the valve.

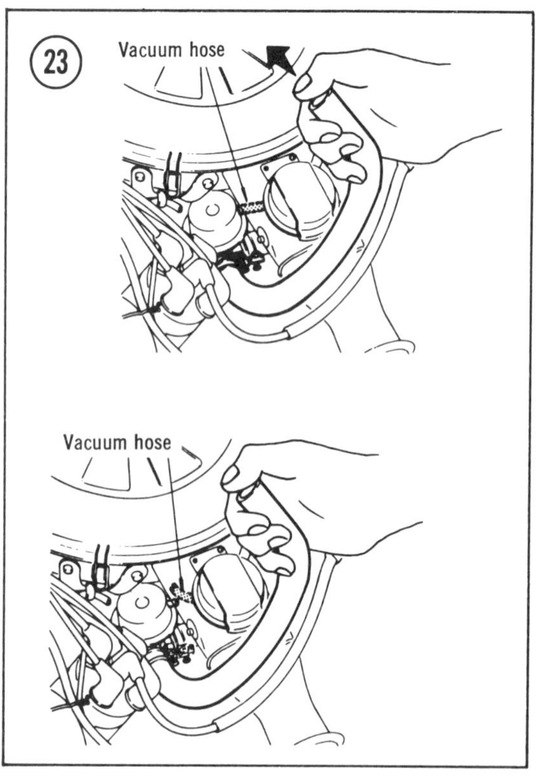

4. Disconnect the vacuum (thin) hose from the valve. Air flow at idle should stop. If not, replace the valve.

Air Injection Tubing

Removal of the air injection tubing is very difficult without bending the tubes. Removal should not be attempted unless the tubes are damaged. To remove, disconnect the short air hose from the check valve. Apply penetrating oil to the 4 nuts attaching the tubes to the exhaust manifold. Remove the nuts and lift the tubing off. Install in the reverse order.

EXHAUST GAS RECIRCULATION SYSTEM

The EGR system, used on 1974-76 vehicles, routes exhaust gas into the intake manifold. The exhaust gas lowers combustion temperature, reducing nitrogen oxide emissions. **Figure 24** shows the 1974 system on the engine. The 1975-76 system (**Figure 25**) is much the same. However, it cuts off EGR flow at low temperatures with a temperature-operated vacuum valve (**Figure 26**), rather than the temperature sensor and electrical solenoid used on 1974 systems.

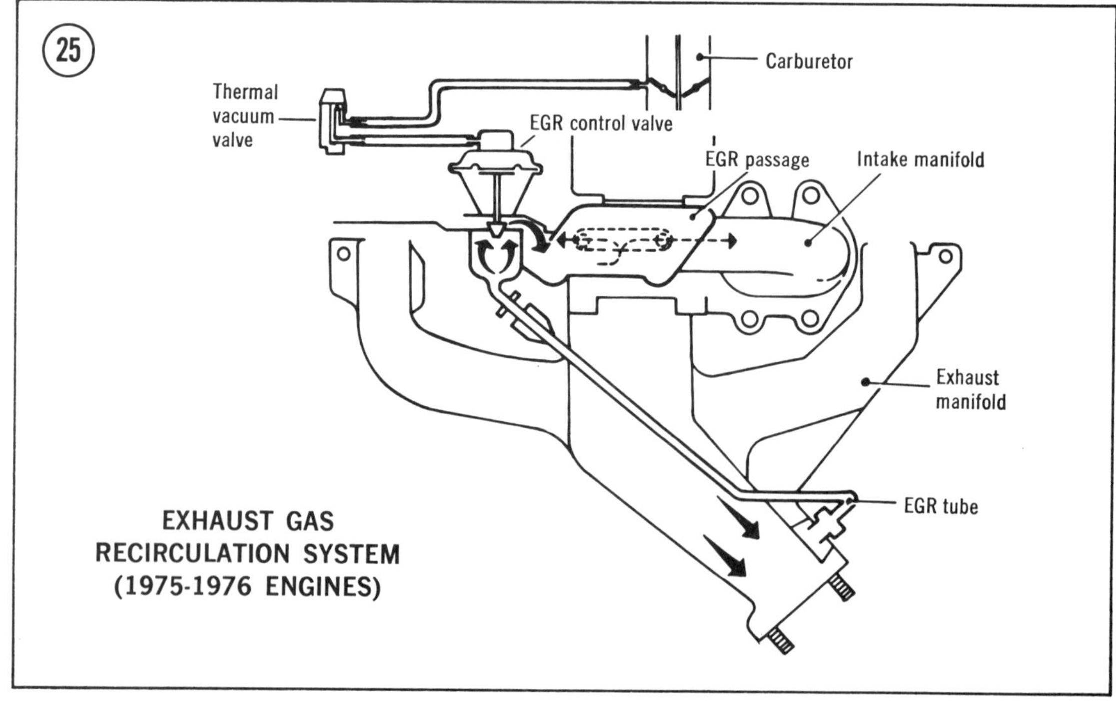

EXHAUST GAS RECIRCULATION SYSTEM (1975-1976 ENGINES)

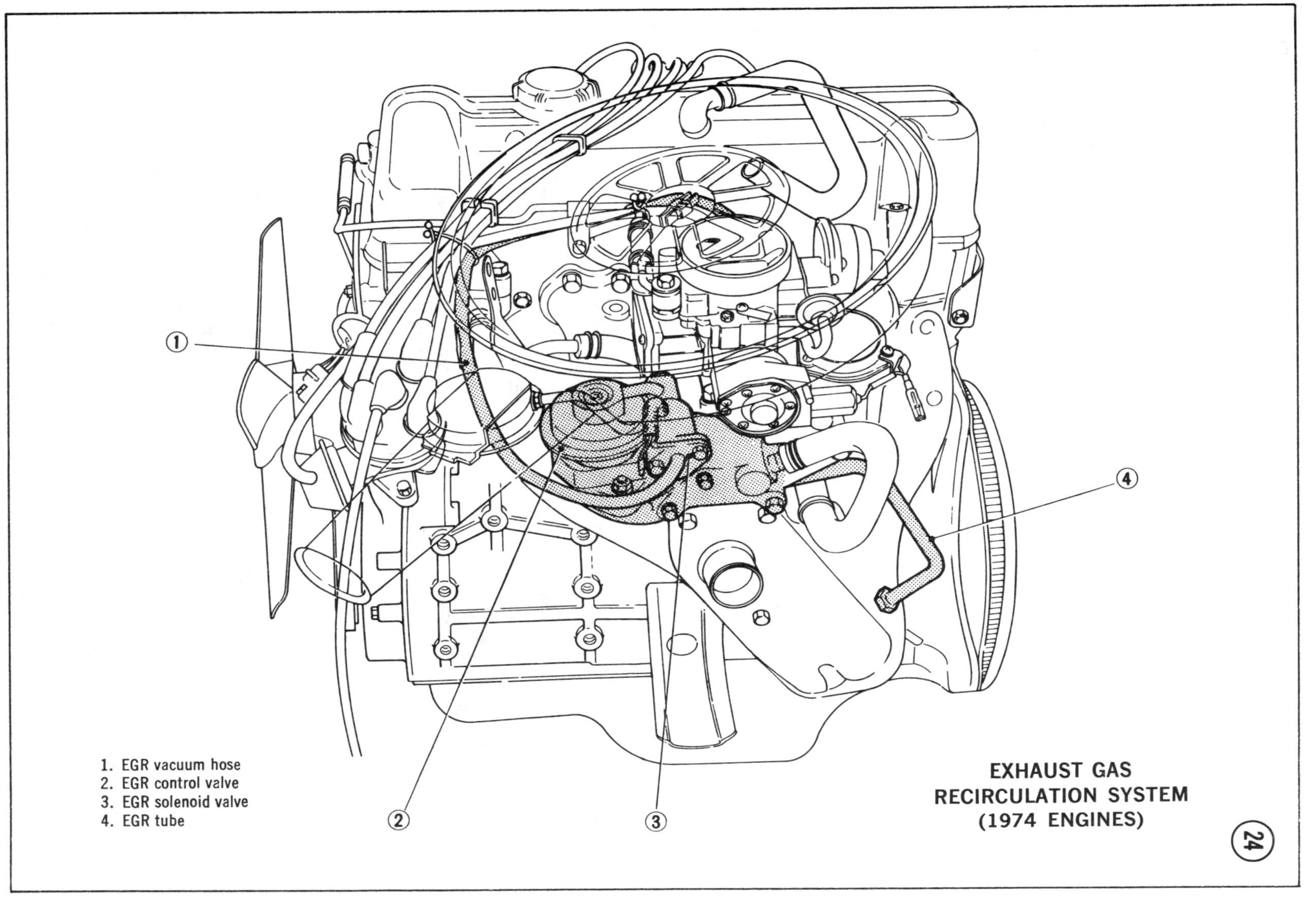

24

EXHAUST GAS RECIRCULATION SYSTEM (1974 ENGINES)

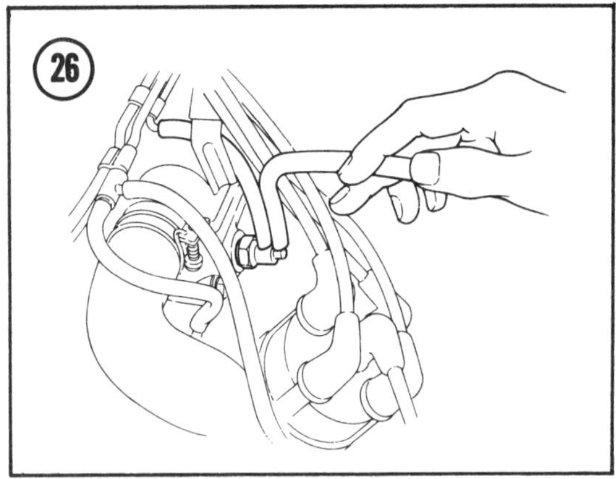

26

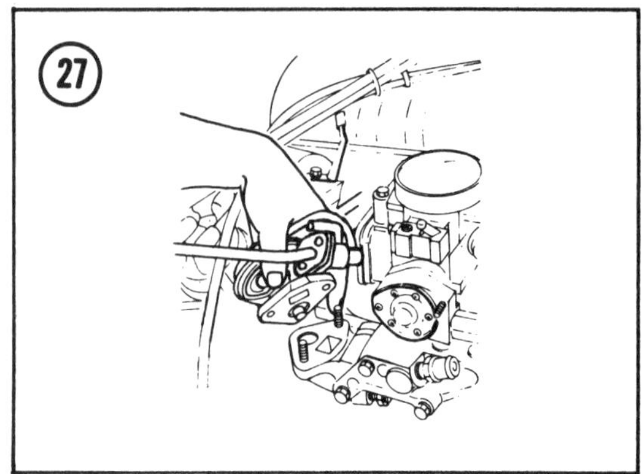

27

Inspection

The system should be inspected at intervals specified in Chapter Two. The EGR valve should be removed and cleaned as part of inspection.

> NOTE: *Since 1975-1976 California cars use unleaded fuel, regular* EGR *valve cleaning is not required.*

1. Examine the EGR system, referring to Figure 24 or 25. Replace cracked or worn hoses and tubes. Replace any parts showing obvious mechanical damage.
2. On 1974 cars, make sure the solenoid valve wire is securely connected.
3. Warm the engine to normal operating temperature.
4. Increase engine speed to 3,000-3,500 rpm. The control valve shaft (visible inside the lower part of the valve) should rise.
5. Disconnect the solenoid valve wire. Connect it to the battery positive terminal with a jumper wire. Again, increase engine speed to 3,000-3,500 rpm. This time the control valve shaft should not rise.
6. With the engine idling, reach into the control valve and push the diaphragm up. The idle should become unstable.

> WARNING
> *The control valve and surrounding area will be hot. Use a screwdriver or similar tool to raise the diaphragm.*

7. Disconnect the control valve vacuum hose, remove 2 attaching nuts, and lift the control valve off the intake manifold (**Figure 27**).
8. Check the control valve for visible wear or damage. Clean the base of the valve with a wire brush and compressed air. Check the intake manifold passage for excessive carbon buildup. If necessary, remove the manifold and clean it.
9. To reset EGR warning light, remove upper grommet from the detector drive counter. This is mounted on the wiper motor at right rear corner of engine compartment. Insert a screwdriver into the hole and press the reset switch.

EXHAUST PIPE AND MUFFLER

The 510 exhaust system consists of a front tube, premuffler, center tube, rear tube, main muffler, and tailpipe. The systems on 1974 cars, and on 1975-76 non-California cars, use a combined center pipe and premuffler, and a combined main muffler and tailpipe. The 1975-76 California cars use a catalytic converter and a main muffler. For construction details, refer to the following illustrations:

Figure 28—510
Figure 29—1974 610
Figure 30—1974 710
Figure 31—1975-76 610 (California)
Figure 32—1975-76 610 (non-California)
Figure 33—1975-76 710 sedan and hardtop (California)
Figure 34—1975-76 710 sedan and hardtop (non-California); 710 wagon (California); and 710 wagon (non-California)

Removal/Installation

1. Prior to removal, soak all bolts, nuts, and

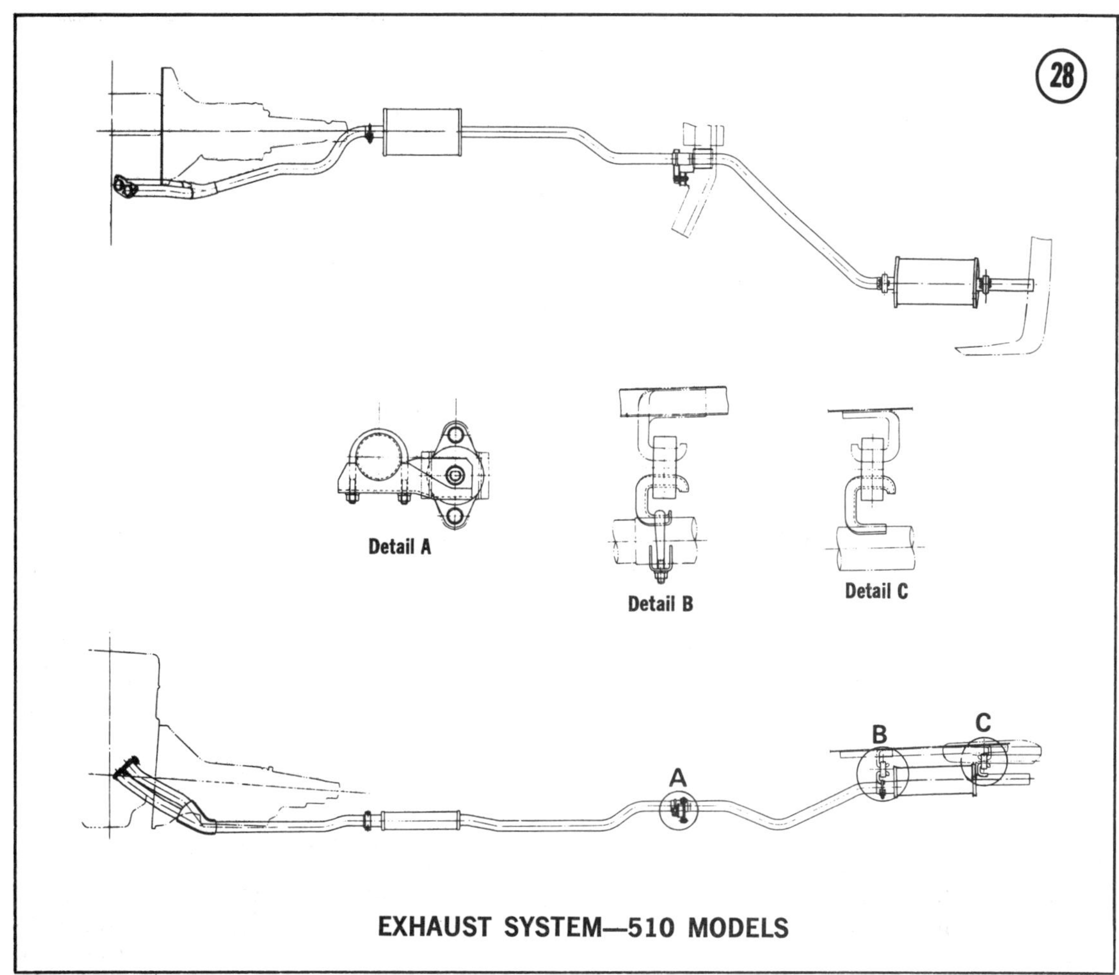

EXHAUST SYSTEM—510 MODELS

pipe joints with penetrating oil such as WD-40.

2. Undo the necessary clamps and hanger brackets, referring to appropriate illustration.

> NOTE: *1974 models use an injected sealer at the front end of the muffler* (**Figure 35**). *1975-76 cars use the sealer at all tube joints. To remove, break the seal by tapping the joint with a metal hammer. Twist the muffler back and forth, then tap it off with a rubber mallet.*

3. Check removed parts for excessive rust, and for damage caused by bottoming the vehicle. Check rubber mounts for melting, cracks, or deterioration. Replace as needed.

4. Install in the reverse order. On 1974-1976 models, inject sealer into the connection (if used). Use a Datsun sealer kit as shown in Figure 35. Let the engine idle for 10 minutes to cure the sealer. Do not accelerate sharply for 20-30 minutes.

EVAPORATIVE EMISSION CONTROL SYSTEM

The evaporative emission control system is designed to prevent gasoline vapor from escaping into the atmosphere. Gasoline fumes around the car may indicate a leaking vapor line. Fuel starvation or a deformed fuel tank may indicate a clogged fuel filler cap valve. If these symptoms occur, have the system tested by a Datsun dealer or certified emission control station.

> NOTE: *If fuel flow is inadequate, also test the fuel pump as described in Chapter Three.*

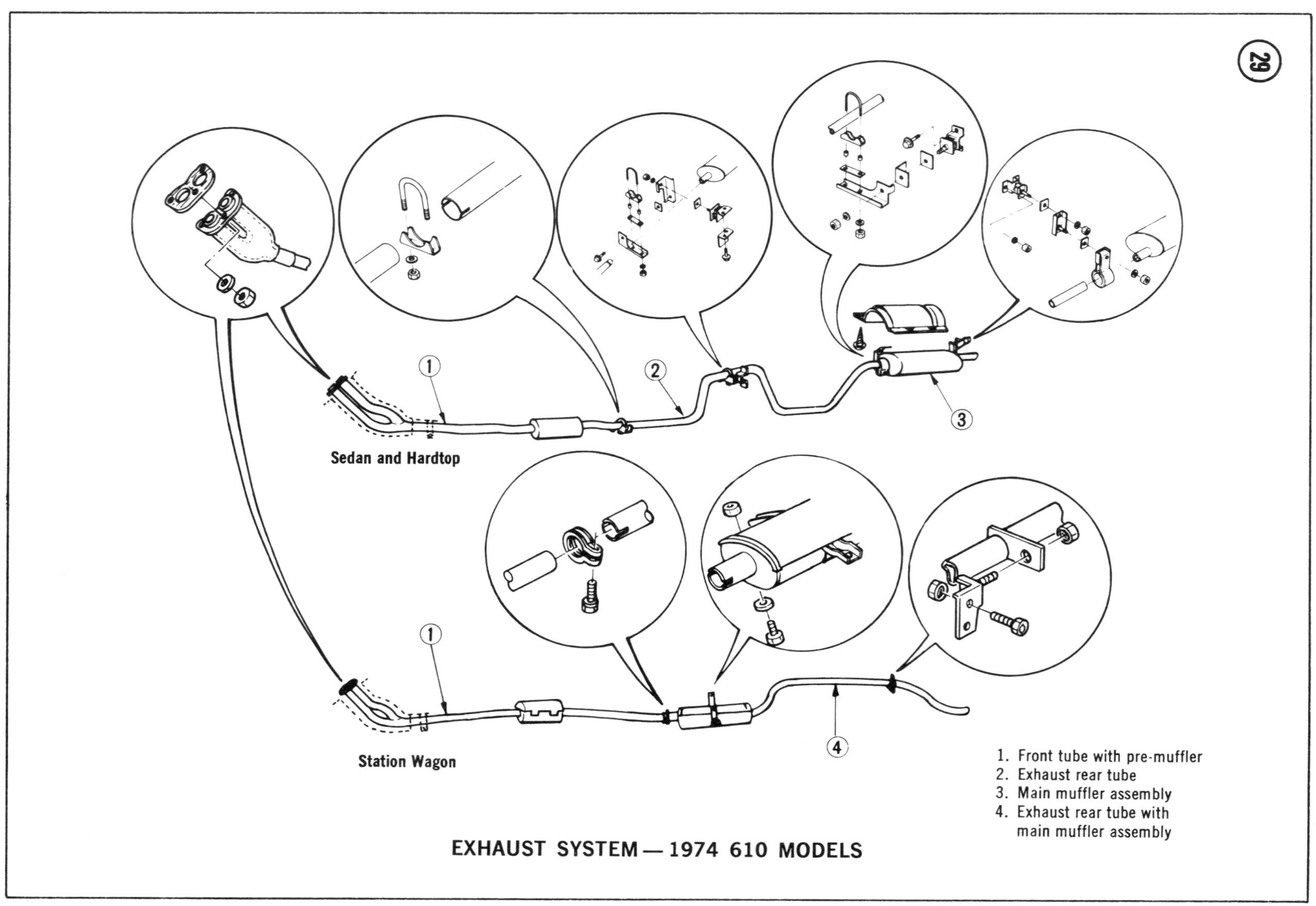

EXHAUST SYSTEM — 1974 610 MODELS

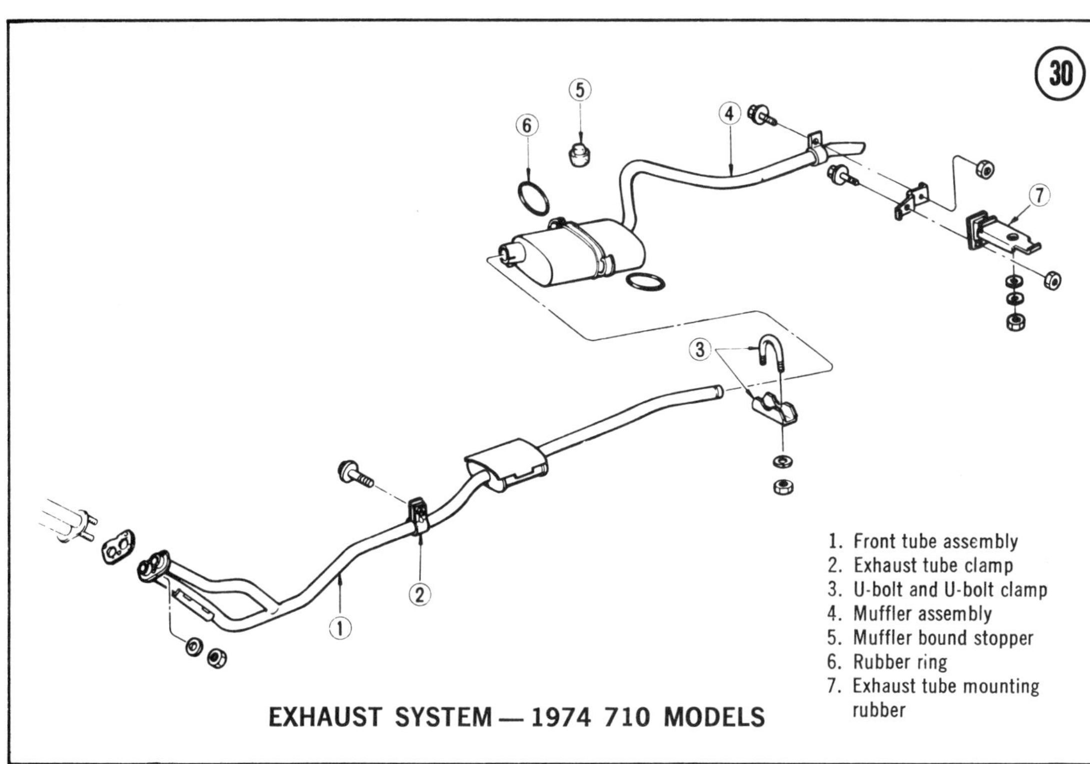

EXHAUST SYSTEM — 1974 710 MODELS

1. Front tube assembly
2. Exhaust tube clamp
3. U-bolt and U-bolt clamp
4. Muffler assembly
5. Muffler bound stopper
6. Rubber ring
7. Exhaust tube mounting rubber

5

31

EXHAUST SYSTEM
1975-76 610 (CALIFORNIA)

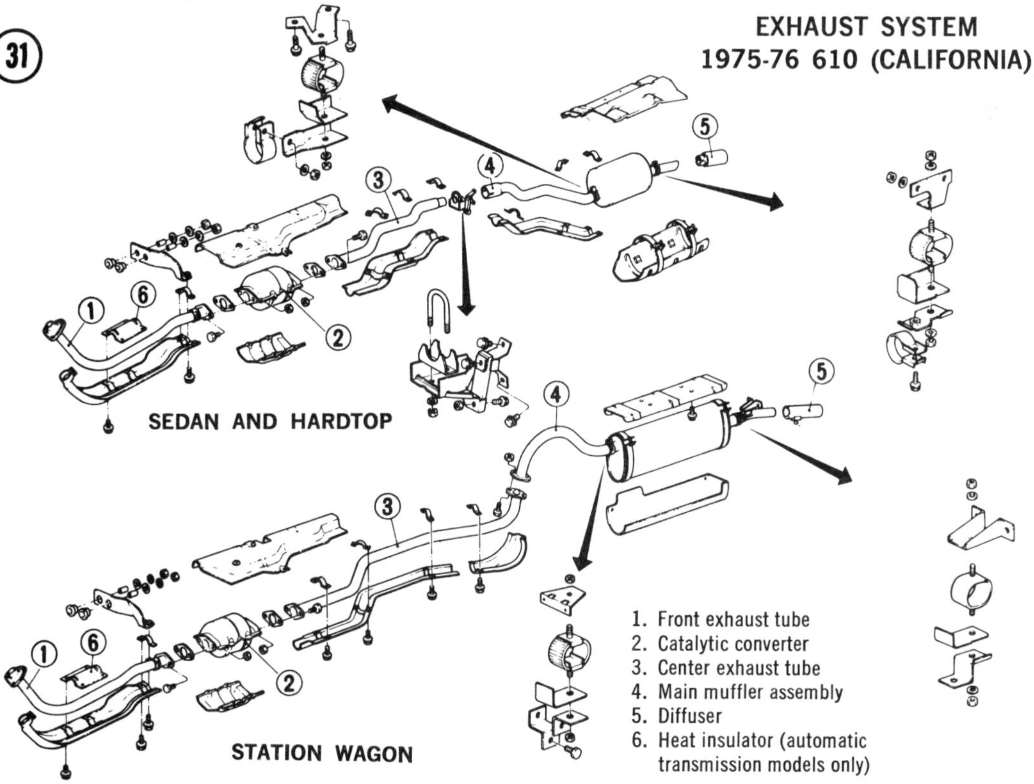

SEDAN AND HARDTOP

STATION WAGON

1. Front exhaust tube
2. Catalytic converter
3. Center exhaust tube
4. Main muffler assembly
5. Diffuser
6. Heat insulator (automatic transmission models only)

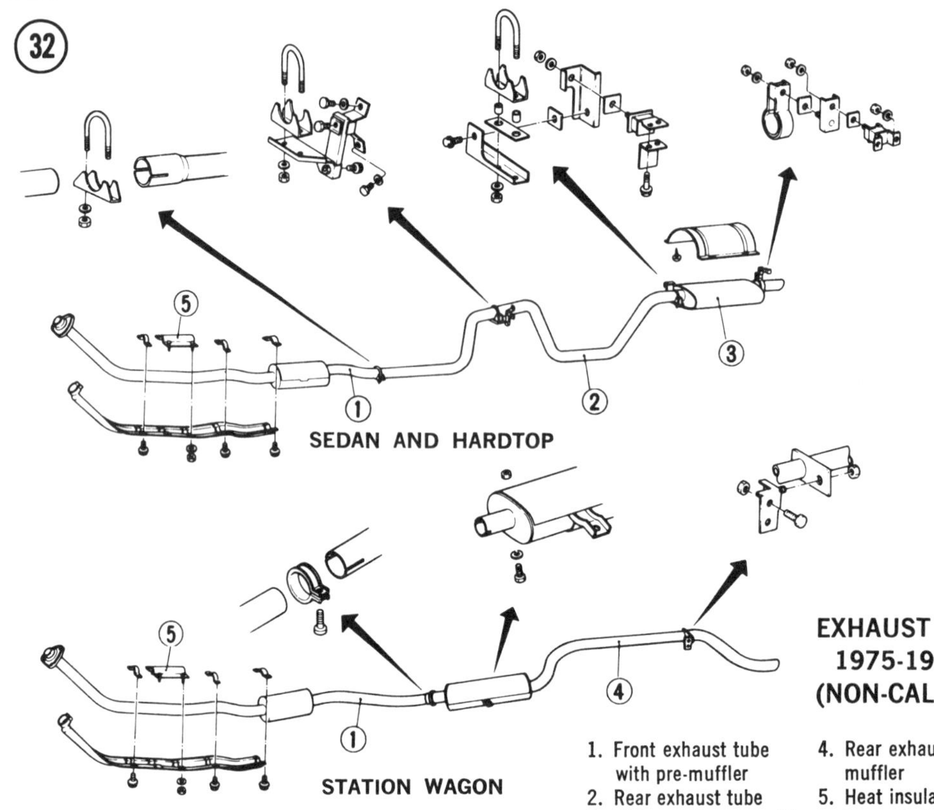

32

SEDAN AND HARDTOP

STATION WAGON

EXHAUST SYSTEM 1975-1976 610 (NON-CALIFORNIA)

1. Front exhaust tube with pre-muffler
2. Rear exhaust tube
3. Main muffler assembly
4. Rear exhaust tube with main muffler
5. Heat insulator (automatic transmission models only)

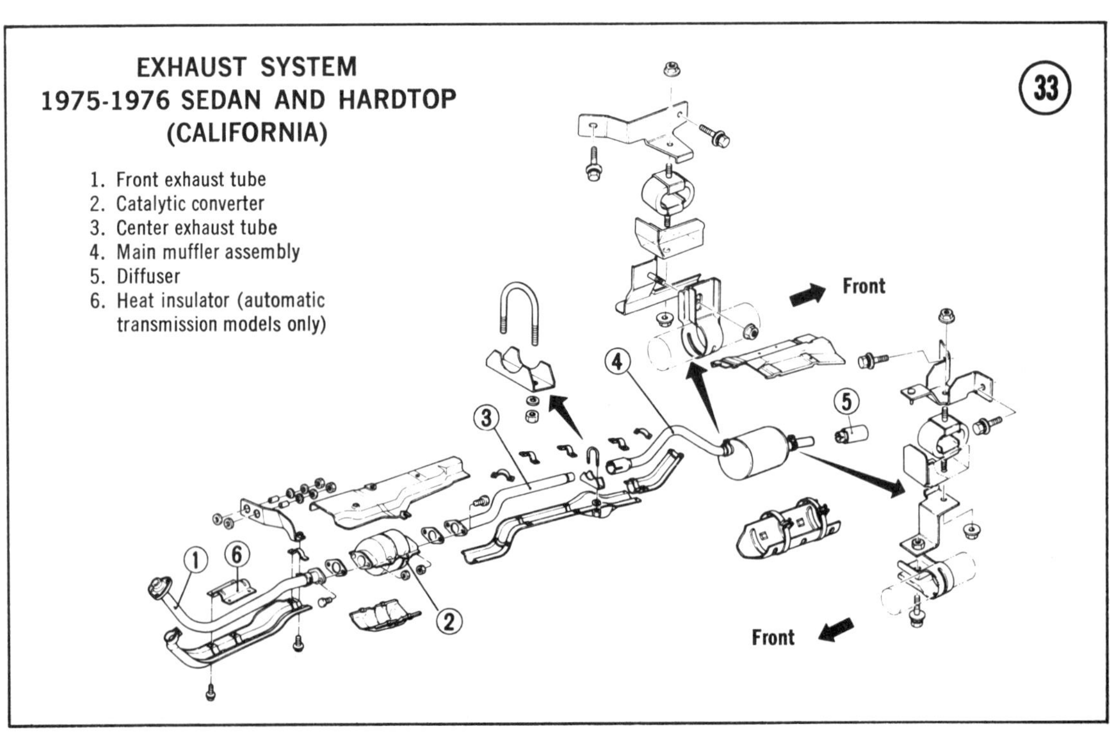

EXHAUST SYSTEM 1975-1976 SEDAN AND HARDTOP (CALIFORNIA)

1. Front exhaust tube
2. Catalytic converter
3. Center exhaust tube
4. Main muffler assembly
5. Diffuser
6. Heat insulator (automatic transmission models only)

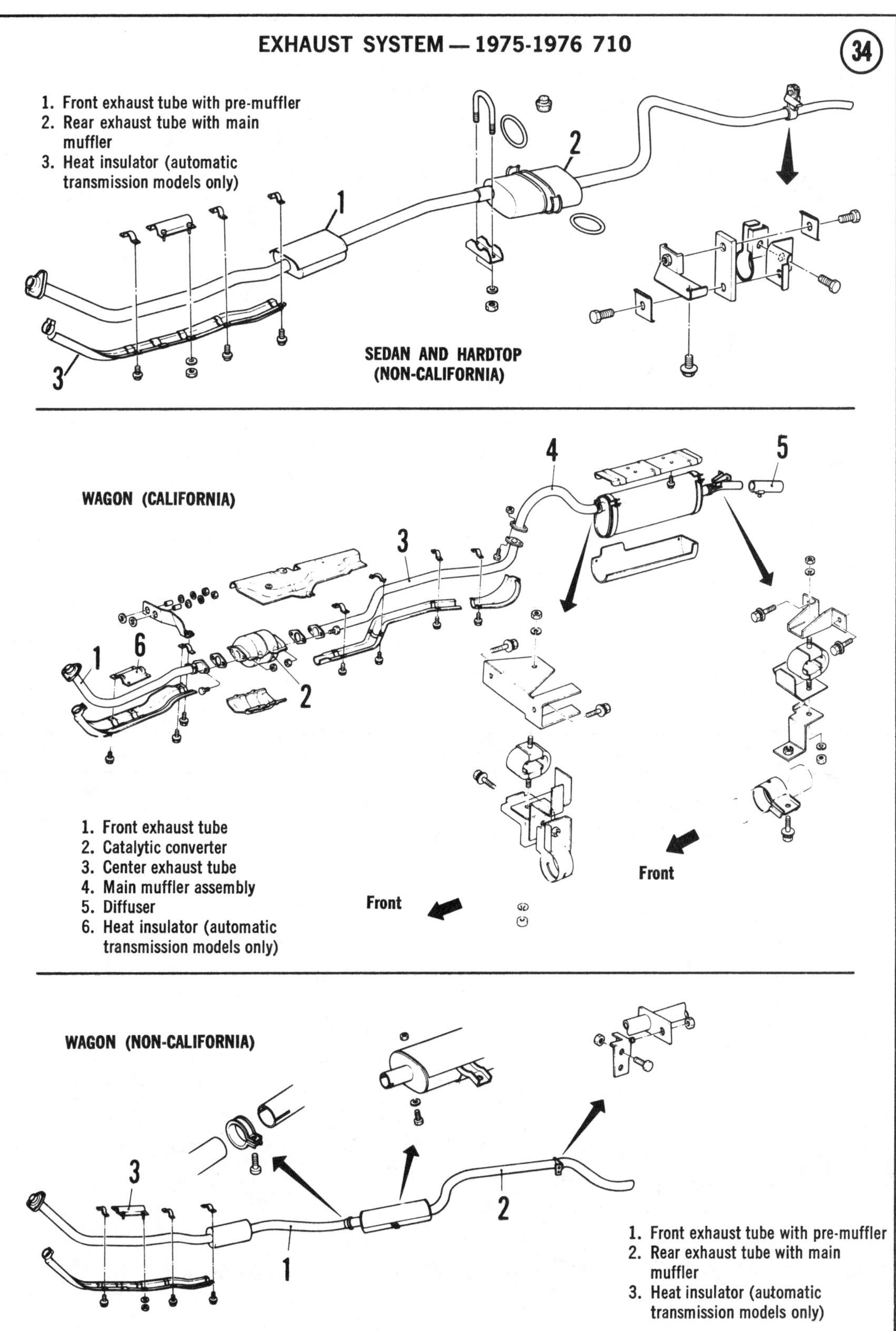
EXHAUST SYSTEM — 1975-1976 710
34
1. Front exhaust tube with pre-muffler
2. Rear exhaust tube with main muffler
3. Heat insulator (automatic transmission models only)
1
2
3
SEDAN AND HARDTOP (NON-CALIFORNIA)
WAGON (CALIFORNIA)
1
2
3
4
5
6
1. Front exhaust tube
2. Catalytic converter
3. Center exhaust tube
4. Main muffler assembly
5. Diffuser
6. Heat insulator (automatic transmission models only)
Front
Front
WAGON (NON-CALIFORNIA)
1
2
3
1. Front exhaust tube with pre-muffler
2. Rear exhaust tube with main muffler
3. Heat insulator (automatic transmission models only)

5

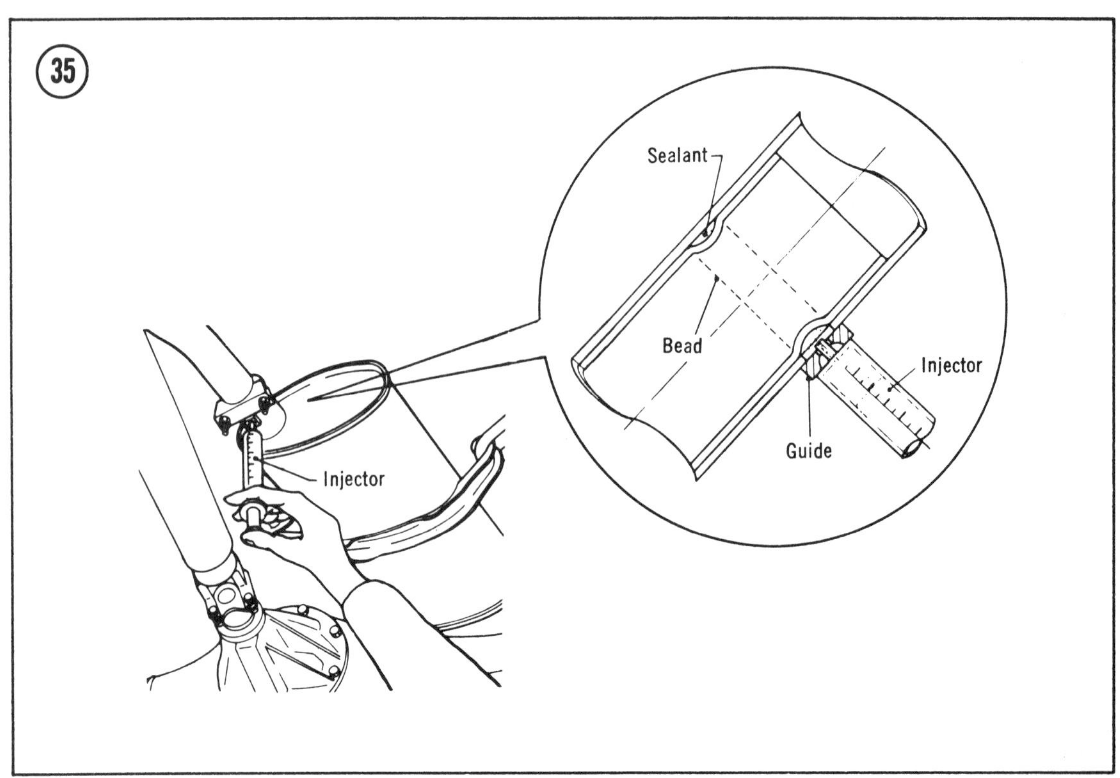
35
Sealant
Bead
Injector
Guide
Injector

CHAPTER SIX

COOLING SYSTEM AND HEATER

Cooling systems on all models use a centrifugal water pump to propel coolant through the radiator, engine, and heating systems. A pellet-type thermostat controls coolant flow.

Fluid-driven fans are used on 1974-76 610's, air conditioned 1974 710's, and all 1975-76 710's. Some 1970-71 510's used clutch-type fans. All others use fixed-blade fans. The heater is a hot water type which circulates engine coolant through a small radiator (heater core) behind the firewall.

This chapter includes service procedures for the thermostat, water pump, radiator, and heater. Cooling system flushing procedures are also described.

COOLING SYSTEM FLUSHING

The recommended coolant for all models is a 50/50 mixture of ethylene glycol-based antifreeze and water. This protects the system to —31°F (—35°C). The system should be drained, flushed, and refilled at intervals specified in Chapter Two. If desired, a chemical flushing agent may be used, following the manufacturer's instructions, prior to the flushing method described here. However, make sure the flushing agent is compatible with the aluminum parts in the engine before using.

Flushing

Refer to **Figure 1**.

1. Drain the cooling system by opening the drain tap at the bottom of the radiator. Do not remove the drain plug from the left side of the engine block.
2. Remove the radiator cap.
3. Disconnect the heater hose from the connection at the rear of the engine. The hose will be a drain during flushing.
4. Turn the heater control on the instrument panel to maximum.
5. Remove the thermostat as described under *Thermostat* later in this chapter.
6. Connect a water supply such as a garden hose to the fitting from which the heater hose was disconnected. This does not have to be a positive fit, as long as most of the water enters the engine. If necessary, temporarily connect a length of heater hose to the fitting to make the garden hose connection more convenient.
7. Turn the water on and flush for 3 to 5 minutes. Do not run the engine. During the last minute of flushing, repeatedly squeeze the upper radiator hose to expel all trapped coolant.
8. Turn off the water and reconnect the heater hose to the engine.

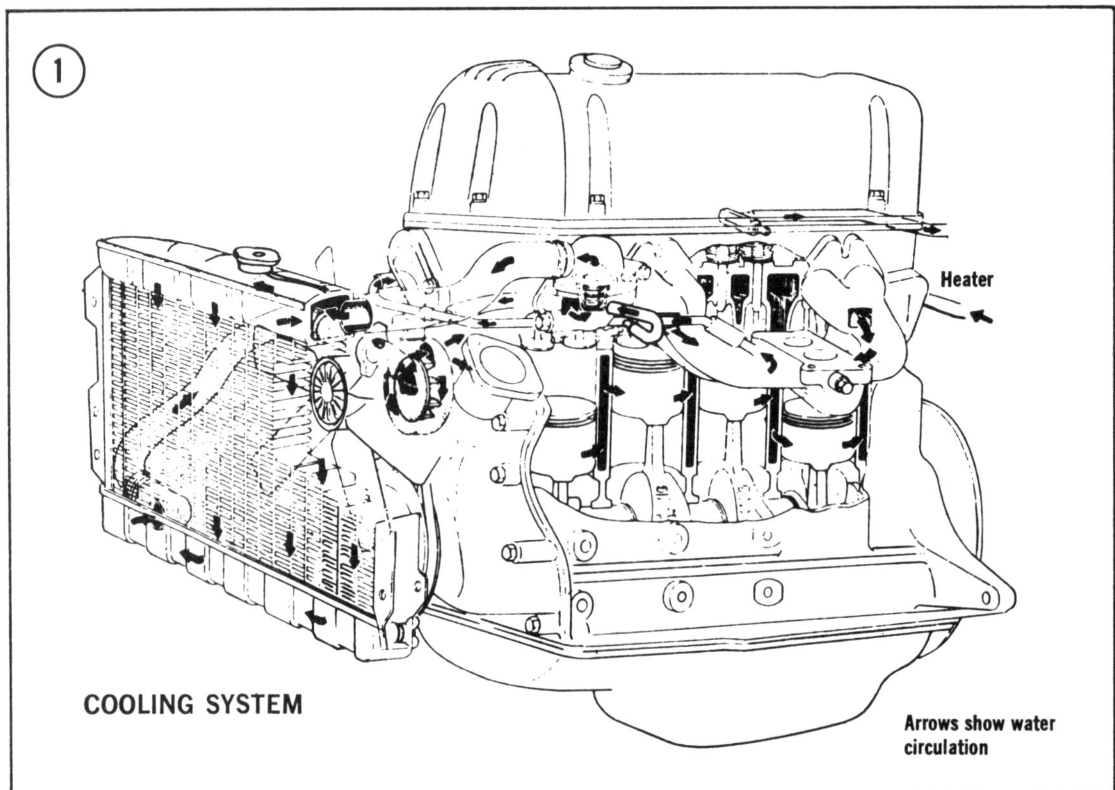

COOLING SYSTEM

9. Drain the entire system by opening the radiator drain tap and removing the threaded plug from the left side of the cylinder block.

Refilling

1. Be sure all hoses are connected and the drains closed.
2. Fill the cooling system with a 50/50 mixture of ethylene glycol-based anti-freeze and water, even if you live in a climate which doesn't require this degree of freeze protection. The anti-freeze is also a good corrosion inhibitor. Coolant capacity is given in **Table 1**.

Table 1 COOLING SYSTEM CAPACITY

	Quarts	Liters
510	7¼	6.8
1973 610	6⅞	6.5
1974 - 76 610	7¼	6.8
1974 710	6⅞	6.5
1975 - 76 710	7¼	6.8

3. When the system is full, install the radiator cap.
4. Run the engine at a fast idle and recheck the coolant level in the radiator. Top up if more than one inch below the filler neck. Also check the system for leaks.
5. After driving several miles, recheck the coolant level. It takes some time for all the air to be removed from the system.

THERMOSTAT

Opening and closing of the thermostat is controlled by a wax pellet which expands when heated and contracts when cooled. The pellet is connected through a piston to a valve. When the pellet expands, the valve is forced open. As the pellet contracts, it allows a spring to close the valve.

Removal and Testing

1. Drain coolant by detaching the upper radiator hose from the water outlet elbow (**Figure 2**).

2. Remove the water outlet elbow and take out the thermostat (**Figure 3**).

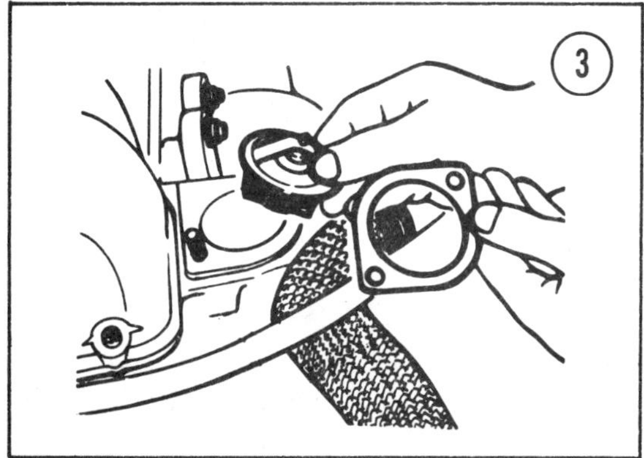

3. Submerge the thermostat in water with a thermometer (**Figure 4**).

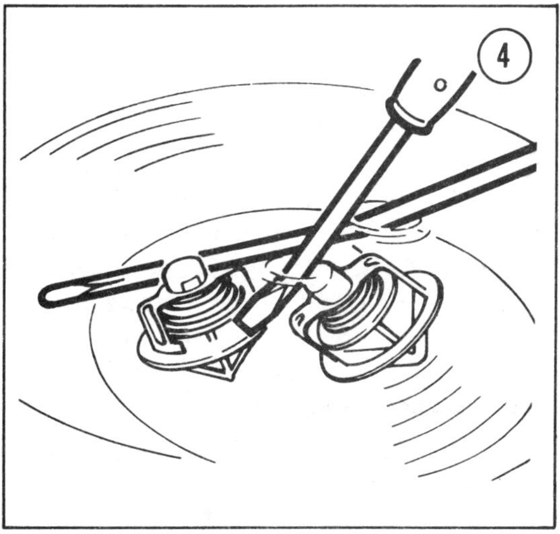

4. Heat the water until the thermostat just begins to open, then check the water temperature. It should be approximately 180°F (82°C). If the valve opens at the wrong temperature or fails to open, replace the thermostat.

5. Measure the maximum lift of the thermostat valve. To do this, mark a screwdriver at a point 0.315 in. (8mm) from the tip. The screwdriver is used as a measuring device. Heat the water to specified opening temperature and measure the lift of the valve with the marked screwdriver. If valve lift is less than 0.315 in. (8mm), replace the thermostat.

Installation

1. If a new thermostat is being installed, test as described in the previous procedure.
2. Install the thermostat in the engine.
3. Install the water outlet elbow, using a new gasket coated on both sides with gasket sealer.
4. Tighten the outlet elbow securing bolts or nuts. Reconnect the hose to the elbow.

6

RADIATOR

Figure 5 shows a typical radiator.

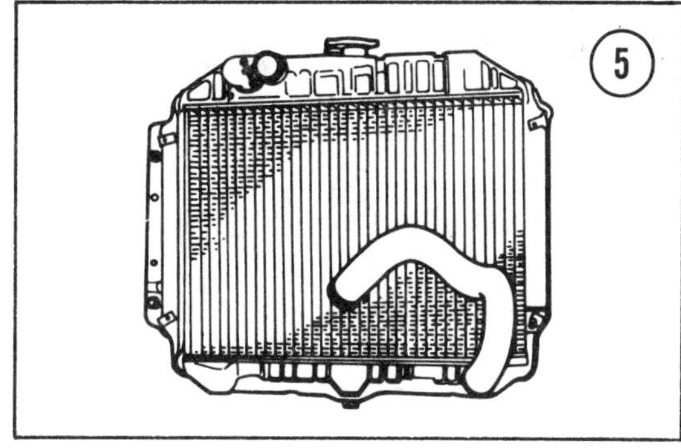

Removal/Installation

1. Remove the radiator cap. Drain coolant by opening the tap at the bottom of the radiator.
2. Disconnect upper and lower radiator hoses.
3. On automatic transmission models, disconnect the transmission fluid cooler lines from the bottom of the radiator.
4. Remove the fan shroud (if so equipped).
5. Remove the radiator securing bolts. Lift the radiator up and out.

6. Install by reversing Steps 1-5. Fill the radiator with a 50/50 mixture of ethylene glycol-based anti-freeze and water. Run the engine and check for leaks.

WATER PUMP

All engines use an aluminum-bodied, non-repairable water pump. On cars with a viscous-hub fan, the fan hub is an integral part of the water pump.

Removal/Installation

1. Remove the radiator as described earlier.
2. Remove 4 fan securing bolts and take the fan off. If equipped with a fixed-blade or clutch-type fan, remove the fan pulley.
3. Undo the water pump securing bolts and remove the pump (**Figure 6**).

> NOTE: *Inspect the pump after removal. If the vanes are badly corroded, replace the pump.*

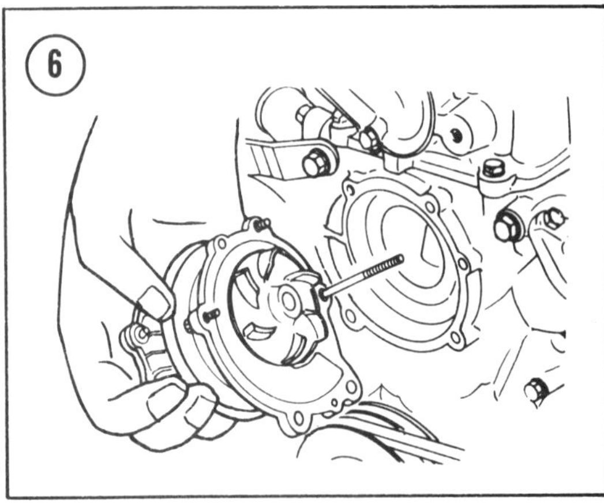

4. Installation is the reverse of these steps. Use a new gasket that is coated on both sides with gasket sealer.

HEATER

Removal/Installation (510)

Figure 7 shows the heater used on early 510's. **Figure 8** shows the later version.

1. Disconnect negative cable from battery.
2. Drain the cooling system by opening the tap at the bottom of the radiator and removing the plug from the left side of the engine block.
3. Place a plastic sheet (such as a painting drop-cloth) on the floor to catch any coolant left in heater hoses or core.
4. Disconnect the heater hoses from the heater.
5. On early models, label and disconnect the heater wires. On later models, disconnect the wiring connector.
6. Label the control cables and detach them from the heater.
7. On late models, remove 4 screws and take out the heater vent.
8. Detach the defroster ducts, then remove the heater securing bolts. Withdraw the heater into the passenger compartment.
9. Installation is the reverse of these steps. Fill the cooling system with a 50/50 mixture of ethylene glycol-based anti-freeze and water.

Removal/Installation (610 and 710)

Figure 9 shows the 610 heater. **Figure 10** shows the 710 heater.

1. Disconnect negative cable from battery.
2. Drain the cooling system by opening the tap at the bottom of the radiator and removing the plug from the left side of the engine block.
3. Place a plastic sheet (such as a painting drop-cloth) on the floor to catch any coolant remaining in the heater core.
4. Detach the heater hoses from the firewall fitting.
5. Remove the console (if so equipped).
6. On 610's, remove the center ventilator (6, Figure 9).
7. Remove the heater duct hose.
8. Detach the defroster hoses from the heater.
9. Label and disconnect heater control cables.
10. Disconnect heater electrical wires. One connector has 4 wires; the other has a single wire.
11. Remove 3 heater attaching screws, one from each side and one from the top. Withdraw the heater into the passenger compartment.
12. Installation is the reverse of these steps. Fill the cooling system with a 50/50 mixture of ethylene glycol-based anti-freeze and water.

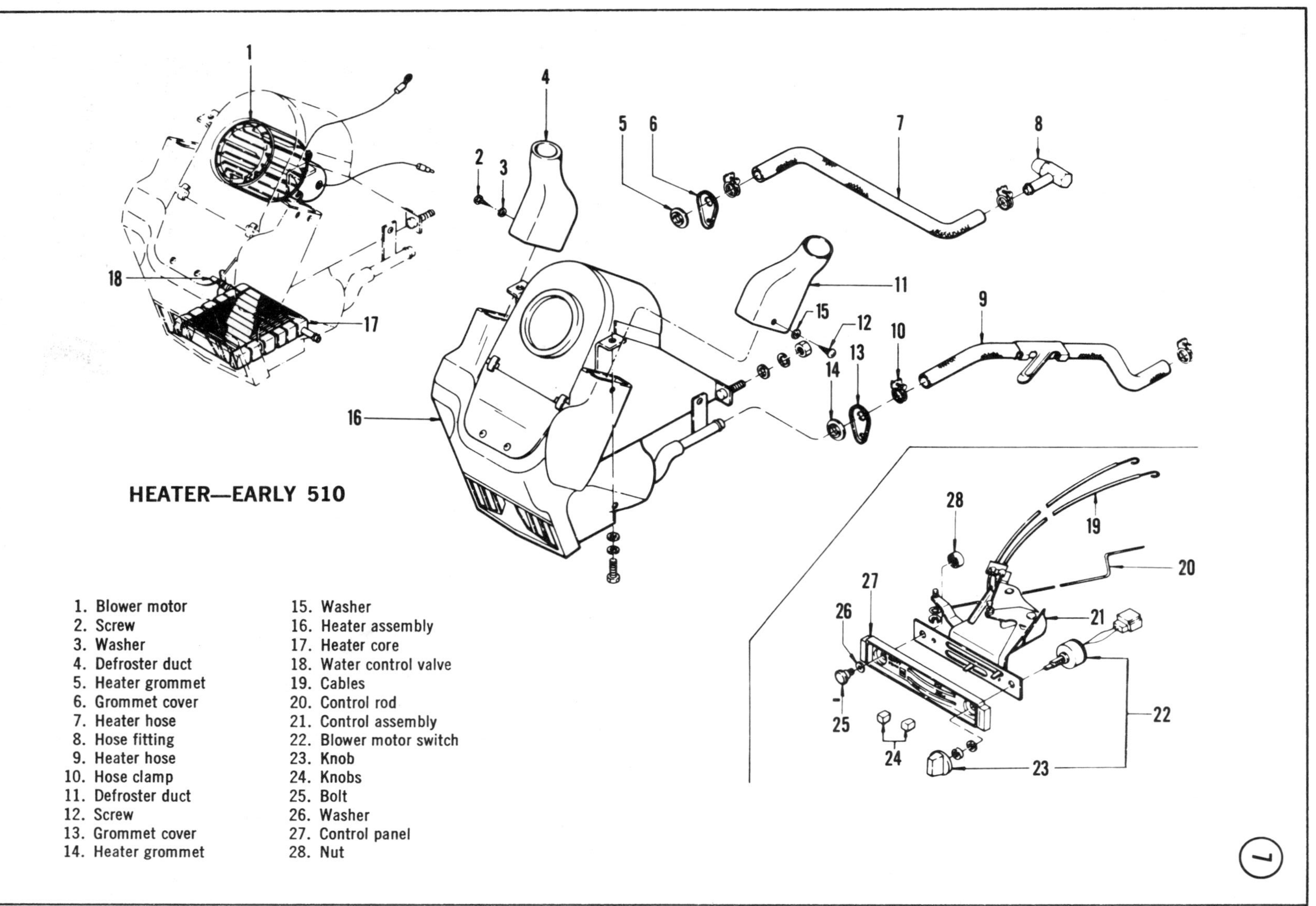

HEATER—EARLY 510

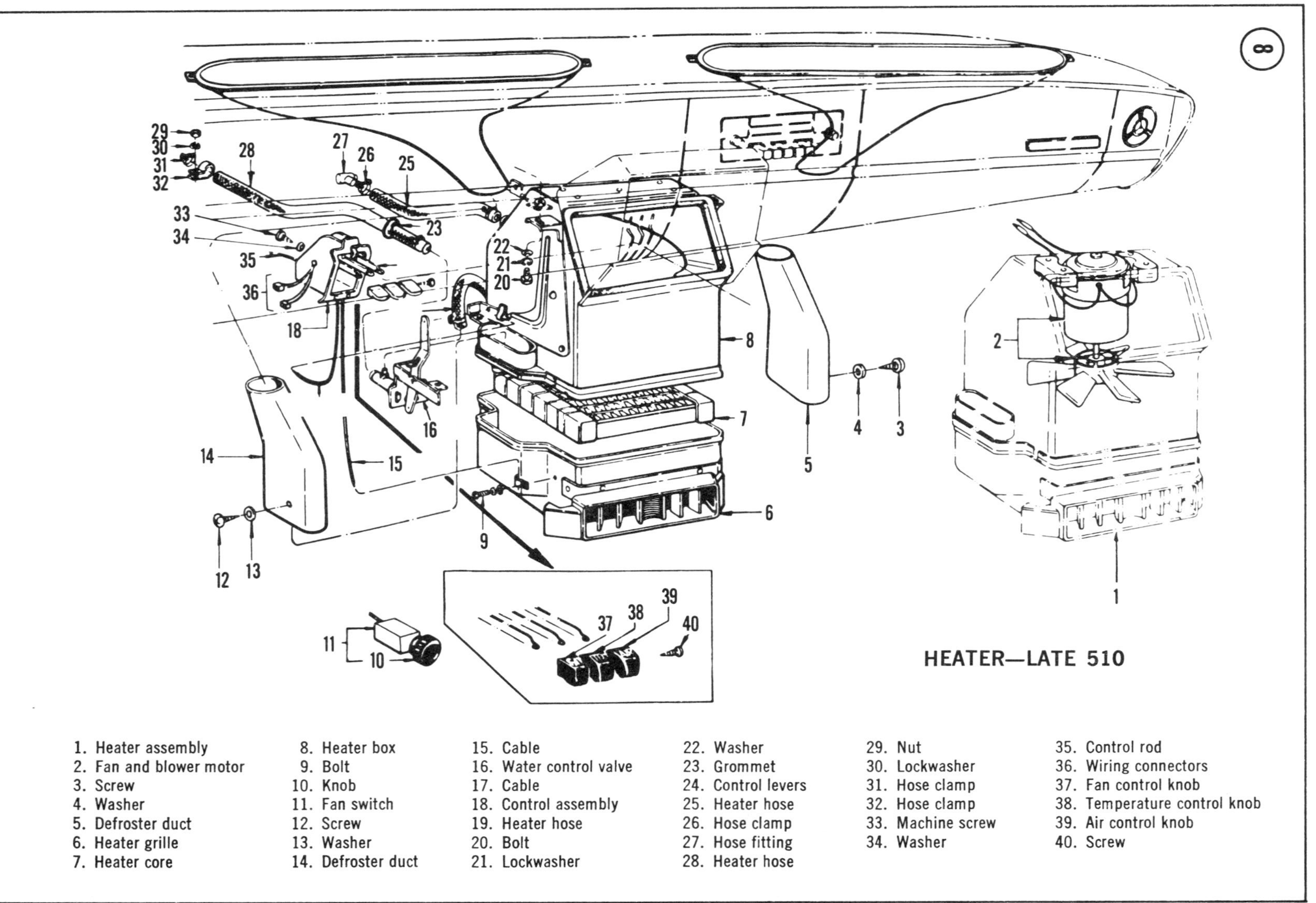
8
HEATER—LATE 510
1. Heater assembly
2. Fan and blower motor
3. Screw
4. Washer
5. Defroster duct
6. Heater grille
7. Heater core
8. Heater box
9. Bolt
10. Knob
11. Fan switch
12. Screw
13. Washer
14. Defroster duct
15. Cable
16. Water control valve
17. Cable
18. Control assembly
19. Heater hose
20. Bolt
21. Lockwasher
22. Washer
23. Grommet
24. Control levers
25. Heater hose
26. Hose clamp
27. Hose fitting
28. Heater hose
29. Nut
30. Lockwasher
31. Hose clamp
32. Hose clamp
33. Machine screw
34. Washer
35. Control rod
36. Wiring connectors
37. Fan control knob
38. Temperature control knob
39. Air control knob
40. Screw

9
HEATER—610 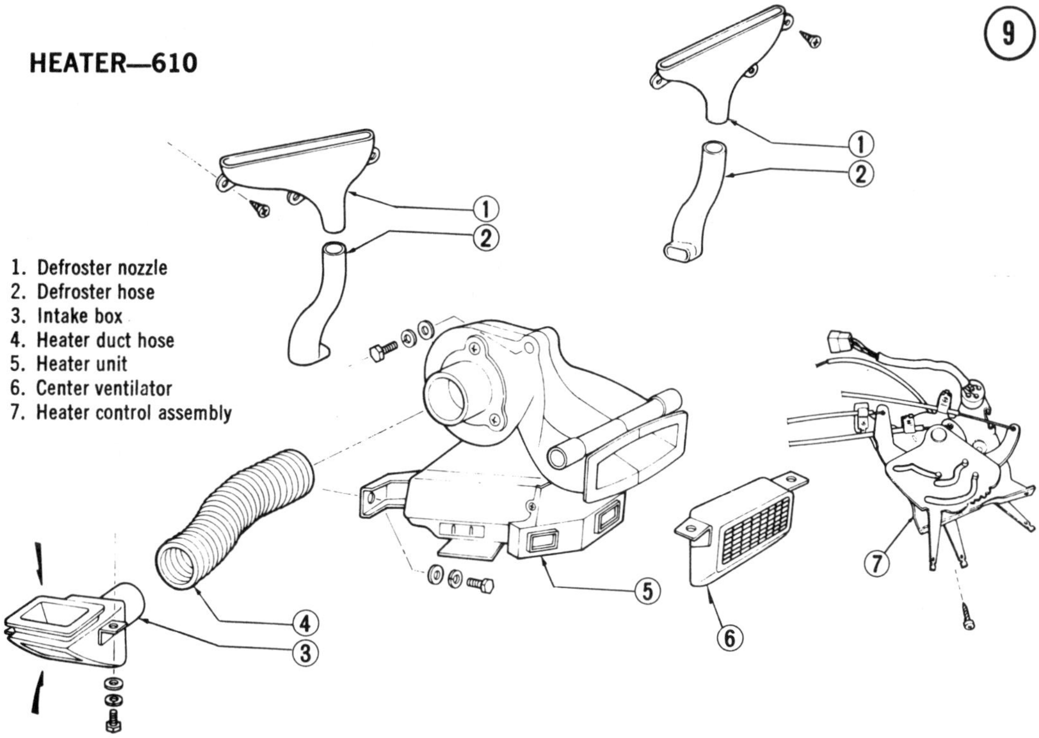
1. Defroster nozzle
2. Defroster hose
3. Intake box
4. Heater duct hose
5. Heater unit
6. Center ventilator
7. Heater control assembly
1
2
3
4
5
6
7

10
HEATER — 710 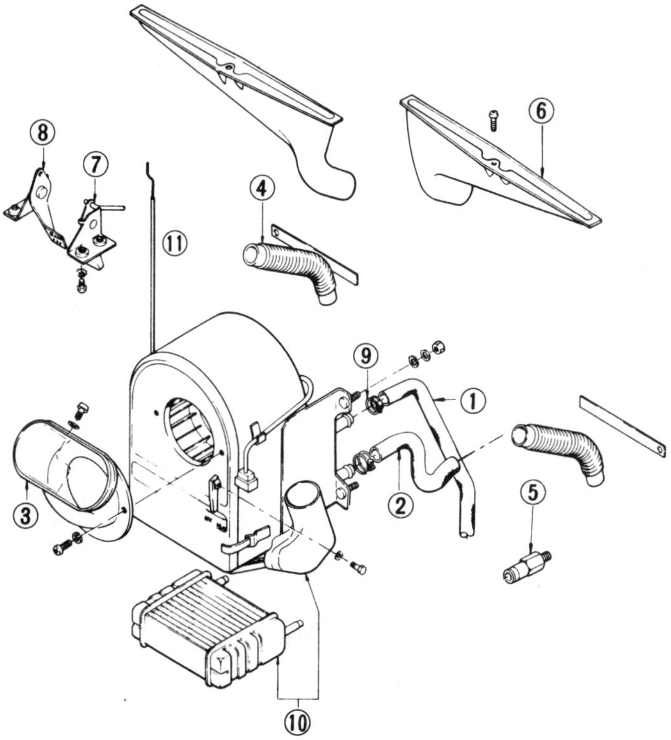
1. Inlet hose
2. Outlet hose
3. Air duct
4. Defroster hose
5. Hose connector
6. Defroster nozzle
7. Heater control lever
8. Air control lever
9. Clamp
10. Heater unit
11. Heater control cable
1
2
3
4
5
6
7
8
9
10
11

CHAPTER SEVEN

ELECTRICAL SYSTEM

All models use a 12-volt battery, negative ground, and a 3-phase alternator. This chapter includes service procedures for the battery, starter, charging system, lighting system, ignition system, fuses, instruments, and windshield wipers.

BATTERY

Care and Inspection

1. Disconnect both battery cables and remove the battery.
2. Clean the top of the battery with a baking soda and water solution. Scrub with a stiff bristle brush. Wipe battery clean with a cloth moistened in ammonia or baking soda solution.

CAUTION

Keep cleaning solution out of battery cells or the electrolyte will be seriously weakened.

3. Clean battery terminals with a stiff wire brush or one of the many tools made for this purpose.
4. Examine entire battery case for cracks.
5. Install the battery and reconnect the battery cables. Be sure the cables are connected to the proper terminals.
6. Coat the battery connections with light mineral grease or Vaseline after tightening.
7. Check electrolyte level and top up with distilled water if necessary.

Testing

Hydrometer testing is the best way to check battery condition. Use a hydrometer with numbered graduations from 1.100 to 1.300 rather than one with just color-coded bands. To use the hydrometer, squeeze the rubber ball, insert the tip in the cell and release the ball (**Figure 1**).

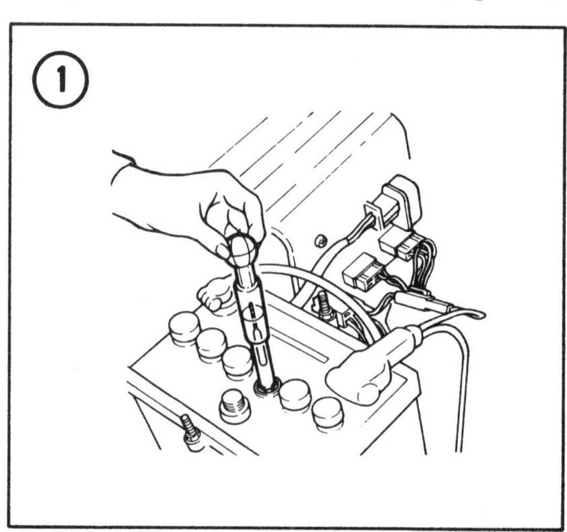

Draw enough electrolyte to float the weighted float inside the hydrometer. Note the number in line with the surface of the electrolyte. This is the specific gravity for the cell. Return the electrolyte to the cell from which it came.

The specific gravity of the electrolyte in each battery cell is an excellent indicator of that cell's condition. A fully charged cell will read from 1.240 to 1.260 at 68°F (20°C). If the cells test below 1.200, the battery must be recharged. Charging is also necessary if specific gravity varies more than 0.025 from cell to cell. **Table 1** converts specific gravity readings into battery charge percentages.

CAUTION

Battery electrolyte must be fully topped up and the negative battery cable disconnected before charging. Keep the electrolyte temperature below 113°F (45°C) during charging.

The hydrometer, together with Table 1, can be used to check the progress of the charging operation.

ALTERNATOR

The alternator generates 3-phase alternating current in the armature coils. Silicon diodes act as one-way valves for the alternating current, letting only charging current through. In this manner, the AC is converted to DC. Models through 1972 use 6 removable diodes, mounted in positive and negative heat sinks. 1973-1976 cars use a one-piece diode assembly.

Service procedures are similar for all models. Differences are noted when they occur. **Figure 2** shows the early design; **Figure 3** shows the later version.

Alternator Output Test

This test requires a 30-volt voltmeter and a fully charged battery.

1. Disconnect the alternator wires.
2. Connect the voltmeter positive lead to the alternator "N" terminal. Connect the negative lead to ground. The voltmeter must indicate battery voltage.
3. Set up the test circuit shown in **Figure 4**.
4. Start the engine. Gradually increase engine speed to 1,100 rpm, then note the voltmeter reading.

CAUTION

Do not run the engine at speeds above 1,100 rpm. Do not race the engine.

The voltmeter should indicate 12.5 volts or more. If the reading is low, the alternator should be disassembled and tested as described later in this chapter.

Alternator Removal/Installation

1. Disconnect the negative battery cable.
2. Detach the electrical connector from the alternator. Label and detach the single wires.
3. Loosen the alternator mounting bolts and remove the fan belt from the alternator pulley.
4. Remove the alternator mounting bolts and take the alternator out.

Table 1 BATTERY CHARGE PERCENTAGE

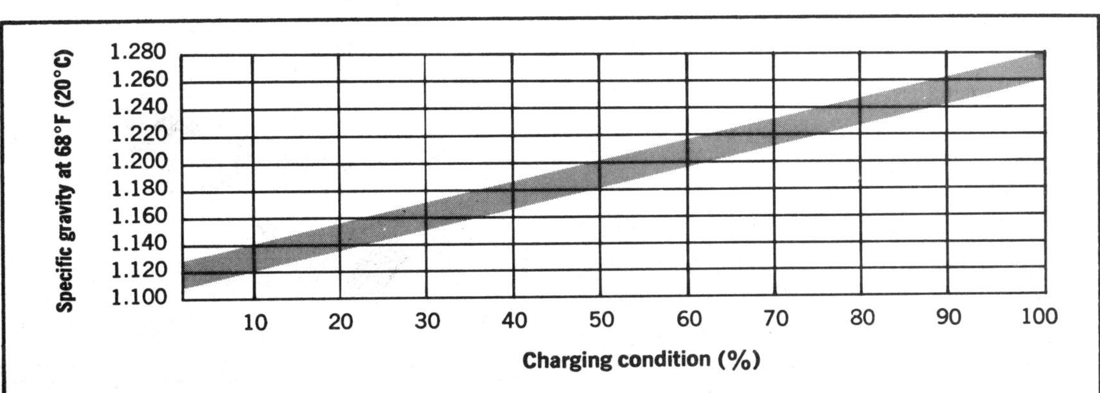

2

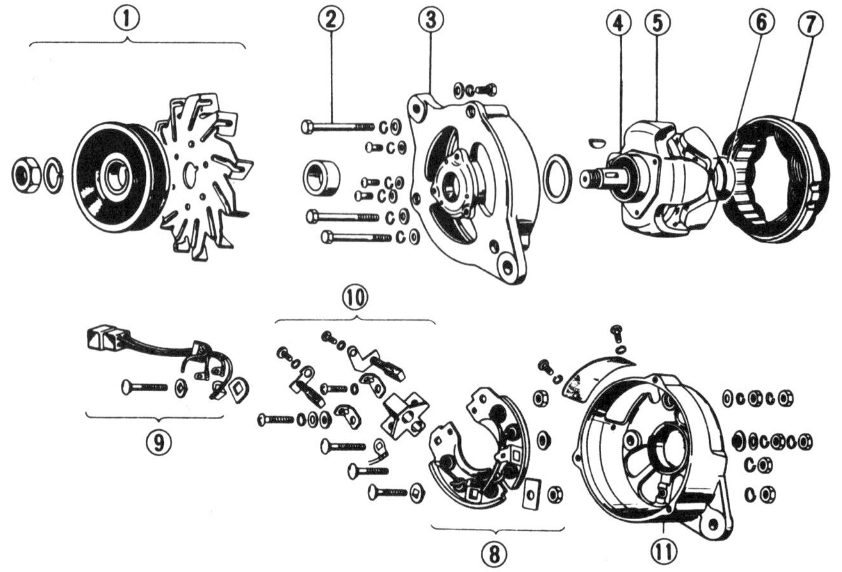

EARLY ALTERNATOR

1. Pulley assembly
2. Through bolt
3. Front cover
4. Front bearing
5. Rotor
6. Rear bearing
7. Stator
8. Diode set plate assembly
9. Lead wire assembly
10. Brush assembly
11. Rear cover

5. Installation is the reverse of these steps. After installation, adjust fan belt tension as described in Chapter Two.

Brush and Diode Replacement (Early Type)

1. Unscrew 3 thru-bolts.

2. Separate the diode end (rear) housing from the drive end (front) housing by tapping the front housing lightly with a wooden mallet. **Figure 5** shows the thru-bolts and separated housings.

3. Unsolder 3 coil lead wires from the negative diodes, then unsolder the wires between the diodes (**Figure 6**).

4. Remove 2 setscrews and take off the brush cover (**Figure 7**). Unsolder and disconnect the "N" terminal wire.

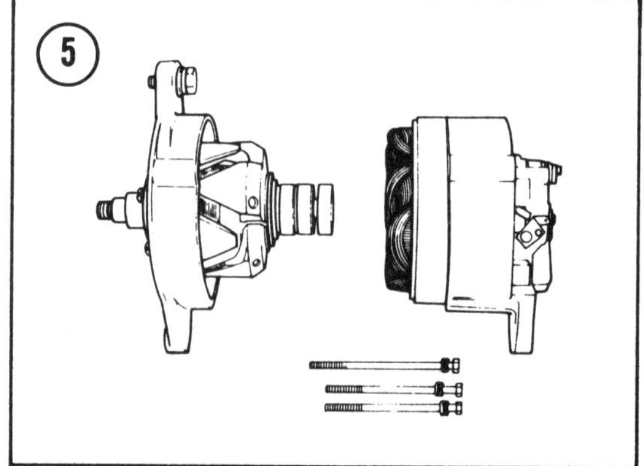

5. Separate the diode end (rear) housing from the stator.

6. Remove the setscrews from the rear cover, then take out the heat sink and brush holder (**Figure 8**).

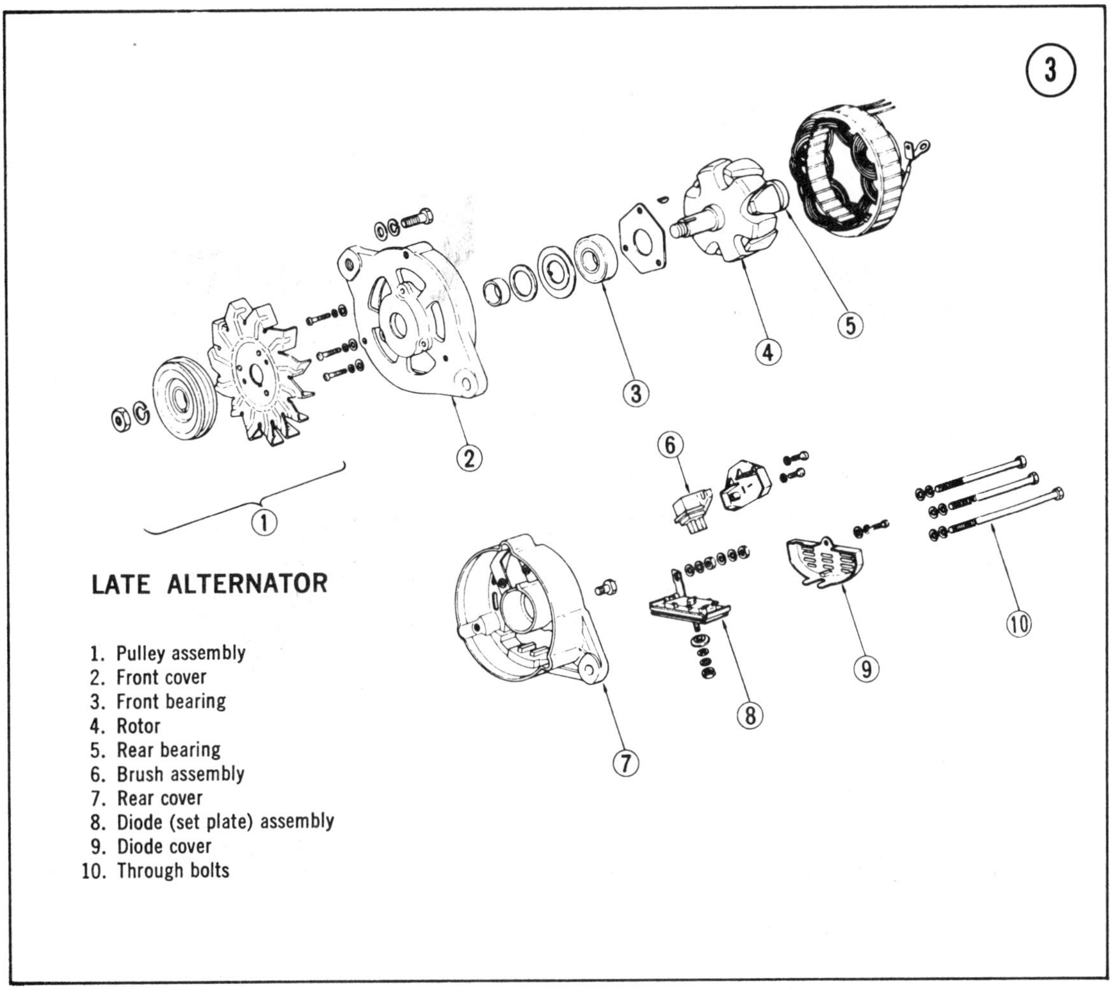

3
LATE ALTERNATOR
1. Pulley assembly
2. Front cover
3. Front bearing
4. Rotor
5. Rear bearing
6. Brush assembly
7. Rear cover
8. Diode (set plate) assembly
9. Diode cover
10. Through bolts

4
ALTERNATOR TEST CIRCUIT
Alternator
E
A
Battery
V
Voltmeter

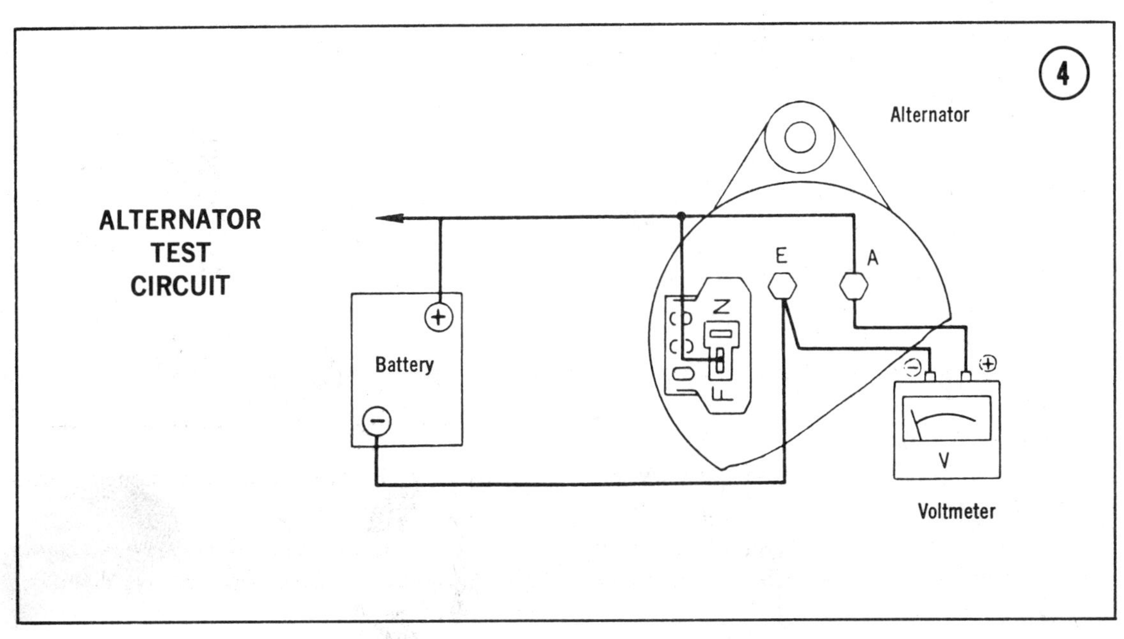

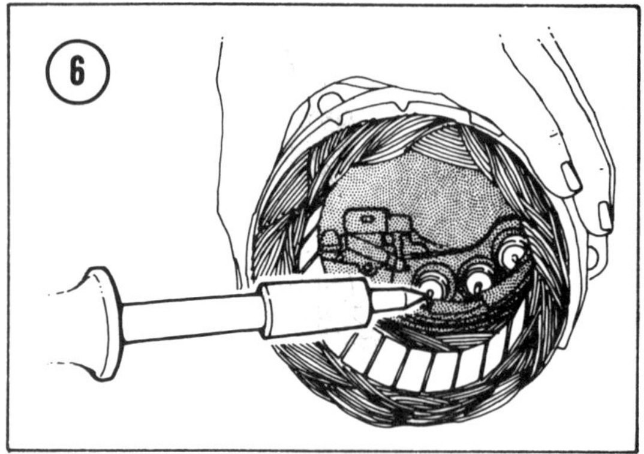

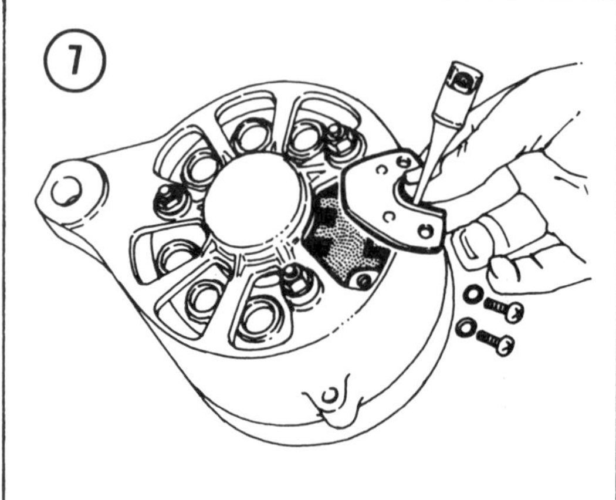

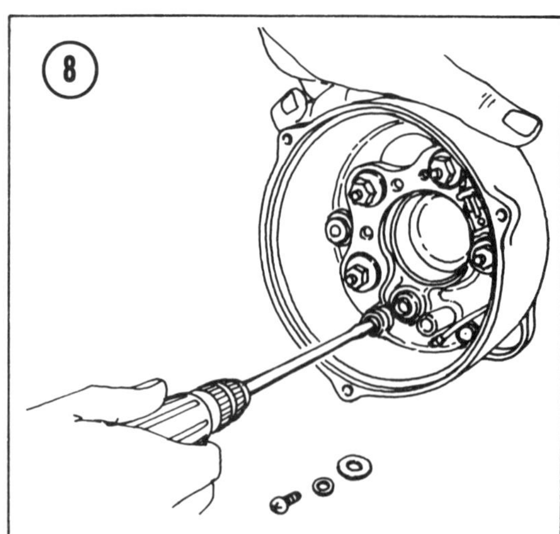

7. To disengage the brush holder, unsolder the black-and-white "F" wire and the brush holder wires.

8. Test the individual diodes with an ohmmeter.

NOTE: *Positive diodes are marked with red numbers; the negative diodes are marked with black numbers (***Figure 9***).*

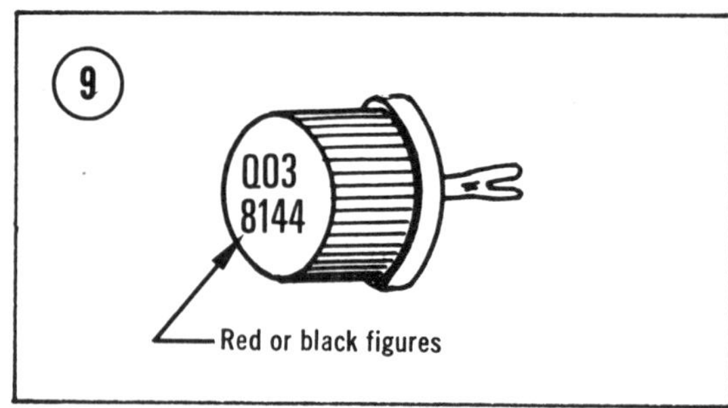

Figure 10 shows the direction of diode current flow. Connect one test lead to the diode terminal and the other to the heat sink (**Figure 11**). Note the resistance. Reverse the test leads and note the resistance again. High resistance in one direction and low resistance in the other direction indicate a satisfactory diode. Low resistance in both directions indicates a shorted diode. High resistance in both directions indicates an open diode. Open or shorted diodes must be replaced.

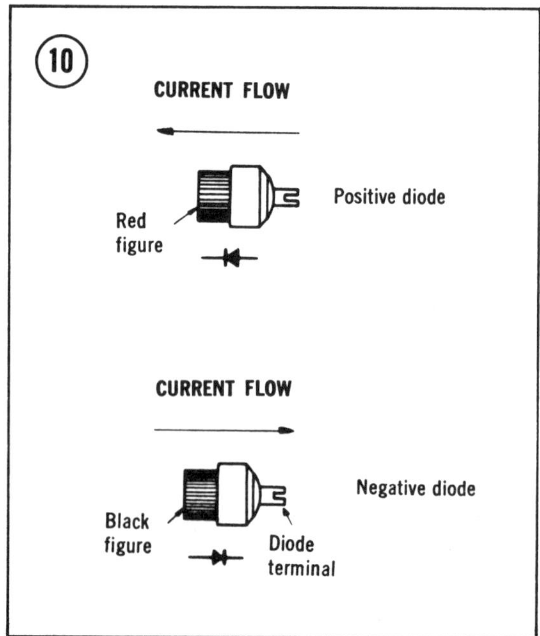

9. To remove diodes, place the heat sink in a suitable support and press the diodes out (**Figure 12**).

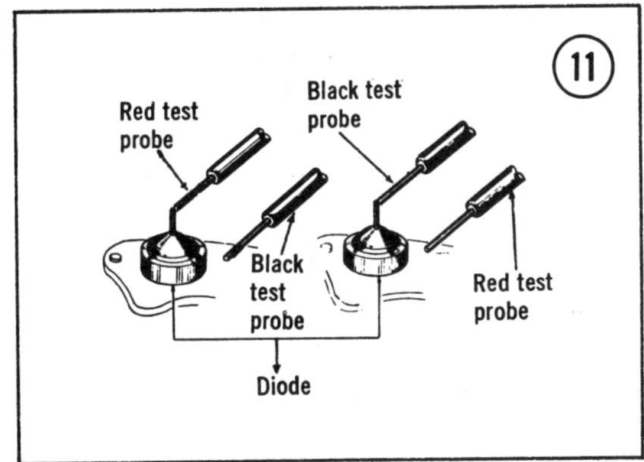

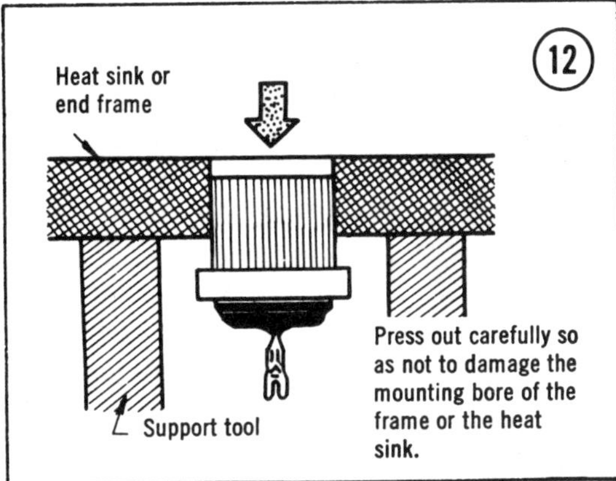

CAUTION

Do not attempt to remove diodes with a hammer. The shock could damage all the diodes in the heat sink.

10. Check the movement of the brushes in the holder. If the brushes do not move freely, clean the holder.

11. Measure brush wear (**Figure 13**). If brushes are worn to less than 0.295 in. (7.5mm) replace them.

Brush Replacement (Late Type)

1. Remove 2 screws and lift off the brush holder cover (**Figure 14**).

2. Remove the brush holder together with the brushes.

CAUTION

Do not disconnect the "N" terminal (1, Figure 14) from its wire.

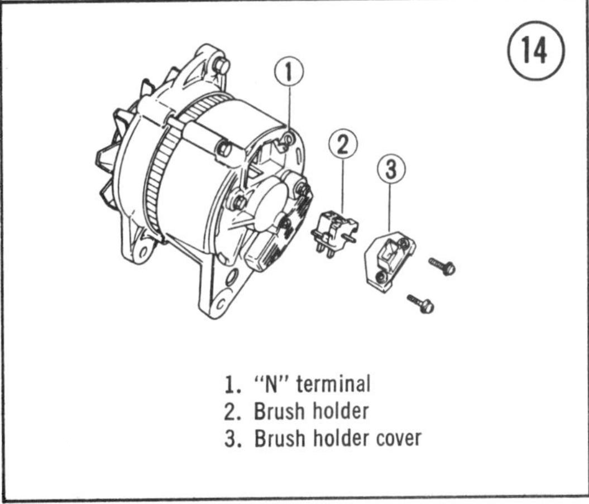

1. "N" terminal
2. Brush holder
3. Brush holder cover

3. Check movement of brushes in the holder. If the brushes don't move freely, clean the holder.

4. Check brushes for wear. If worn to the limit line (**Figure 15**), replace the brush assembly.

5. Inspect brush wiring. Replace if damaged.

6. Press brushes into the holder with a spring scale (**Figure 16**). On new springs, pressure should range from 9.0-12.2 oz. (255-345 gm) when the brushes protrude 0.079 in. (2mm). The pressure decreases approximately ¾ oz. (20gm) per 0.004 in. (1mm) of brush wear. Replace the brush assembly if the springs are weak.

7. Install by reversing Steps 1 and 2.

Diode Replacement (Late Type)

1. Remove one screw and take off the diode cover (**Figure 17**).

2. Unsolder 3 stator wires from diode terminal.

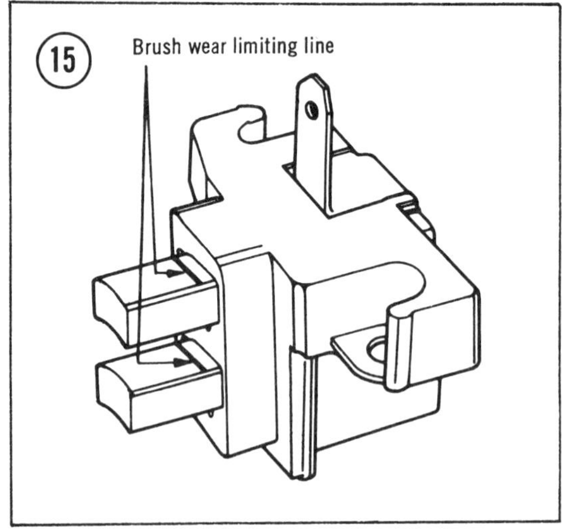

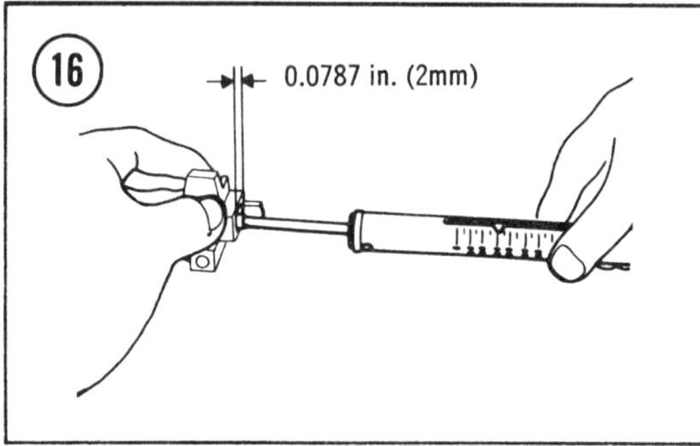

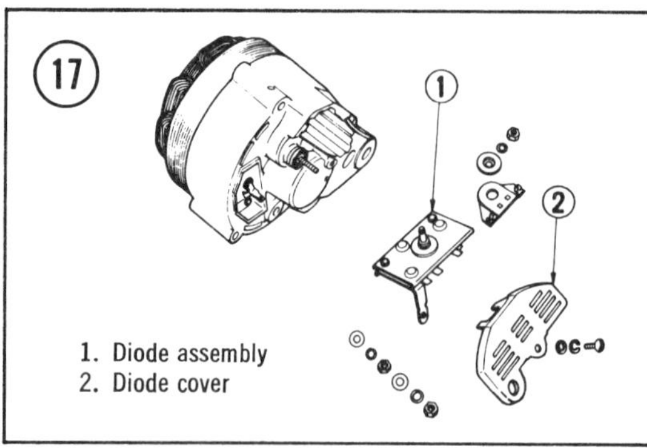

1. Diode assembly
2. Diode cover

CAUTION

Unsolder the wires as quickly as possible. Heat can damage diodes.

3. Remove the "A" terminal nut and diode installation nut. Lift the diode assembly out.

4. On later cars, check the diode assembly. **Figure 18** shows the direction of current flow. Connect the tester leads between the positive plate and the positive diode terminal (**Figure 19**).

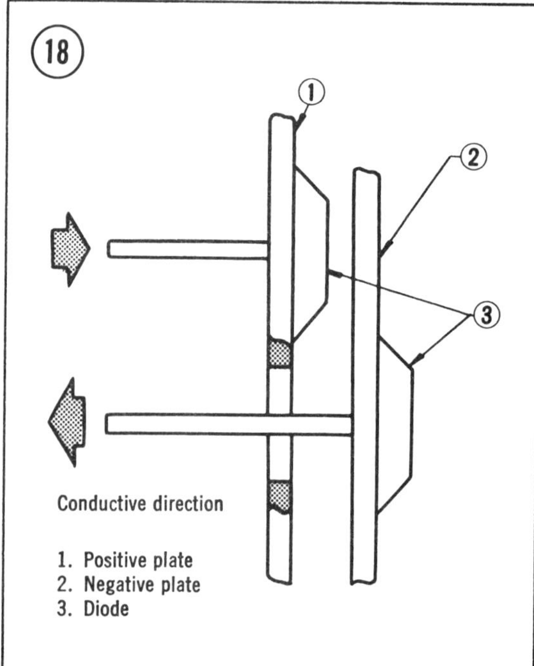

1. Positive plate
2. Negative plate
3. Diode

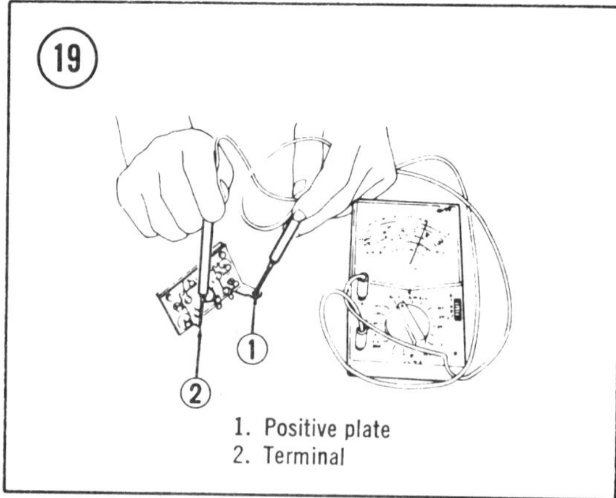

1. Positive plate
2. Terminal

Current should flow only from the terminals to the plate. Connect the tester leads from the negative plate to each negative diode terminal (**Figure 20**). Current should flow only from the plate to the terminals.

If any diode fails this test, replace the diode assembly as a unit.

5. Install by reversing Steps 1 and 2.

STARTER

Figure 21 shows the 1968-74 starter design. **Figure 22** shows the 1975-76 version.

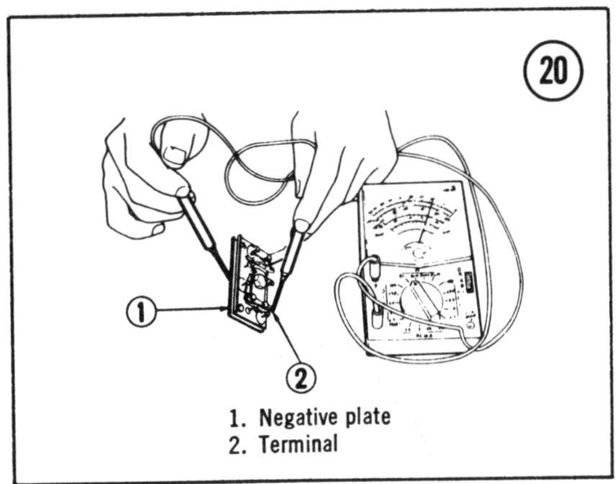

1. Negative plate
2. Terminal

Removal/Installation

1. Disconnect negative cable from battery.
2. Disconnect the wires from solenoid terminals "S" and "B". Figure 21 shows the 1968-74 version. The 1975-76 design is the same.
3. Remove 2 starter securing bolts. Pull the starter forward until it is clear, then lift it out.
4. Install in the reverse order.

Solenoid Replacement

1. Remove the starter as described earlier.
2. Disconnect the wire running from the solenoid to the starter.
3. Remove the solenoid attaching bolts.
4. Unhook the solenoid plunger from the shift lever inside the starter. Lift the solenoid off.
5. Installation is the reverse of these steps.

Brush Replacement

1. Remove the starter as described earlier.
2. On 1975-76 starters, remove the dust cover, snap ring, and thrust washers from the starter's front end. See **Figure 23**.

22

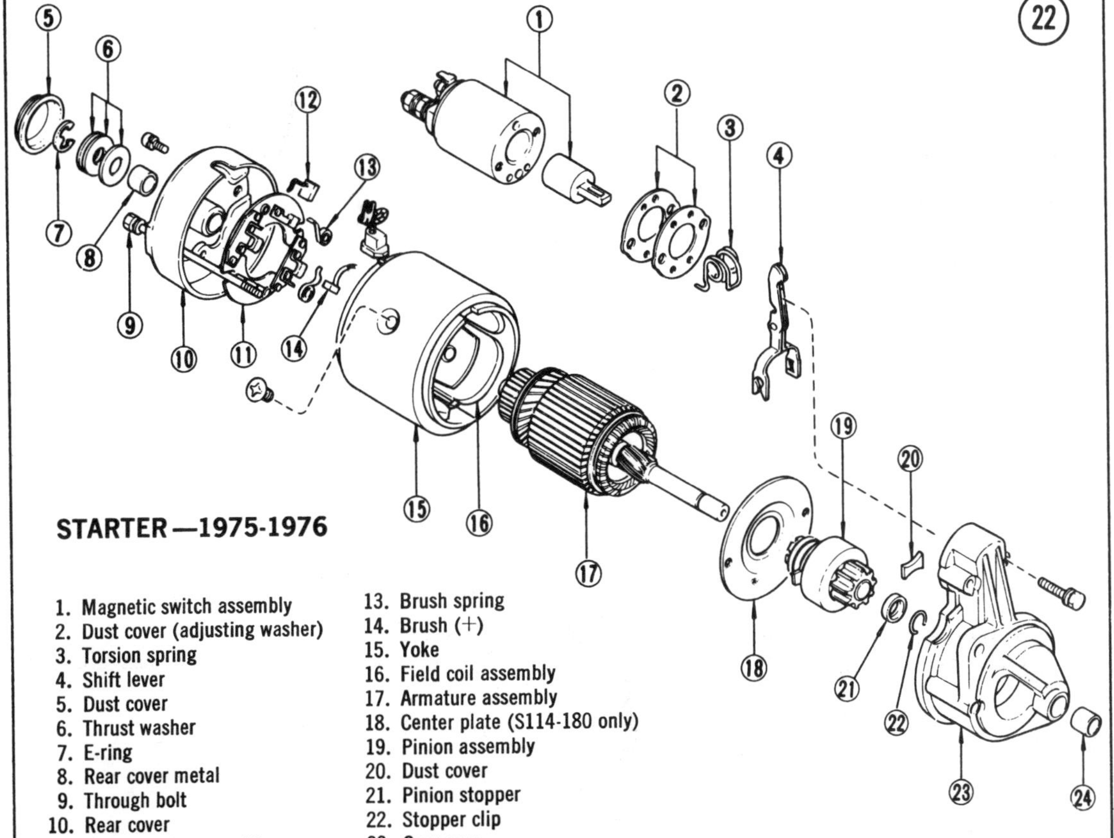

STARTER—1975-1976

1. Magnetic switch assembly
2. Dust cover (adjusting washer)
3. Torsion spring
4. Shift lever
5. Dust cover
6. Thrust washer
7. E-ring
8. Rear cover metal
9. Through bolt
10. Rear cover
11. Brush holder assembly
12. Brush (—)
13. Brush spring
14. Brush (+)
15. Yoke
16. Field coil assembly
17. Armature assembly
18. Center plate (S114-180 only)
19. Pinion assembly
20. Dust cover
21. Pinion stopper
22. Stopper clip
23. Gear case
24. Gear case metal

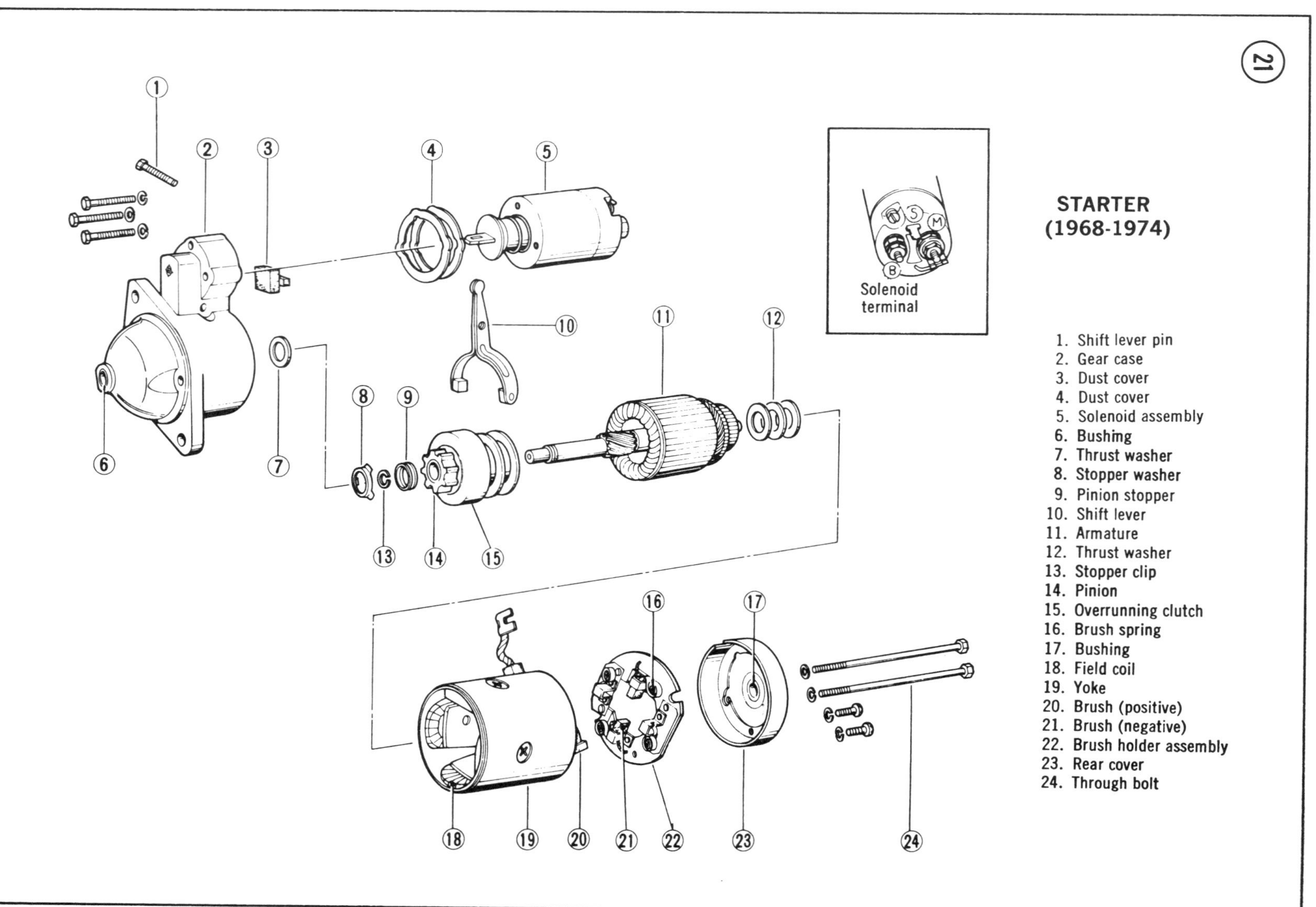
21
STARTER
(1968-1974)
1. Shift lever pin
2. Gear case
3. Dust cover
4. Dust cover
5. Solenoid assembly
6. Bushing
7. Thrust washer
8. Stopper washer
9. Pinion stopper
10. Shift lever
11. Armature
12. Thrust washer
13. Stopper clip
14. Pinion
15. Overrunning clutch
16. Brush spring
17. Bushing
18. Field coil
19. Yoke
20. Brush (positive)
21. Brush (negative)
22. Brush holder assembly
23. Rear cover
24. Through bolt
S
M
B
Solenoid terminal
1
2
3
4
5
6
7
8
9
10
11
12
13
14
15
16
17
18
19
20
21
22
23
24

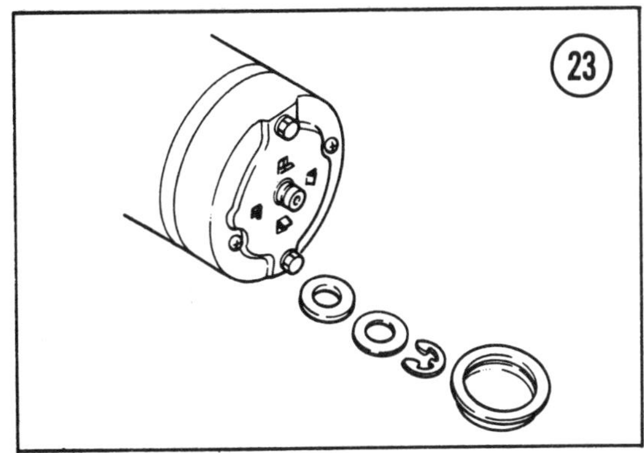

3. Remove 2 through-bolts and 2 setscrews (**Figure 24**). Take the end cover off the starter.

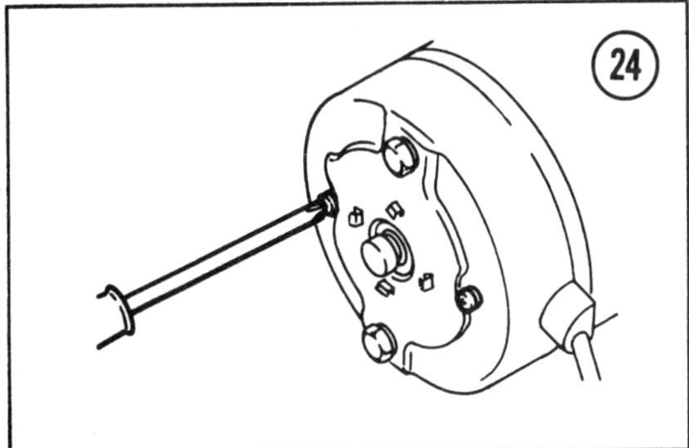

4. Make a wire hook and pull back the brush springs (**Figure 25**). Slide the brushes out of their slots.

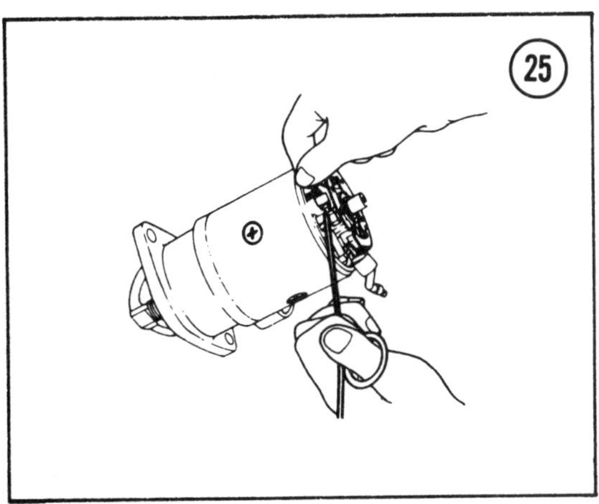

5. Measure brush length. Minimum length is 0.492 in. (12.5mm) on 1968-74 cars; 0.47 in. (12.5mm) on 1975-76 models. Replace brushes if any are shorter than minimum.

6. Check brush movement in the slots. Clean the slots and brushes if the movement is not smooth. Examine brush springs. Replace if weak or damaged.

7. Check the brush holder for shorts to ground. Use an ohmmeter or a continuity tester such as the one shown in **Figure 26**. Touch one tester lead to the brush holder and the other to the positive brush slots. If the ohmmeter shows continuity (test lamp lights), a short circuit exists. Replace insulator or brush holder.

8. Install brushes by reversing Steps 1-4.

CAUTION

Use resin core solder when resoldering brush leads. Do not use acid core solder.

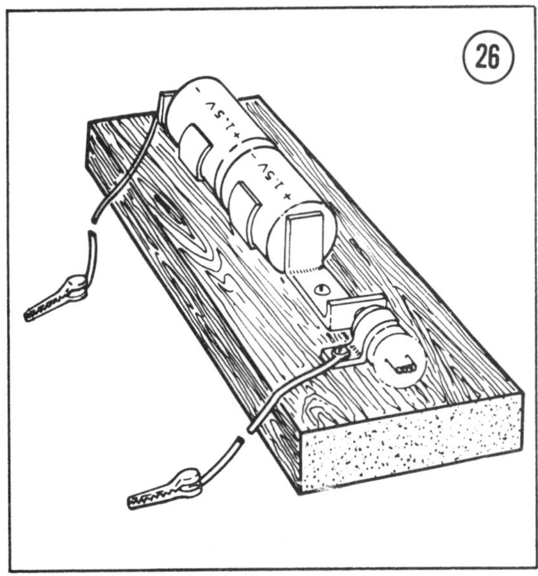

LIGHTING SYSTEM

Headlight Replacement

Figure 27 shows a typical headlight assembly.

1. Remove the radiator grille.

2. On 610 models, disconnect the side marker light wires.

3. Loosen 3 screws securing the headlight retaining ring. Rotate the ring clockwise and take it off.

4. Take the bulb out of its socket. Disconnect the wires.

5. Installation is the reverse of these steps. The 3 locating tabs in the bulb fit into the

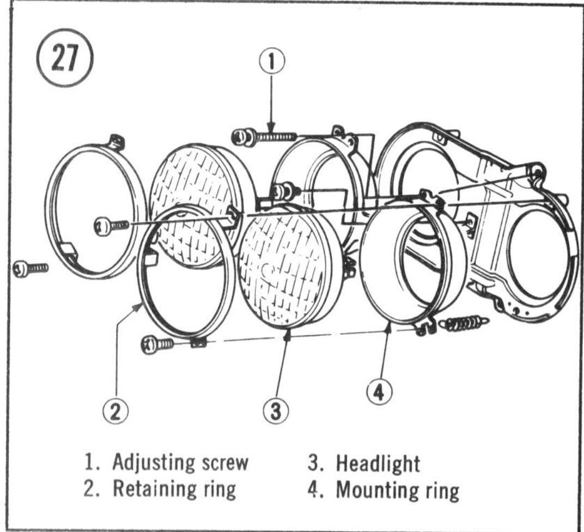

1. Adjusting screw
2. Retaining ring
3. Headlight
4. Mounting ring

indentations in the mounting ring. Be sure the word TOP (molded in the lens) is up.

Rear Combination Lights

1. To replace bulbs on sedans and hardtops, turn the bulb socket counterclockwise and remove it from the lamp body. Push the bulb into the socket, turn counterclockwise, and remove. Install in the reverse order.

2. To replace bulbs on 510 and 610 station wagons, remove the lens securing screws and take the lens off. Push the bulb into the socket, turn counterclockwise, and remove. Install in reverse order.

3. To replace bulbs on 710 station wagons, remove 3 screws and take off the lens. Then turn the bulb socket counterclockwise and remove it from the lamp body. Push the bulb into the socket and turn counterclockwise to remove. Install in the reverse order.

Front Parking/Turn Signal Lights—Side Marker Lights

To replace a bulb (all models), remove the lens securing screws and take the lens off. Push the bulb into the socket, turn counterclockwise, and remove. Install in the reverse order.

License Plate Light

1. *510's, 610 hardtops and station wagons, 710 sedans and hardtops*—Remove the lens cover securing screws and lens cover. Push the bulb into the socket, turn counterclockwise, and pull out. Install in the reverse order.

2. *610 sedans*—Open the trunk. Turn bulb socket counterclockwise and remove (**Figure 28**).

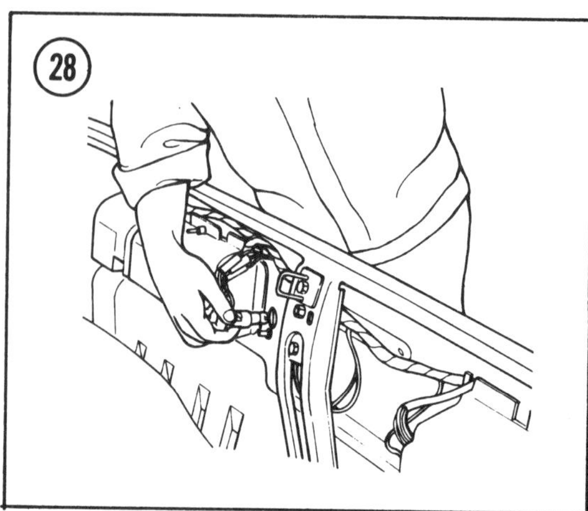

3. *710 station wagons*—Remove 3 screws and take off the lens(es). See **Figure 29**. Push the bulb(s) in, turn counterclockwise, and pull out. Install in the reverse order.

Headlight Switch Removal/Installation

1. Press the switch knob in, turn it counterclockwise, and pull it off.

2. Reach behind the instrument panel and disconnect the switch wires.

3. On 510's, remove the instrument panel. On 610's, remove the instrument cluster cover. See *Instruments* later in this chapter.

4. On 610's, remove cluster lid "A" (**Figure 30**). This is secured by 5 screws at the front and one screw at the rear.

5. Remove the switch securing nut and take the switch out.

6. Install in the reverse order.

Turn Signal-Dimmer Switch Removal/Installation

1. Disconnect negative cable from battery.

2. Remove the steering wheel and steering column shell. See Chapter Twelve.

3. Disconnect the turn signal-dimmer switch wiring connectors.

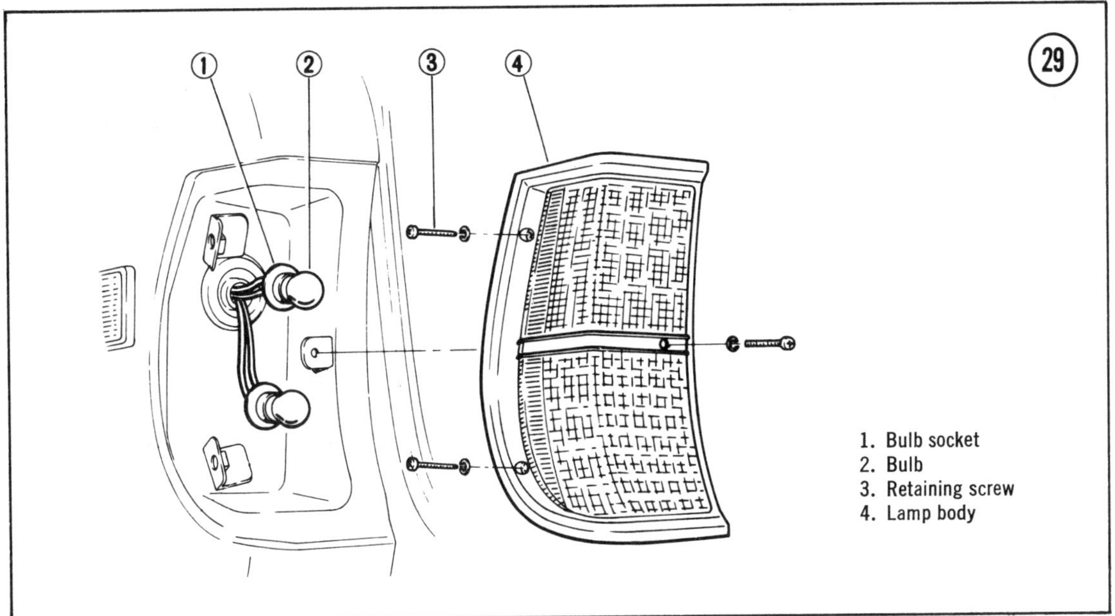

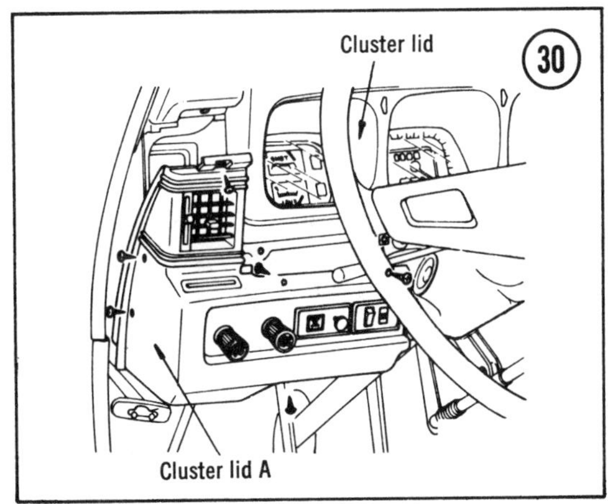

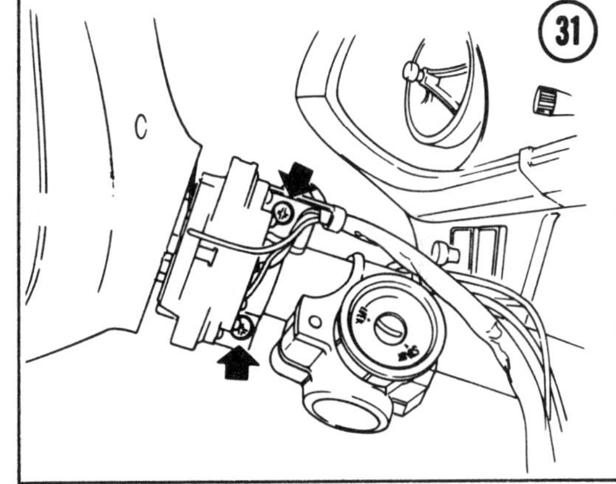

4. Loosen 2 screws clamping the switch to the steering column (**Figure 31**). Slide the switch off.

5. Installation is the reverse of these steps.

INSTRUMENTS

Cluster Removal/Installation (510)

Figure 32 shows the cluster used on early 510's. **Figure 33** shows the later version.

1. Working behind the instrument panel, disconnect the speedometer cable and multi-pole wiring connector. If equipped with a tachometer or clock, disconnect its wires.

2. Remove the front panel from the instrument cluster. Remove the cluster securing screws and take it out. Individual gauges can then be removed.

3. Installatoin is the reverse of these steps.

Cluster Removal/Installation (610)

1. Disconnect negative cable from battery.

2. Remove 4 screws securing the steering column shell. Separate and remove the shell halves.

3. Remove 4 screws securing the cluster (see **Figure 34**).

4. Pull the cluster forward. Reach behind it and disconnect the speedometer cable and multi-pole wiring connector. If equipped with a tachometer or clock, disconnect its wires.

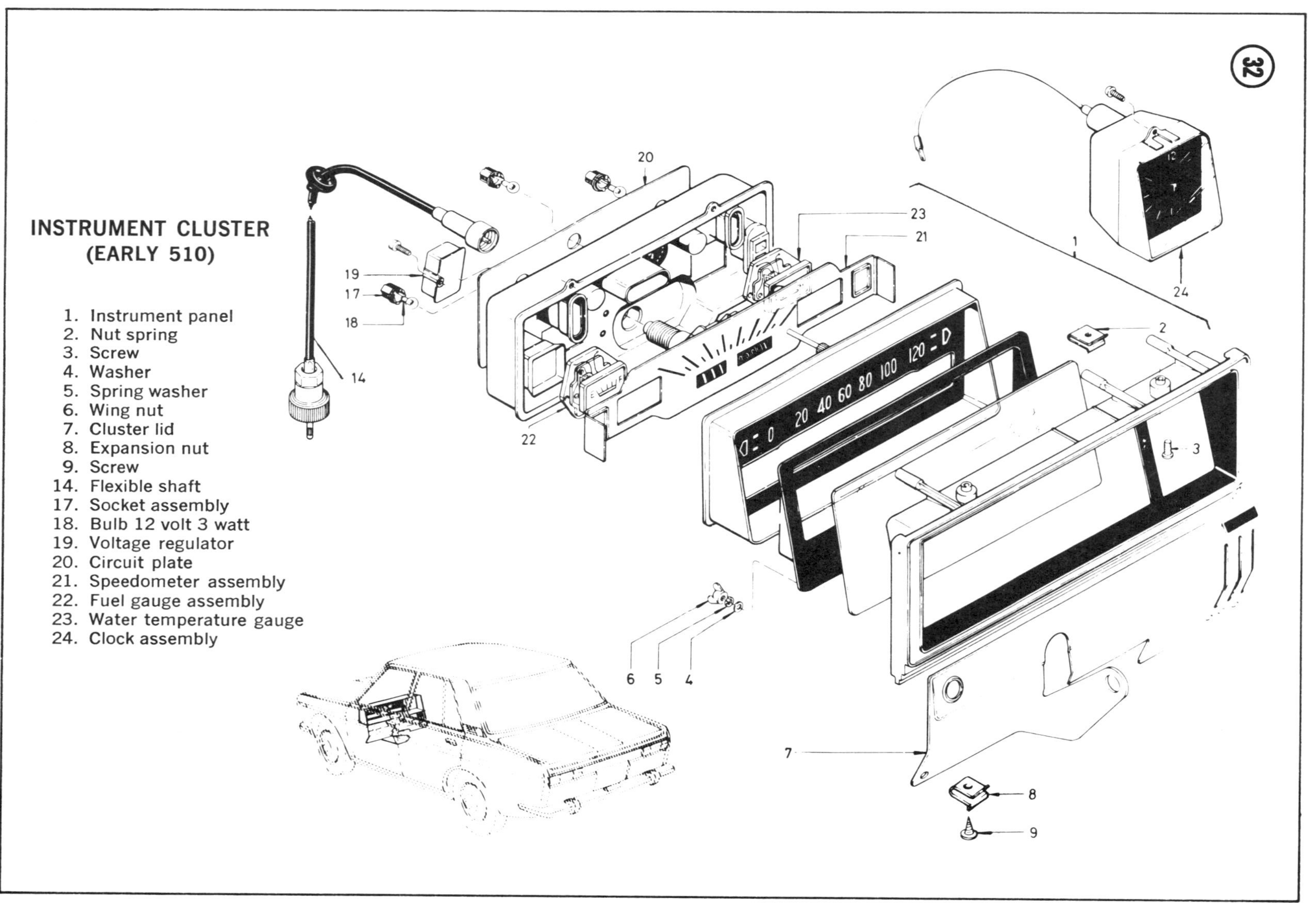
32
INSTRUMENT CLUSTER
(EARLY 510)
1. Instrument panel
2. Nut spring
3. Screw
4. Washer
5. Spring washer
6. Wing nut
7. Cluster lid
8. Expansion nut
9. Screw
14. Flexible shaft
17. Socket assembly
18. Bulb 12 volt 3 watt
19. Voltage regulator
20. Circuit plate
21. Speedometer assembly
22. Fuel gauge assembly
23. Water temperature gauge
24. Clock assembly

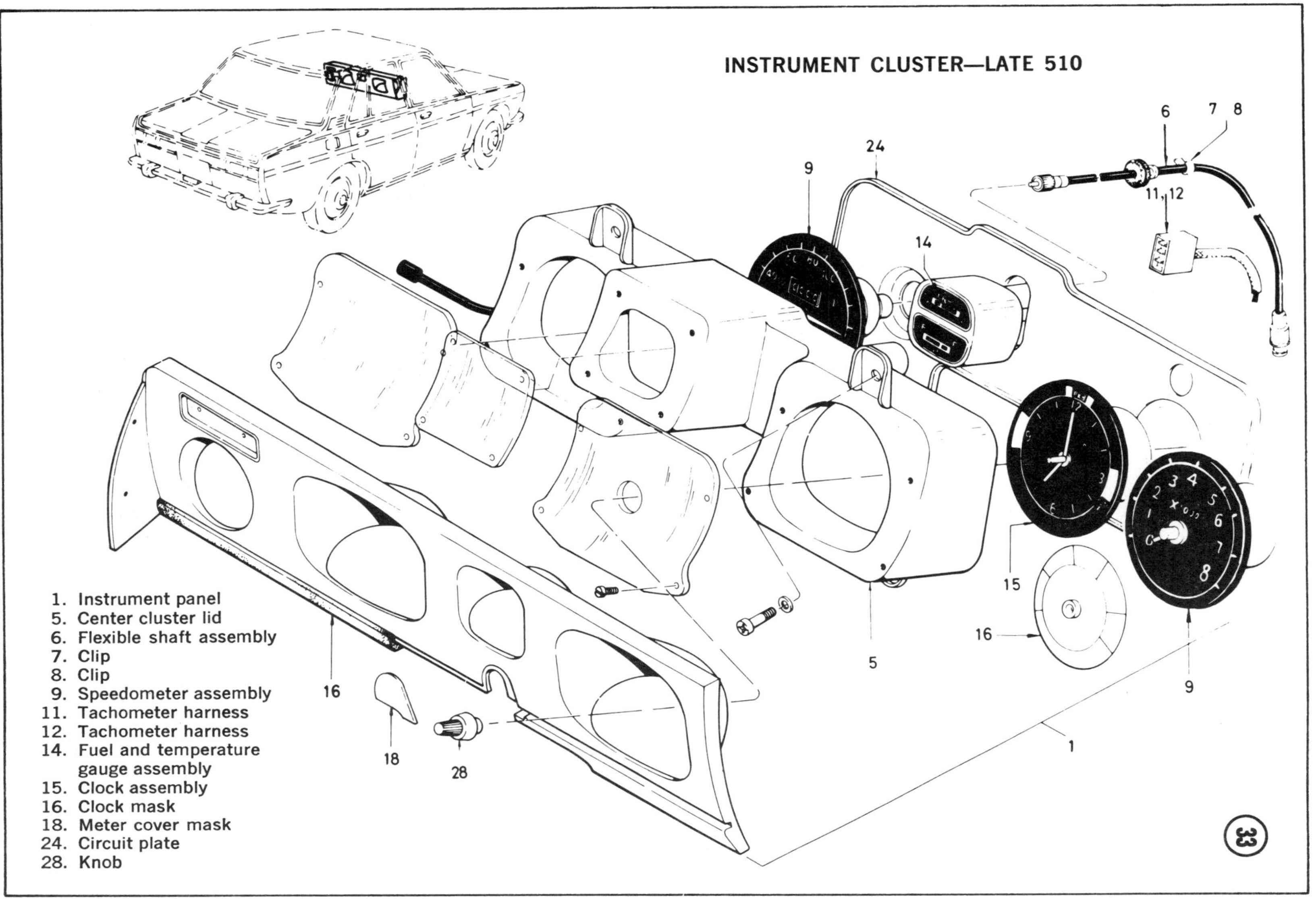
INSTRUMENT CLUSTER—LATE 510
33
1. Instrument panel
5. Center cluster lid
6. Flexible shaft assembly
7. Clip
8. Clip
9. Speedometer assembly
11. Tachometer harness
12. Tachometer harness
14. Fuel and temperature gauge assembly
15. Clock assembly
16. Clock mask
18. Meter cover mask
24. Circuit plate
28. Knob

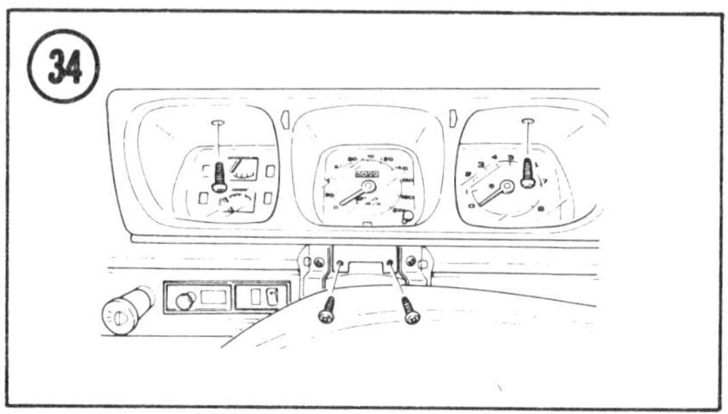

5. Lift the cluster out of the instrument panel.
6. To remove the speedometer, undo 6 screws securing the printed circuit and gauges to the cluster. See **Figure 35**. Take the printed circuit and gauges out. Remove 2 speedometer screws and take the speedometer out.
7. To remove the fuel or water temperature gauge, remove 2 screws and lift the gauge out.
8. Installation is the reverse of these steps.

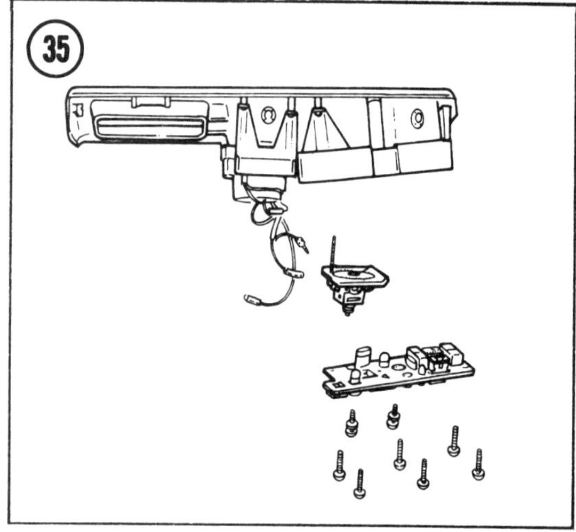

Cluster Removal/Installation (710)

See **Figure 36** for this procedure.

1. Disconnect negative cable from battery.

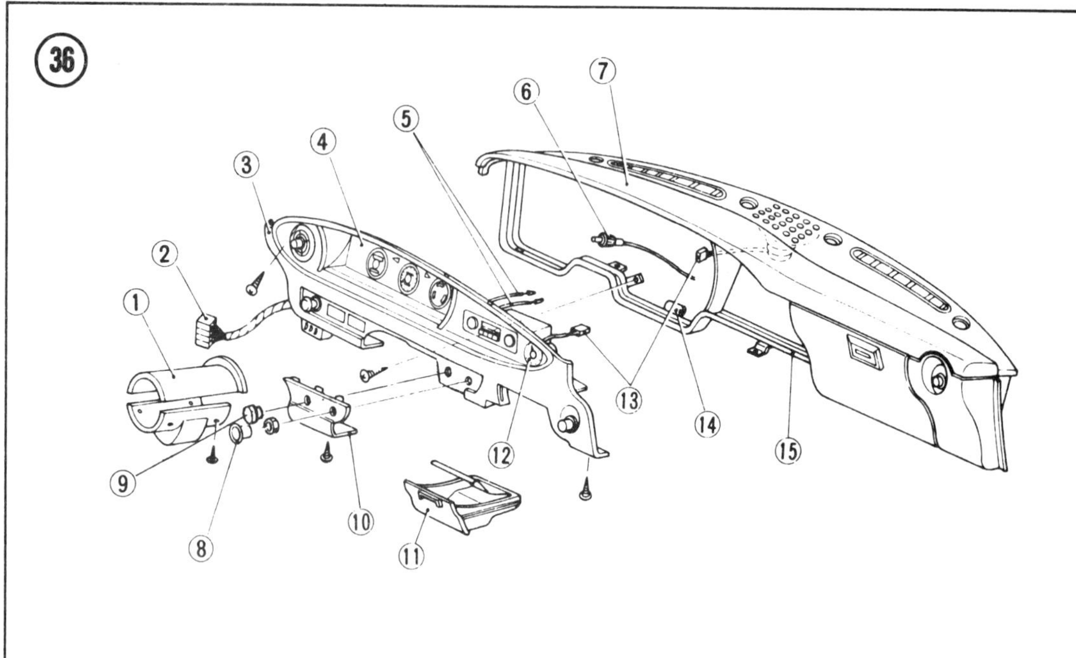

INSTRUMENT CLUSTER—710

1. Shell covers
2. Instrument harness
3. Cluster lid A
4. Combination meter
5. Illumination fiber scope
6. Speedometer cable
7. Instrument upper pad
8. Wiper and washer switch knob
9. Illumination control switch
10. Cluster lid C
11. Ash tray
12. Clock
13. Speaker harness
14. Bulb
15. Instrument panel

2. Remove the steering wheel and steering column shell (Chapter Twelve).

3. Remove the turn signal-dimmer switch as described earlier in this chapter.

4. Remove the wiper knob, its ring nut, and the instrument light dimmer knob (8 and 9, Figure 36). Remove the wiper knob by pressing in and turning counterclockwise. The dimmer knob can be pulled straight off.

5. Remove 2 screws securing cluster lid "C" (10, Figure 36), then take it out.

6. Remove the ashtray.

7. Disconnect 4 wiring connectors behind the left side of the instrument panel.

8. Remove 12 screws securing cluster lid "A".

9. Disconnect the speedometer cable, radio and antenna wires, tachometer wire (if so equipped), and instrument light wires.

10. Disconnect the fiber optic illuminators for the wiper and headlight switches (5, Figure 36) as well as the hazard switch illuminator.

> NOTE: *Disconnect the illuminators from the bulb (14, Figure 36), not from the switches.*

11. Remove the trip odometer knob.

12. Detach the multi-pole wiring connector from the printed circuit board behind the gauges.

13. Remove 6 screws securing the instrument housing to the panel. The housing and gauges can then be removed.

14. To remove a gauge, remove 2 attaching screws and take it out of the housing.

15. Installation is the reverse of these steps.

HORN

All models use 2 horns, mounted at the front of the engine compartment. **Figure 37** shows a typical installation. If the horns work, but are not loud enough, make sure the wires are making good contact and the horns are properly grounded to the body. Horn volume can be adjusted by turning the screw at the back of the horn (**Figure 38**).

If only one horn works, check the wiring to the non-working horn. If the horn is receiving current and is grounded properly, it is probably defective.

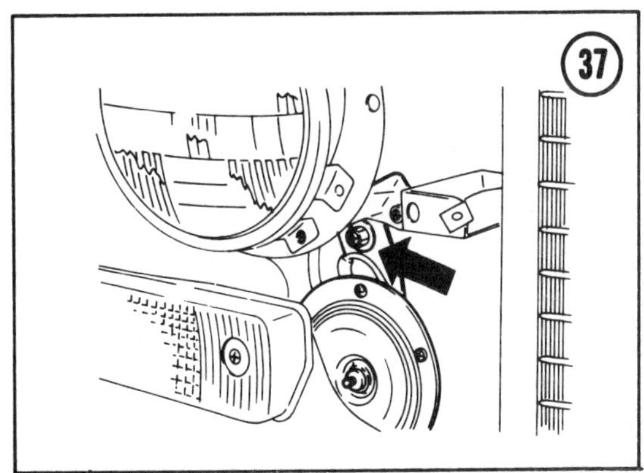

37

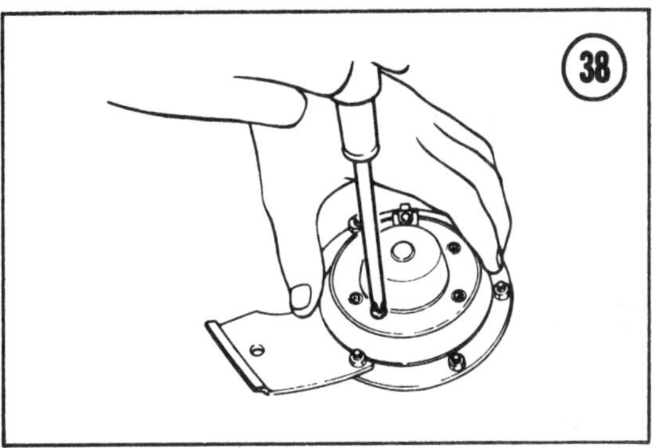

38

If neither horn works, check the horn fuse, then the battery. If these are good, connect a jumper wire between the horn relay "H" and "B" terminals. If the horn sounds, the relay is probably defective. Replace it as described later.

If the horn still doesn't work, ground the relay "S" terminal with a jumper wire. If the horn sounds, the horn button is probably defective; have it tested by a dealer or electrical shop.

Horn Relay Replacement

On 510's, the horn relay is located at the right rear corner of the engine compartment. It can be identified by its wire colors: green, green-and-yellow, and black-and-green.

On 1973-74 610's and 710's, the horn relay is mounted on the bracket forward of the right-hand strut housing (**Figure 39**). On 1975-76 cars, the relay is on the same bracket, but in a different position (**Figure 40**).

On early models with separate relay wires, disconnect one wire at a time and connect it to

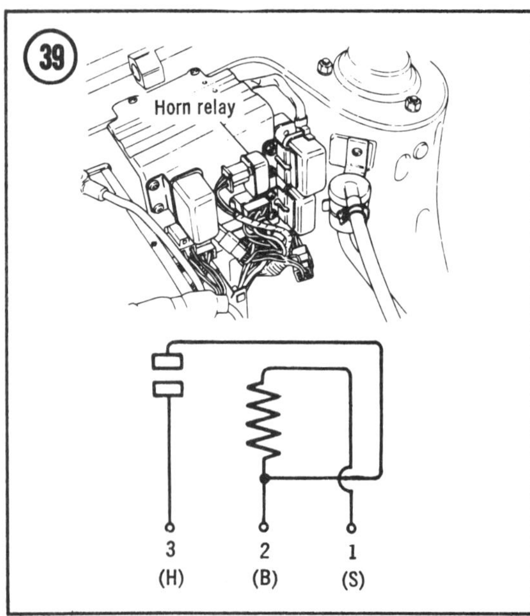

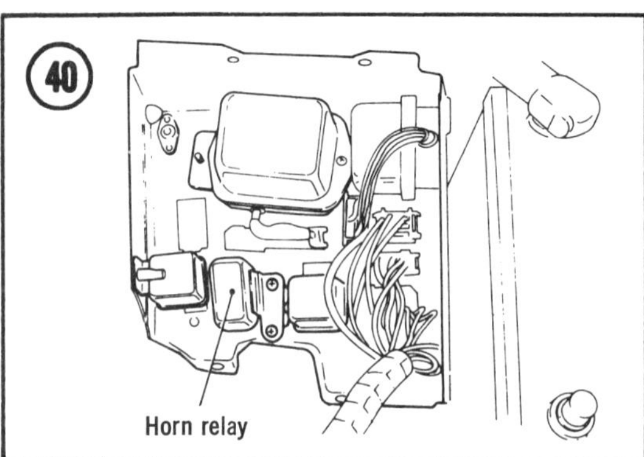

the new relay. This ensures that the wires will be connected properly.

On late models with a one-piece wiring connector, simply remove the old relay, install the new one, and attach the wiring connector.

WINDSHIELD WIPERS AND WASHERS

Wiper Motor Replacement (510)

1. Disconnect the wiring connector from the motor. See **Figure 41**.
2. Reach behind the motor and remove the stop ring securing it to wiper linkage connecting rod.
3. Remove 3 motor securing screws and take the motor out.
4. Installation is the reverse of these steps.

Wiper Motor Replacement (610)

1. Detach the wiring connector from the wiper motor. See **Figure 42**.
2. Remove the cowl top grille.
3. Remove 3 bolts securing the wiper motor.
4. Disconnect the wiper motor from the linkage at the ball-joint.
5. Installation is the reverse of these steps.

Wiper Motor Replacement (710)

1. Disconnect the wiper motor wiring connector (**Figure 43**).

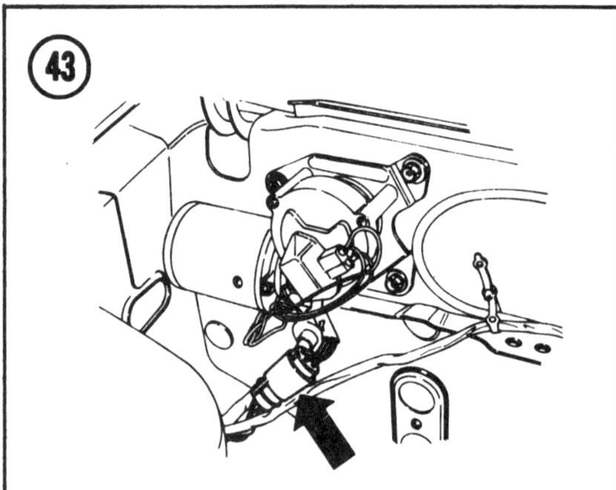

2. Remove the cowl top grille.
3. Disconnect the wiper motor from the linkage (**Figure 44**).

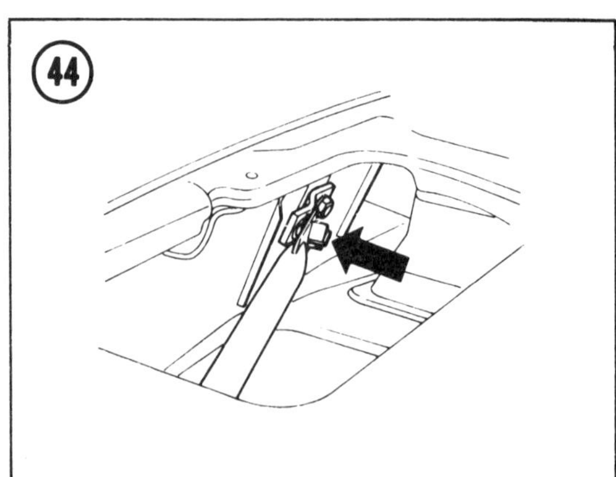

4. Remove 3 motor attaching bolts and take the motor out.
5. Installation is the reverse of these steps.

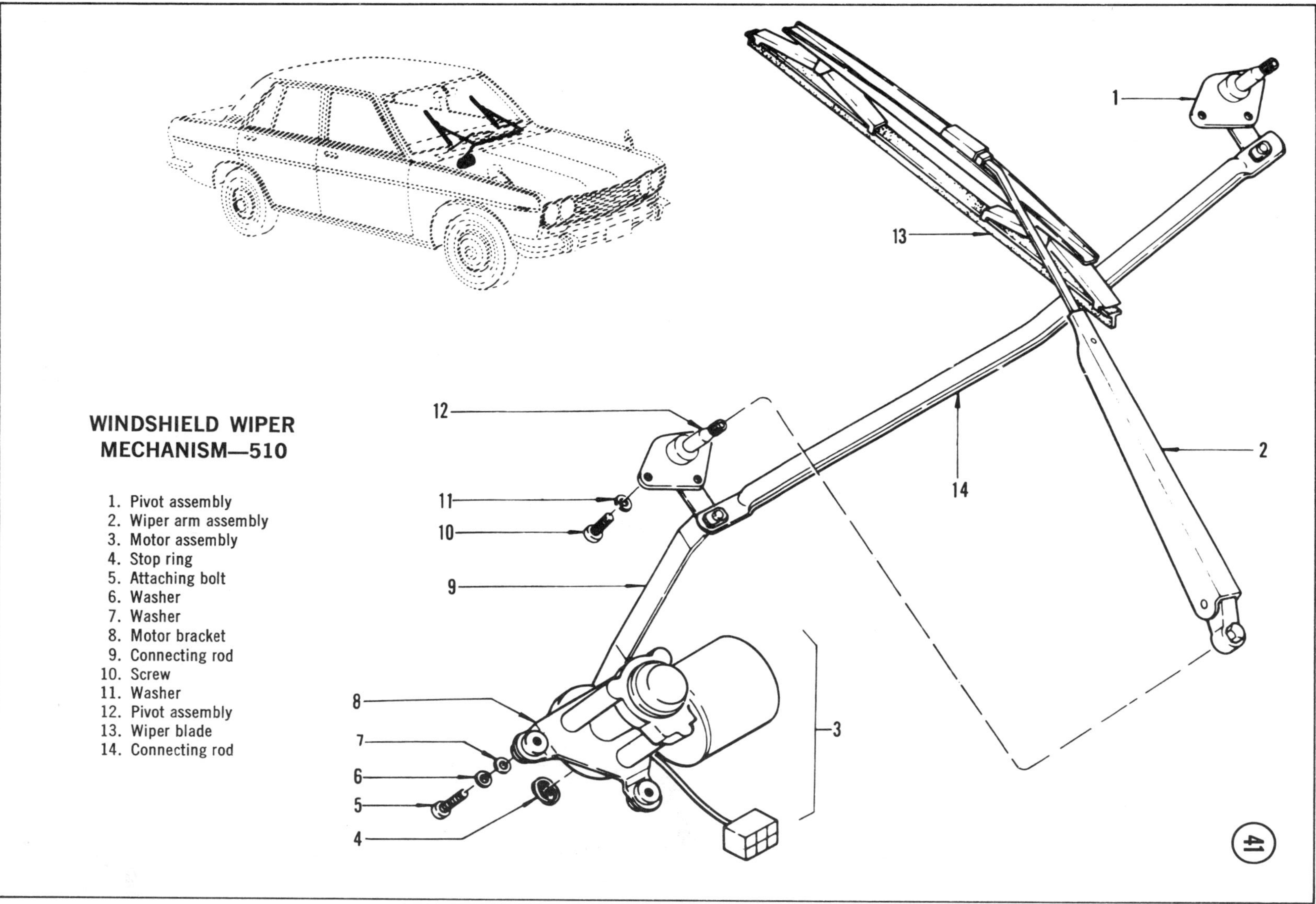

WINDSHIELD WIPER MECHANISM—510

1. Pivot assembly
2. Wiper arm assembly
3. Motor assembly
4. Stop ring
5. Attaching bolt
6. Washer
7. Washer
8. Motor bracket
9. Connecting rod
10. Screw
11. Washer
12. Pivot assembly
13. Wiper blade
14. Connecting rod

42

WINDSHIELD WIPER MECHANISM—610

1. Pivot
2. Wiper arm
3. Pivot
4. Wiper arm
5. Wiper motor

Washer Motor and Tank Replacement

Figure 45 shows a typical windshield washer system. The motor and tank are replaced as an assembly. Before replacing the motor and tank, check for a blown fuse, clogged fluid lines, and defective wiring.

To replace the motor and tank assembly, simply disconnect the motor wires and fluid line. Then remove the assembly from its bracket, install a new one, and reconnect the wires and line.

FUSES AND FUSIBLE LINKS

Fuse Replacement

The 510 fuse block is located at the right rear corner of the engine compartment (**Figure 46**). The 610 and 710 fuse blocks are located on the right-hand side of the passenger footwell (**Figure 47**). Fuse specifications are printed on the inside or outside of the fuse block cover.

Whenever a fuse blows, find out the cause before replacing. Usually the trouble is a short circuit in the wiring. This may be caused by worn-through insulation or by a wire that works its way loose and shorts to ground. Carry several spare fuses in the glove compartment.

46

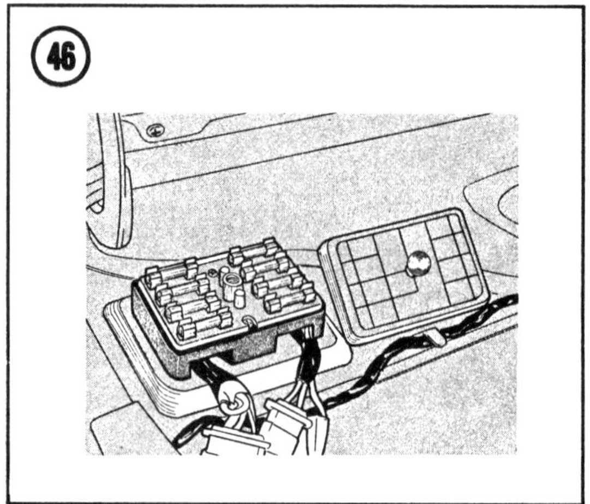

CAUTION

Never substitute tinfoil or wire for a fuse. An overload could cause a fire and complete loss of the vehicle.

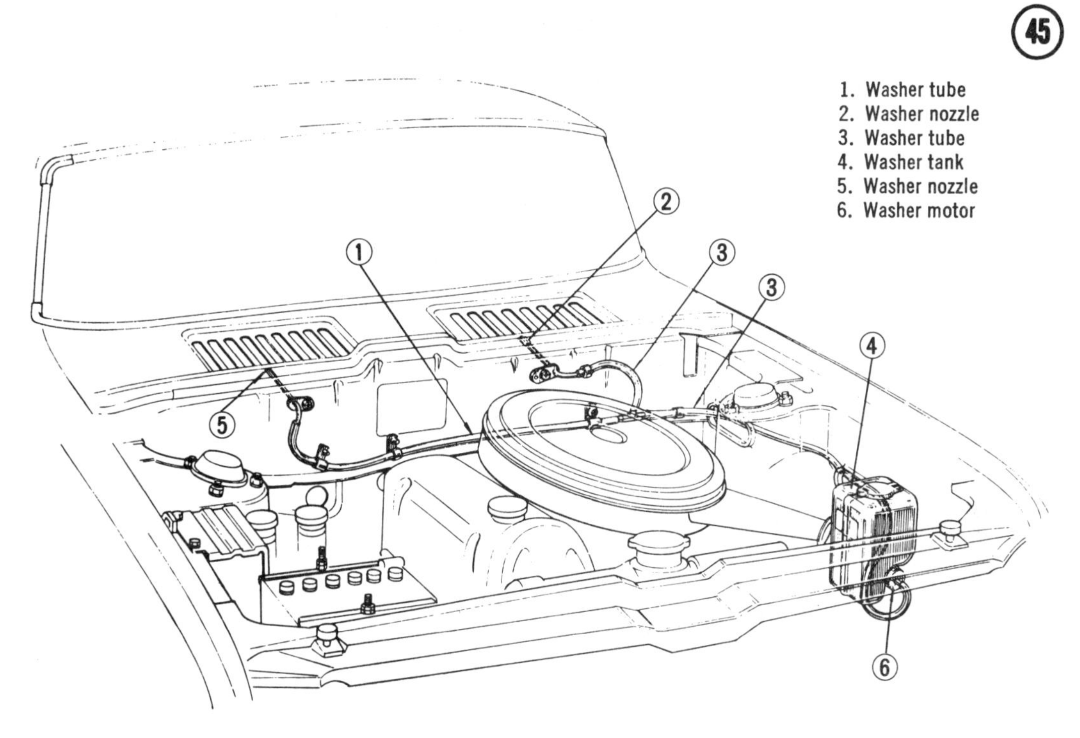

45

1. Washer tube
2. Washer nozzle
3. Washer tube
4. Washer tank
5. Washer nozzle
6. Washer motor

WINDSHIELD WASHER SYSTEM

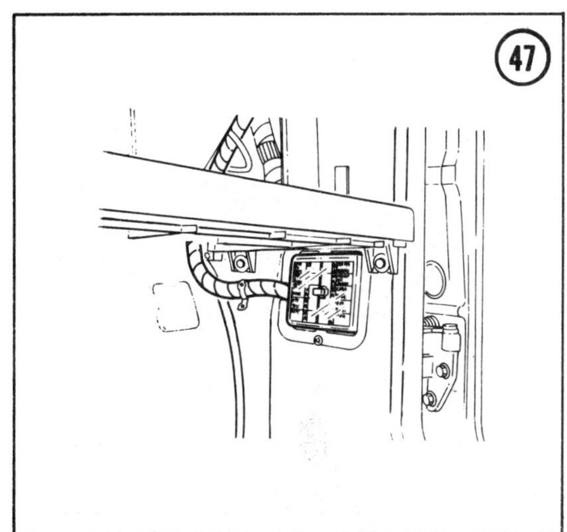

Fusible Link Replacement

Fusible links are short sections of thin wire in a larger wire. They are intended to burn out if an overload occurs, thus protecting the wiring harnesses.

The 510 fusible link is located in the red-and-white wire running from alternator terminal "A" to the starter solenoid. It can be identified by its red color. **Figure 48** shows the 610 fusible links; **Figure 49** shows the 710 version.

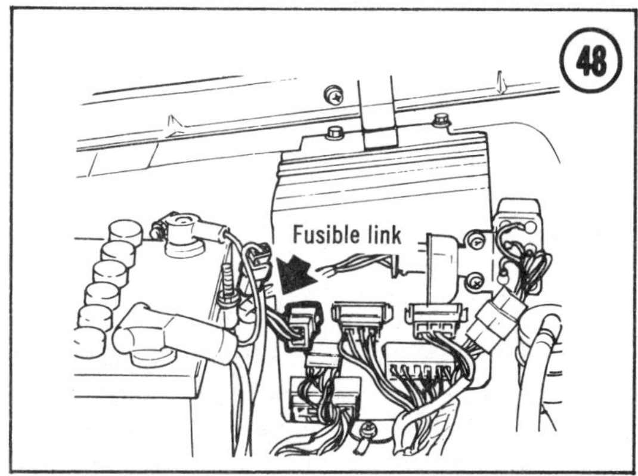

Burned-out fusible links can usually be detected by melted or burned insulation. Suspect links with no apparent damage can be tested for

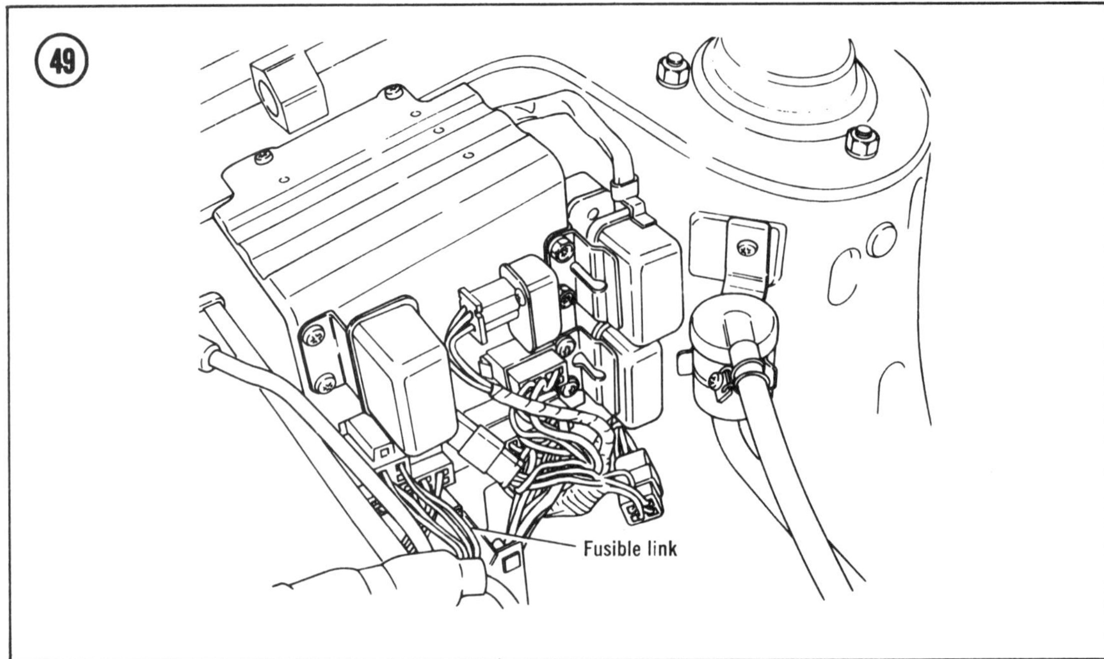

continuity with an ohmmeter or test lamp like the one shown in Figure 26. If a link burns out, unplug it and plug in a new one.

CAUTION

Never replace a fusible link with a link of larger capacity. Never wrap fusible links with tape.

IGNITION SYSTEM

All 1968-74 cars, and 1975-76 non-California cars, use a conventional breaker point ignition system. The system comprises the battery, ignition switch, ignition coil, distributor, spark plugs, and associated wiring. 1970-73 models use 2 sets of breaker points; all others use one set. **Figure 50** shows a dual-point system; **Figure 51** shows a single-point system.

1975-76 California cars use a pulse-controlled transistor ignition system. See **Figure 52**. A reluctor is used in place of the conventional distributor cam, and the breaker points are replaced by a pickup coil. The reluctor has 4 protrusions, one for each cylinder. As each protrusion faces the pick-up coil, it causes the coil to send an electrical signal to the transistor ignition unit. The transistor unit then triggers production of high-voltage current in the coil. This current runs through the coil wire to the distributor, which routes it to the appropriate spark plug.

The following sections describe replacement procedures. No ignition components except the distributor are repairable.

Ignition Switch and Steering Lock Replacement

The ignition switch is combined into a unit with the steering lock. The switch itself is secured to the lock with a single screw. **Figure 53** shows a typical ignition switch.

1. Remove the steering column shell.
2. Place ignition key in unlocked position.
3. Disconnect the ignition switch wiring connector. If equipped with a key warning buzzer, disconnect both of its wires.
4. Drill out the self-shearing screws and remove them with a screw extractor (easy-out). Remove 2 plain screws (if used).
5. If necessary, remove the screw securing the ignition switch to the steering lock. Take the switch off.
6. Install in the reverse order. Use new self-shearing screws and tighten them until the heads snap off.

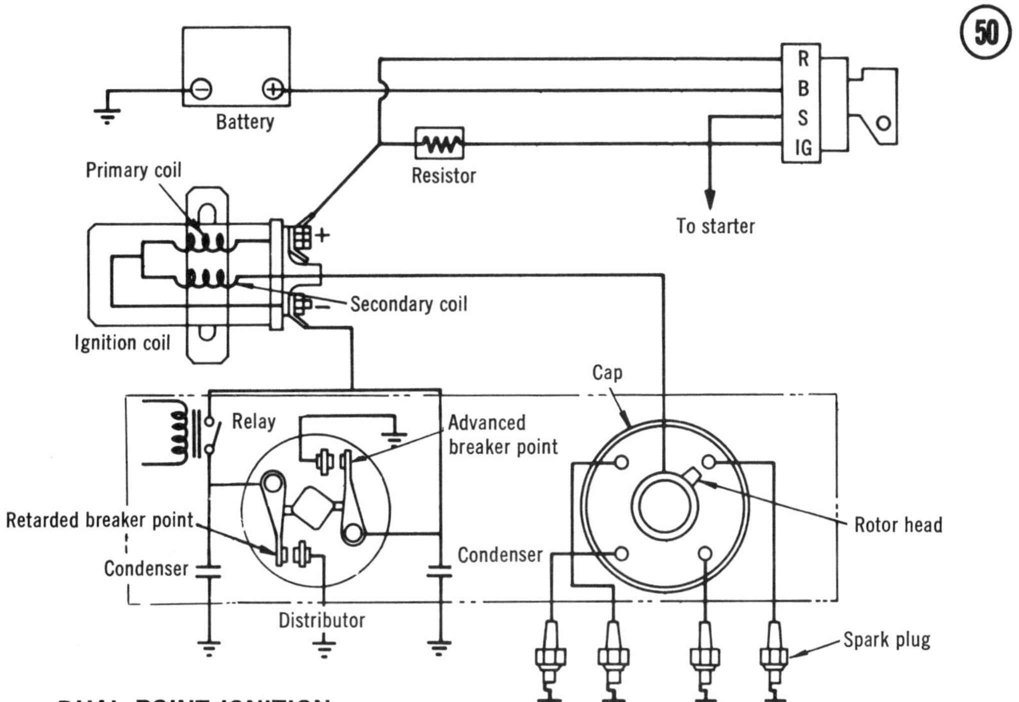

50

Battery
R
B
S
IG
Resistor
Primary coil
To starter
Secondary coil
Ignition coil
Cap
Relay
Advanced breaker point
Retarded breaker point
Rotor head
Condenser
Condenser
Distributor
Spark plug

DUAL POINT IGNITION

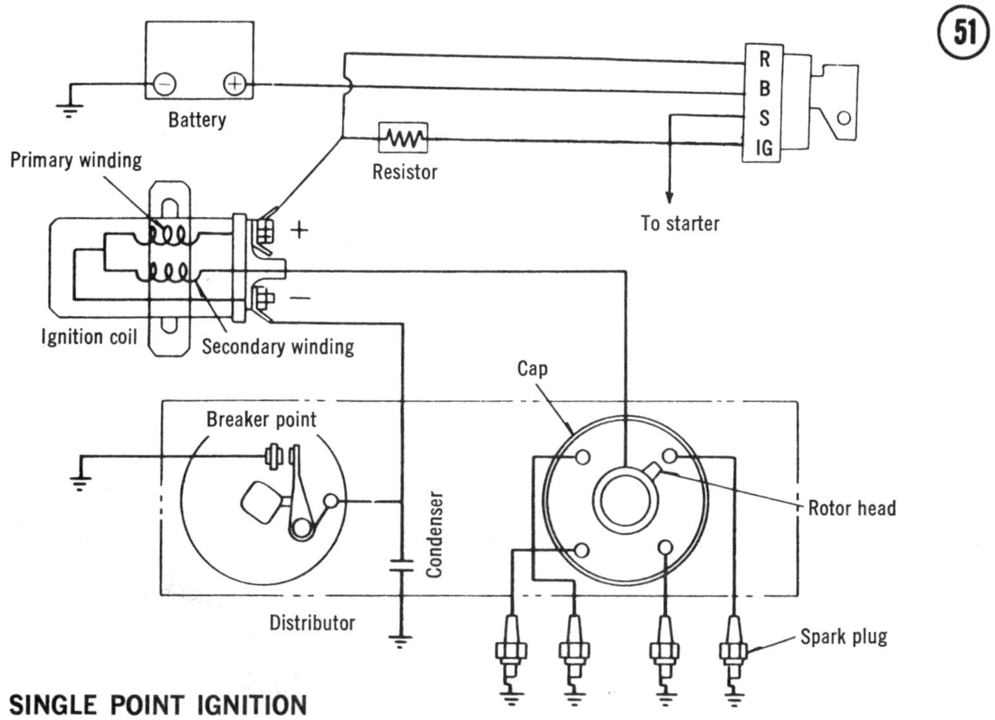

7

51

Battery
R
B
S
IG
Resistor
Primary winding
To starter
Ignition coil
Secondary winding
Cap
Breaker point
Rotor head
Condenser
Distributor
Spark plug

SINGLE POINT IGNITION

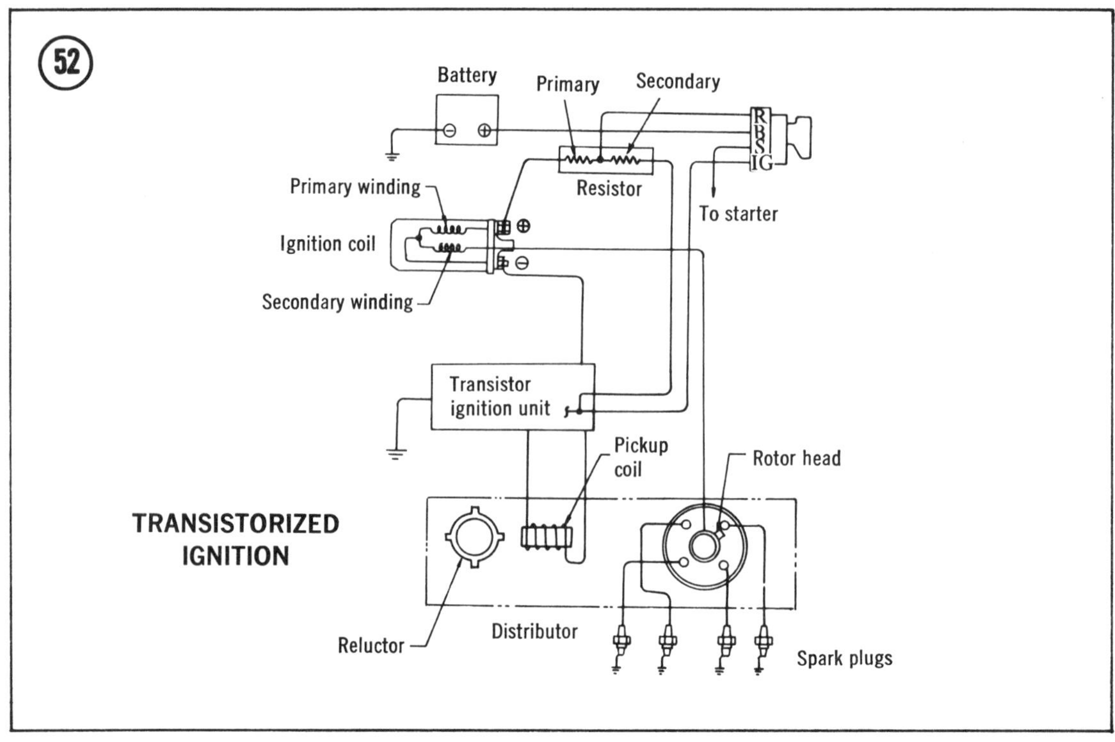

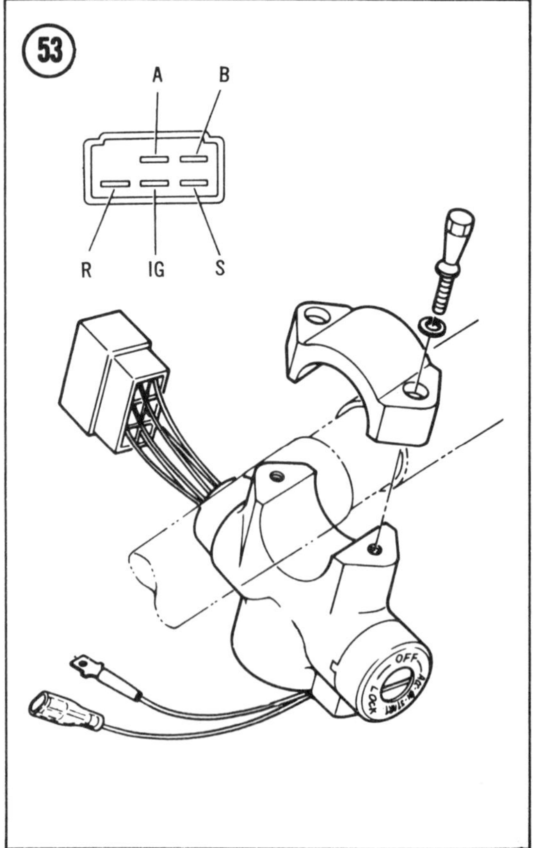

Ignition Coil Replacement

On all models, the coil is mounted on the left side of the engine compartment. The coil and its resistor should be replaced as a matched set.

To replace, disconnect the coil and resistor wires. Remove the coil and resistor, then install the new ones.

> NOTE: *On 1975-76 cars, be sure the coil wire cover fits securely into the rubber ignition coil cap. See* **Figure 54**.

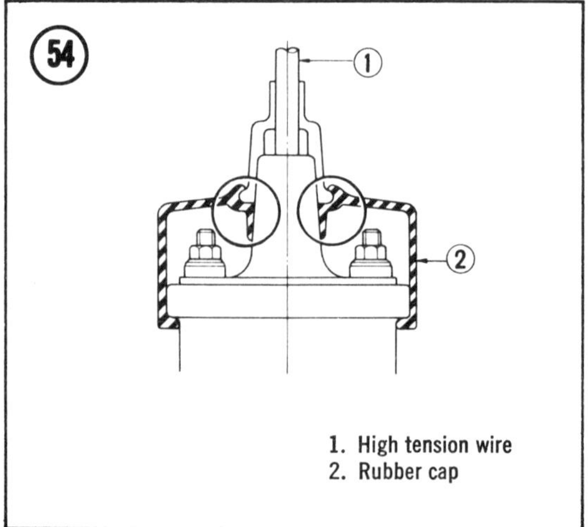

1. High tension wire
2. Rubber cap

DISTRIBUTOR

Proper engine operation depends very heavily on distributor advance characteristics. Advance is controlled by centrifugal and vacuum mechanisms, as well as by the spark timing control system on dual-point distributors. Adjustment of the advance mechanisms is critical and requires special test fixtures. Take the job to a Datsun dealer or automotive electrical specialist.

Removal

1. Remove the distributor cap clips and take off the cap.
2. Disconnect the primary lead wire(s) from the distributor terminal(s).
3. Disconnect the vacuum line from the vacuum advance unit.
4. Turn the engine over until No. 1 piston is at top dead center on its compression stroke. This occurs when the 0° timing mark at the front of the engine aligns with the timing pointer, and the distributor rotor points at No. 1 terminal in the distributor cap. Be sure to check rotor position as well as the timing marks, because the 0° mark also lines up when No. 4 cylinder is at TDC on its compression stroke.
5. To simplify installation, make alignment marks on the distributor body and engine.
6. Remove 2 distributor body setscrews. Lift the distributor out of the engine.

Installation

1. If the engine was turned over after distributor removal, place No. 1 piston at top dead center on its compression stroke. See *Removal*, Step 4.
2. Note the position of the distributor driving spindle. See **Figure 55**. Note that the spindle tooth is slightly offset toward the front of the engine.
3. Insert the distributor so it engages with the driving spindle. Make sure the rotor points toward No. 1 terminal in the distributor cap. Align the marks on engine and distributor body.
4. Install the body setscrews and distributor cap. Connect primary lead(s) to distributor.

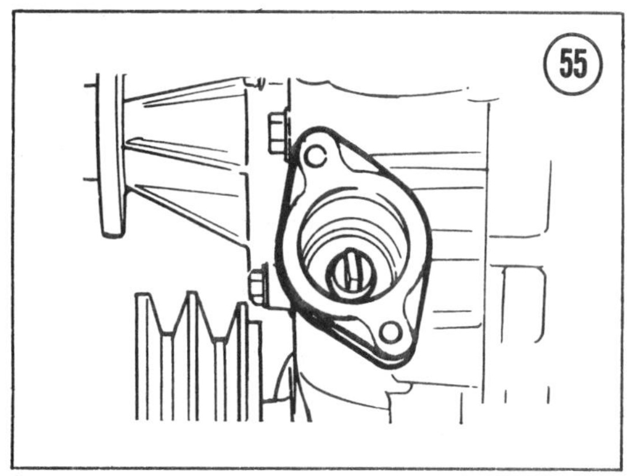

5. Adjust the ignition timing as described in Chapter Two.

SPARK TIMING CONTROL SYSTEMS

These systems are used on 1970-73 and 1975-76 cars to advance or retard ignition timing under specific driving conditions. The 1970-73 systems use a dual-point distributor. One set of points has a more advanced timing setting than the other. Various switches and relays determine which set of points is in use.

The 1975-76 systems use a single-point or breakerless distributor. Vacuum to the distributor's vacuum advance unit is cut off in the lower 3 gears (manual transmission) or delayed in all gears (automatic transmission).

Figure 56 shows the system used on 1970-72 cars. **Figure 57** shows the 1973 system. **Figure 58** shows the 1975-76 manual transmission system. **Figure 59** shows the 1975-76 automatic transmission version.

System Test (1970-72 Manual Transmission)

1. Warm passenger compartment above 55°F. Use the car's heater if necessary.
2. Disconnect the thin wires from the side of the distributor.
3. Connect an ammeter between the retarded wire (not the retarded terminal) and ground (any bare metal in the engine compartment). See **Figure 60**.
4. Turn ignition on, but don't start the engine.
5. Place the shift lever in third gear and press the accelerator. The ammeter should show approximately 3 amps when the pedal is partway

56

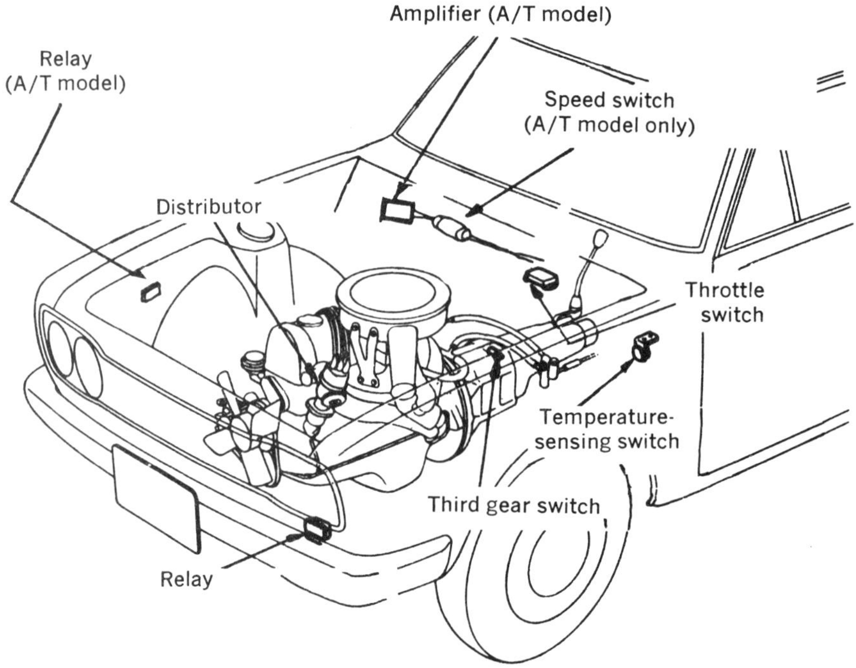

Amplifier (A/T model)
Relay
(A/T model)
Speed switch
(A/T model only)
Distributor
Throttle
switch
Temperature-
sensing switch
Third gear switch
Relay

57

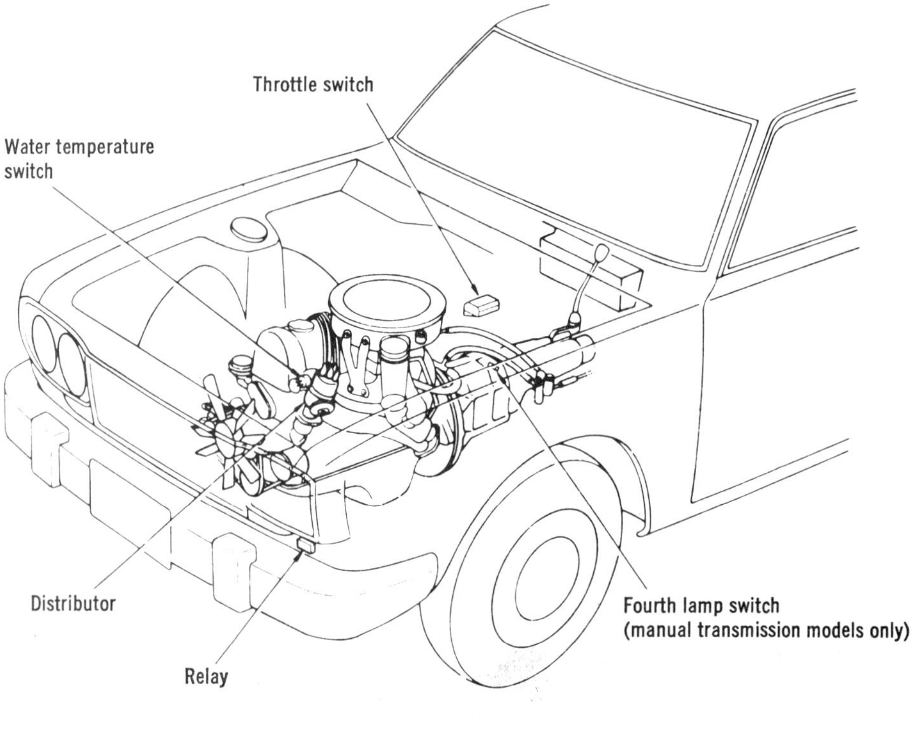

Throttle switch
Water temperature
switch
Distributor
Relay
Fourth lamp switch
(manual transmission models only)

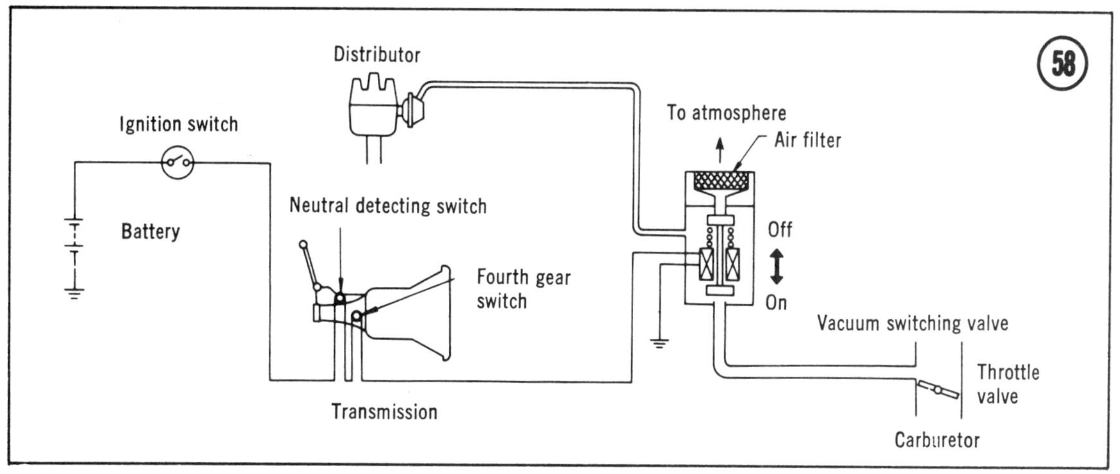

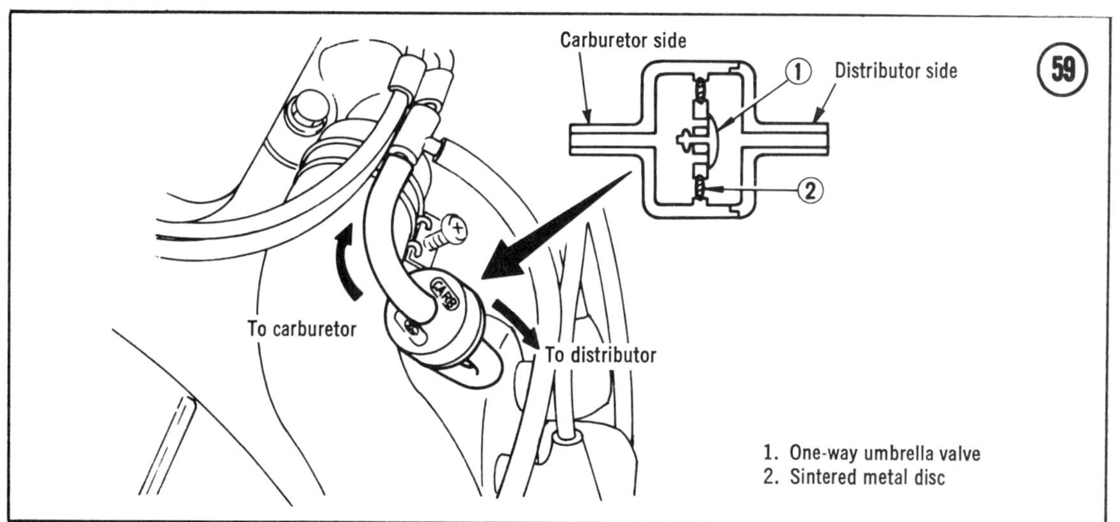

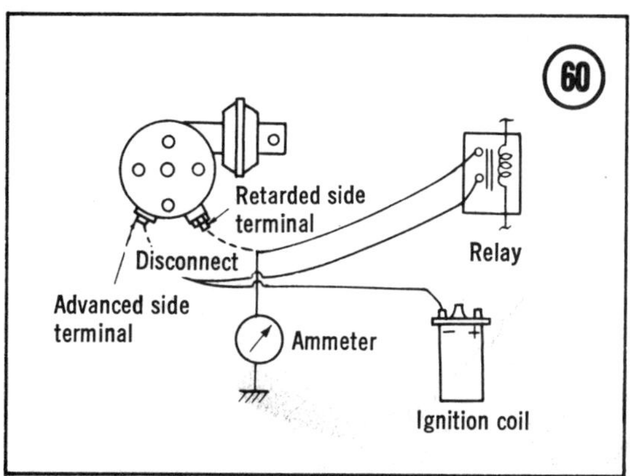

down. The ammeter should indicate zero when the pedal is on the floor or nearly all the way up, and also when the shift lever is taken out of third gear position.

6. If the ammeter shows zero when it should show 3 amps, check the relay. To do this, disconnect the relay wires. Connect a voltmeter positive lead to No. 1 relay terminal's wire (not to the terminal). Connect the voltmeter negative lead to ground (any bare metal in the engine compartment). With the key on, the voltmeter should indicate 12 volts. If it does, replace the relay. If not, check the wiring. Also test the system components as described later in this chapter.

System Test (1970-72 Automatic Transmission)

1. Disconnect the wire from the distributor's retarded terminal. This is the thin wire connected to the side of the distributor, closest to the vacuum advance unit.

2. Connect an ammeter between the disconnected wire and its terminal. Position the ammeter so it can be seen while the car is driven. If necessary, connect extension wires to the ammeter leads.

3. Drive the car and watch the ammeter. Below 13 mph, the ammeter should indicate zero. Above that speed, with the throttle partly open, it should indicate current flow. If not, test the system components as described later in this chapter.

System Test (1973)

The 1973 system is tested as part of ignition timing adjustment. This is part of each tune-up. See Chapter Two.

System Test (1975-76 Manual Transmission)

1. Make sure all wires are connected properly. See Figure 58.

2. Make sure all vacuum lines are connected properly. See **Figure 61**.

3. Connect a timing light and accurate tune-up tachometer to the engine.

4. Run the engine at 1,800 rpm. With the clutch pedal floored, move the shift lever through all gear positions. Ignition timing should advance approximately 5° farther in fourth and neutral than in the other gears.

5. If ignition timing fails to advance only in fourth or neutral, replace the switch for that gear (**Figure 62**). Use Loctite on the switch threads.

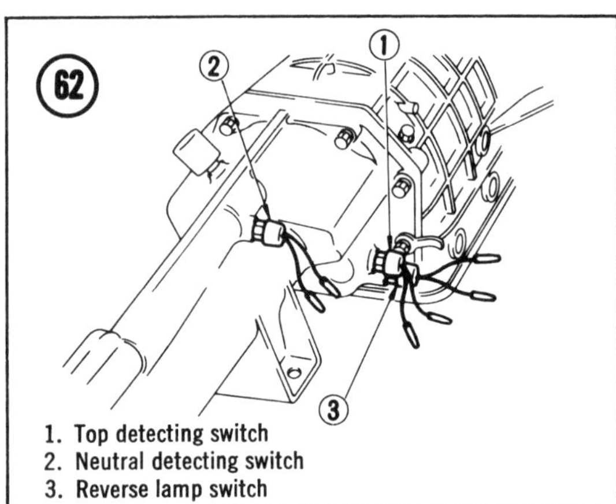

1. Top detecting switch
2. Neutral detecting switch
3. Reverse lamp switch

6. If ignition timing doesn't advance in any gear, disconnect the green wire from the vacuum switching valve (Figures 58 and 61). With the engine at 1,800 rpm, connect the green wire directly to the battery positive terminal. Note ignition timing.

7. Disconnect the green wire from the battery terminal. Timing should advance approximately 5°. If it does, replace the neutral and fourth gear switches. If not, replace the vacuum switching valve.

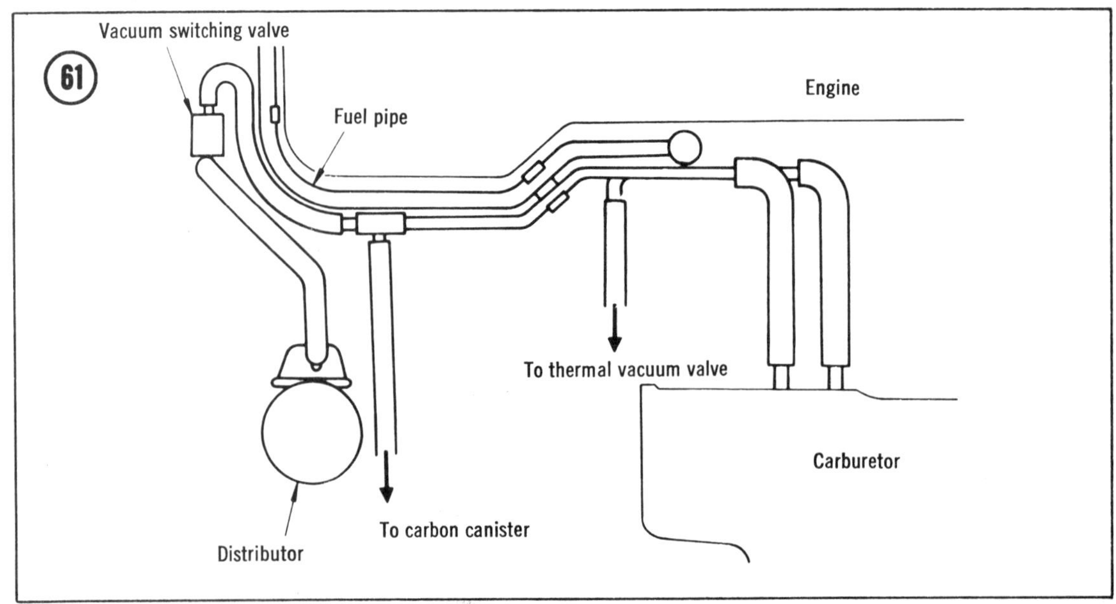

System Test (1975-76 Automatic Transmission)

This system has only one major component and does not require periodic testing. Replace the spark delay valve at intervals specified in Chapter Two.

Transmission Switch Test (1970-73)

1. Locate the switch, mounted on the right-hand side of the transmission. On 510's and 610's, both switch wires are blue-and-yellow.

2. Connect an ohmmeter or self-powered test lamp to the wires coming from the switch.

3. Turn the ignition on, but don't start the engine.

4. On 1970-1972 models, the ohmmeter should show zero resistance (test lamp should light) when the transmission is in third gear. In all other gears, the ohmmeter should show infinite resistance (test lamp should stay out).

5. On 1973 models, the ohmmeter should show infinite resistance (test lamp should stay out) when the transmission is in fourth gear. In all other gears, the ohmmeter should show zero resistance (test lamp should light).

6. If the switch fails to pass this test, unscrew it and install a new one. Use Loctite on the switch threads.

Temperature Switch Test (1970-72)

The temperature switch is located near the hood release lever or handle (**Figure 63**).

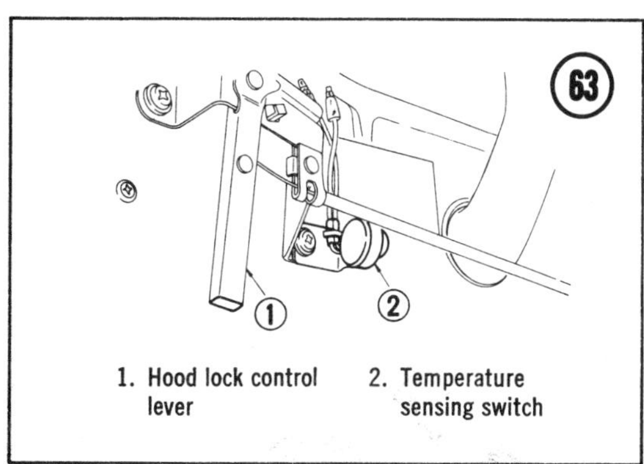

1. Hood lock control lever
2. Temperature sensing switch

1. Disconnect the switch wires. Connect an ohmmeter or self-powered test lamp between the wires coming from the switch.

2. Be sure switch temperature is above 55°F. If necessary, place a sponge soaked in hot water on the switch. At this point, the ohmmeter should indicate zero resistance (the test lamp should light).

3. Make sure switch temperature is below 34°F. If necessary, use an ice pack to cool the switch. The ohmmeter should now show infinite resistance (test lamp should go out).

4. If the switch fails either part of this test, remove it and install a new one. Test the switch as described in Steps 2 and 3.

Throttle Switch (1970-73)

1. Remove the cover from the switch.

2. Turn the ignition on, but don't start the engine. Slowly floor the accelerator and listen for clicks from the switch. Turn the ignition off.

3. Check switch wires for damaged insulation.

> NOTE: *Steps 4 and 5 apply to 1970-72 models only.*

4. Check the gap between cam and switch body (**Figure 64**). It should be 0.032 in. If it is incorrect, loosen both adjusting screws (1, Figure 64) and rotate the switch to change it.

5. Connect an ohmmeter or self-powered test lamp between terminals 1 and 2, then between terminals 1 and 3. The ohmmeter should indicate infinite resistance (test lamp should stay out) when the accelerator is pressed partway. At full throttle or with the accelerator backed all the way off, the ohmmeter should show zero resistance (test lamp should light).

> NOTE: *Steps 6 and 7 apply to 1973 models only.*

6. Make sure the idle marks are aligned (**Figure 65**). If necessary, loosen the adjusting screws and turn the switch to align the marks.

7. Connect an ohmmeter or self-powered test lamp between the wires running from the throttle switch. With the pedal fully depressed, the ohmmeter should indicate infinite resistance (test lamp should go out). With the pedal partly depressed or backed all the way off, the ohmmeter should show zero resistance (the test lamp should light).

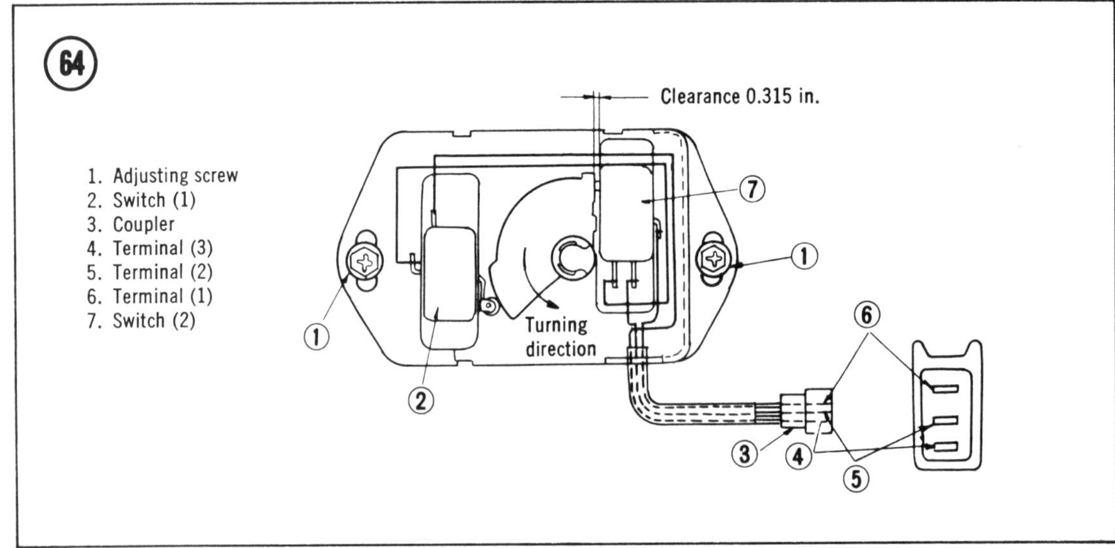

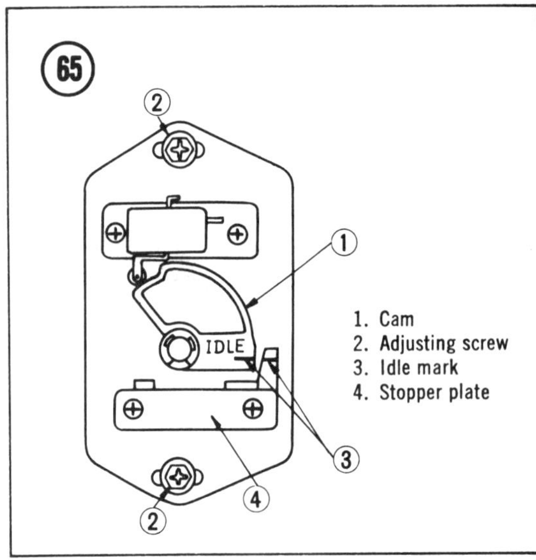

8. If the throttle switch does not work properly, replace it. Adjust the new switch as described in Step 4 or 6.

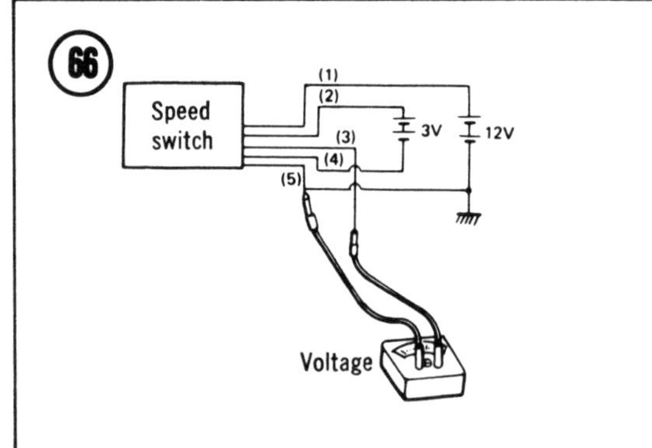

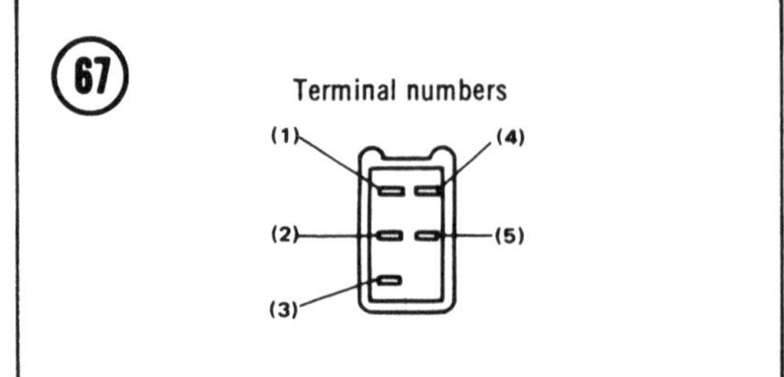

Speed Switch (1970-72 Automatic Transmissions)

1. Locate the speed detector, mounted in the speedometer cable just behind the speedometer. Follow the wires from the speed detector to the speed switch. Disconnect the wires from the speed switch.

2. Set up the test circuit shown in **Figure 66**. **Figure 67** identifies the terminals.

3. With the test circuit set up as shown, the voltmeter should indicate 12 volts. This should drop to zero when terminal 2 is disconnected from its power source.

4. If the switch doesn't respond properly, remove the cover. Make sure the armature and return spring are positioned properly, then test again. If the switch still doesn't respond, replace it.

CHAPTER EIGHT

CLUTCH

All models use a single, dry-plate clutch with diaphragm spring. Major components are the pressure plate, disc, release mechanism, and hydraulic linkage. **Figure 1** shows clutch parts.

The release mechanism, which controls engagement and disengagement, consists of a bearing, sleeve, and withdrawal lever. The release mechanism is in turn controlled by the hydraulic linkage, which transmits pedal pressure through the clutch master cylinder, hydraulic line, and operating cylinder. The operating cylinder pushrod moves the withdrawal lever.

This chapter includes all service procedures practical for home mechanics. For specifications see **Table 1** at the end of the chapter.

PART IDENTIFICATION

Many clutch parts have two or more names. To prevent confusion, the following list gives part names used in this chapter and common synonyms.

Withdrawal lever—release lever, throw-out arm

Release bearing—throw-out bearing

Operating cylinder—slave cylinder

Pressure plate—pressure plate assembly, clutch cover assembly

Disc—driven plate

CLUTCH PEDAL

Adjustment (510)

1. Back off the pedal stopper (**Figure 2**) until it is clear of the pedal.

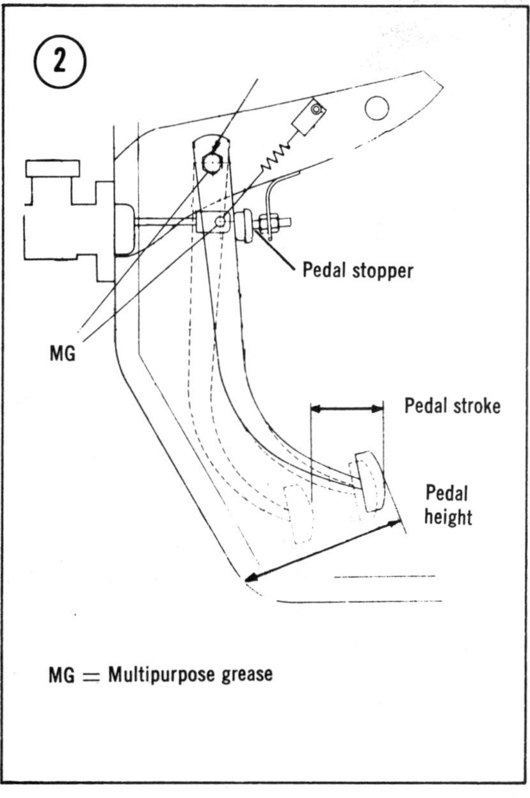

8

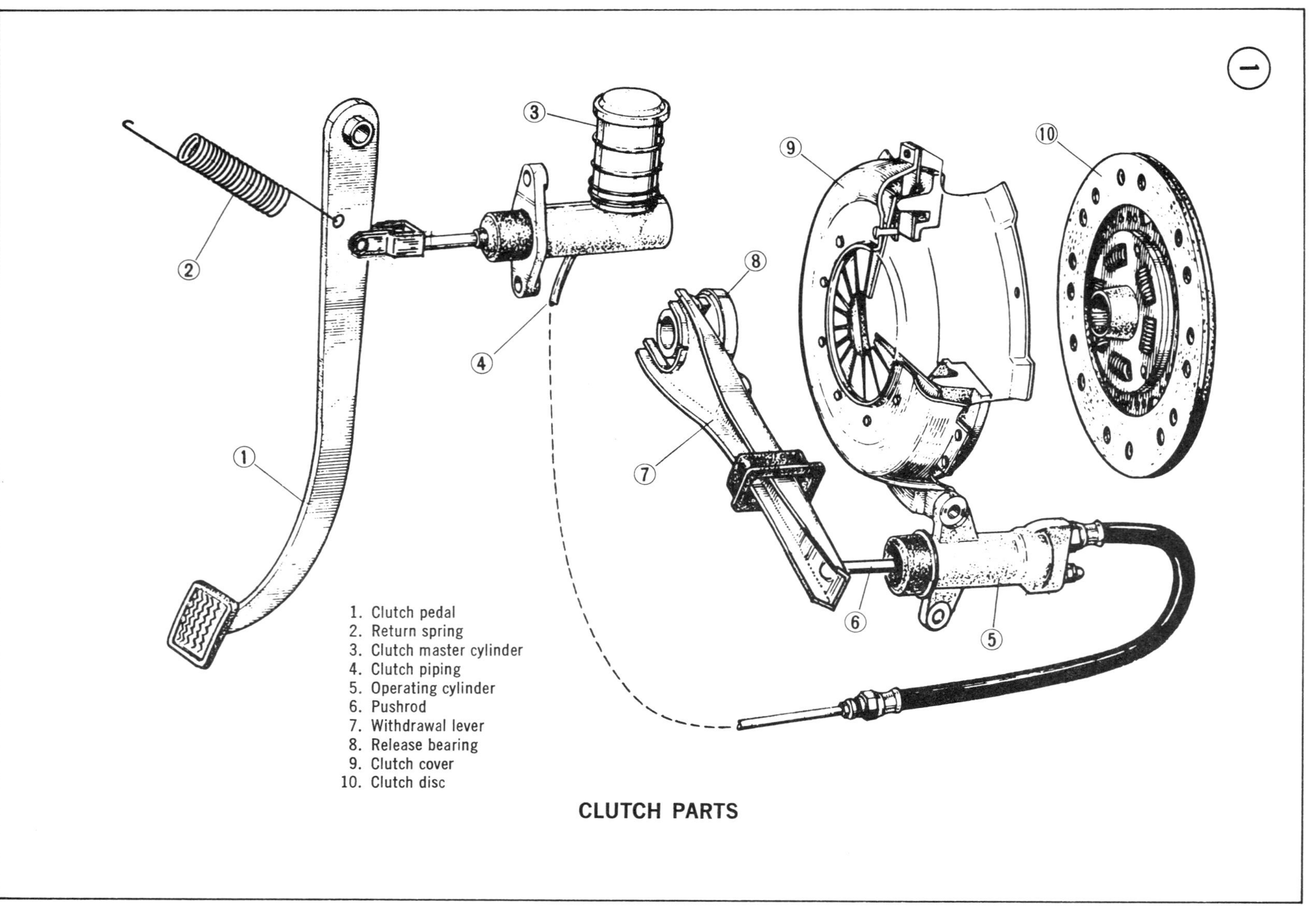

CLUTCH PARTS

2. Loosen the locknut on the master cylinder pushrod. Set pedal height at 8.224 in. (209mm) by rotating the pushrod. Tighten the locknut.

3. Lower the pedal to 8.15 in. (207mm) by turning the pedal stopper. Tighten the pedal stopper locknut.

Adjustment (610, 710)

1. Loosen pedal stopper locknut. See **Figure 3**.

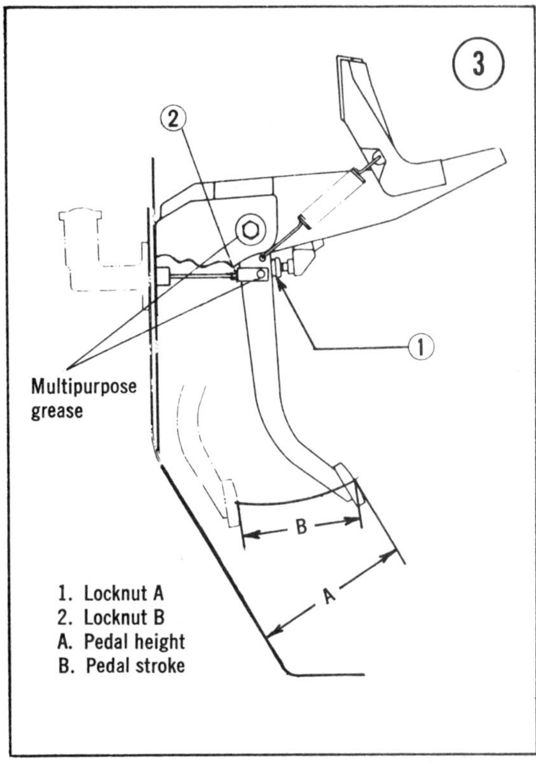

2. Turn the pedal stopper in or out to change pedal height. It should be 6.89 in. (175mm) on 610's and 7.09 in. (180mm) on 710's.

3. Tighten the pedal stopper locknut.

4. Loosen the locknut on the master cylinder pushrod. Rotate the pushrod in or out to adjust play at the clevis pin. After adjustment, you should be able to move the pedal slightly without moving the master cylinder pushrod. Specified pedal movement is 0.04-0.20 in. (1-5mm).

MASTER CYLINDER

Figure 4 shows typical master cylinders. Refer to it as needed for the following procedures.

Removal/Installation

1. Remove the clevis pin attaching the master cylinder pushrod to the clutch pedal.

2. With a container handy to catch dripping hydraulic fluid, disconnect the hydraulic line from the master cylinder.

CAUTION

Hydraulic fluid will damage paint. Wipe up any spilled fluid immediately, then wash the area of the spill with soap and water.

3. Remove both master cylinder installation nuts and lift the cylinder out.

4. Installation is the reverse of these steps. Adjust pedal height. Bleed air out of the hydraulic system as described later in this chapter.

Disassembly

Refer to Figure 4.

1. Remove the filler cap from the fluid reservoir. Pour the fluid from the cylinder.

2. Pull back the dust cover and remove the stopper ring.

3. Take the stopper out of the cylinder. Remove the pushrod, then the piston assembly.

4. Take the piston cup off the piston and discard it.

NOTE: *Do not remove the fluid reservoir unless absolutely necessary.*

Inspection

1. Thoroughly clean all parts in brake fluid before inspection. Never use gasoline or kerosene for cleaning.

2. Check the piston for excessive or uneven wear, scoring, cracks, or corrosion. Replace the piston if any of these defects are found.

3. Check the cylinder bore for wear, cracks, scoring, or corrosion. Replace the cylinder if defects are visible.

4. As a final check on a suspect cylinder and piston, measure the outside diameter of the piston and inside diameter of the cylinder. If the difference between these two figures exceeds 0.006 in. (0.15mm), replace the master cylinder.

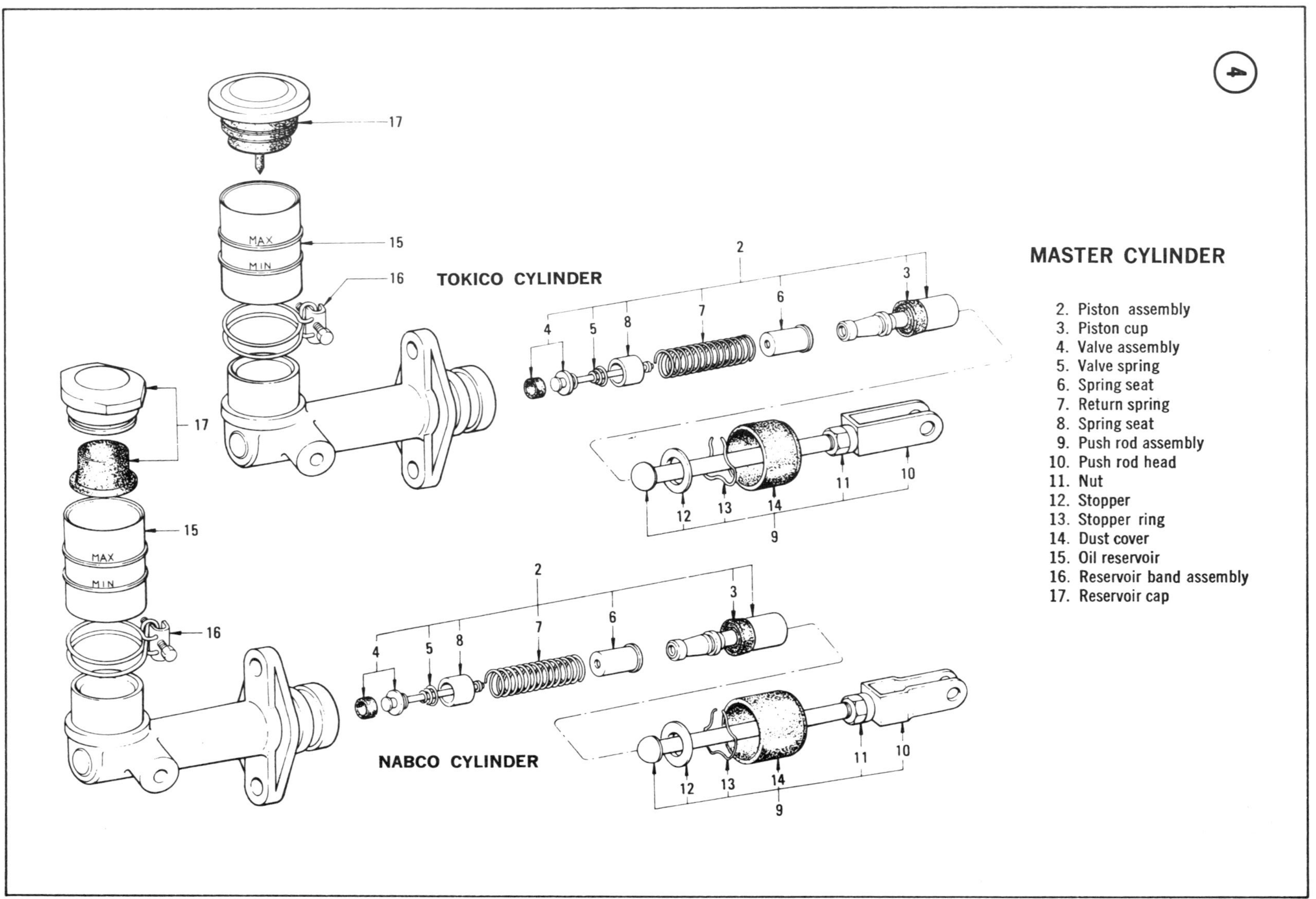
4
MASTER CYLINDER
2. Piston assembly
3. Piston cup
4. Valve assembly
5. Valve spring
6. Spring seat
7. Return spring
8. Spring seat
9. Push rod assembly
10. Push rod head
11. Nut
12. Stopper
13. Stopper ring
14. Dust cover
15. Oil reservoir
16. Reservoir band assembly
17. Reservoir cap
TOKICO CYLINDER
NABCO CYLINDER
MAX
MIN
MAX
MIN

5. Check the dust cover for wear, cracks, or signs of deterioration. Replace if these are detected. Check the fluid reservoir, filler cap, and hydraulic line for wear or damage. Replace as needed.

Assembly

1. Coat the cylinder bore with hydraulic fluid.
2. Install the piston return spring assembly.
3. Soak the piston cup with hydraulic fluid, then install it on the piston. The lip of the cup faces the front of the car when the piston is installed.
4. Coat the piston with hydraulic fluid and insert it into the cylinder. Be careful not to bend back the lip of the piston cup.
5. Place the dust cover on the pushrod. Insert the pushrod and stopper into the cylinder. Install the stopper ring and push the lip of the dust cover over the cylinder.

OPERATING CYLINDER

Early cylinders use an external return spring and an adjustable pushrod. Later models use a non-adjustable pushrod and no return spring.

Removal/Installation

1. Unhook and remove the external spring (if so equipped).
2. With a container handy to catch dripping hydraulic fluid, disconnect the flexible clutch line from the metal tube. See Figure 1.
3. Disconnect the fluid hose from the operating cylinder.
4. Remove 2 cylinder mounting bolts. Separate the pushrod from the clutch withdrawal lever. Take the cylinder out.
5. Installation is the reverse of these steps. Adjust withdrawal lever play (if applicable). Bleed the clutch as described later in this chapter.

Disassembly and Inspection

Figure 5 shows a typical operating cylinder.

1. Remove the dust cover.
2. Remove the snap ring (if so equipped), then take out the piston and cup. Discard the cup.
3. Remove the internal spring (if so equipped).

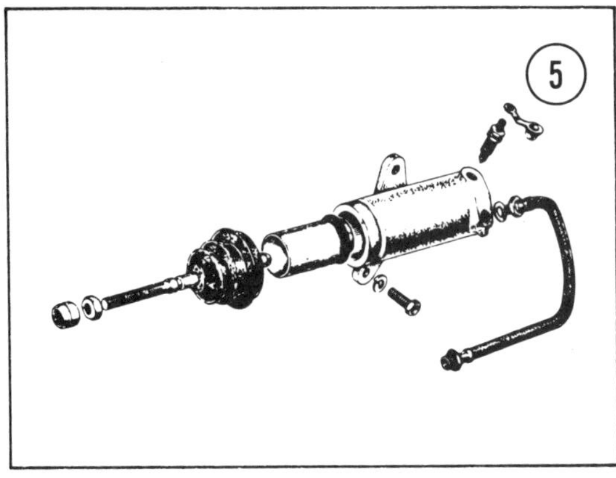
5

4. Remove the bleed valve.
5. Thoroughly clean all parts in brake fluid. Do not use gasoline or kerosene.
6. Check the piston for excessive or uneven wear, scoring, cracks, or corrosion. Replace the piston if these conditions are found.
7. Check the cylinder bore for the defects described in Step 6. Replace the entire cylinder if any of these are found.

Assembly

Assembly is the reverse of the disassembly procedure, plus the following:

1. Soak the piston cup in brake fluid before installation. Make sure the lip of the cup faces into the cylinder before installing.
2. On cylinders with an internal spring, assemble the spring to the piston before installing the spring and piston.
3. Coat the cylinder bore and piston with brake fluid before installing the piston.

WITHDRAWAL LEVER PLAY

Withdrawal lever play is regulated by the length of the operating cylinder pushrod. On adjustable-pushrod models, adjustment is necessary whenever the operating cylinder is removed.

Figure 6 is a cutaway of the operating cylinder, withdrawal lever, and release bearing. Refer to it as needed for this procedure.

1. Loosen the locknut. Rotate the adjusting nut until the top of the withdrawal lever contacts the release bearing inside the clutch housing. All withdrawal lever play should be eliminated.

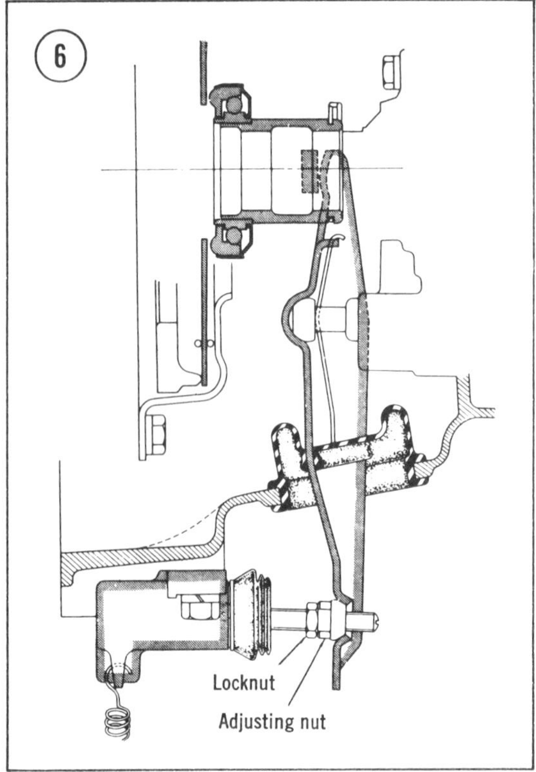

2. Back off the adjusting nut 1¾ turns and secure it with the locknut.

BLEEDING THE CLUTCH

Bleeding air out of the clutch hydraulic system is necessary whenever air enters the system. This occurs when the hydraulic line is disconnected at either end. It can also result from a very low clutch fluid level, or from defective master or operating cylinders. Air in the system can make shifting gears very difficult.

> NOTE: *This procedure requires two people, one to operate the clutch pedal and the other to open and close the bleed valve.*

1. Remove the dust cap from the bleed valve on the operating cylinder.
2. Attach a plastic tube to the bleed valve. Place the other end of the tube in a clear glass jar containing several inches of clean brake fluid.

> NOTE: *Do not allow the end of the tube to come out of the brake fluid during bleeding. If this happens, air may be sucked into the system, and the procedure will have to be repeated.*

3. Top up the clutch master cylinder reservoir with fluid.
4. Have an assistant pump the clutch pedal two or three times, then hold it to the floor.
5. While the pedal is down, open the bleed valve to let air escape. Close the valve before letting the pedal up.
6. Repeat Steps 4 and 5 until the fluid entering the jar is free of air bubbles. Remove the tube, put the dust cover on the bleed valve, and top up the master cylinder.

CLUTCH REMOVAL

The engine and clutch housing must be separated to remove the clutch. This can be done either by removing the engine and transmission and separating them (Chapter Four) or by removing only the transmission (Chapter Nine). The release mechanism is incorporated in the clutch housing (front part of the transmission).

Once the engine and transmission have been separated, do the following:

1. Mark the edges of the pressure plate and flywheel so they may be reassembled in the same relative positions.
2. Remove the clutch cover bolts gradually in a diagonal pattern to prevent warping the pressure plate.

CLUTCH INSPECTION

Clutch Disc

Check the clutch disc for the following:

1. Oil or grease on the facings.
2. Glazed facings.
3. Warped facings.
4. Loose or missing rivets.
5. Facings worn to within 0.012 in. (0.3mm) of any rivet.
6. Broken springs.
7. Loose fit or rough movement on transmission main drive shaft splines.

Small amounts of oil or grease may be removed from the disc with trichloroethylene, and the facings dressed with a wire brush. However, if the facings are soaked with oil or grease, the disc must be replaced. The disc must also be replaced if any of the other defects are present, or if facings are worn and a new pressure plate is being installed.

Pressure Plate

Check the pressure plate for:

1. Scoring
2. Burn marks (blue-tinted areas)
3. Cracks

Replace the pressure plate if these are evident. If the clutch trouble is still not apparent, take the pressure plate and disc to a competent garage. Have the disc and pressure plate checked for excessive runout, and the diaphragm spring for incorrect finger height. Do not attempt to readjust the fingers or dismantle the pressure plate without proper tools and experience.

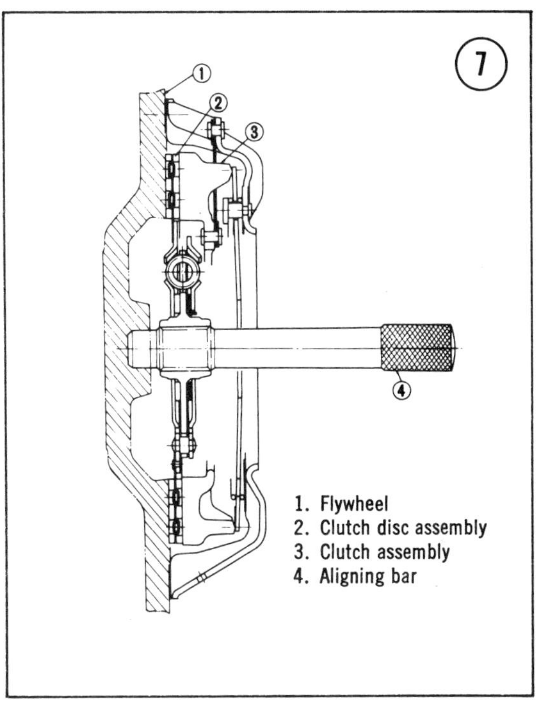

1. Flywheel
2. Clutch disc assembly
3. Clutch assembly
4. Aligning bar

CLUTCH INSTALLATION

1. Be sure your hands are clean.
2. Inspect the disc facings, pressure plate, and flywheel to be sure they are free of grease, oil, or other foreign material.
3. Clean the clutch pilot bushing and fill it with multipurpose grease.
4. Place the clutch disc and pressure plate in position on the flywheel. The long side of the disc hub faces the rear of the car. Line up the alignment marks made during removal.
5. Center the disc and pressure plate with an aligning bar such as the one shown in **Figure 7**. A main drive shaft from a junk transmission can be substituted if special tool isn't available.
6. Install the clutch cover bolts, tightening gradually in a diagonal pattern. Tighten to specifiications given at the end of the chapter.

RELEASE MECHANISM

Removal

As with the clutch, release mechanism removal requires that the engine and transmission be separated first. The release mechanism is mounted in the clutch housing. Either remove the engine and transmission and separate them (Chapter Four) or remove only the transmission (Chapter Nine).

Disassembly

1. Referring to **Figure 8**, remove the dust cover from the clutch housing.

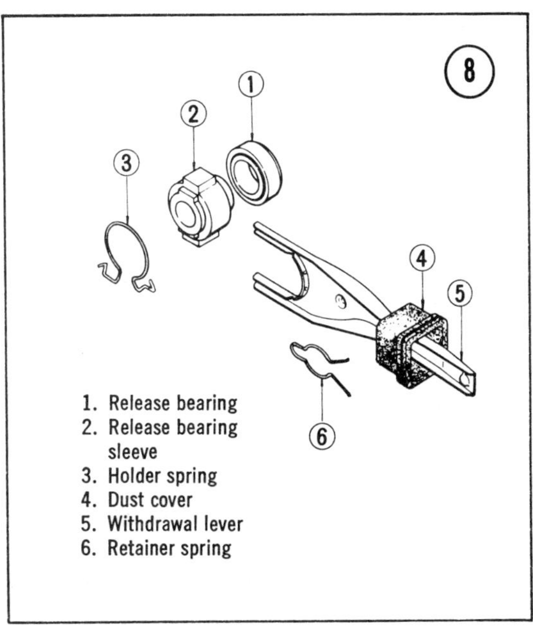

1. Release bearing
2. Release bearing sleeve
3. Holder spring
4. Dust cover
5. Withdrawal lever
6. Retainer spring

2. Remove the holder spring. Take out the release bearing and sleeve.

3. If the operating cylinder has an external return spring, unhook it from withdrawal lever.

4. Detach the retainer spring from the withdrawal lever. Remove the withdrawal lever from its ball pin.

5. Remove the release bearing from its sleeve with a puller (**Figure 9**). The bearing is a press fit on the sleeve.

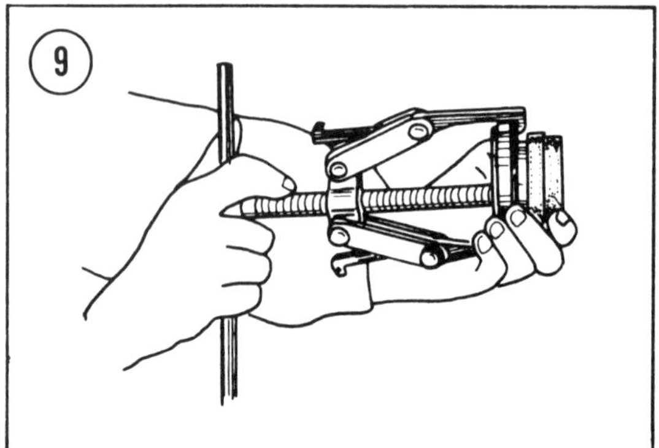

Inspection

Check release mechanism for the following:

1. *Wear at the contact point of the withdrawal lever and release bearing sleeve.* Replace the sleeve if worn.

2. *Grease leaking from the release bearing.* Replace the bearing if this is evident.

CAUTION
Do not clean the release bearing in solvent, since it is prelubricated at the factory. Clean with a lint-free cloth.

3. *A worn release bearing.* To check, hold the inner face with fingers and rotate the outer race while applying light pressure to it. If the bearing feels rough or makes noise, replace it.

Assembly

1. Press the release bearing onto the sleeve (**Figure 10**). When it is in place, rotate the bearing to make sure it operates smoothly.

2. Referring to **Figure 11**, apply a *light* coat of multipurpose grease to the following:

Contact points of withdrawal lever and release bearing sleeve

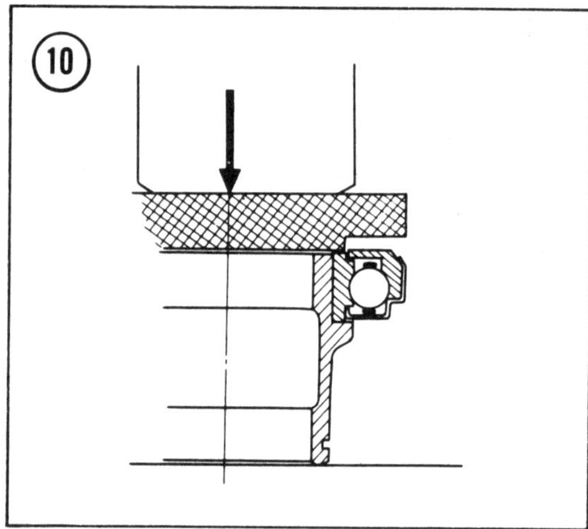

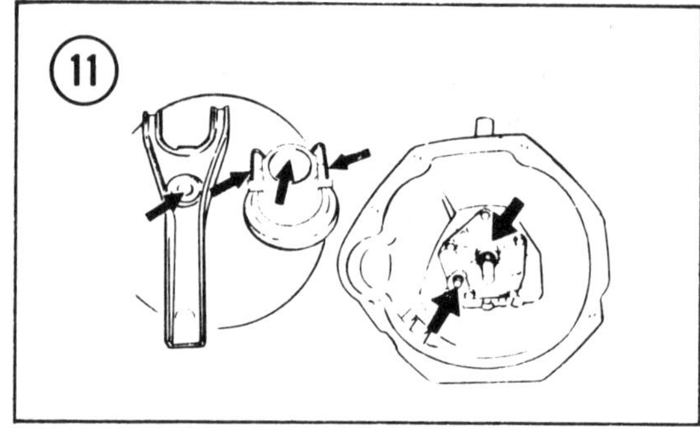

Contact points of withdrawal lever and ball pin

Contact points of release bearing sleeve and transmission front cover

3. Pack the recess inside the bearing sleeve with multipurpose grease. See **Figure 12**.

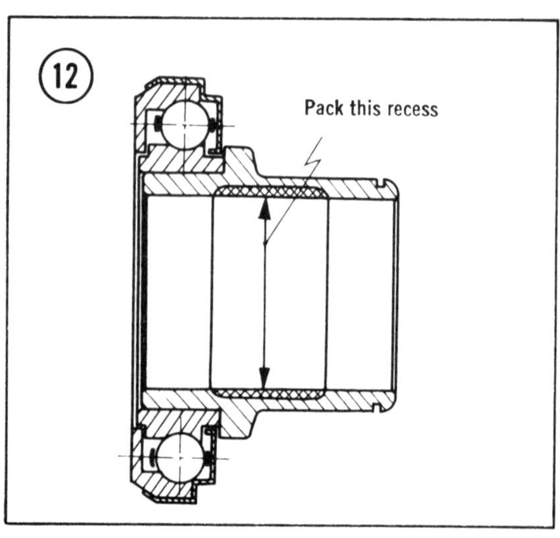

4. Apply a small amount of molybdenum disulphide grease to the transmission main drive shaft splines.

5. Place the withdrawal lever in position over the transmission main drive shaft, with the operating cylinder end through the hole in the clutch housing.

6. Position the release bearing and sleeve on the withdrawal lever. Install the holder spring.

7. Install the dust cover in the clutch housing.

8. If the operating cylinder uses an external return spring, attach it to the withdrawal lever.

9. Install the transmission as described in Chapter Nine.

10. Bleed air from the clutch hydraulic system as described earlier in this chapter.

11. Check and adjust pedal height as described earlier.

12. On cars with adjustable operating cylinders, adjust withdrawal lever play as described earlier.

Table 1 CLUTCH SPECIFICATIONS

Disc diameter	7.87 in. (200mm)
Master cylinder bore diameter	5/8 in. (15.87mm)
Tightening torque, clutch cover bolts	
510	17½-19 ft.-lbs. (2.4-2.6 mkg)
1973-74 610	12-16 ft.-lbs. (1.6-2.2 mkg)
1975-76 610, all 710's	12-15 ft.-lbs. (1.6-2.1 mkg)

CHAPTER NINE

TRANSMISSION

All models use a 4-speed manual transmission as standard equipment. A 3-speed automatic is optional. This chapter includes removal and inspection procedures for the manual transmission, as well as testing and adjustment procedures for the automatic.

MANUAL TRANSMISSION

Removal/Installation

1. Disconnect the negative cable from battery.
2. Remove the console (if so equipped). Remove the shift lever hole cover from the floor.
3. Remove the nut from the base of the shift lever (**Figure 1**).

4. Jack up all 4 corners of the vehicle and place it on jackstands. Be sure the stands are securely positioned.
5. Drain the transmission oil. If this isn't done, the oil will run onto the floor when the transmission is removed.
6. Remove the drive shaft (Chapter Eleven).
7. On 1975-76 California cars, remove the catalytic converter heat shield. On all 610's and 710's, disconnect both ends of the front exhaust tube.
8. Disconnect the wires from the reverse lamp switch, third gear switch, and neutral switch (if so equipped). **Figure 2** shows the reverse and neutral switches. The third gear switch is similar.

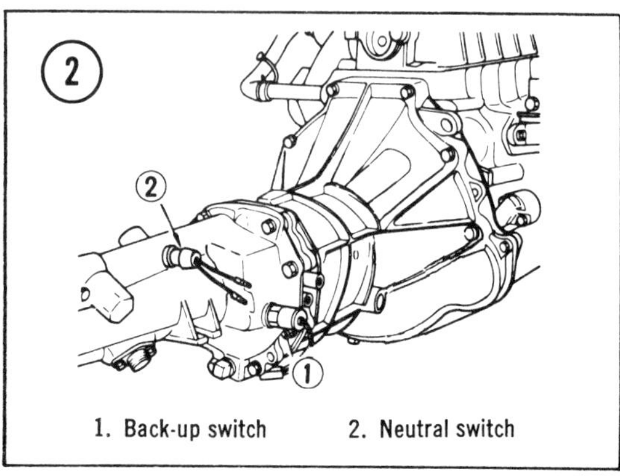

1. Back-up switch 2. Neutral switch

9. Detach the speedometer cable from the rear extension.

10. Remove clutch operating cylinder (Chapter Eight).

11. Remove the starter (Chapter Seven).

12. Place a jack beneath the engine. Use a block of wood beneath the jack and oil pan to prevent damage.

13. Place a transmission jack beneath the transmission. These are available from rental dealers.

14. Detach the mounting member from the vehicle frame, then from the transmission. **Figure 3** shows a typical mounting member.

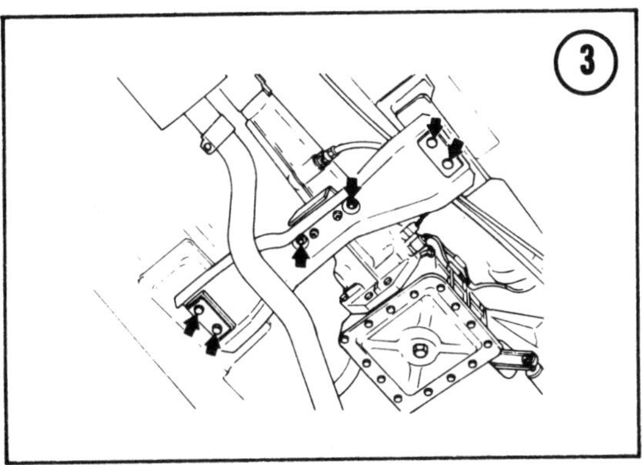

15. On 610 sedans and hardtops and all 710's, unbolt the gussets from the engine block and clutch housing (**Figure 4**).

16. Remove the engine-to-transmission bolts.

17. Lower the jacks beneath the engine and transmission. Slide the transmission backward and down until it is clear of the engine. Lower transmission and take it out from under the car.

CAUTION

To prevent damage to the transmission main drive gear, never remove the transmission partway. Be sure the main drive gear seperates completely from the engine when removing transmission.

18. Install by reversing Steps 1-17. Tighten nuts and bolts to specifications (Table 2, end of chapter). Fill the transmission with an oil recommended in Chapter Two. Fill and bleed the clutch hydraulic system. If the vehicle has an adjustable-pushrod operating cylinder, adjust withdrawal lever play. See Chapter Eight.

Inspection

1. Before cleaning, check the transmission for oil leaks. Check at front and rear ends of the transmission, as well as at the mating surfaces of transmission case and rear extension.

2. Clean the transmission with solvent.

3. Examine the clutch release mechanism (Chapter Eight). This is also a good time to inspect the clutch disc and pressure plate, especially if there is oil in the clutch housing.

4. Check the shaft at each end of the transmission for movement. Loose, wobbly shafts indicate worn transmission bearings.

5. Remove the inspection cover from the bottom of the transmission. Loosen the bolts a little at a time to prevent warping the cover.

6. Check the internal transmission parts for obvious wear or damage. If you aren't sure what to look for, this can be done by a mechanic for a nominal fee.

7. If you have a dial indicator, mount it as shown in **Figure 5** and measure gear backlash. To measure, hold the mainshaft from turning. Turn the countershaft against the dial indicator's plunger as far as possible without turning the mainshaft. The gauge reading is gear backlash. Repeat the procedure for the other gears. Backlash should be 0.002-0.008 in. (0.05-0.20mm). If incorrect, the mainshaft gear and countershaft gear must be replaced as a set.

8. Unless the transmission is being replaced or overhauled, use a new gasket when installing the inspection cover. Coat the gasket on both sides with gasket sealer. Tighten the cover bolts

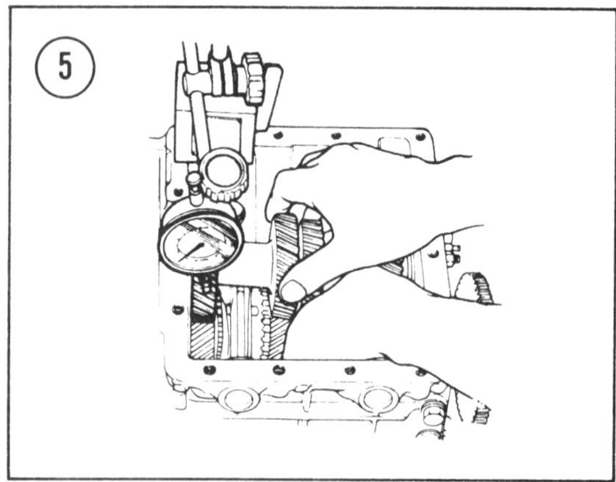

evenly, a little at a time, to specifications (Table 1), end of chapter.

AUTOMATIC TRANSMISSION

Sedans through car No. PL510-117463 and wagons through car No. WPL510-853594 use the British-made Borg Warner model 35 (Letchworth) automatic transmission.

Sedans from car No. PL510-117464 and wagons from car No. WPL510-853595 use the American-made Borg Warner Model 41 (Muncie) automatic. However, the Model 35 torque converter is still used.

The 1972-1976 vehicles use the Nissan Model 3N71B automatic, made by Japan Automatic Transmission Company.

Many automatic transmission problems can be corrected by the simple adjustments described in this section. Automatic transmission repair, however, requires professional skills, many special tools, and extremely high standards of cleanliness. Jobs requiring disassembly should be left to a Datsun dealer or competent automatic transmission specialist.

Fluid Level Check

1. Warm the engine to normal operating temperature. Do this by driving at least 15 miles (Borg Warner) or letting the engine idle for at least 10 minutes (3N71B).

> NOTE: *On some models, the dipstick has 2 scales, labeled* HOT *and* COLD. *The cold scale may be used instead of warming up the engine.*

2. Move the shift lever through all gear positions to P. Leave the engine running.

> NOTE: *On Borg Warner Model 41 transmissions, the fluid level can be checked with the engine off. The level shown on the dipstick will be approximately ¼ in. higher than it would be with the engine running.*

3. Pull out the dipstick, located at the rear of the engine compartment on the right-hand side. Fluid level should be at the H or F mark. If necessary, add fluid through the dipstick tube to raise fluid level. Use Type A fluid *only* in Model 35 transmissions; use Dexron fluid *only* in Model 41 and 3N71B transmissions.

CAUTION

Do not fill the transmission past the upper line on the dipstick. Overfilling can cause the fluid to foam, resulting in wear and damage.

4. Examine the fluid on the dipstick. Clean transmission fluid is a transparent red. If the fluid has deteriorated to a varnish-like condition, it may cause the control valves to stick. Black fluid may indicate a burned clutch or a burned brake band.

Linkage Adjustment

1. Move the shift lever back and forth from 1 to P (or L to P) several times. A slight click should be heard and felt at each gear position.
2. Place the shift lever in N. Detach the shift lever from the linkage. **Figure 6** shows the floor shift linkage; **Figure 7** shows the column shift linkage.
3. Working beneath the car, make sure the range selector lever on the side of the transmission is in N. On Borg Warner transmissions, this occurs when the lever is in the center of the 5 detents. On 3N71B transmissions, this occurs when the slot in the range selector lever is vertical.
4. Adjust the linkage so the shift lever in the car and the range selector lever on the transmission are in N at the same time. Adjust floor linkages with the joint trunnion nuts (4, Figure 6). Adjust column linkages with the selector rod adjusting nut (13, Figure 7).

AUTOMATIC TRANSMISSION FLOOR SHIFT LINKAGE

(6)

1. Range selector
2. Selector rod
3. Joint trunnion
4. Control lever bracket

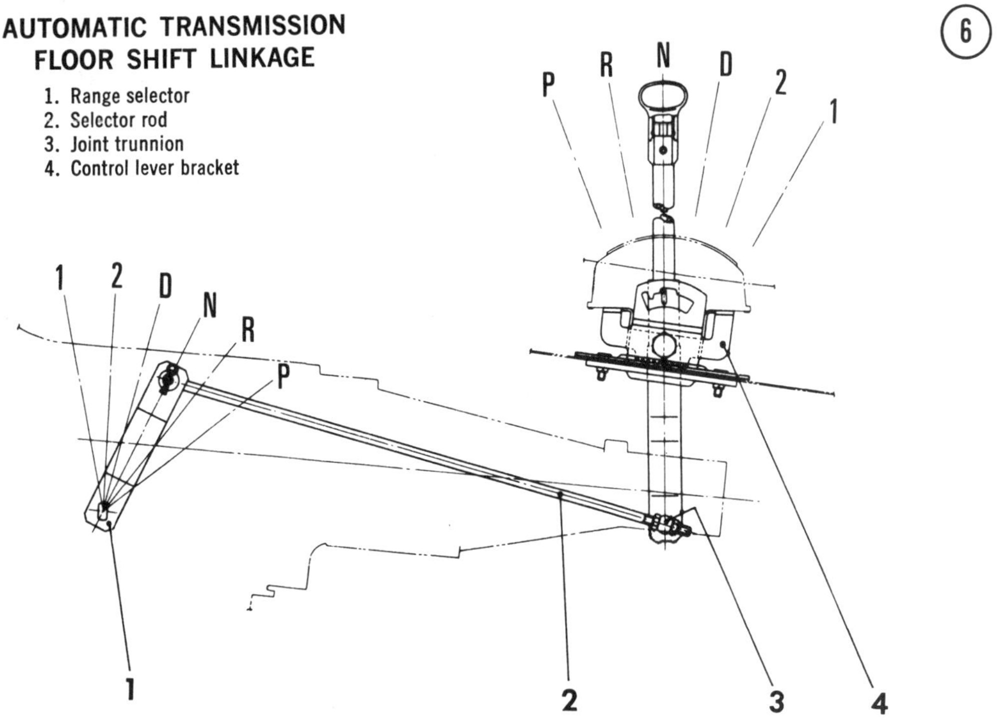

Starter Inhibitor Switch (Borg Warner)

If the starter operates in any gear other than N or P, or if the reverse lamps light in any gear other than R, check linkage adjustment. If the linkage is adjusted properly, check the starter inhibitor switch. The switch is mounted on the left side of the transmission case.

1. Securely block both front wheels so the car will not roll in either direction. Jack up the rear end of the car and place jackstands beneath the axle.
2. Sketch the inhibitor switch wires so they can be reconnected properly, then disconnect them from the switch.
3. Connect the wires from terminals 1 and 3 together. Do the same with the wires from terminals 2 and 4. **Figure 8** shows the terminal numbers. The starter and reverse lamps should now operate in any gear position.

WARNING

Lower the car onto its wheels before operating the starter. Otherwise, the vibration may knock the car off the jackstands. Do not operate the starter in any gear other than N or P, or the car may take off suddenly.

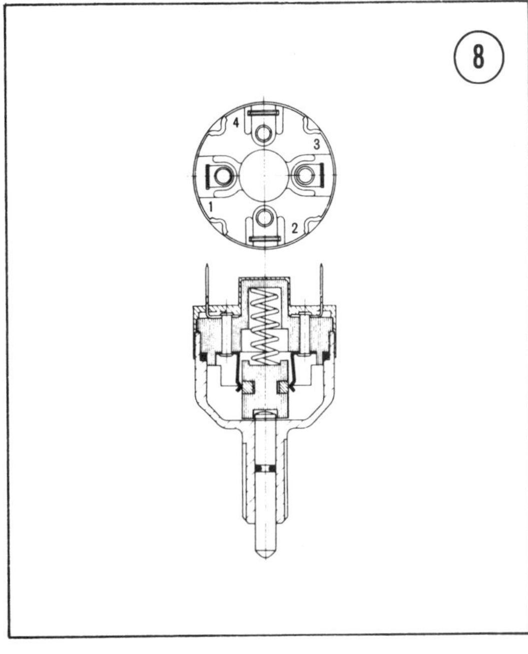

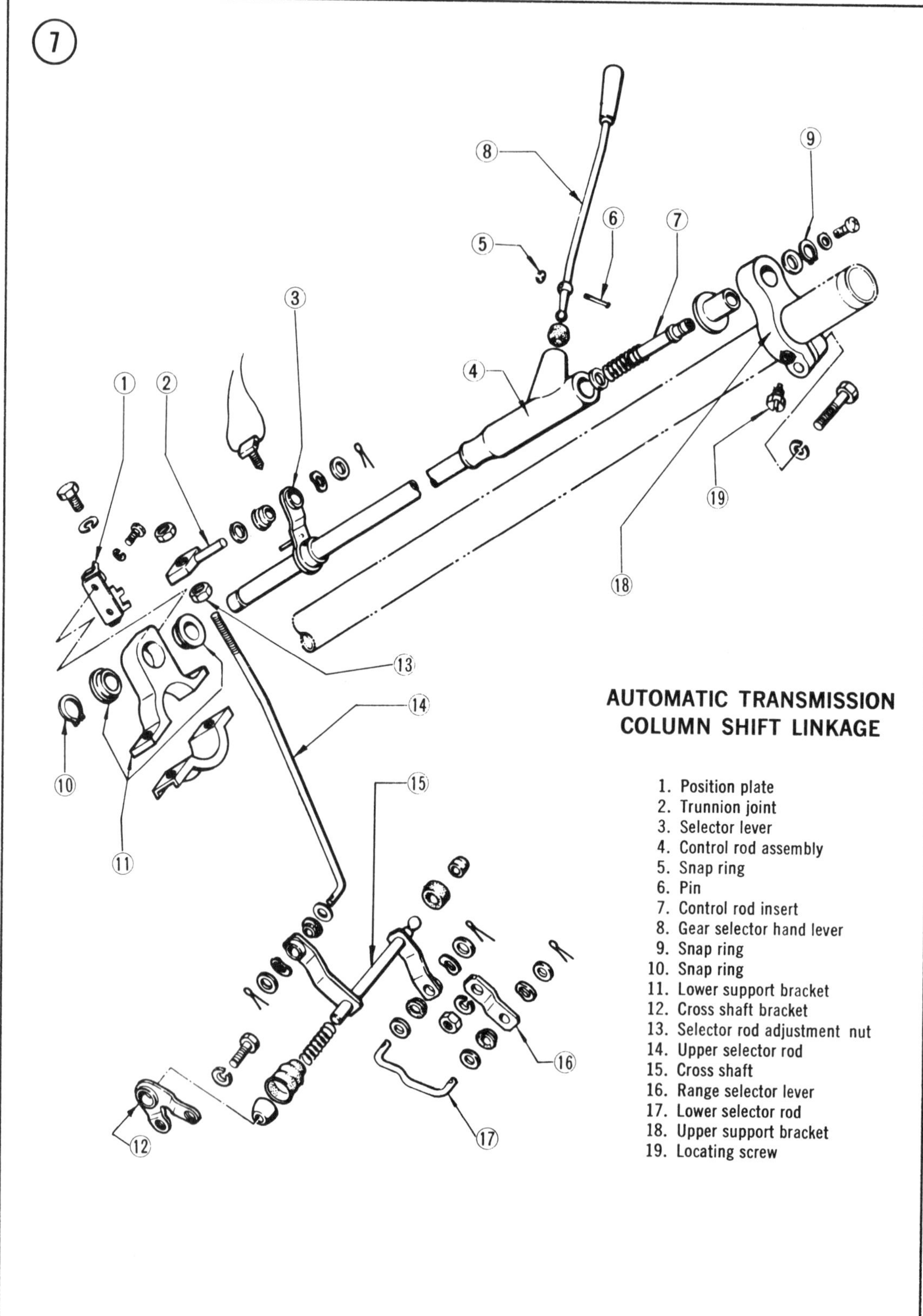
7
AUTOMATIC TRANSMISSION
COLUMN SHIFT LINKAGE
1. Position plate
2. Trunnion joint
3. Selector lever
4. Control rod assembly
5. Snap ring
6. Pin
7. Control rod insert
8. Gear selector hand lever
9. Snap ring
10. Snap ring
11. Lower support bracket
12. Cross shaft bracket
13. Selector rod adjustment nut
14. Upper selector rod
15. Cross shaft
16. Range selector lever
17. Lower selector rod
18. Upper support bracket
19. Locating screw

If the starter and reverse lamps now operate, the starter inhibitor switch is probably out of adjustment. If the problem still exists, the car's wiring may be defective.

4. Loosen the locknuts behind the switch. Use an open-end wrench or a special socket such as Datsun tool ST 25390000 (**Figure 9**).

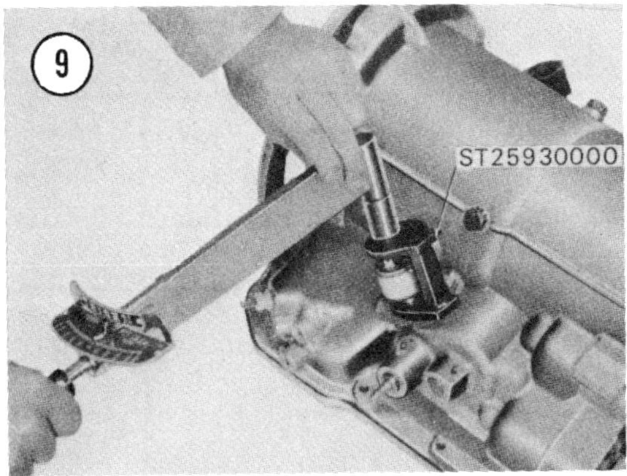

5. On Model 35 transmissions, connect an ohmmeter or self-powered test lamp across terminals 2 and 4. On Model 41 transmissions, connect the tester across terminals 1 and 3. Screw the switch in until the test lamp goes out (ohmmeter shows open-circuit). At this point, make match marks on switch body and transmission case.

6. Move the tester wires to the 2 remaining switch terminals. Again, screw the switch in until the test lamp goes out (ohmmeter shows open-circuit). Mark the switch position in relation to the transmission case.

7. Turn the switch back to halfway between the 2 marks, then tighten the locknut to 5 ft.-lb. Connect the wires to the switch.

8. Make sure the starter operates only in N and P, and the reverse lamps light only in R. If the problem still exists, replace the starter inhibitor switch.

Starter Inhibitor Switch (3N71B)

If the starter operates in any gear other than N and P, or if the reverse lamps light in any gear other than R, check linkage adjustment. If the linkage is adjusted correctly, check the inhibitor switch.

1. Detach the range selector lever (9, **Figure 10**) from the transmission shift linkage. Move the range selector lever to the N position. This occurs when the slot in the lever is vertical.

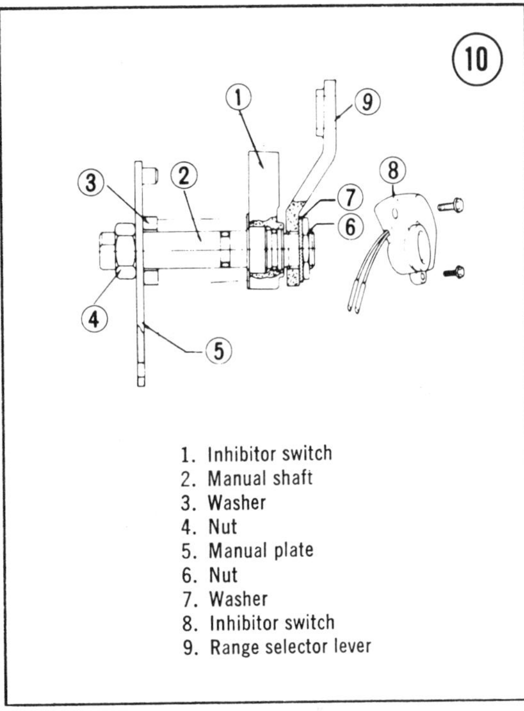

1. Inhibitor switch
2. Manual shaft
3. Washer
4. Nut
5. Manual plate
6. Nut
7. Washer
8. Inhibitor switch
9. Range selector lever

2. Attach an ohmmeter or self-powered test lamp to the black-and-yellow inhibitor switch wires. The ohmmeter should indicate continuity (test lamp should light) while the range selector lever is within 3° of the N position.

3. Repeat Step 2 with the range selector lever in the P position.

4. Move the lever to the R position, and connect the tester to the red-and-black wires on the inhibitor switch. Again, the tester should indicate continuity in a 3° range on either side of the R position.

5. If the tester shows continuity when the lever is obviously more than 3° away from the N, R, or P positions, adjust the inhibitor switch. To do this, first move the range selector lever to the N position. Then remove the lever retaining nut (6, Figure 10), 2 inhibitor switch installation bolts, and the machine screw under the switch. Align the machine screw hole with the pinhole in the manual shaft (2, Figure 10). Check the alignment by inserting a drill bit or piece of

wire 0.059 in. (1.5mm) thick through the 2 holes. Then install the switch bolts, pull out the wire, and install the machine screw. Install the nut on the manual shaft and recheck switch adjustment as described in Steps 2, 3, and 4.

6. If the switch doesn't work properly after adjustment, replace it.

Kickdown Cable Adjustment (Borg Warner Model 35)

1. Connect an oil pressure gauge to the line pressure outlet at the left rear corner of the transmission case (**Figure 11**). This is an inch fitting (not metric). Place the gauge where it can be seen from the driver's seat.

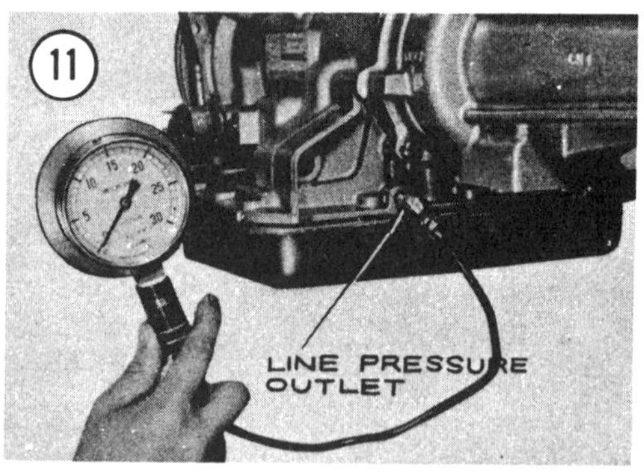

2. Start the car and place it in D. When engine speed is increased from 500 rpm to 1,000 rpm, line pressure should rise 15-20 psi. If pressure increase is below 15 psi, turn the adjuster on the carburetor end of the cable (**Figure 12**) to decrease effective cable length. If pressure increases more than 20 psi, turn the adjuster to increase the cable's effective length.

> NOTE: *The cable is impregnated with molybdenum disulphide or graphite. Do not oil it.*

Kickdown Switch Adjustment (Borg Warner Model 41, Jatco Model 3N71B)

The kickdown switch is located on a bracket beneath the instrument panel. **Figure 13** shows the Jatco switch and downshift solenoid. The Borg Warner version is similar.

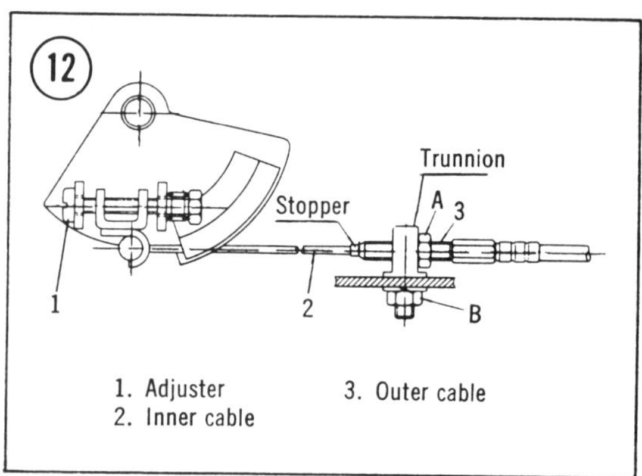

1. Adjuster
2. Inner cable
3. Outer cable

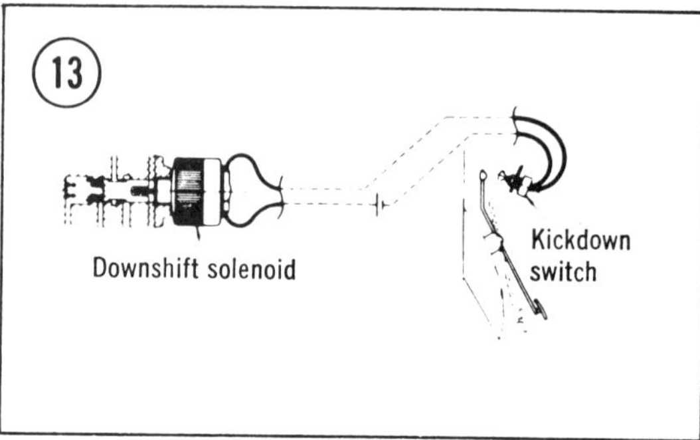

1. Disconnect the wires from the kickdown switch. Connect an ohmmeter or self-powered test lamp between them.

2. Floor the accelerator. The ohmmeter should show continuity (test lamp should light). If not, adjust switch position. Replace the switch if it fails to respond to adjustment.

Table 1
MANUAL TRANSMISSION TIGHTENING TORQUES

	Ft.-lb.	mkg
Engine-to-transmission bolts		
510	18-29	2.5-4.0
610 and 710	29-35	4.0-4.8
Transmission-to-gusset bolts (610 and 710 sedans and hardtops, 710 wagons)	2½-3	0.32-0.44
Shift lever nut	14-16	1.9-2.2
Speedometer pinion bolt	2-3	0.3-0.4
Front and bottom covers		
510	8-13	1.1-1.8
All others	6-7	0.8-1.0
Electrical switches	14-22	2-3

CHAPTER TEN

BRAKES

All models use disc brakes at the front and drum brakes at the rear. The front brakes are single-piston floating caliper types. The rear brakes use single-piston wheel cylinders.

A Master-Vac brake booster is used on 610's and 710's. The 610's and 710's also use a proportioning valve to prevent premature rear wheel lockup. The handbrake on all models is a mechanical type that operates the rear brakes.

Specifications (**Table 1**) and tightening torques (**Table 2**) are found at the end of the chapter.

DISC BRAKES (1968-74)

Figure 1 is an exploded view of the disc brake assembly. Refer to it as needed for the following procedures.

Pad Replacement

The pads should be checked for wear at intervals specified in Chapter Two. Pads should be replaced when the friction material is worn to 0.039 in. (1mm) or less.

1. Loosen the front wheel nuts, jack up the front end of the car, place it on jackstands, and remove the front wheels.
2. Remove the pad retaining clip (**Figure 2**).

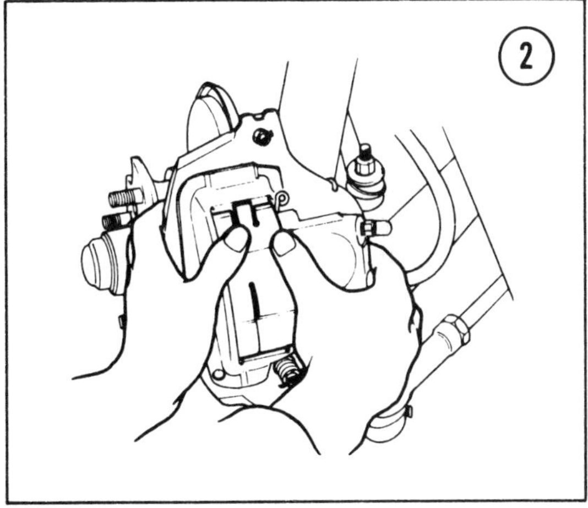

3. Insert a screwdriver between the outer pad and caliper plate. Pry the caliper plate outward as far as it will go.
4. Pull the pads out.
5. Inspect the pads for wear and damage caused by overheating. Check for grease, oil, or brake fluid on the friction material. If the pads are only slightly oily or greasy, and not excessively worn, they can be cleaned in trichloroethylene and reused. If they are saturated with oil or grease, wet with brake fluid, or damaged from overheating, replace the pads. Always replace pads in full sets.

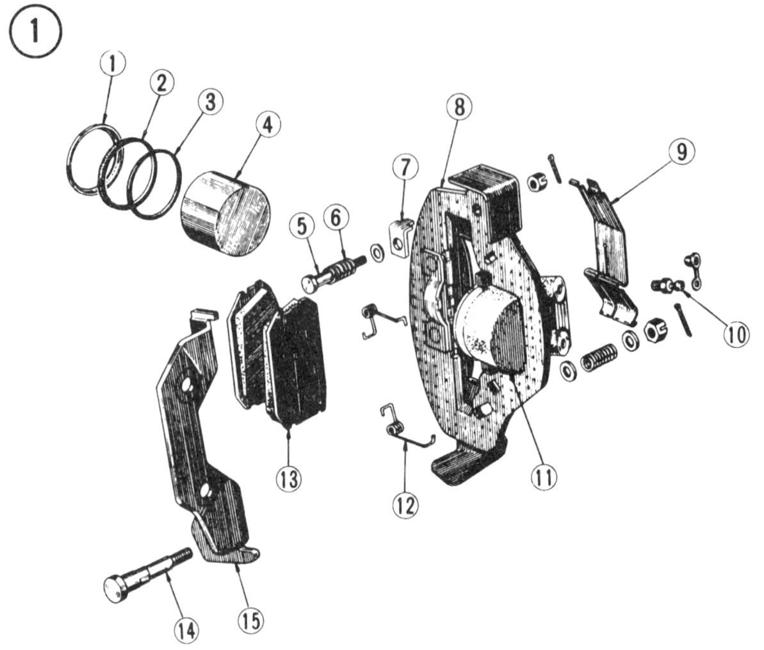

1. Retainer
2. Wiper seal
3. Piston seal
4. Piston
5. Hold-down pin
6. Spring
7. Supporting bracket
8. Caliper plate
9. Clip
10. Bleeder screw
11. Cylinder
12. Torsion spring
13. Pad
14. Mounting bracket
15. Pivot pin

DISC BRAKE ASSEMBLY

6. Carefully clean out the space which holds the brake pads. Inspect the cylinder. If the piston appears dirty or rusty, recondition the caliper as described later. The caliper must also be overhauled if brake fluid has been leaking past the piston seals.

7. Place rags beneath the master cylinder in case it overflows. Open the caliper bleed valve far enough to let brake fluid escape. Press the piston into the cylinder far enough to install the pads. Close the bleed valves.

8. Install the pads and anti-squeal shim. Install the pad retaining clip.

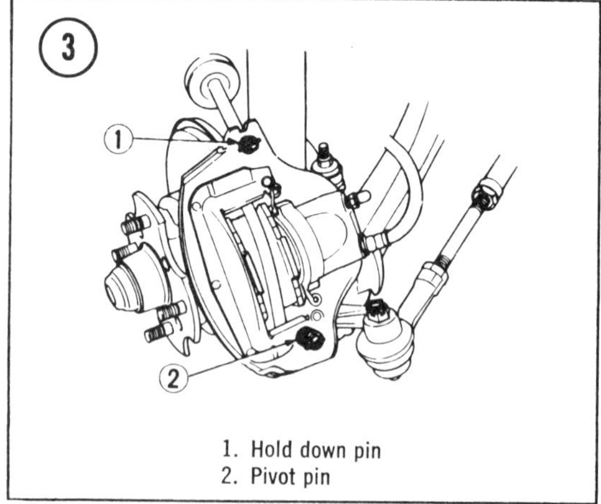

1. Hold down pin
2. Pivot pin

Caliper Removal

1. Remove the brake pads as described earlier. Disconnect the brake hose from its connection to the metal brake line, then unscrew it from the caliper.

2. Remove the cotter pins from the hold-down and pivot pins (**Figure 3**). Remove the nuts and take the pins out.

3. Separate the caliper assembly from its mounting bracket.

4. If necessary, remove 2 bolts attaching the mounting bracket to the car (**Figure 4**).

Caliper Disassembly

1. Thoroughly clean the outside of the caliper before disassembly.

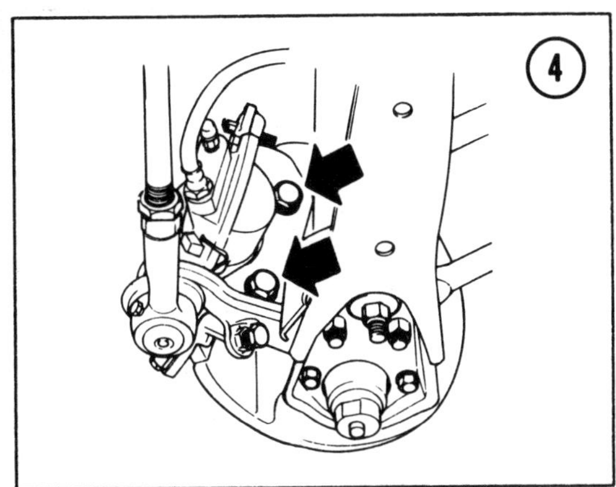

2. Remove the torsion springs (**Figure 5**). Remove the cylinder from the caliper plate.

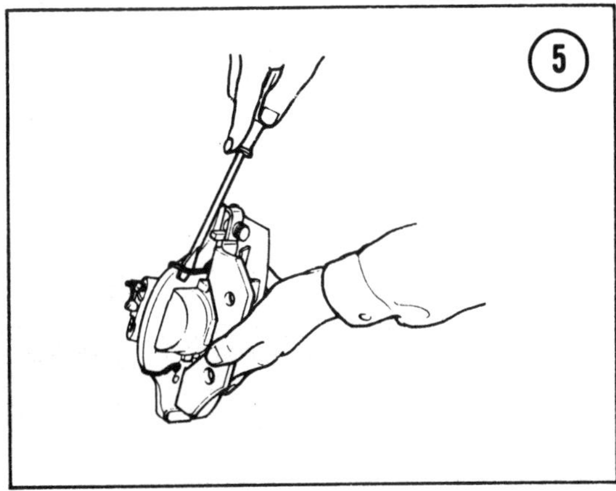

3. Point the piston at a block of wood. Blow compressed air into the brake hose hole to force the piston out. Use a service station air hose if you don't have a compressor.

WARNING

The piston may come out with considerable force. Be sure your fingers are out of the way.

4. Remove the retainer, wiper seal, and piston seal from the cylinder bore.

Inspection and Repair

1. Thoroughly clean all parts in alcohol or brake fluid before inspection. Do not use gasoline or kerosene.

CAUTION

Do not allow brake fluid to come in contact with brake pads. Brake fluid will ruin the pads, and they will have to be replaced.

2. Inspect the pads as described earlier under *Pad Replacement*.
3. Check the cylinder walls for wear or damage. If these conditions are apparent, replace the cylinder. The cylinder must also be replaced if walls are excessively corroded. Slight amounts of corrosion may be removed with fine emery paper.
4. Check the piston for excessive or uneven wear, damage, scoring, or corrosion. Replace the piston if these are evident.

NOTE: *The piston friction surface is chrome plated. Therefore, the piston cannot be cleaned with emery paper. If the pistons cannot be cleaned with solvent and a rag, replace them.*

5. Discard the wiper and piston seals. They must be replaced whenever the cylinder is disassembled.

Caliper Assembly

1. Coat a new piston seal with rubber grease. Using only your fingers, carefully install the piston seal, wiper seal, and retainer in the cylinder.

NOTE: *Never reuse a piston seal. In addition to preventing brake fluid leaks, the seals retract the pistons when the brake pedal is let up. They are also critical to self-adjustment of the front brakes. Very minor damage or age deterioration can make the seals useless.*

2. Apply a thin coat of rubber grease to the piston. Install it in the cylinder.
3. Slide the cylinder into the caliper plate. Secure it with the torsion springs.

Caliper Installation

1. If the caliper mounting bracket was removed, bolt it to the steering knuckle (Figure 4). Tighten the bolts to 53-65 ft.-lb. (7.3-9.0 mkg) on 510's; or 53-72 ft.-lb. (7.3-9.9 mkg), 610's and 710's.
2. Position the caliper plate next to the mounting bracket. Secure it with the pivot pin and hold-down pin.

3. Install the pads as described earlier in this chapter.

4. Bleed the brakes as described later in this chapter.

5. Press the brake pedal several times to seat the pads. Make sure the caliper plate moves smoothly and that there are no fluid leaks.

Disc Inspection

1. Loosen the front wheel nuts, jack up the front end of the car, place it on jackstands, and remove the front wheels.

2. Remove the caliper as described earlier.

3. Check wheel bearing adjustment as described in Chapter Twelve.

4. With a dial gauge contacting the center of the disc's swept area (**Figure 6**), rotate the disc one full turn and measure runout. Maximum permissible runout (total indicator reading) is 0.0024 in. (0.06mm) on 510's and 710's; or 0.0048 in. (0.12mm) on 610's.

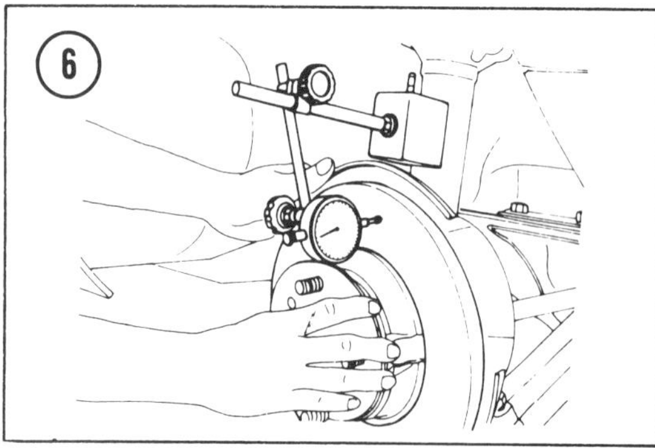

5. Measure parallelism around the circumference of the disc. Use a micrometer contacting the center of the disc's swept area (**Figure 7**). Variation in thickness around the disc should be within 0.0012 in. (0.03mm) if the disc is new. Maximum permissible thickness variation is 0.0028 in. (0.07mm). If the variation exceeds this limit, have the disc turned to correct it. Do not cut the disc thinner than 0.331 in. (8.4mm).

6. Using the micrometer, measure the thickness of the disc at several points around the circumference and at varying distances from the center. Normal disc thickness is 0.394 in. (10mm). If the disc is thinner than 0.331 in. (8.4mm), replace it.

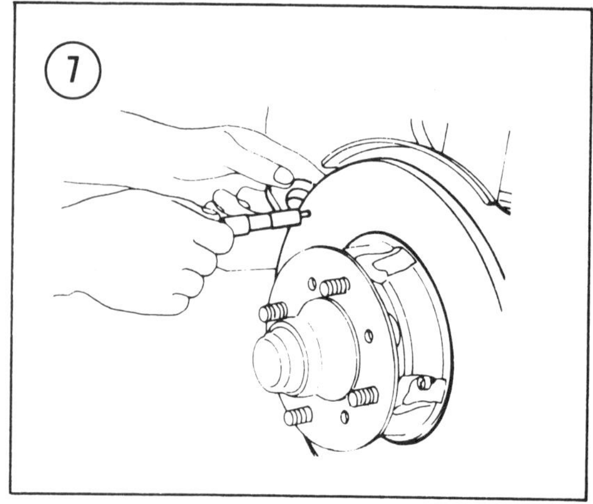

Disc Removal/Installation

1. Loosen the front wheel nuts, jack up the front end of the car, place it on jackstands, and remove the front wheels.

2. Remove the caliper as described earlier.

3. Remove the wheel bearing grease cap and locknut as described in Chapter Twelve.

4. Remove the brake disc together with the wheel hub (**Figure 8**).

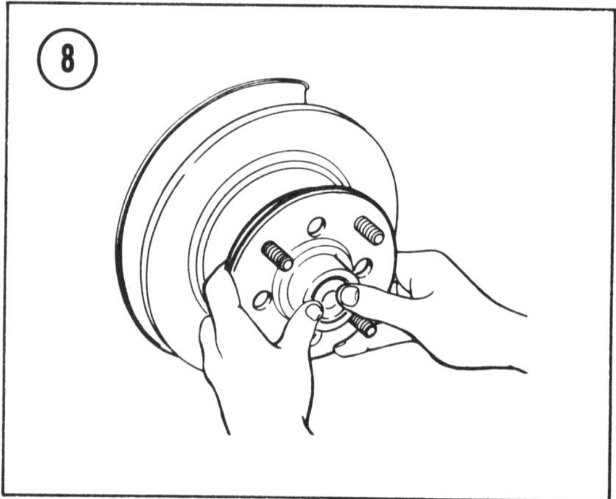

5. Remove 4 bolts and separate the brake disc from the hub (**Figure 9**).

6. Bolt the disc to the hub. Tighten the bolts to 28-38 ft.-lb. (3.9-5.3 mkg).

7. Repack and adjust the wheel bearings as described in Chapter Twelve.

8. Install the caliper.

9. Install the front wheels, lower the car, and bleed brakes as described later in this chapter.

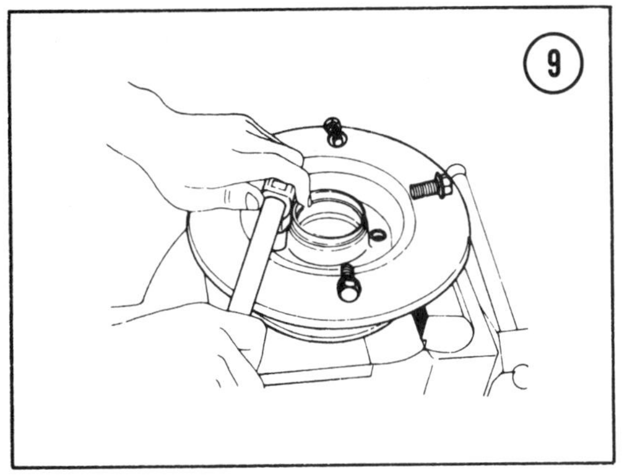

DISC BRAKES (1975-76 610)

Figure 10 shows the disc brake design used on 1975-76 610's.

Pad Replacement (1975-76 610)

1. Loosen the front wheel nuts, jack up the front end of the car, place it on jackstands, and remove the front wheels.
2. Remove the retaining clip from each retaining pin.
3. Pull the retaining pins out, then remove the pad springs.
4. Remove the pads with pliers (**Figure 11**).

CAUTION

Do not press the brake pedal with the pads removed, or the pistons will fall out.

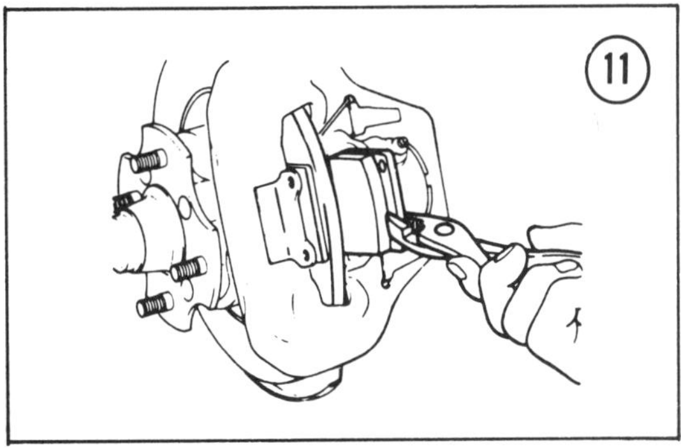

5. Inspect pads. A light layer of grease or dirt may be sanded off or removed with trichloroethylene. If dirt or grease is heavy, or if pad friction material is worn to 0.079 in. (2mm) or less, replace the pads.

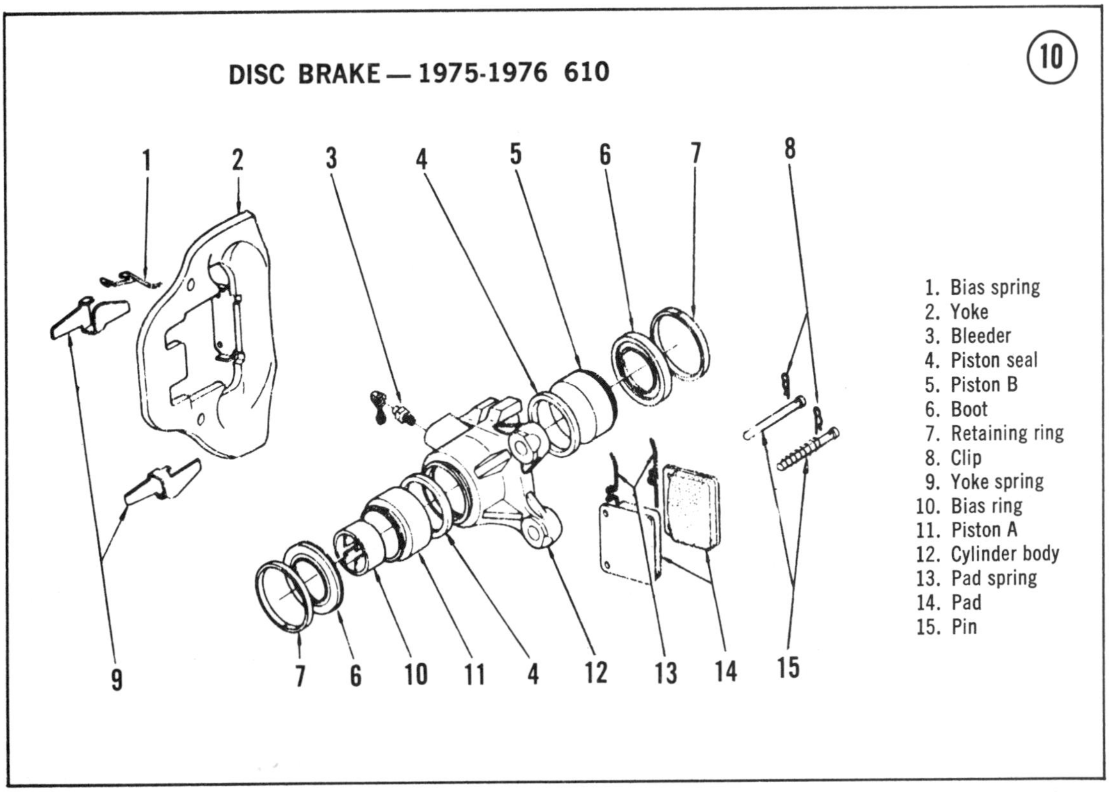

(10)

DISC BRAKE—1975-1976 610

1 2 3 4 5 6 7 8

9 7 6 10 11 4 12 13 14 15

1. Bias spring
2. Yoke
3. Bleeder
4. Piston seal
5. Piston B
6. Boot
7. Retaining ring
8. Clip
9. Yoke spring
10. Bias ring
11. Piston A
12. Cylinder body
13. Pad spring
14. Pad
15. Pin

> NOTE: *Always replace pads in sets of 4.*

6. Carefully clean out the space which holds the brake pads. Inspect the cylinder. If brake fluid has leaked from the cylinder, overhaul the caliper as described later.

7. Open the caliper bleed valve. Push piston B into the cylinder (**Figure 12**). Push piston A into the cylinder by pulling on the yoke (**Figure 13**). This makes room to install the pads.

> CAUTION
> *Do not push the pistons in past the seals, or they will hang up on the seals (**Figure 14**). If this happens, the caliper will have to be disassembled to install new seals.*

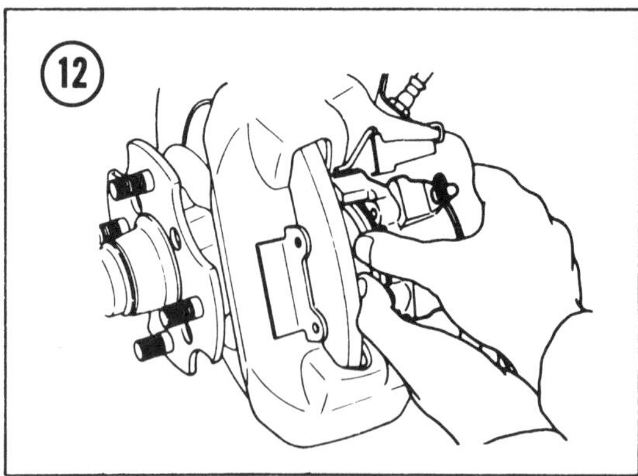

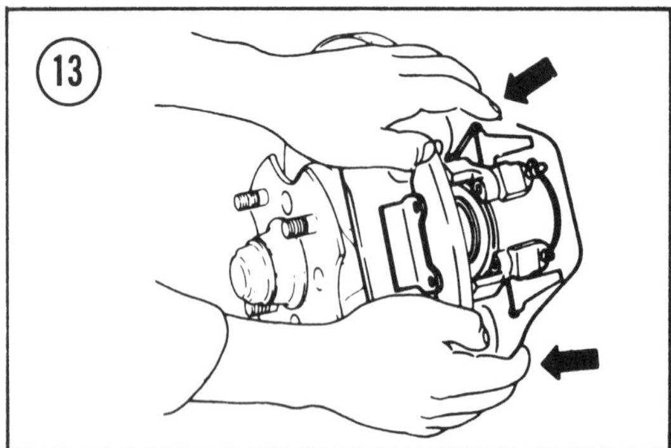

8. Once the pistons are pushed in, close the bleed valve. Wipe up any spilled brake fluid.

9. Install the pads and pad springs. Install the retaining pins, with the coil spring on the lower pin.

10. Secure the retaining pins with the retaining clips.

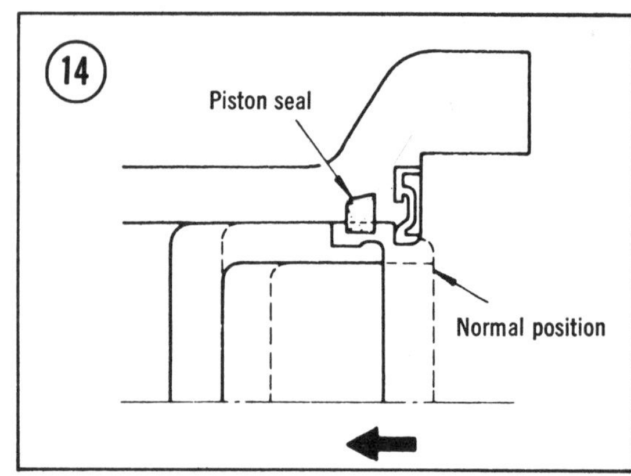

11. Install the wheels and lower the car. Pump the brake pedal several times to seat the pads.

Caliper Removal/Installation

Refer to Figure 10 for this procedure.

1. Remove the brake pads as described in the previous procedure.

2. Disconnect the metal brake line from the caliper.

> NOTE: *The factory recommends using special tool GG94310000 (brake line torque wrench, **Figure 15**) when connecting and disconnecting brake lines. Never use an adjustable wrench.*

3. Remove caliper mounting bolts (**Figure 16**).

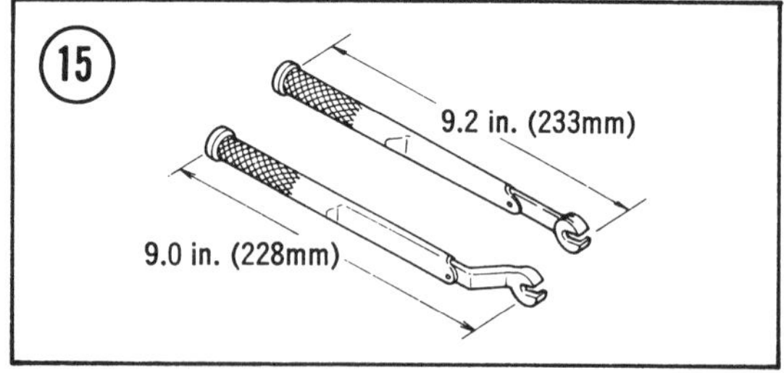

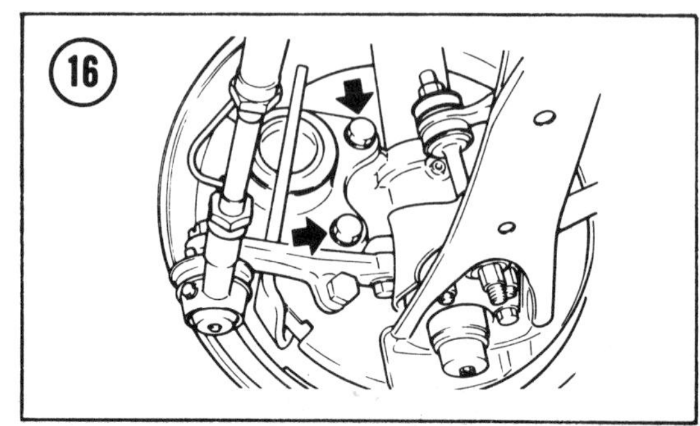

4. Install in the reverse order. Tighten caliper mounting bolts to 53-72 ft.-lb. (7.3-9.9 mkg). Tighten the brake line nut(s) to 11-13 ft.-lb. (1.5-1.8 mkg). Bleed the brakes as described under *Brake Bleeding* later in this chapter.

Caliper Overhaul (1975-76 610)

Refer to Figure 10 for this procedure.

1. Remove the caliper as described in the previous procedure.
2. Pour the brake fluid out through the brake line hole.
3. Remove the bleed valve.
4. Push both pistons into the cylinder. Place the yoke in a vise (**Figure 17**) and tap it lightly with a hammer. This will separate the cylinder body from the yoke.

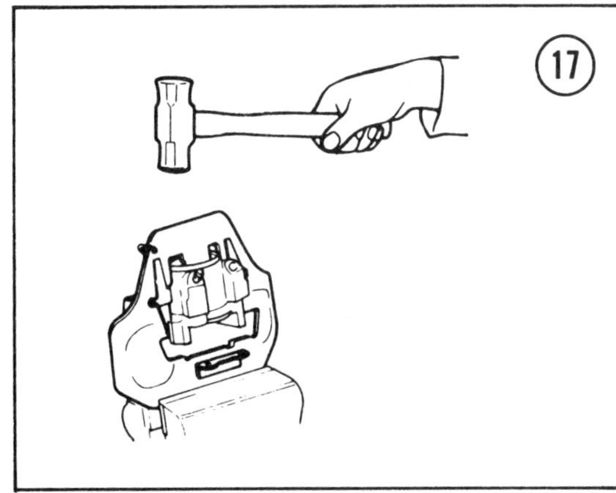

5. Remove the bias ring (**Figure 18**) from piston A. Remove the retaining ring and boot from each end of the cylinder.

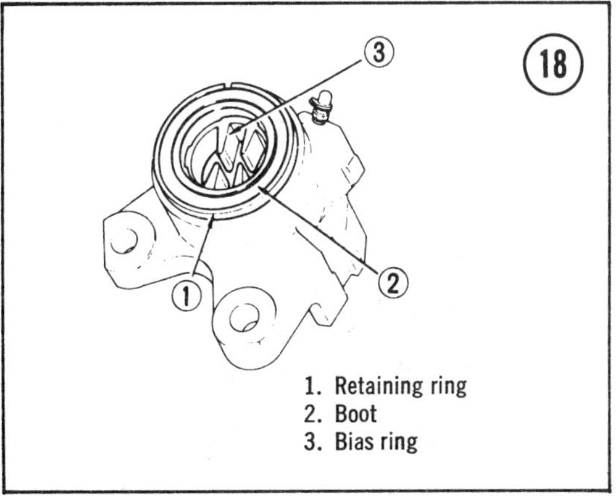

6. Push both pistons out in one direction.
7. Remove the piston seals. Use fingers only, so the cylinder bore won't be scratched.
8. Remove the yoke springs and bias spring from the yoke.
9. Thoroughly clean all parts in alcohol or brake fluid. Do not use solvent or kerosene.
10. Inspect brake pads as described under *Pad Replacement*.
11. Inspect the pistons. Since they are chrome plated, the pistons cannot be cleaned with emery paper. If the pistons can't be cleaned with a rag and chrome cleaner, replace them.
12. Inspect the cylinder bore. If scored or worn, replace the cylinder body. Small amounts of dirt or corrosion may be removed with fine emery paper. Replace the cylinder body if dirt or corrosion is severe.
13. Coat the cylinder bore with brake fluid and install new piston seals.

> NOTE: *Never reuse a piston seal. In addition to stopping leaks, the seals retract the pistons when the brake pedal is let up. Very minor damage or deterioration can make the seals useless.*

14. Place the bias ring (Figure 18) in piston A.

> NOTE: *Piston A has a dimple in the bottom (**Figure 19**). Piston B does not.*

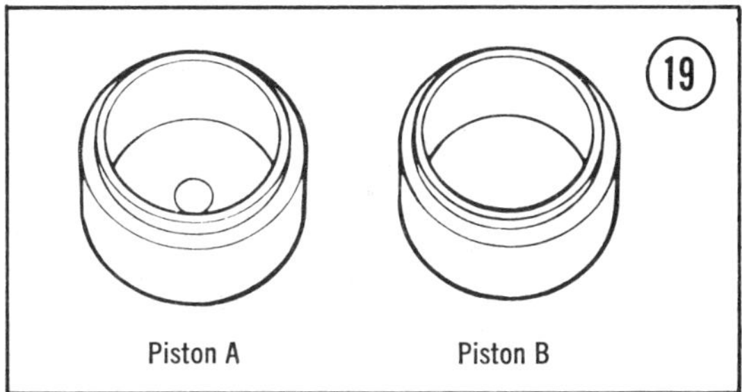

15. Coat the cylinder bore with brake fluid. Coat the pistons with brake grease or brake fluid, then install them in the cylinder. Refer to Figure 10 to make sure pistons are installed correctly.

CAUTION

Don't push the pistons in past the normal position (Figure 14). If pushed

10

in too far, the pistons will hang up on the seals. The seals will then have to be thrown away and replaced with new ones.

16. Align the yoke grooves in the cylinder body and bias ring.

17. Install the rubber boots and retaining rings.

18. Install the yoke springs and bias springs on the yoke. See **Figure 20**.

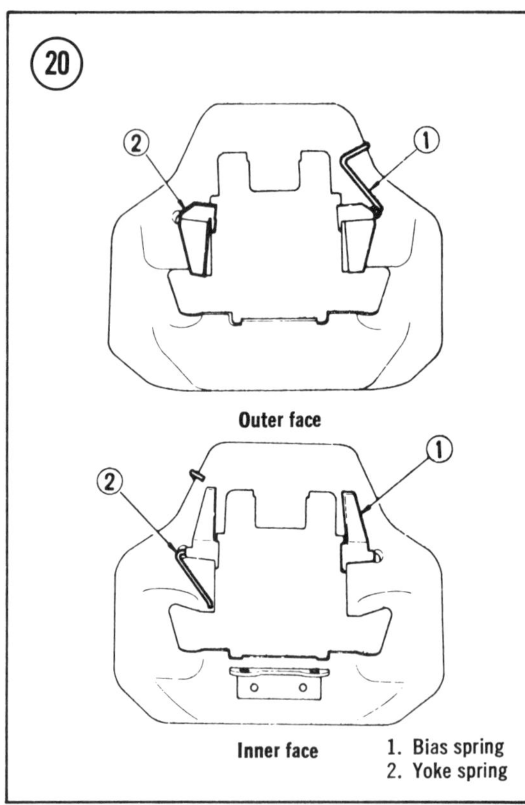

1. Bias spring
2. Yoke spring

19. Coat the cylinder body's yoke grooves with disc brake grease. Install the cylinder body in the yoke (**Figure 21**).

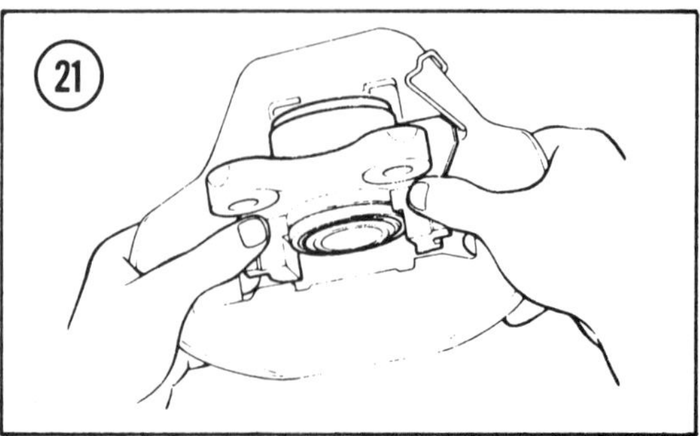

Disc Inspection, Removal/Installation

These procedures are the same as for 1968-74 cars, described earlier in this chapter. Micrometer and torque wrench specifications are the same.

DISC BRAKES (1975-76 710)

The 1975-76 710's use a double-piston, single-cylinder caliper.

Pad Replacement

1. Loosen the front wheel nuts, jack up the front end of the car, place it on jackstands, and remove the front wheels.

2. Remove the clip (1, **Figure 22**) securing the pad retaining pins.

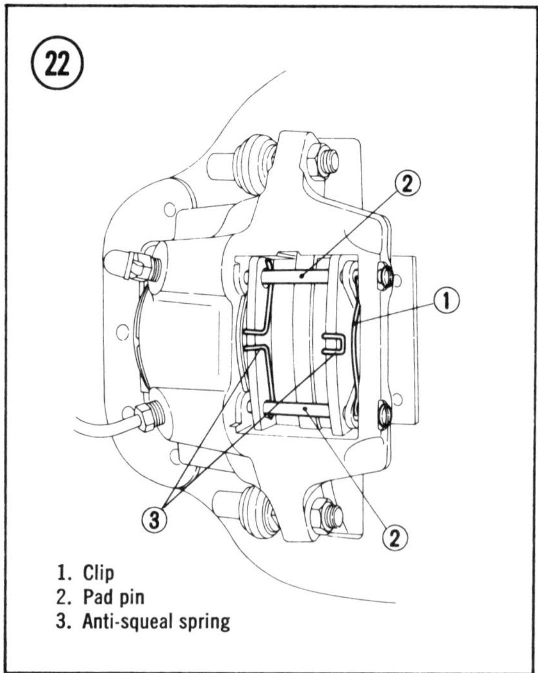

1. Clip
2. Pad pin
3. Anti-squeal spring

3. Hold down the anti-squeal springs, then pull out the pad retaining pins. Release the springs and pull out the pads.

CAUTION

Do not press the brake pedal with the pads removed, or the pistons will fall out.

4. Inspect pads. A light layer of grease or dirt may be sanded off or removed with trichloro-

ethylene. If dirt or grease is heavy, or if pad friction material is worn to 0.079 in. (2mm) or less, replace the pads.

NOTE: *Always replace pads in complete kits. These include all pads, retaining pins, retaining pin clips, and anti-squeal springs necessary to service both front brake assemblies.*

5. Check the cylinder body for brake fluid leaks. If fluid has leaked from the cylinder, overhaul the caliper as described later.

6. Carefully clean the space which holds the brake pads. Clean with rubbing alcohol only. Open the bleed valve.

7. Push piston B into the cylinder with a pry bar (**Figure 23**). Push piston A in by prying the caliper yoke outward (**Figure 24**).

CAUTION

*Do not push the pistons in past the normal position (***Figure 25***). This will cause the pistons to hang up on the seals. The caliper will then have to be disassembled and the seals replaced with new ones.*

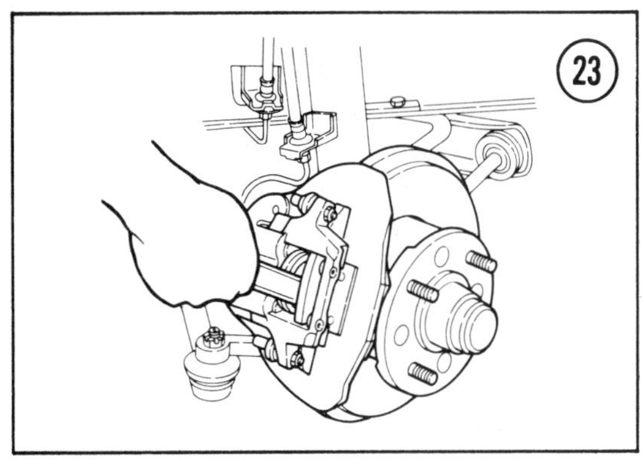

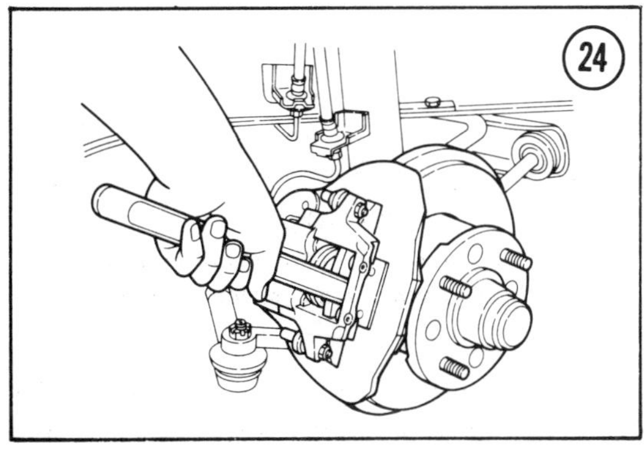

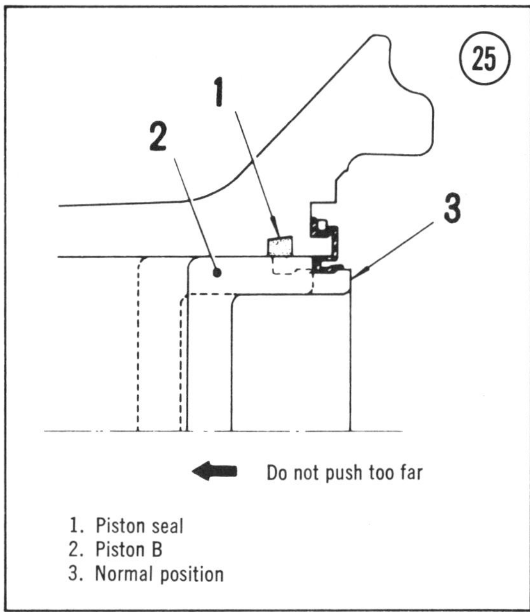

1. Piston seal
2. Piston B
3. Normal position

8. Apply disc brake grease to the following friction points: Cylinder body and brake pads; pad retaining pins and pads; pad retaining pins and pin bracket on caliper yoke.

CAUTION

Apply very small amounts of grease. Do not let grease touch the pad friction surfaces.

9. Close the bleed valve. Install the wheels and lower the car.

10. Pump the brake pedal several times to seat the pads. If necessary, bleed the brakes as described later in this chapter.

Caliper Removal/Installation (1975-76 710)

1. Remove the brake pads as described in the previous procedure.

2. Disconnect the brake line from the caliper. The factory recommends tool GG94310000 (brake line torque wrench, Figure 15) to connect and disconnect brake lines. Do not use an adjustable wrench.

3. Remove the caliper mounting bolts (**Figure 26**). Lift the caliper off.

4. Install in the reverse order. Tighten the mounting bolts to 53-72 ft.-lb. (7.3-9.9 mkg). Tighten brake line to 11-13 ft.-lb. (1.5-1.8 mkg).

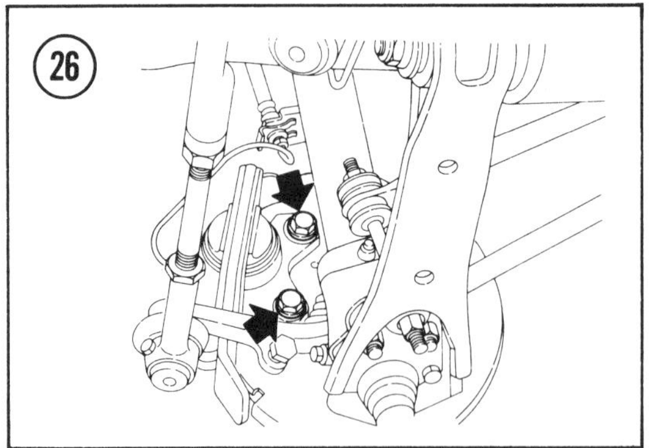

5. Bleed the brakes as described later in this chapter. Tighten the bleed valve to 5-6½ ft.-lb. (0.7-0.9 mkg).

Caliper Overhaul (1975-76 710)

Refer to **Figure 27** for this procedure.

1. Pour the brake fluid out of the caliper. Clean the outside of the caliper with rubbing alcohol.
2. Remove the gripper pin nuts (**Figure 28**). Take the cylinder body out of the yoke.

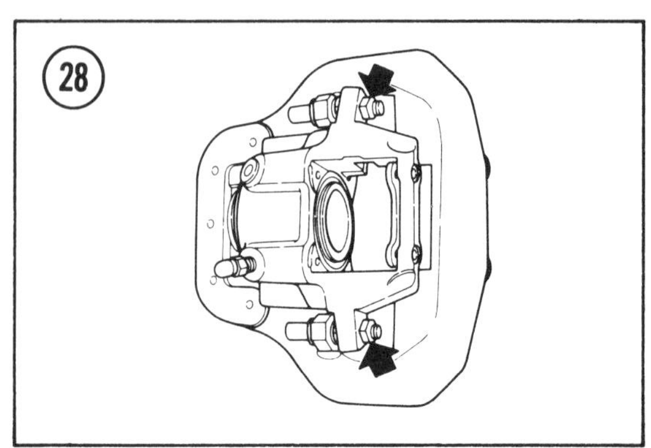

3. Remove the yoke holder (**Figure 29**) from piston A. Remove the retaining ring and dust seal from each end of the cylinder body.
4. Remove the pistons. If necessary, force the pistons out with compressed air. Service station air hoses work well for this.

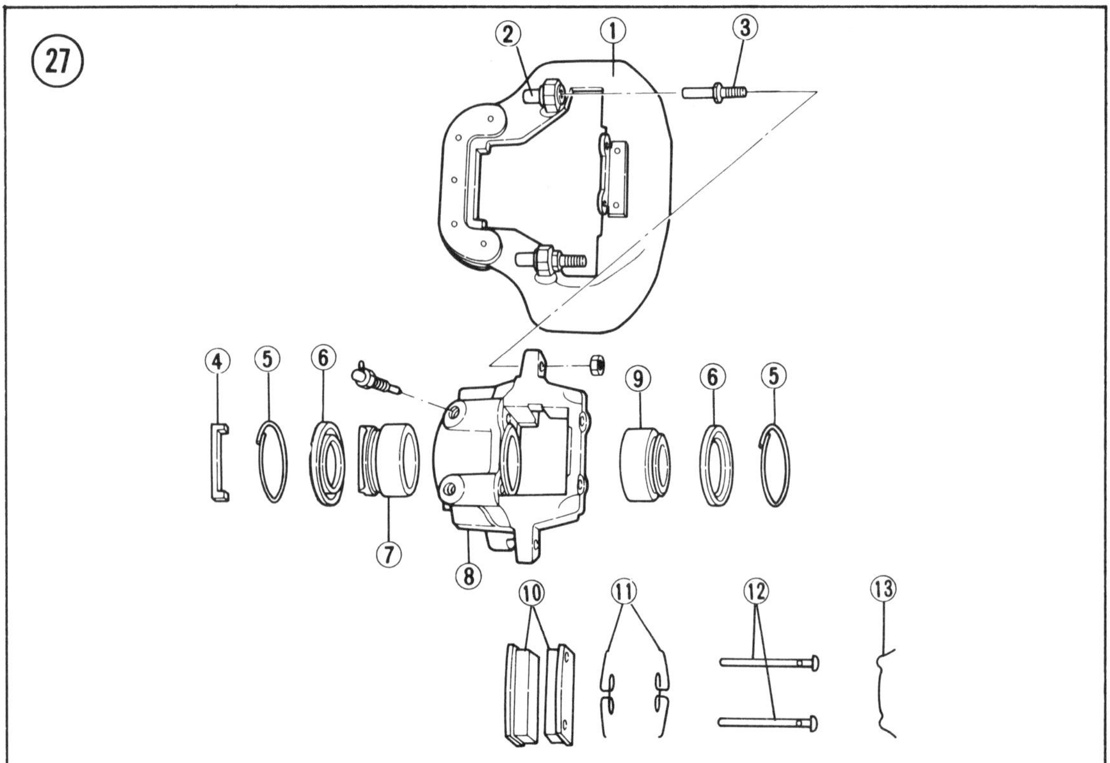

27

1. Yoke
2. Gripper
3. Gripper pin
4. Yoke holder
5. Retainer ring
6. Dust seal
7. Piston A
8. Cylinder body
9. Piston B
10. Pad
11. Anti-squeal spring
12. Pad pin
13. Clip

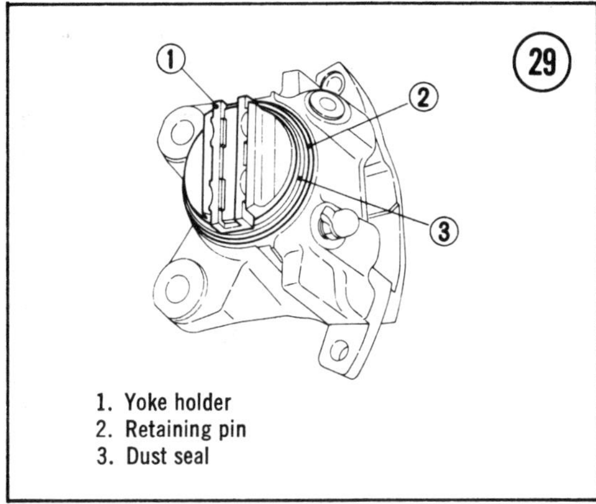

1. Yoke holder
2. Retaining pin
3. Dust seal

WARNING

The pistons may shoot out with extreme force. Place a block of wood in the space which holds the brake pads. Point piston A (7, Figure 27) at a block of wood on the ground. Apply compressed air gradually.

5. Once the pistons are out, remove the piston seals. Use fingers only so the cylinder bore won't be scratched.

6. If the grippers are worn or damaged, remove them from the yoke. Otherwise, leave them in place.

7. Check the yoke for wear, cracks, or other visible defects. Replace if any of these can be seen. If serviceable, clean the yoke with rubbing alcohol.

8. Inspect the cylinder bore. Replace the cylinder body if wear or damage can be seen. Light rust or dirt may be removed with fine emery paper. Replace the cylinder body if dirt or rust is severe. If serviceable, clean the cylinder body with rubbing alcohol.

9. Inspect the pistons. Since they are chrome plated, the pistons cannot be sanded. If the pistons can't be cleaned with chrome cleaner and a rag, replace them.

10. Install new piston seals, using fingers only so the cylinder won't be scratched.

NOTE: *Never reuse piston seals. In addition to stopping leaks, the seals retract the pistons when the brake pedal is let up. Very minor damage or deterioration can ruin the seals.*

11. Coat the cylinder bore with brake fluid. Apply rubber grease or brake fluid to the pistons, then insert them into the cylinder. Insert piston A from direction Q1 and piston B from direction Q2. See **Figure 30**. Align the yoke grooves in piston A and in the cylinder body.

CAUTION

Do not push the pistons in past the point shown in Figure 30, or they may hang up on the seals. If this happens, the seals will have to be thrown away and replaced with new ones.

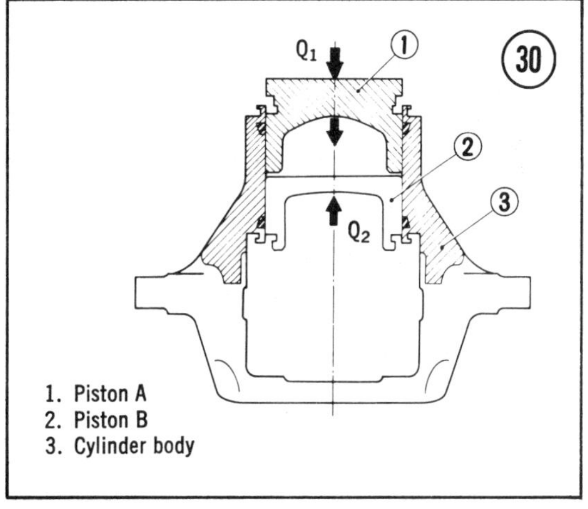

1. Piston A
2. Piston B
3. Cylinder body

12. Apply disc brake grease to the sealing surfaces on the dust seals. Install the dust seals and retaining rings. Wipe off any excess grease with alcohol.

13. Install the yoke holder (Figure 29) in piston A.

14. If the grippers were removed, install them (**Figure 31**). Use a one per cent soap solution (one teaspoon soap in 2 cups of water) to lubricate the grippers. Do not use a stronger soap solution.

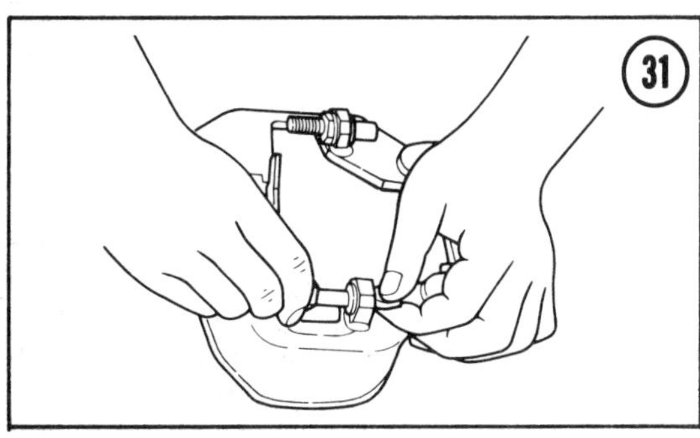

10

15. Position the cylinder body in the yoke. Align the yoke holder with the yoke, then press them together (**Figure 32**). This requires a force of 44-66 lb. (20-30 kg).

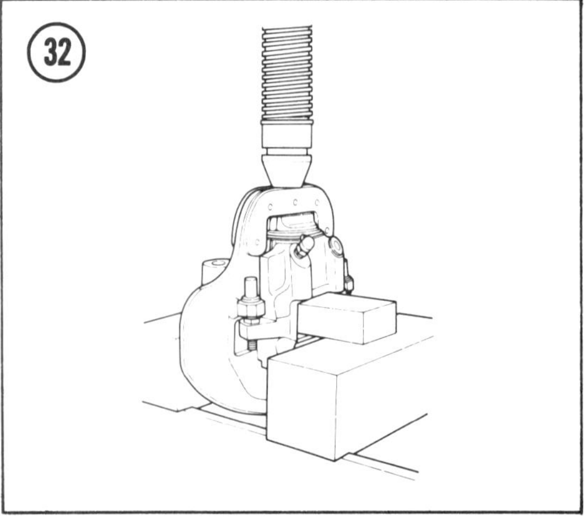

Disc Inspection, Removal/Installation

These procedures are the same as for 1968-74 cars, described earlier in this chapter. Micrometer and torque wrench specifications are the same.

REAR DRUM BRAKES

Figure 33 is an exploded view of the rear brakes for 510's and 610's. **Figure 34** is an assembled view. 710 rear brakes are basically the same, but the upper spring has only one coil.

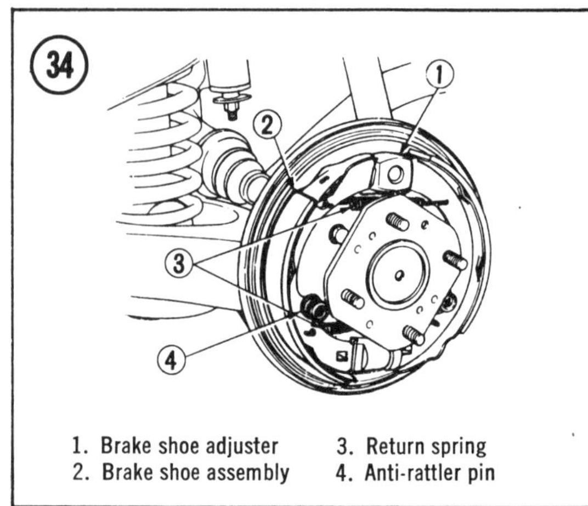

1. Brake shoe adjuster
2. Brake shoe assembly
3. Return spring
4. Anti-rattler pin

Removal

1. Loosen the rear wheel nuts, jack up the rear end of the car, place it on jackstands, and remove the rear wheels.

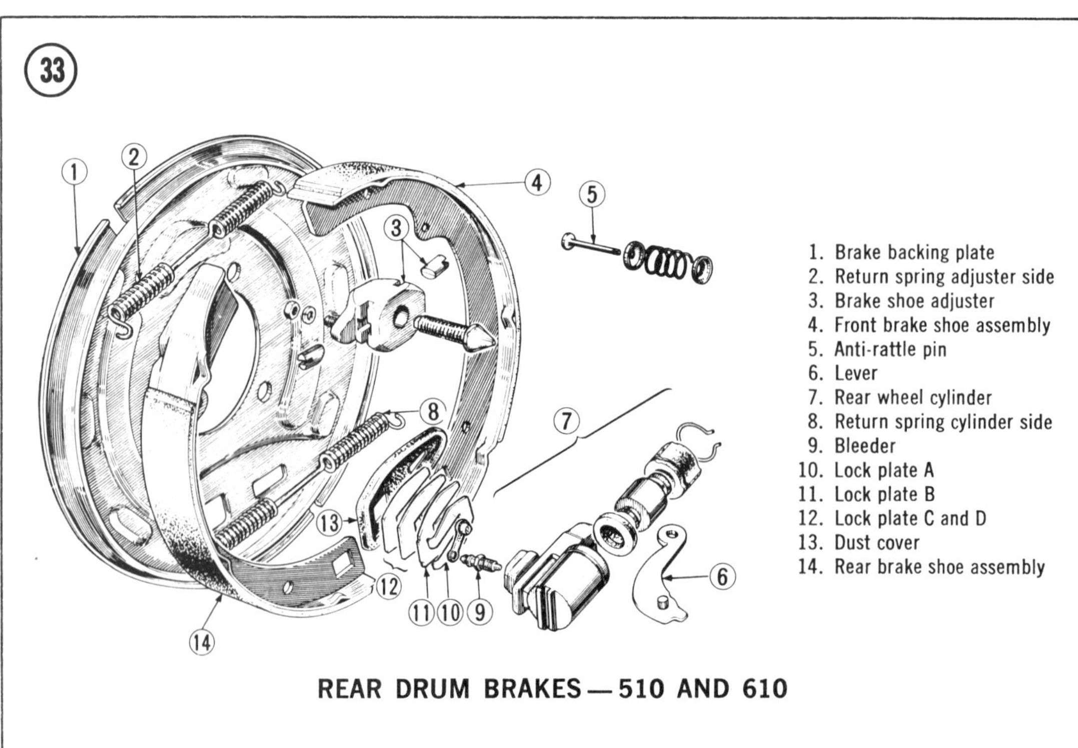

1. Brake backing plate
2. Return spring adjuster side
3. Brake shoe adjuster
4. Front brake shoe assembly
5. Anti-rattle pin
6. Lever
7. Rear wheel cylinder
8. Return spring cylinder side
9. Bleeder
10. Lock plate A
11. Lock plate B
12. Lock plate C and D
13. Dust cover
14. Rear brake shoe assembly

REAR DRUM BRAKES—510 AND 610

2. Make sure the handbrake is all the way off.

3. Pull the drum off. If it is difficult to remove, back off the brake adjuster.

4. Turn the anti-rattle pins (4, **Figure 35**) 90° with pliers. Remove the pins, retaining collars, springs, and spring washers.

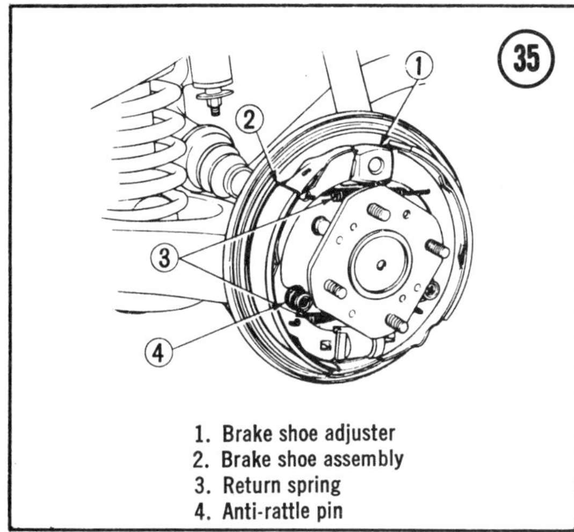

1. Brake shoe adjuster
2. Brake shoe assembly
3. Return spring
4. Anti-rattle pin

5. Remove the return springs (3, Figure 35). Lift the brake shoes off.

6. Remove the adjuster securing nut and take the adjuster off.

7. If wheel cylinder overhaul is planned, disconnect the brake hose from the cylinder. Detach the handbrake rod or cable, remove the lock plates, and take the cylinder out.

8. Backing plate removal requires removal of the rear axle shaft or spindle. Removal is rarely necessary for normal brake service. If necessary, refer to procedures in Chapter Eleven.

Inspection

1. Clean all parts except the wheel cylinder in rubbing alcohol or brake fluid. Do not use gasoline or kerosene.

CAUTION

If cleaning with brake fluid, keep it off the brake linings. Brake fluid will ruin the linings, and they will have to be replaced.

2. Check drums for visible scoring, excessive or uneven wear, and corrosion. If you have precision measuring equipment, measure the drum for wear and out-of-roundness. If you don't have the equipment, this measurement can be done by a dealer or machine shop. Maximum permissible out-of-roundness is 0.0008 in. (0.05mm). If the drum is out of round or otherwise defective, it can be turned to correct it. However, the inside diameter must not exceed 9.055 in. (230mm). If it would have to be cut larger than this to smooth it, the drum must be replaced.

3. Inspect the lining material on the brake shoes. Make sure it is not cracked, unevenly worn, or separated from the shoes. If linings are only slightly oily or greasy, and not excessively worn, they may be cleaned in trichloroethylene and reused. If linings are saturated with oil or grease, or contaminated with brake fluid, they must be replaced. Linings must also be replaced if worn thinner than 0.059 in. (1.5mm).

4. Check the anti-rattle pins, adjuster mechanism, and handbrake operating arm for worn or damaged parts. Replace as needed.

5. Check return springs for weakness or deformation. Replace if these conditions are detected.

Wheel Cylinder Overhaul

Figure 36 shows the wheel cylinder used on 510's and 610's. The 710 wheel cylinder is basically the same, but uses a slightly different snap ring and dust cover.

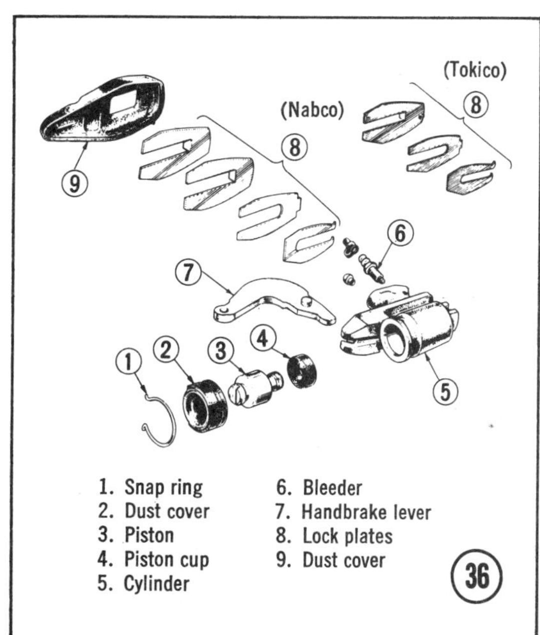

1. Snap ring
2. Dust cover
3. Piston
4. Piston cup
5. Cylinder
6. Bleeder
7. Handbrake lever
8. Lock plates
9. Dust cover

36

10

1. Remove the snap ring. The dust cover, piston, and piston cup can then be removed.
2. Discard the piston cup.
3. Clean the piston and cylinder in alcohol or brake fluid. Do not use gasoline or kerosene.
4. Check the cylinder bore and piston for scoring, cracks, corrosion, dirt, or excessive wear. Check the outside of the cylinder for wear at its contact point with the brake shoes. Replace the cylinder if these conditions are detected.
5. As a final check on a suspect cylinder and piston, measure piston diameter and cylinder bore. If there is more than 0.006 in. (0.15mm) difference between these figures, replace the cylinder.
6. Coat the piston cup with rubber grease and install it on the piston.
7. Coat the cylinder bore with brake fluid.
8. Install the piston. The lip of the cup faces into the cylinder. Install the dust cover and secure it with the snap ring.

Installation

Installation is the reverse of the removal procedure, plus the following:

1. Tokico wheel cylinders use 3 lock plates; Nabco wheel cylinders use 4. Install the lock plates in the order and directions shown in **Figure 37.**

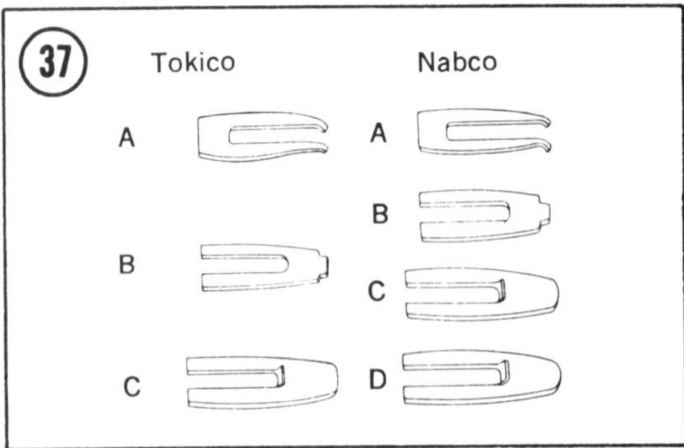

2. Apply brake grease to the metal-to-metal friction points shown in **Figure 38**.

CAUTION
Do not let grease touch brake linings.

3. Tighten the adjuster securing nut to 10-13 ft.-lb. (1.4-1.8 mkg).

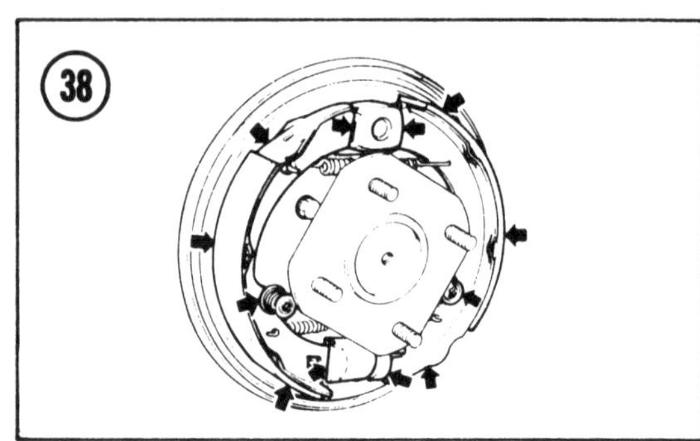

4. After installation, bleed and adjust the brakes as described later in this chapter.

MASTER CYLINDER

All models use dual-piston master cylinders. **Figure 39** shows the master cylinder used in 510's. **Figure 40** shows the 610-710 cylinder. The 1975-76 models have a brake fluid level indicator built into the fluid reservoir. The indicator must not be removed or disassembled.

Removal/Installation

1. On 510's, disconnect the master cylinder pushrod from the brake pedal.
2. Disconnect brake lines from the master cylinder.

CAUTION
Place rags beneath the master cylinder to keep brake fluid off the paint.

3. Remove 2 master cylinder installation nuts. **Figure 41** shows a typical installation. Lift the master cylinder out.

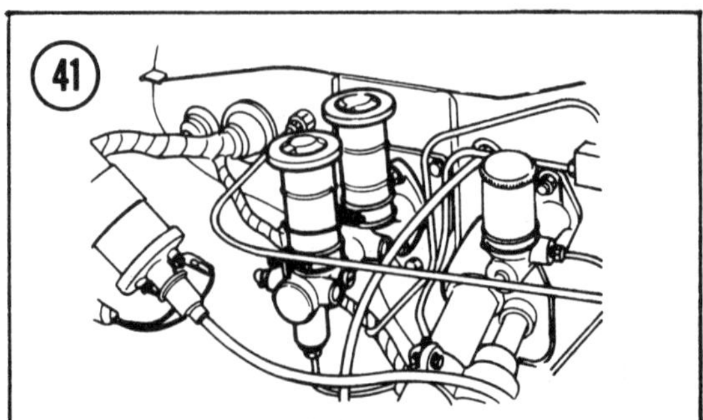

4. Installation is the reverse of these steps. Bleed the brakes as described later in this chapter.

(39)

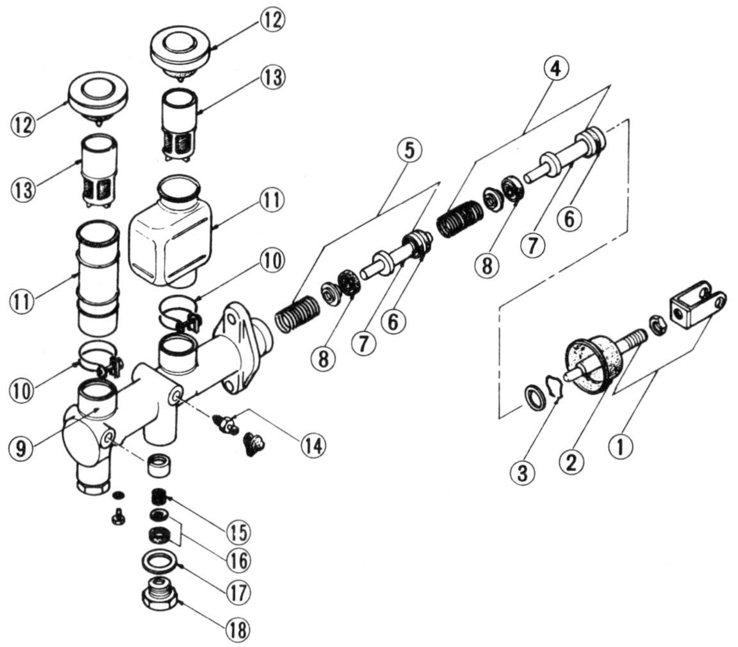

1. Pushrod assembly
2. Dust cover
3. Stopper ring
4. Piston assembly (A)
5. Piston assembly (B)
6. Secondary piston cap
7. Piston
8. Primary piston cap
9. Master cylinder body
10. Reservoir band assembly
11. Reservoir
12. Reservoir cap assembly
13. Filter
14. Bleeder screw
15. Check valve spring
16. Check valve assembly
17. Valve cap gasket
18. Valve cap

MASTER CYLINDER—510

(40)

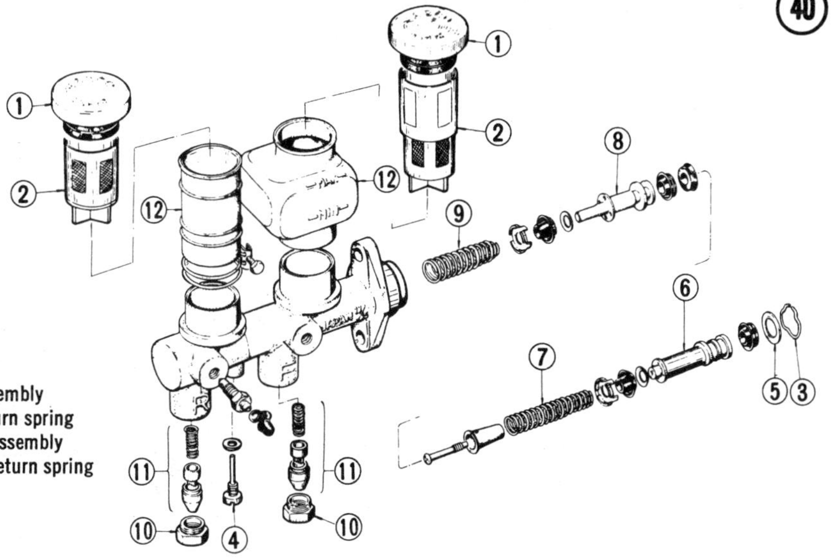

1. Reservoir cap
2. Filter
3. Stopper ring
4. Stopper screw
5. Stopper
6. Primary piston assembly
7. Primary piston return spring
8. Secondary piston assembly
9. Secondary piston return spring
10. Plug
11. Check valve
12. Reservoir

MASTER CYLINDER—610 AND 710

Disassembly

Refer to the appropriate exploded view for this procedure.

1. Remove the stopper bolt(s) and drain the brake fluid from the cylinder.
2. Remove the snap ring. Take out the stopper, piston assemblies, and return springs.

CAUTION
Remove the piston(s) carefully to prevent damaging the piston and cylinder friction surfaces.

3. Remove the cap screw(s). Take out the check valve(s) and spring(s).

NOTE: *Do not remove the brake fluid reservoirs unless installing new ones.*

Inspection

1. Thoroughly clean all parts in alcohol or brake fluid. Do not use gasoline or kerosene.
2. Discard the piston cups, check valves, and packing rings.
3. Check the cylinder bore and piston(s) for excessive or uneven wear, scoring, or corrosion. Wear is excessive if clearance between cylinder walls and pistons exceeds 0.006 in. (0.15mm). Replace cylinder and piston if these conditions are evident.
4. Check spring for wear, damage, or weakness. Replace as needed.
5. Inspect the bleed valves, stopper screws, check valve cap screws, and fluid reservoirs for wear or damage. Replace as needed.

Assembly

Assembly is the reverse of the disassembly procedure, plus the following:

1. Coat the cylinder bore, piston, and cups with brake fluid before assembly.

CAUTION
Do not scratch the cylinder bore or piston(s) when installing.

2. After installation, bleed the brakes and check for brake fluid leaks.
3. Check pedal pad height. If necessary, adjust as described later in this chapter.

BRAKE BOOSTER

The Master-Vac brake booster uses intake manifold vacuum to reduce braking effort. The booster is used on 610's and 710's. The booster and its check valve should be tested at intervals specified in Chapter Two.

Check Valve Test

1. Remove the check valve from its clip on the firewall. (**Figure 42**).

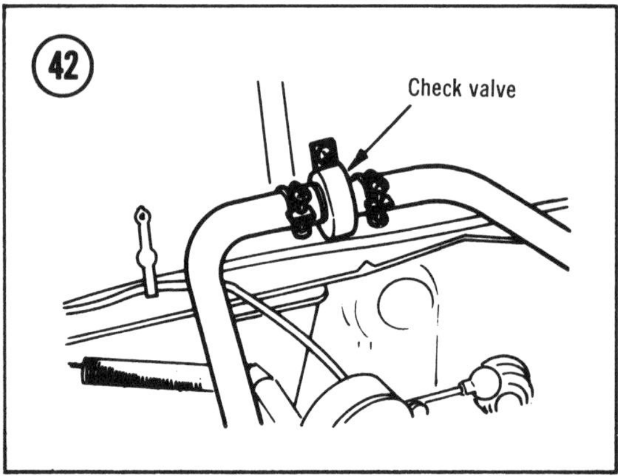

2. Disconnect the hose from the brake booster side of the valve. Connect a vacuum gauge in its place.
3. Run the engine at a fast idle. Turn the engine off when vacuum reaches approximately 20 in. (500mm).
4. With the engine off, watch the vacuum gauge for 15 seconds. Any vacuum drop, even a slight one, indicates a defective check valve or vacuum line. If no defect can be seen in the vacuum line, replace the check valve.

Airtightness Test (No Load)

1. Using a T-fitting, connect a vacuum gauge into the line between check valve and brake booster. See **Figure 43**.
2. Run the engine at a fast idle. Turn it off when vacuum reaches approximately 20 in. (500mm).
3. With the engine off, watch the vacuum gauge for 15 seconds. Any vacuum drop indicates a defective vacuum line or brake booster. If no defects can be found in the vacuum line, replace the brake booster as described later.

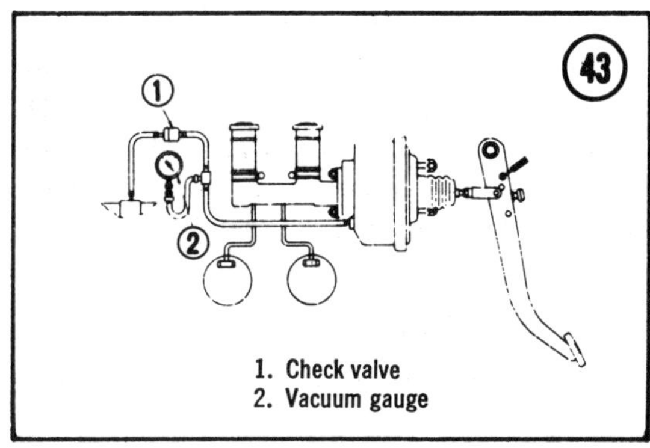
1. Check valve
2. Vacuum gauge

Airtightness Test (Under Load)

1. Connect a vacuum gauge as described in Step 1 of the previous procedure. Place the gauge where it can be seen from the driver's seat, or have an assistant watch it for you.

2. With the engine running, press the brake pedal as far as it will go.

3. When vacuum reaches approximately 20 in. (500mm), shut the engine off. Keep the brake pedal down.

4. Watch the vacuum gauge for 15 seconds after the engine is shut off. Any vacuum drop indicates a defective brake booster. Overhaul as described later in this chapter.

Booster Removal/Installation

Refer to **Figure 44** for this procedure.

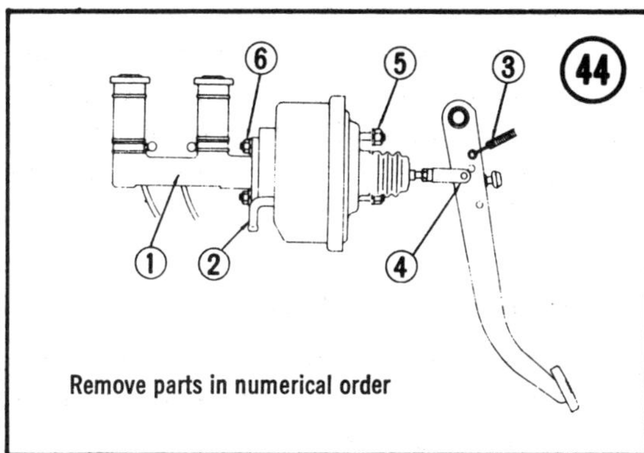
Remove parts in numerical order

1. Disconnect the brake lines (1, Figure 44) from the master cylinder.

2. Detach the vacuum line from the fitting on the brake booster (2).

3. Detach the return spring (3) and booster pushrod (4) from the pedal.

4. Remove the nuts attaching the booster to the firewall (5). Lift the booster out of the engine compartment.

5. Remove the nuts attaching the master cylinder to the booster (6). Separate the master cylinder and booster.

6. Installation is the reverse of these steps. After installation, bleed the brakes, test the brake booster as described earlier, and check pedal height. If necessary, adjust pedal height as described later in this chapter.

Disassembly

Refer to **Figure 45** for this procedure. During disassembly lay parts on a bench in order of removal, even if they are going to be replaced. Having the parts in order will ease reassembly.

1. Thoroughly clean the outside of the booster before disassembly. Be sure your working area is *clean.*

2. Paint or scribe mating marks on the front shell, rear shell, and stud assembly. This ensures that the parts will be reassembled in their original positions.

3. Place the booster in a soft-jawed vise as shown in **Figure 46**. Remove the pushrod, locknut, and valve body guard.

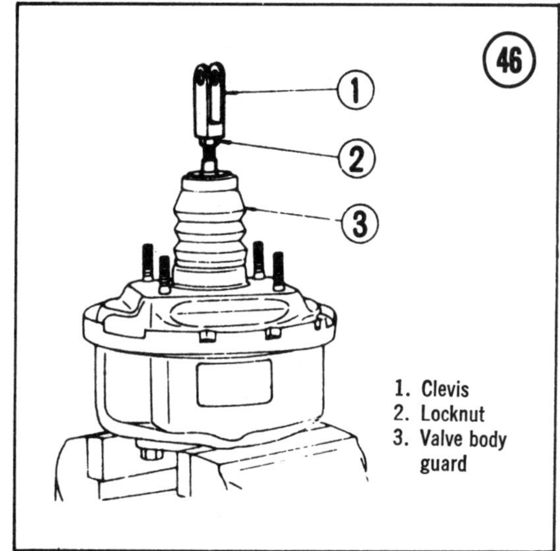
1. Clevis
2. Locknut
3. Valve body guard

4. Separate the front and rear shells. Use the Datsun special tool shown in **Figure 47** or improvise a substitute.

10

45

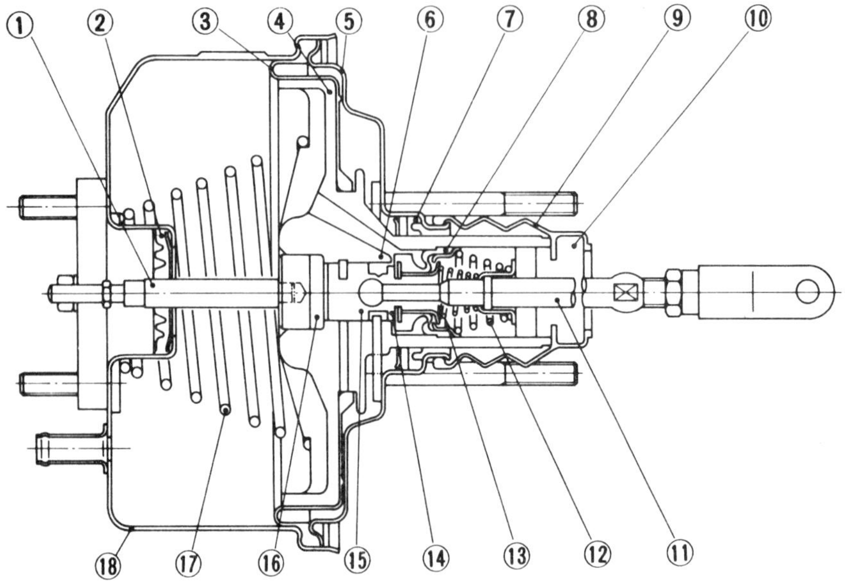

BRAKE BOOSTER

1. Pushrod
2. Plate and seal
3. Diaphragm
4. Diaphragm plate
5. Rear shell
6. Vacuum valve
7. Seal
8. Poppet assembly
9. Valve body guard
10. Air silencer filter
11. Valve operating rod
12. Valve return spring
13. Poppet return spring
14. Exhaust valve
15. Valve plunger
16. Reaction disc
17. Diaphragm return spring
18. Front shell

47

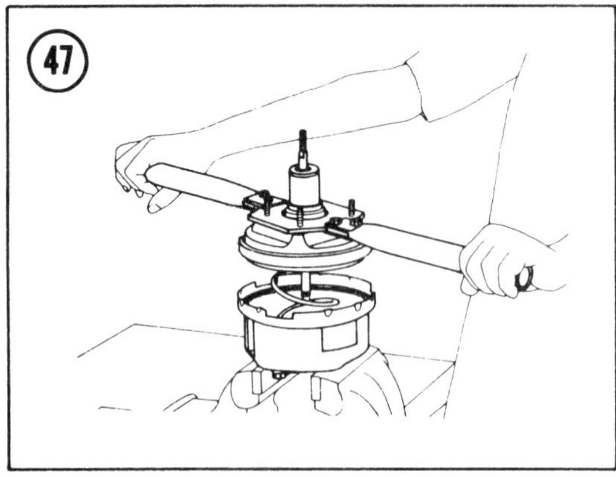

48

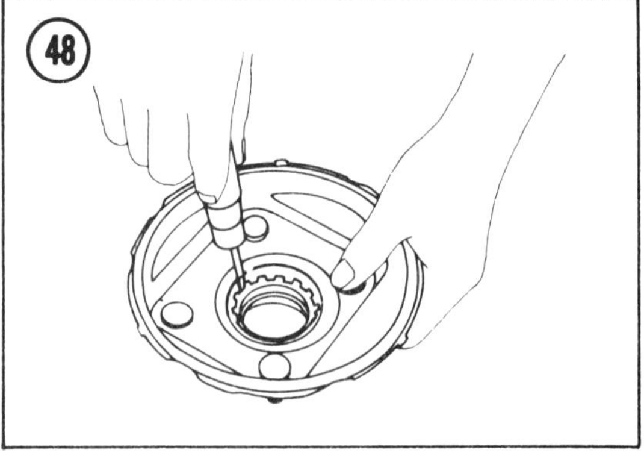

5. Carefully pry the seal retainer loose with a screwdriver (**Figure 48**). Remove the seal and discard it.

6. Remove the diaphragm from the diaphragm plate (**Figure 49**). Throw the diaphragm away.

7. Carefully pry the air silencer retainer loose from the valve body (**Figure 50**).

CAUTION

Don't tap on the screwdriver with a hammer, or the valve body may be damaged.

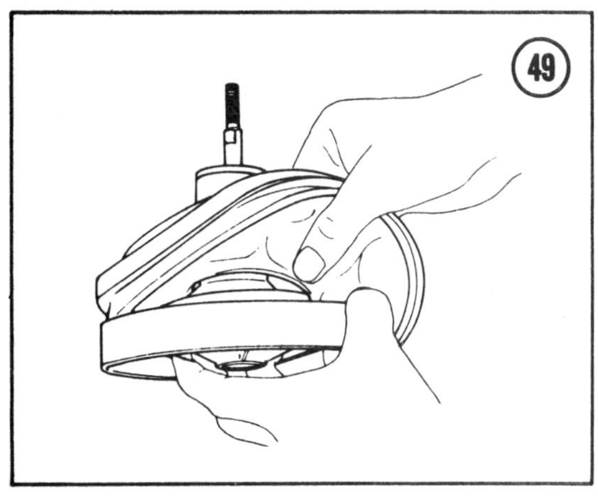

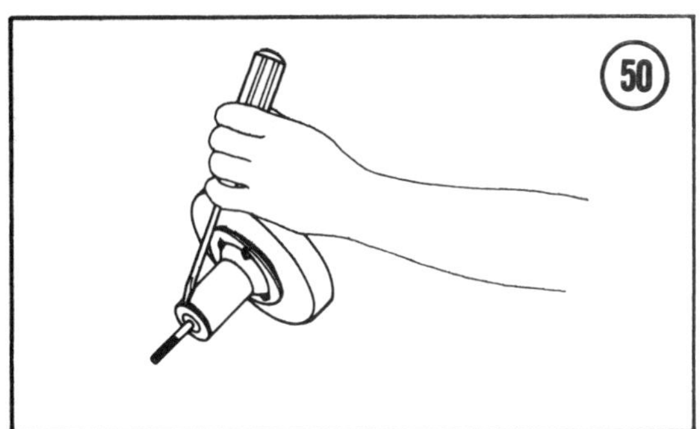

8. Press in the valve operating rod and take out the stop key. See **Figure 51**.

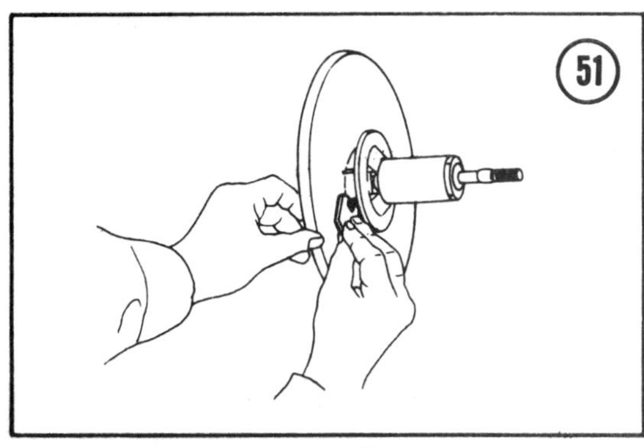

9. Pull the valve plunger assembly, together with the air silencer filter and air silencer, out of the valve body. See **Figure 52**. Take the air silencer filter and air silencer off the valve operating rod.

10. Remove the reaction disc (**Figure 53**).

11. Detach the flange from the front shell (**Figure 54**).

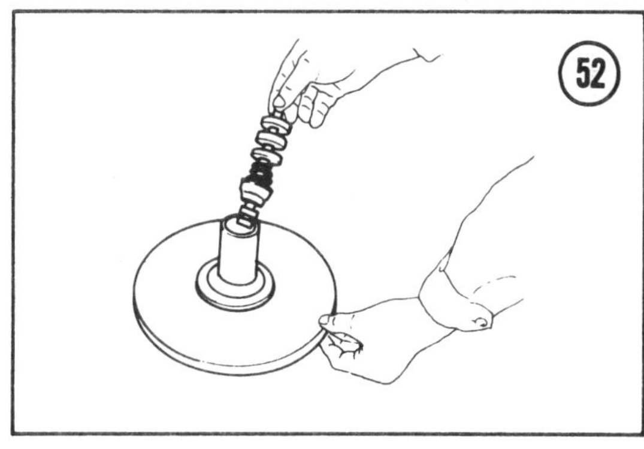

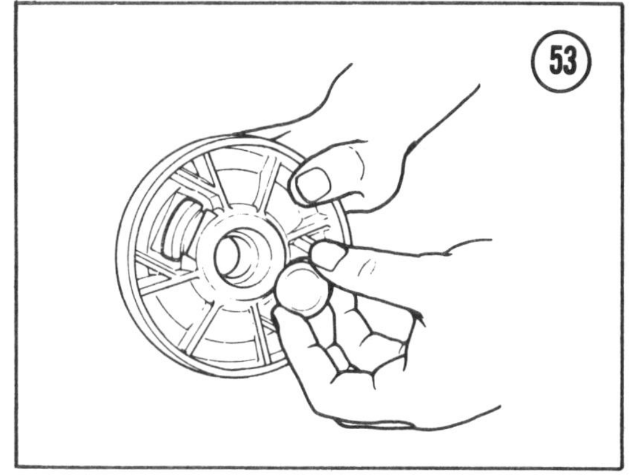

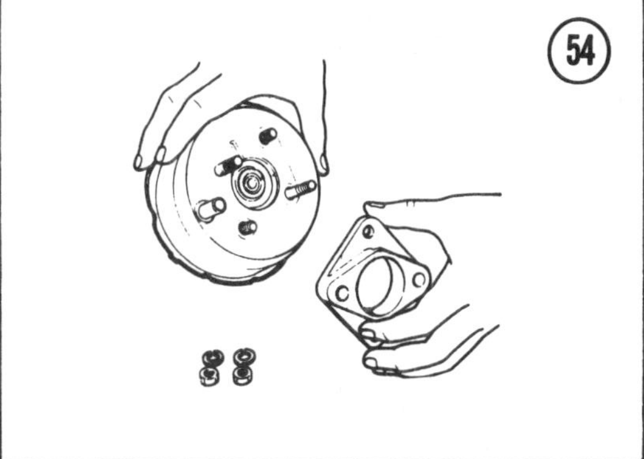

12. Remove the plate and seal assembly from beneath the flange.

Inspection

1. Thoroughly clean all parts with alcohol before inspection.

2. Check front and rear shells for wear or damage. Replace if these conditions are found.

3. Examine stud threads. Repair lightly damaged threads with a die. Replace parts with

severely damaged threads.Check welds at bases of the studs for cracks. Replace cracked parts.

4. Check for corrosion on the areas marked "D" in **Figure 55**. Clean off light corrosion with emery paper. Replace heavily corroded parts.

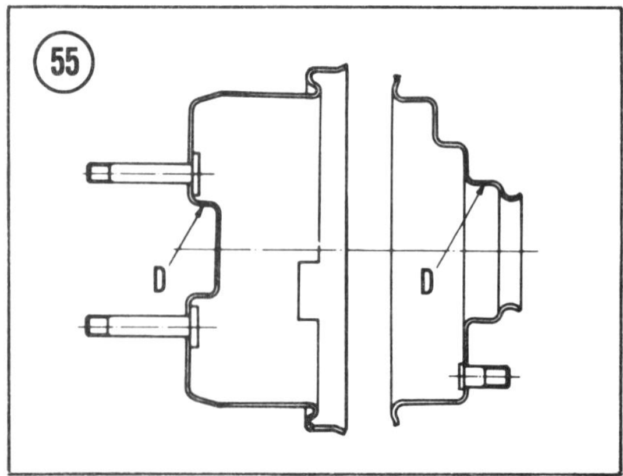

5. Inspect the outer surface of the valve body (E, **Figure 56**). Any visible damage, including slight scratches, is cause for replacement.

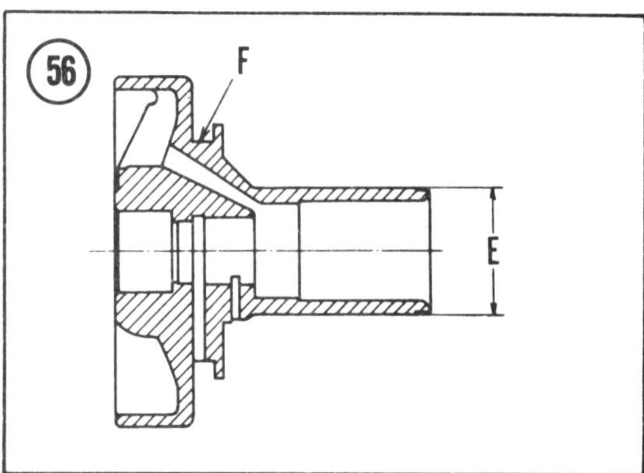

6. Check bearing movement on the valve body. Replace the bearing if it doesn't move smoothly.

7. Check the diaphragm plate and valve body for cracks. Replace if cracks can be found.

8. Carefully examine the groove in the diaphragm plate (F, Figure 56). Replace the diaphragm plate if wear or damage can be seen.

9. Check the flange for cracks or rust. Replace if these can be found.

10. Check the diaphragm spring for weakness, rust, or deformation. Replace as needed.

11. Check the pushrod for rust. Remove light rust with emery paper. Replace heavily rusted pushrods. The pushrod must also be replaced if the friction surface (**Figure 57**) is scored.

12. Check the stop key and pedal-to-booster clevis for wear and damage. Replace as needed.

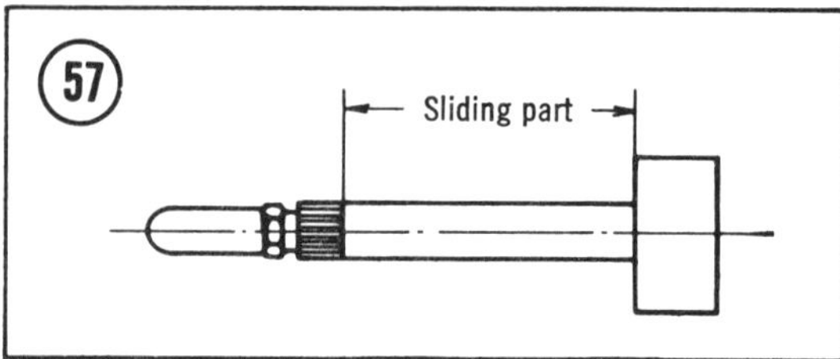

Assembly and Adjustment

Assembly is the reverse of the disassembly procedure, plus the following steps.

1. Replace the following parts whenever the booster is disassembled:
   a. Bearing and valve body seal
   b. Diaphragm
   c. Air silencer retainer, silencer, and filter
   d. Valve plunger assembly
   e. Reaction disc
   f. Plate and seal assembly
   g. Valve body seal

2. Apply a light coat of silicon grease (contained in the repair kit) to the following:
   a. On the seal (7, Figure 45) the lip and face contacting the rear shell.
   b. Friction surfaces of the valve plunger assembly (**Figure 58**).

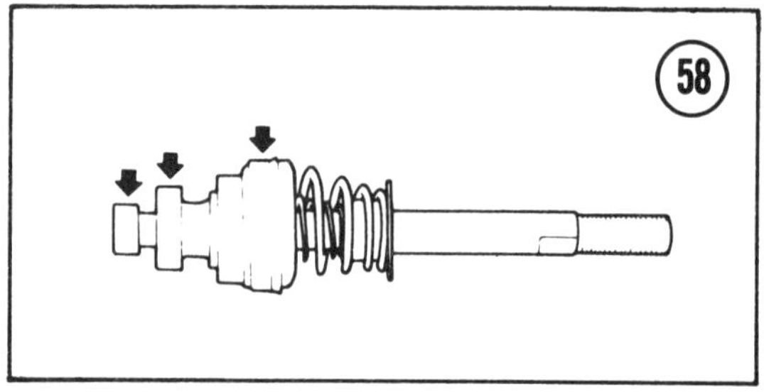

   c. Both surfaces of the reaction disc.
   d. The edge of the diaphragm where it makes contact with the front and rear shells.
   e. The surfaces on the plate and seal assembly (2, Figure 45) that contact the front shell and pushrod.

f. The pushrod surface that contacts the diaphragm plate.

3. Apply a thin coat of mica powder to the diaphragm. Don't get any powder on the outer edge.

4. When inserting the valve operating rod in the valve body, be sure the rod goes straight in and is not tilted to either side. When the rod is in, press it down against its spring and insert the stop key. See **Figure 59**.

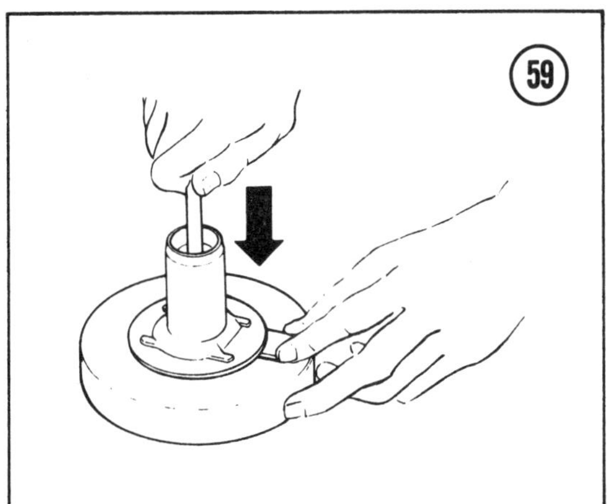

5. When installing the bearing and seal retainer on rear shell, use a drift such as ST 08060000 (**Figure 60**). Tap the retainer in until the flange on the drift contacts the rear shell. If you can't get the special tool, tap the retainer in until it is 0.264-0.276 in. (6.7-7.0mm) deep in its recess. See **Figure 61**.

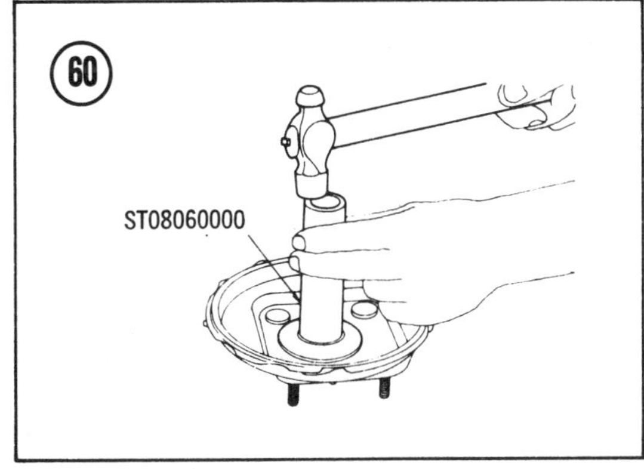

6. After assembly, adjust pushrod protrusion (B, **Figure 62**). Correct protrusion is 0.384-0.394 in. (9.75-10.0mm) on 610's and 710's; and 0.394-0.413 in. (10.0-10.5mm) on pickups.

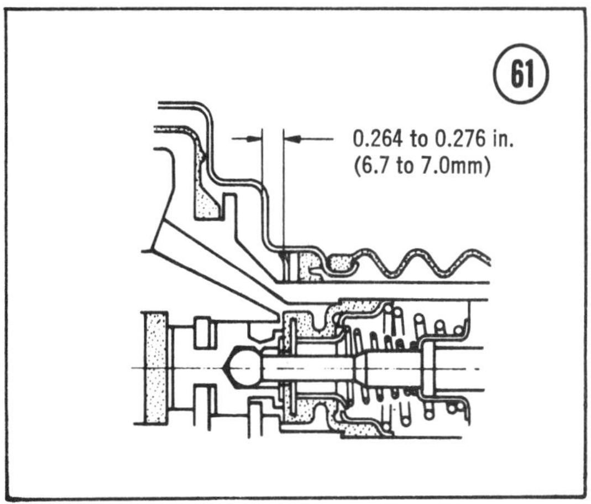

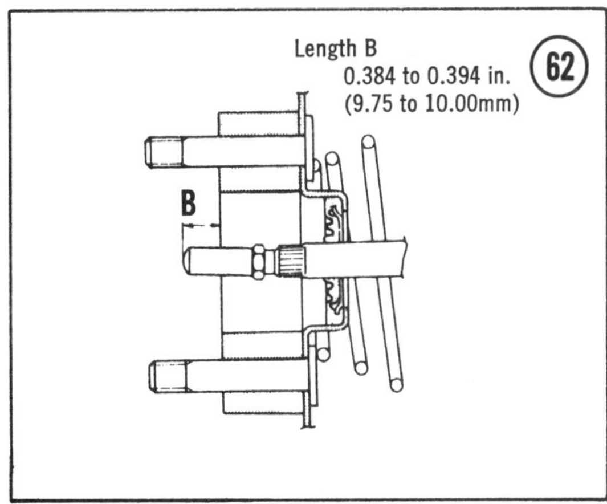

STOPLIGHT SWITCH REPLACEMENT

The stoplight switch is located on the pedal bracket (**Figure 63**). To remove it, disconnect the wires, loosen the locknut, and unscrew the switch. Screw the new switch in far enough to the brake lights go on when the pedal is moved slightly. Secure with the locknut.

WARNING LIGHT SWITCH REPLACEMENT

If the warning light switch is defective, replace it. Do not attempt to repair the switch. Refer to **Figure 64**.

1. Disconnect the warning light wire.
2. Disconnect the brake lines.
3. Remove the attaching bolt and take out the switch.

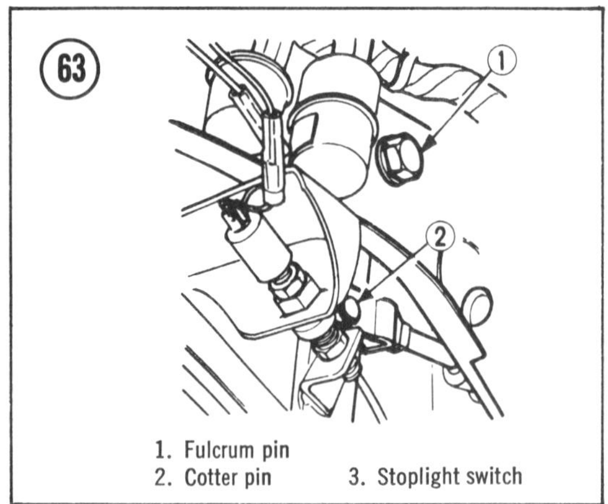

1. Fulcrum pin
2. Cotter pin
3. Stoplight switch

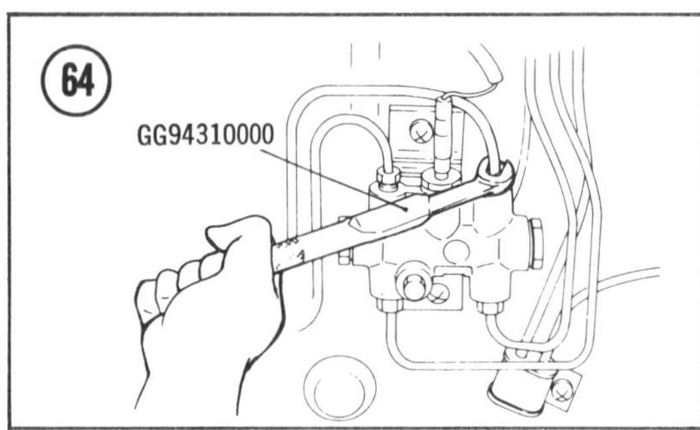

4. Install by reversing Steps 1-3. Bleed the brakes after installation.

PROPORTIONING VALVE

The proportioning valve, used on cars with disc brakes, prevents premature rear wheel lockup.

Testing

Test the proportioning valve at intervals specified in Chapter Two. To test, drive the car at a speed in excess of 31 mph (50 kph). Brake hard enough to lock the wheels *slightly*. If the front wheels lock before or at the same time as the rear wheels, the valve is good. If the rear wheels lock first, the valve is defective and must be replaced.

CAUTION
Do not lock the wheels completely when braking, or the tires will be flat-spotted.

To remove the valve, disconnect the brake lines, noting carefully how they are connected. Remove the securing bolt and take the valve out. Install in the reverse order. Bleed the brakes after installation.

BRAKE BLEEDING

The hydraulic system should be bled whenever air enters it and reduces braking effectiveness. If the pedal feels spongy, or if pedal travel increases considerably, brake bleeding is usually called for. Bleeding is also necessary whenever a hydraulic line is disconnected or the system is repaired.

This procedure requires handling brake fluid. Be careful not to get any fluid on brake pads, shoes, drums, or discs. Clean all dirt from bleed valves before beginning. Two people are required, one to operate the brake pedal and the other to open and close the bleed valves.

Bleeding should be conducted in the following order: master cylinder, right rear, left rear, right front, left front.

1. Clean away any dirt around the master cylinder. Top up the reservoir with brake fluid marked DOT 3 or DOT 4.
2. Attach a plastic tube to the bleed valve. Dip the end of the tube in a jar containing several inches of clean brake fluid.

NOTE: *Do not allow the end of the tube to come out of the brake fluid during bleeding. This could allow air into the system, requiring that the bleeding procedure be done over.*

3. Press the brake pedal as far as it will go 2 or 3 times, then hold it down.
4. With the brake pedal down, open the bleed valve until the pedal goes to the floor, then close the bleed valve. Do not let the pedal up until the bleed valve is closed.
5. Let the pedal back up slowly.
6. Repeat Steps 3-5 until the fluid entering the jar is free of air bubbles.
7. Repeat the process for the other bleed valves.

NOTE: *Keep an eye on the brake fluid level in the master cylinder throughout the bleeding process. If the reservoirs are allowed to become empty, air will be sucked into the hydraulic system and the procedure will have to be repeated.*

ADJUSTMENTS

Brake Pedal (510)

1. Loosen the stoplight switch locknuts. Back off the switch until it is clear of the pedal. See **Figure 65**.
2. Loosen the locknut on the master cylinder pushrod. Set pedal height at 7.36 in. (187mm) on manual transmission cars; or 7.95 in. (202mm) on automatic transmission cars. Tighten the pushrod locknut.
3. Adjust the stoplight switch so the threaded portion is flush with the front surface of the switch bracket (surface A, Figure 65). Secure the switch with the locknuts.
4. Turn the pedal stopper out far enough so the stoplight switch plunger is pushed in all the way. The stoplight switch should go on when the pedal is moved slightly, and go off when the pedal is released.

Brake Pedal (610 and 710)

1. Adjust the stoplight switch so the threaded portion is flush with the front surface of its bracket (surface A, Figure 65). Secure the switch with the locknut.
2. Set pedal height at 7.28 in. (185mm) with the pedal stopper.
3. Loosen the pushrod locknut. Adjust pushrod length by rotating the pushrod. After adjustment, you should be able to move the brake pedal slightly without moving the pushrod. Specified free movement is 0.039-0.197 in. (1-5mm).

Front Disc Brakes

Front disc brakes are adjusted automatically by the piston seals. Manual adjustment is never necessary, and no means of adjustment is provided.

Rear Drum Brakes

Rear drum brakes are adjusted by turning a cam. **Figure 66** shows a typical adjusting cam.

1. Securely block both front wheels so the car will not roll in either direction. Jack up the rear end of the car and place it on jackstands.
2. Turn the cam with a wrench to tighten the brake shoes. Tighten until the shoes begin to drag.

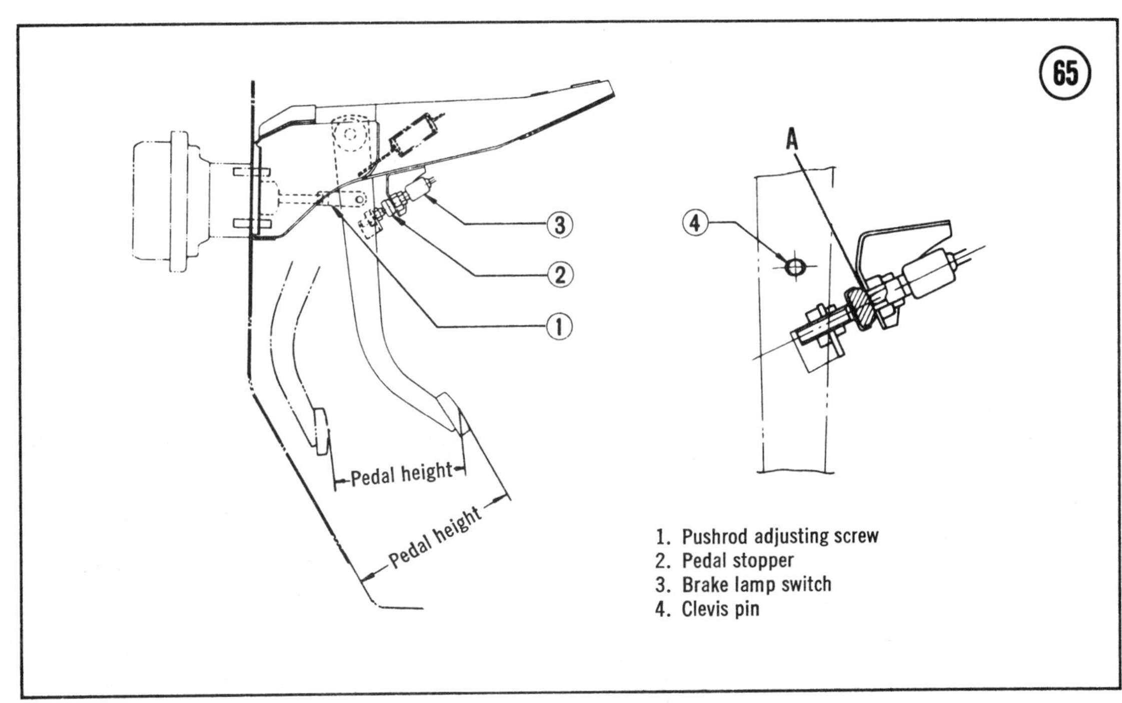

1. Pushrod adjusting screw
2. Pedal stopper
3. Brake lamp switch
4. Clevis pin

10

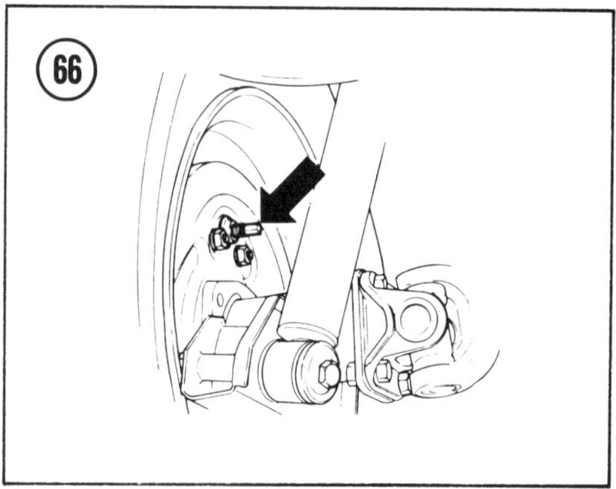

3. Back off the adjuster just enough so the shoes do not drag. Remove the jackstands and lower the car.

Handbrake (510 and 610 Sedan and Hardtop)

1. Before adjusting the handbrake, adjust the rear brakes as described earlier.

2. If necessary, tighten the rear cable adjuster (**Figure 67**) to take up slack in the rear cable.

NOTE: *Do not tighten cable enough to move the wheel cylinder levers.*

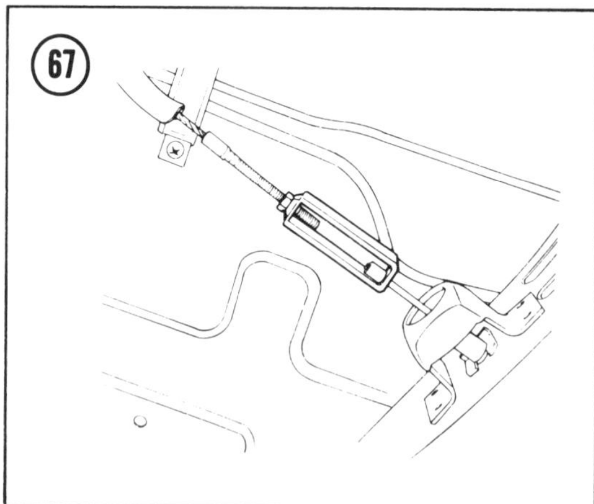

3. Check the stroke of the handbrake lever or control stem. A 44 lb. pull should give a stroke of approximately 3⅓ to 3¾ in. (510); 3½ to 4 in. (1973 610); or 3¼ to 3¾ in. (1974-76 610).

4. If necessary, turn the adjusting nuts on the handbrake rod (**Figure 68**) to change length of the stroke.

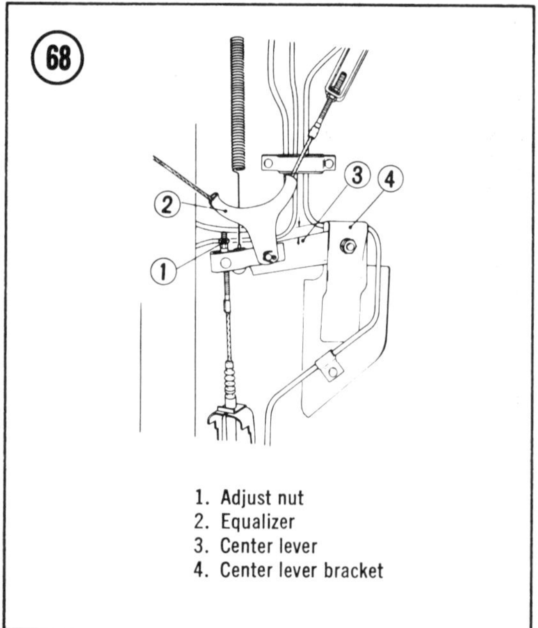

1. Adjust nut
2. Equalizer
3. Center lever
4. Center lever bracket

5. Check handbrake operation. Make sure the wheel cylinder levers return to their original postions when the handbrake is released.

Handbrake (510 and 610 Station Wagons)

1. Adjust the rear brakes as described earlier in this chapter.

2. Check control stem or lever stroke. A 44 lb. pull should give a stroke of 2-3 in. (510 wagon) or 3¼ to 3¾ in. (610 wagon).

3. If necessary, adjust the front cable or rod to change stroke length. **Figure 69** shows the adjusting nuts on 610's. The 510 arrangement is similar.

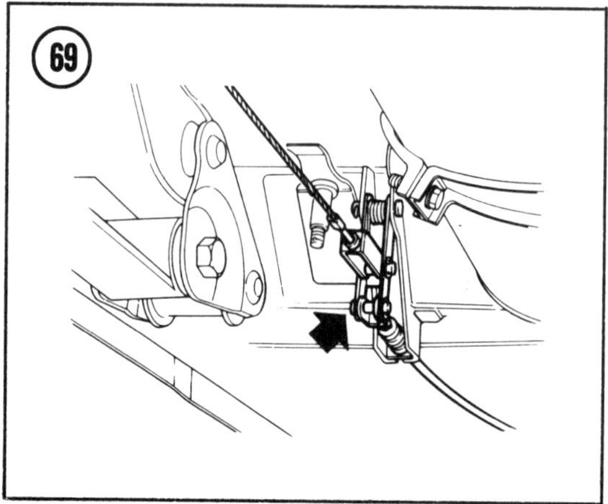

Handbrake (710)

1. Before adjusting the handbrake, adjust the rear brakes as described earlier in this chapter.

2. Check handbrake stroke. A 44-lb. (20kg) pull should raise the handbrake lever to the 6th or 7th notch.

3. To adjust the stroke on sedans and hardtops, loosen the locknut and adjusting nut (**Figure 70**). Turn the adjusting nut as needed, then secure with the locknut. After adjustment, dimension "A" (Figure 70) should be about 0.2 in. (5mm).

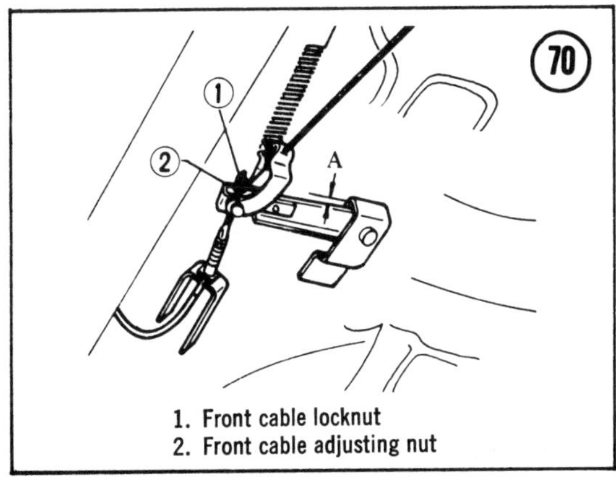

1. Front cable locknut
2. Front cable adjusting nut

4. To adjust the stroke on station wagons, loosen the locknut (**Figure 71**) and rotate the turnbuckle as needed. Then tighten the locknut.

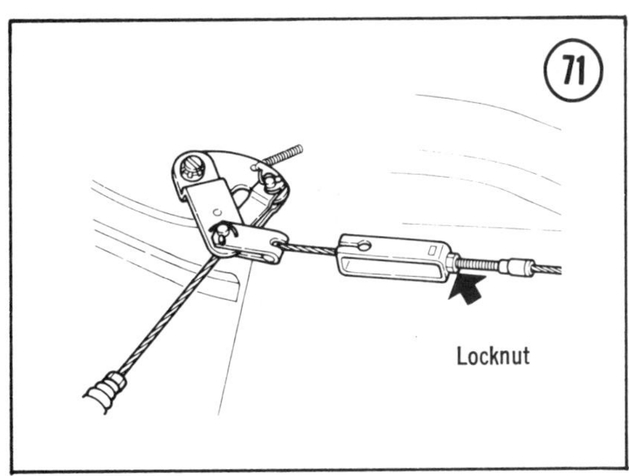

5. After adjustment, make sure the wheel cylinder levers (**Figure 72**) return to their original positions when the handbrake is released.

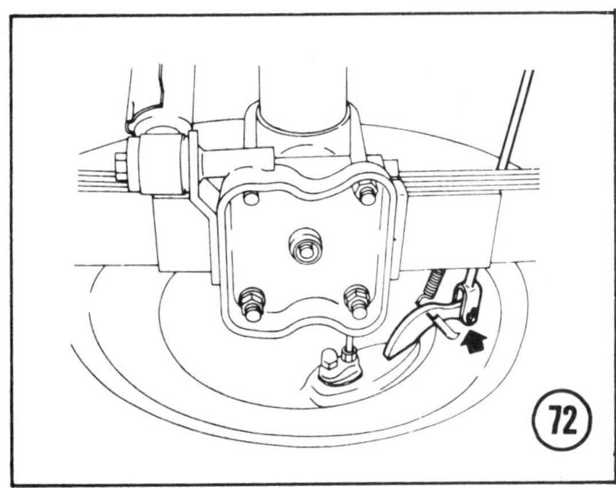

Table 1 BRAKE SPECIFICATIONS

Disc diameter	
1968-74	9.134 in. (232mm)
1975-76	9⅝ in. (245mm)
Drum diameter	9.0 in. (228.6mm)
Master cylinder diameter	¾ in. (19.05mm)
Caliper bore diameter	
1968-74	2.0 in. (50.8mm)
1975-76	2.012 in. (51.10mm)
Rear wheel cylinder diameter	
510 and 710	13/16 in. (20.64mm)
610	⅞ in. (22.2mm)

Table 2 TIGHTENING TORQUES

	Ft.-lb.	Mkg
Brake lines, 510	12-14	1.7-2.0
Metal brake lines, 610 and 710	11-13	1.5-1.8
Flexible brake hoses, 610 and 710	12-14	1.7-2.0
Caliper mounting bolts		
510	53-65	7.3-9.0
610 and 710	53-72	7.3-9.9
Disc-to-hub bolts	28-38	3.9-5.3

CHAPTER ELEVEN

REAR SUSPENSION, DIFFERENTIAL, AND DRIVE SHAFT

The 510 and 610 sedans and hardtops use a semi-trailing arm independent suspension at the rear. Station wagons and 710's use a rigid axle supported by leaf springs. All models use conventional tube shock absorbers. **Figure 1** shows the independent rear suspension (IRS). **Figure 2** shows a typical rigid axle suspension.

On IRS cars, the differential is attached to mounting members at front and rear. On rigid-axle vehicles, the differential is mounted in the axle housing.

IRS cars use exposed axle shafts with universal joints at the ends and ball splines in the centers. This allows the axle shafts to move vertically with the suspension arms and change length as needed. Rigid axle shafts are enclosed in the axle housing.

610 station wagons use a 2-piece, 3-joint drive shaft, supported in the center by a bearing. All other models use a one-piece 2-joint drive shaft.

DRIVE SHAFT

Removal/Installation

1. Securely block both front wheels so the vehicle will not roll in either direction. Jack up the rear end and place it on jackstands.

2. On 510's, loosen the clamps on premuffler and center exhaust pipe. Twist the muffler and pipe to the left to provide removal clearance for the drive shaft.

3. Make match marks on the drive shaft and differential flanges so they can be reassembled in the same relative positions.

4. On 610 wagons, unbolt the center bearing bracket from the vehicle. See **Figure 3**.

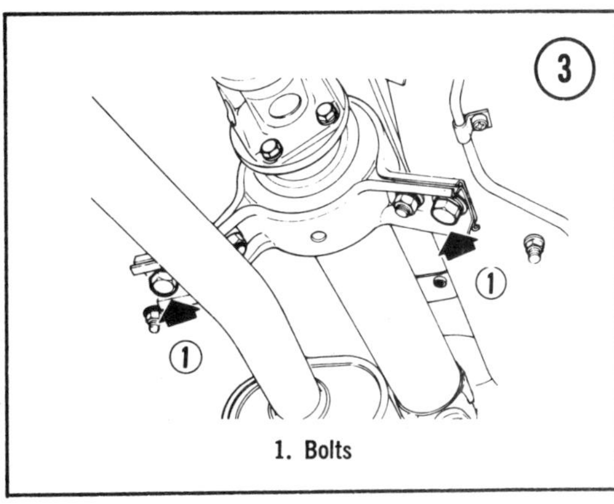

1. Bolts

5. Remove 4 bolts attaching the drive shaft to the differential.

6. Slide the drive shaft rearward out of the transmission.

1

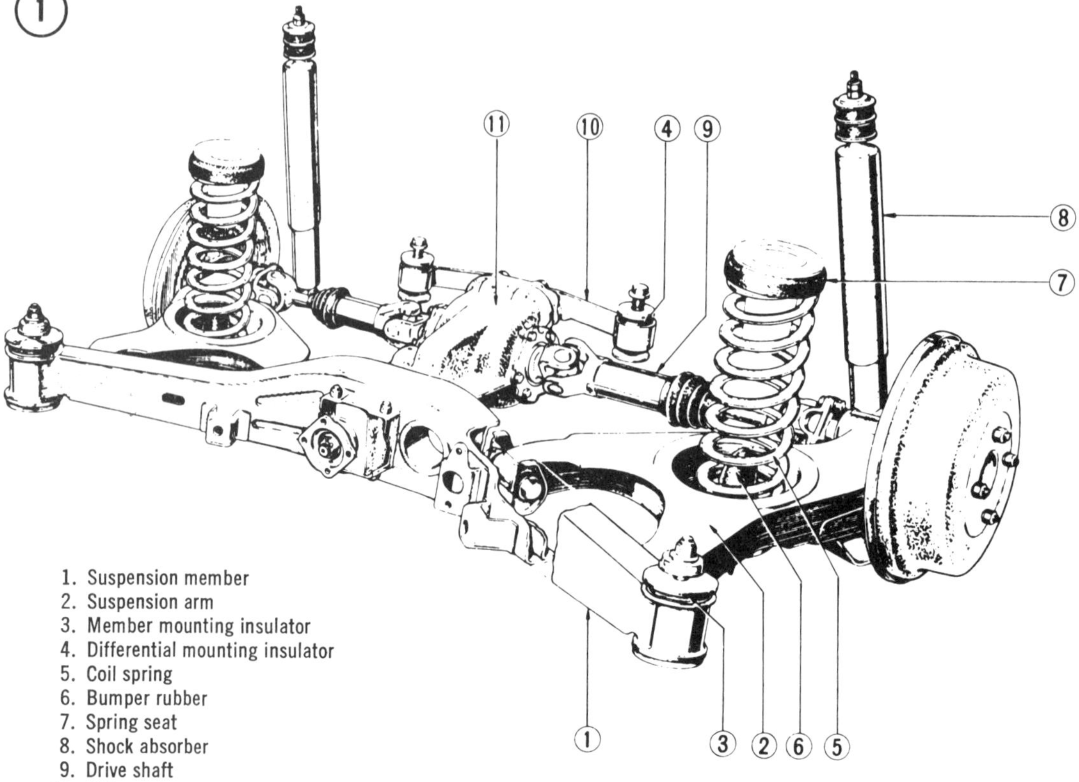

1. Suspension member
2. Suspension arm
3. Member mounting insulator
4. Differential mounting insulator
5. Coil spring
6. Bumper rubber
7. Spring seat
8. Shock absorber
9. Drive shaft
10. Differential mounting member
11. Differential carrier

INDEPENDENT REAR SUSPENSION

2

1. Differential carrier
2. Rear axle case
3. Leaf spring
4. Shock absorber

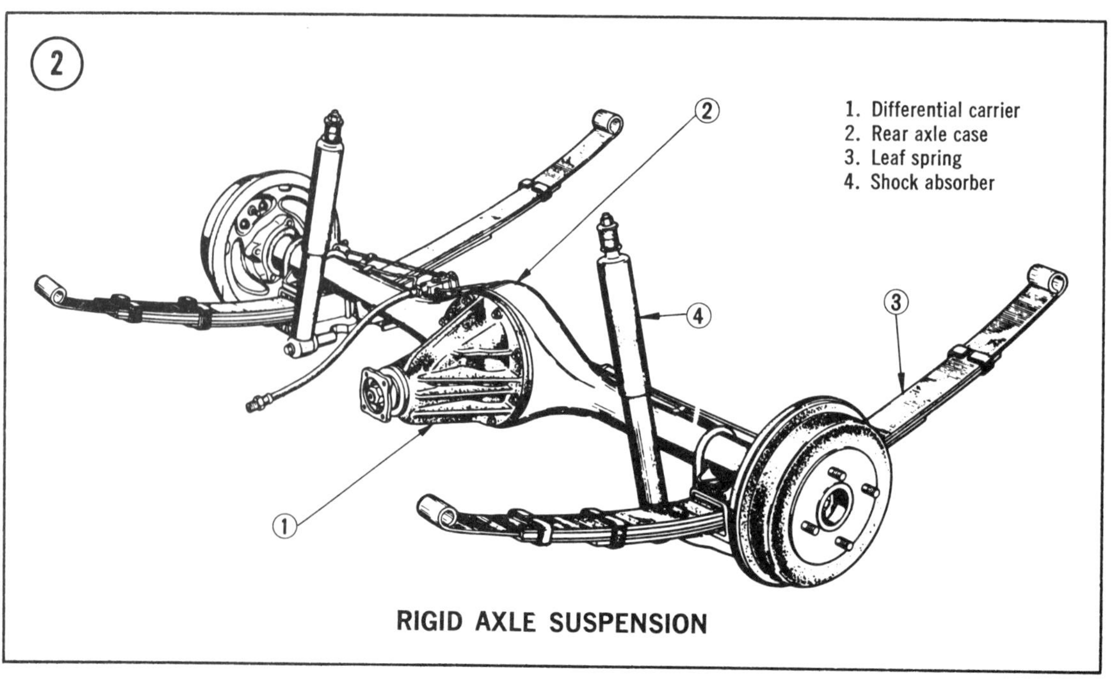

RIGID AXLE SUSPENSION

7. Installation is the reverse of these steps. Tighten all nuts and bolts to specifications (end of chapter).

Universal Joint Repair

The drive shaft should not be disassembled unless the universal joints are worn. Center bearing replacement (3-joint drive shafts) requires special equipment and should be left to a Datsun dealer.

1. Before disassembly, mark all parts so they can be reassembled in the same relative positions.
2. Remove the 4 snap rings from each of the universal joints.
3. Place the drive shaft in a vise as near the U-joint as possible. Be careful not to distort the shaft.
4. Lightly tap the base of the yoke with a hammer (**Figure 4**). Withdraw the opposite bearing race. Do the same for the remaining bearing races. Carefully separate the crosses and yokes.

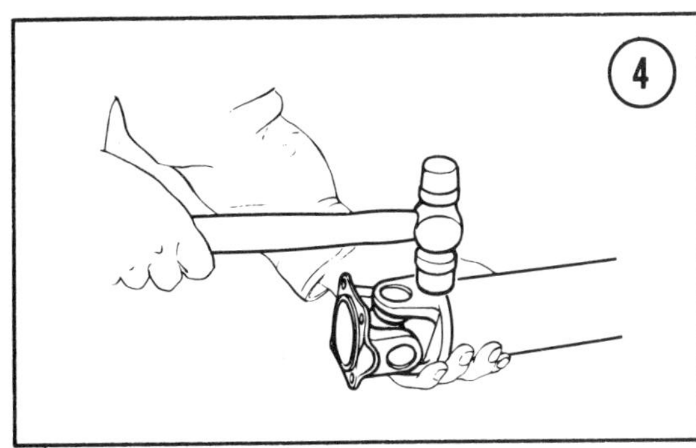

5. Check universal joint components for wear, damage, pitting, rust, or distortion. Replace as needed. If the drive shaft shows signs of damage, have it checked for balance by a dealer.
6. Assemble by reversing Steps 1-4. Apply grease liberally to the bearings and races.

AXLE SHAFTS (IRS)

The axle shafts should be disassembled and lubricated at intervals specified in Chapter Two. Except for this, no maintenance is required. The shafts must be replaced as assemblies if defective, since repair parts are not available.

Removal/Installation

1. Securely block both front wheels so the car will not roll in either direction. Jack up the rear end of the car and place it on jackstands. If necessary, remove wheels to provide working room.
2. Unbolt the axle shaft from the bearing spindle and differential. Cars through 1973 use 4 bolts at each end of the axle shaft while 1974-76 models use a single bolt at the inner end.
3. Remove the axle shaft from under the car. Be careful not to drop the shaft. It is easily damaged.
4. Installation is the reverse of these steps. Tighten all bolts to specifications (end of chapter).

Disassembly/Assembly

Figure 5 shows the axle shaft design used through 1973. The 1974-76 version is the same except for the shape of the inner universal joint yoke. Repair procedures are the same for all models.

1. Disassemble and inspect the universal joints in the same manner as drive shaft universal joints.
2. Referring to Figure 5, remove the snap ring (7) from the sleeve yoke plug (9).
3. Compress the axle shaft and remove the snap ring from the stopper (4). Remove the stopper.
4. Detach the rubber boot and separate the axle shaft sections. Be careful not to lose any of the balls or spacers, since they cannot be replaced.
5. Assembly is the reverse of these steps. Apply multipurpose grease to the universal joints and ball splines. Also grease the area shown in **Figure 6**. Make sure the balls and spacers are assembled in the order shown in Figure 5.

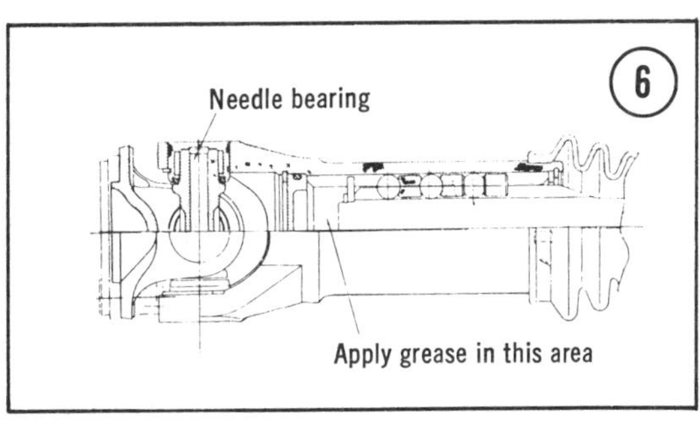

11

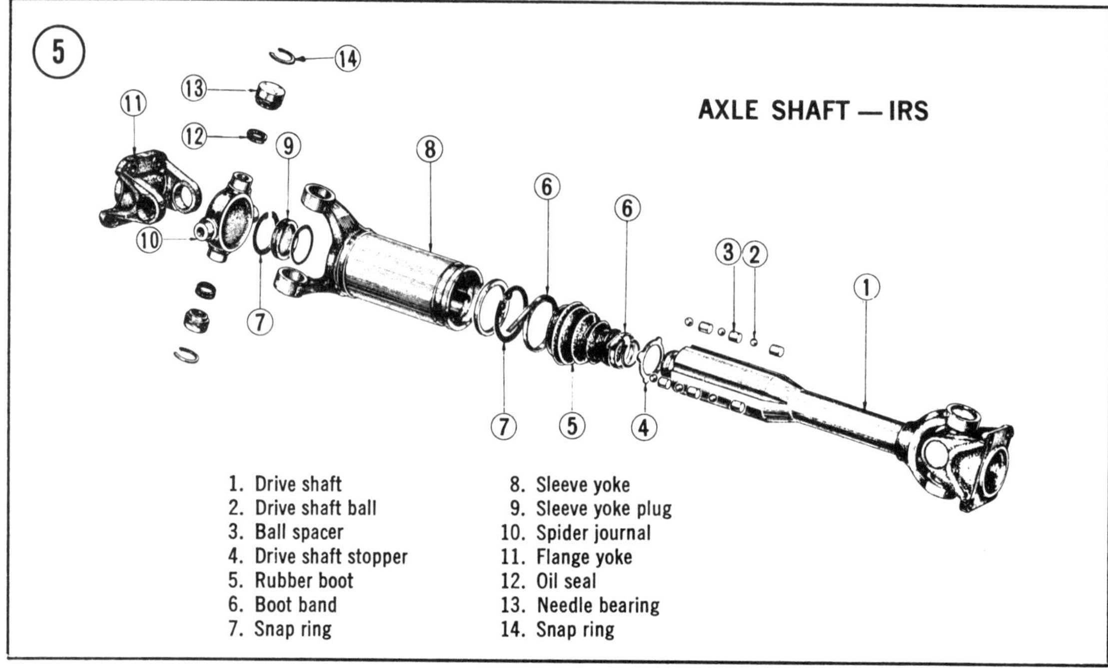

Inspection

1. Check the boot and the O-ring next to the sleeve yoke plug for damage. Replace as needed.
2. Check the shaft for bending, cracks, wear, damage, or distortion. Replace the complete shaft assembly if these are detected.
3. Check the steel balls and spacers for wear, damage, or distortion. Replace the complete shaft assembly if these are found.
4. Check the sleeve yoke (8, Figure 5) for wear or damage. Replace the complete axle shaft if these conditions are found.
5. Check the universal joints for play. If play can be detected in an assembled universal joint, replace the axle shaft.
6. Place the axle shaft in a soft-jawed vise and connect a dial gauge as shown in **Figure 7**. Fully compress the axle shaft and measure play. Replace the complete shaft if play exceeds 0.004 in. (0.1mm).

WHEEL BEARINGS AND SPINDLES (IRS)

Removal/Installation

1. Securely block both front wheels so the car will not roll in either direction.
2. Loosen the rear wheel nuts, jack up the rear end of the car, place it on jackstands, and remove the rear wheels.

CAUTION

This procedure requires undoing the wheel bearing locknuts, which are torqued to 181-239 ft.-lb. Make sure the front wheels are SECURELY blocked. Use good quality jackstands, positioned solidly beneath the car frame. Otherwise, the force required to undo the nuts could knock the car off the jackstands.

3. Unbolt the outer end of the axle shaft from the spindle flange.

4. Hold the spindle flange with a flange wrench such as ST 38060001 (**Figure 8**). Remove the wheel bearing locknut with a socket and breaker bar. If the flange wrench or an acceptable substitute isn't available, install the wheels and lower the car. Apply the handbrake and loosen the wheel bearing locknut. Put the car up on jackstands again.

> NOTE: *The nut is locked by bending the lip against the spindle threads with a punch (**Figure 9**). Do not attempt to bend the lip away from the threads or otherwise unlock the nut before removing it. Simply undo the nut.*

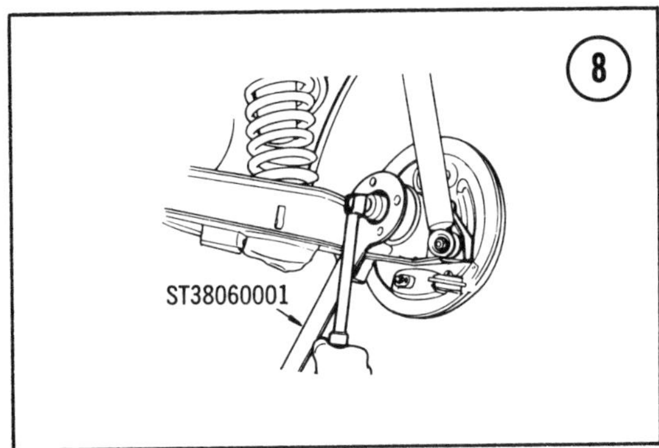

5. Attach a slide hammer to the spindle as shown in **Figure 10.** Pull the spindle out. If these tools aren't available, drive the spindle out from the inside, using a soft-metal drift.

6. Remove the spacer and flange from the bearing housing.

7. Take out the inner bearing and oil seal.

8. Remove the oil seal and inner bearing from the housing. If necessary, drive the bearing out with a drift (such as a piece of pipe) the same diameter as the bearing.

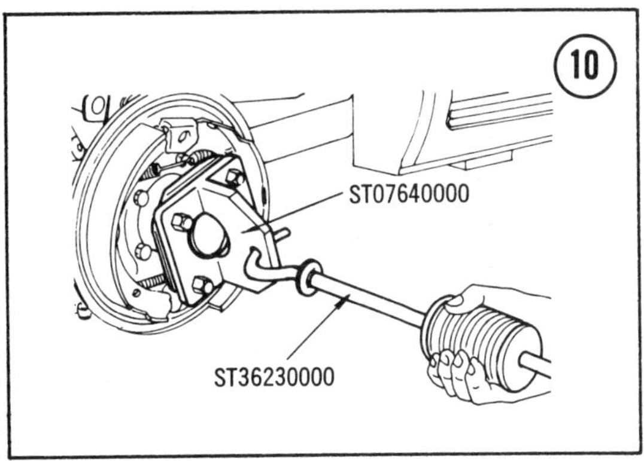

Inspection

1. Clean all parts thoroughly in solvent before inspection. Discard inner bearing grease seals.

2. Check the bearings for play and wear by holding the inner race and rotating the outer race. Check bearing friction surfaces for wear, chips, scoring, signs of seizure, and the bluish tint that indicates overheating. Replace any bearings with these defects.

3. If the outer bearing or its grease seal need replacement, remove the bearing with a gear puller or have a machine shop press it off. Outer bearings may not be reused once they have been removed from the spindle.

4. Check the ends of the bearing spacer. Replace spacers showing signs of compression, distortion, or wear.

5. Check the bearing spindles for signs of wear or damage. Replace as needed.

Assembly and Installation

Assembly and installation are the reverse of the removal and disassembly procedures, plus the following.

1. On outer wheel bearings, the sealed side faces the wheel. On inner wheel bearings, the sealed side faces the differential.

2. If new bearing spacers are being used, select them according to the marks shown in **Figure 11**. Bearing housings are marked "A", "B", or "C" at the point shown in the figure. Select a spacer with a corresponding mark.

3. Before installing the spacer, coat the outside of it with multipurpose grease. See **Figure 12**. Fill the space between the grease seal lips with

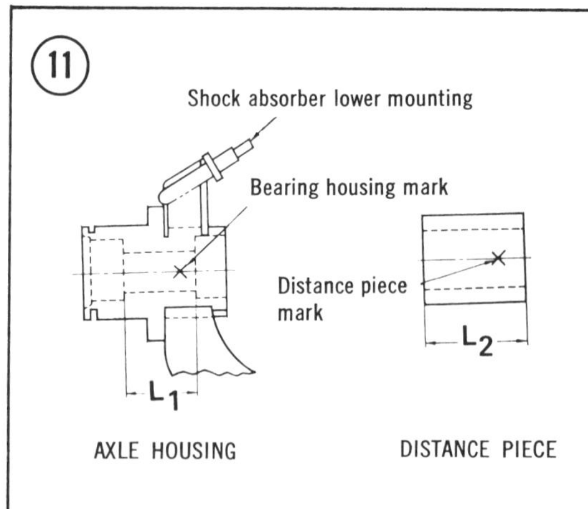

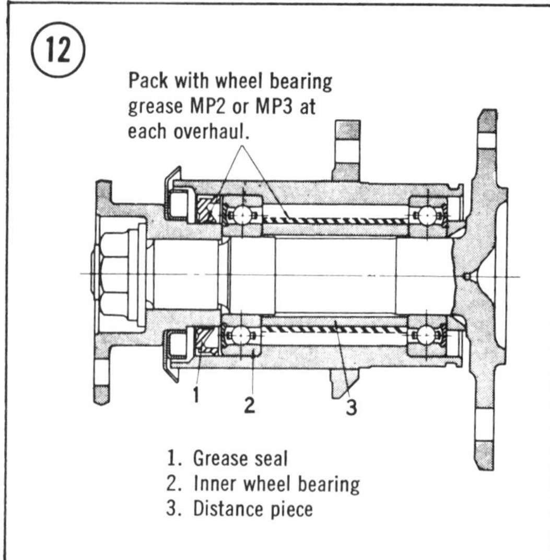

grease. Pack each bearing, working as much grease as possible into the spaces between balls and races.

4. After the spindle and bearings are installed in the housing, tighten the wheel bearing locknut to 181-239-ft.-lb. (25-33 mkg). This should result in spindle end play of zero-0.006 in. (zero-0.15mm). Turn the spindle with a spring scale attached to one of the lug nut studs. Force required to turn the spindle should be 28 oz. (790 gr) or less. If necessary, tighten or loosen the bearing locknut to adjust. However, tightness of nut must remain between 181-239 ft.-lb.

5. After tightening the locknut, bend the lip into the spindle threads at 2 points with a drift (Figure 9).

RIGID REAR AXLES

Axle Shaft Removal

1. Loosen the rear wheel nuts, jack up the rear end of the vehicle, place it on jackstands, and remove the rear wheel(s).

2. Remove the brake drum (Chapter Ten). Disconnect the brake line and handbrake cable at the wheel.

3. Remove 4 nuts or bolts securing the brake backing plate to the axle housing. See **Figure 13**.

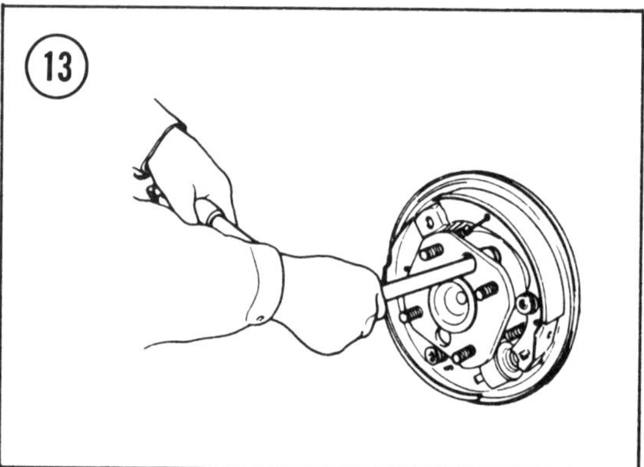

4. Remove the axle shaft, together with the brake backing plate. Use a slide hammer and adapter like the ones shown in **Figure 14**. Similar tools are available from rental dealers.

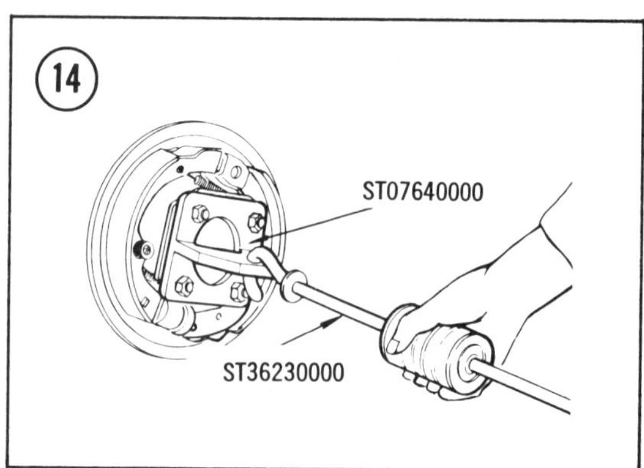

Rear Axle Shaft Inspection

1. Carefully examine the machined surfaces of the axle shaft and housing for wear. Check the shaft for bending, twisting, or damaged splines.

2. Inspect the rear wheel bearing. Rotate it and check for noise, roughness, or excessive play. If in doubt about the bearing, replace it.

Axle Oil Seal Replacement

1. Remove the axle shaft as described earlier.
2. Pry out the old oil seal with a screwdriver (**Figure 15**).

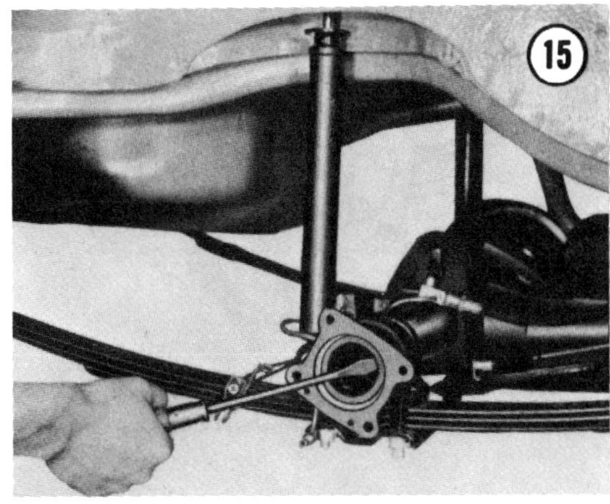

3. Drive the new seal in with a suitable drift.
4. Pack the space between the seal lips with multipurpose grease.

Rear Wheel Bearing Replacement

This procedure requires special equipment, including a press capable of several thousand pounds. It is included in case you are not near a dealer, and your local machine shop is not familiar with Datsuns.

1. Remove the axle shaft as described earlier.
2. Using a hammer and cold chisel, make several nicks in the bearing retaining collar (**Figure 16**). It will then slide easily. The retaining collar must not be reused.

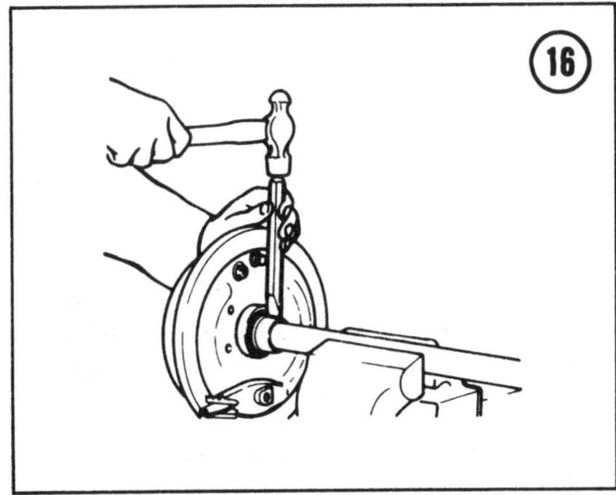

CAUTION
Do not hit the axle shaft with the cold chisel when removing retaining collar.

3. Press off the bearing and retaining collar.
4. Line up the bearing spacer, new wheel bearing, and bearing retaining collar on axle shaft.

NOTE: *On sealed-type bearing, be sure the sealed side faces the wheel.*

5. Place the lined-up parts on a press stand such as ST 38210000 (**Figure 17**). Press the spacer, bearing, and new retaining collar onto the shaft.

NOTE: *If the collar can be pressed on with less than 6,600 pounds force, it is too loose.*

6. Pack the bearing with multipurpose grease.

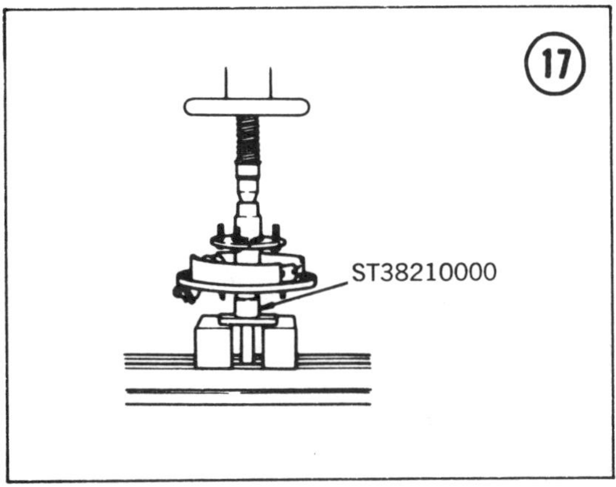

Axle Shaft Installation

1. Install a new axle housing oil seal as described earlier. Make sure the wheel bearing is packed with grease.
2. Install the axle shaft in the housing. Be careful not to damage the oil seal.
3. Check clearance between the wheel bearing and housing face (clearance C, **Figure 18**). It should be 0.004 in. (0.1mm) or less. If necessary, add or remove shims to adjust.

After installation, connect a dial gauge as shown in **Figure 19** and measure axle shaft end-play. Compare with specifications (**Table 1**).

4. Tighten the axle shaft nuts or bolts to specifications (**Table 3**, end of chapter).

11

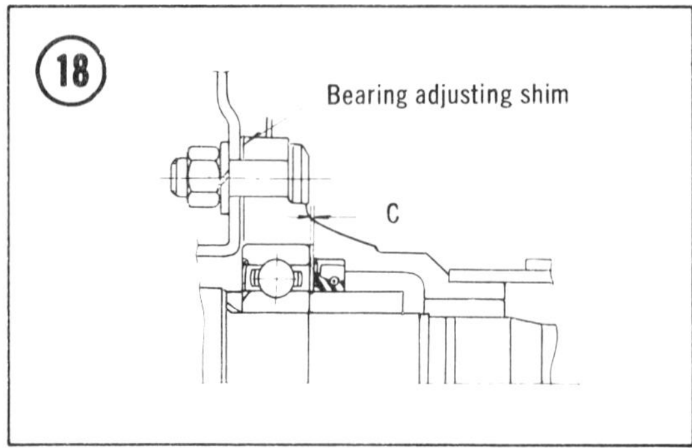

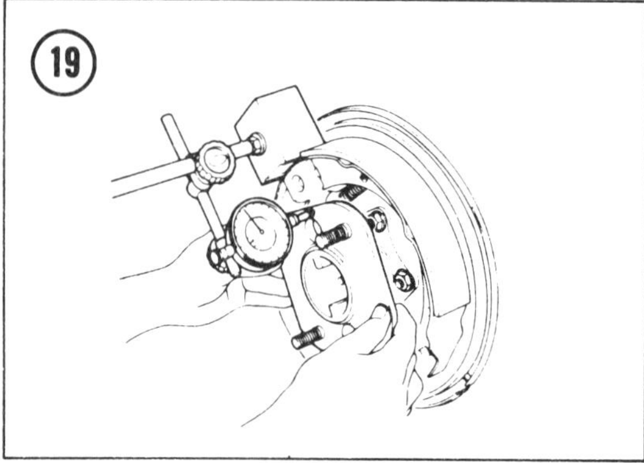

Table 1 AXLE SHAFT END PLAY

510 wagon	0.012-0.020 in. (0.3-0.5mm)
610 wagon (1974)	0.004-0.018 in. (0.10-0.45mm)
610 wagon (1975-76)	Less than 0.006 in. (0.15mm)
710 wagon (all)	0.018 in. (0.45mm)

5. Install the brake drum and wheel. Connect the brake line and handbrake cable. Install the wheels and lower the car.

DIFFERENTIAL

This section includes removal, inspection, and installation procedures. Differential repair requires special skills and tools, and should be left to a dealer. The inspection procedures will tell you if repair is necessary.

Removal/Installation (IRS)

1. Securely block both front wheels so the car will not roll in either direction. Jack up the rear end of the car and place it on jackstands.

2. Disconnect the rear handbrake cable and drive shaft (1 and 2, **Figure 20**). Mark the drive shaft and differential flanges so they may be reassembled in the same relative positions.

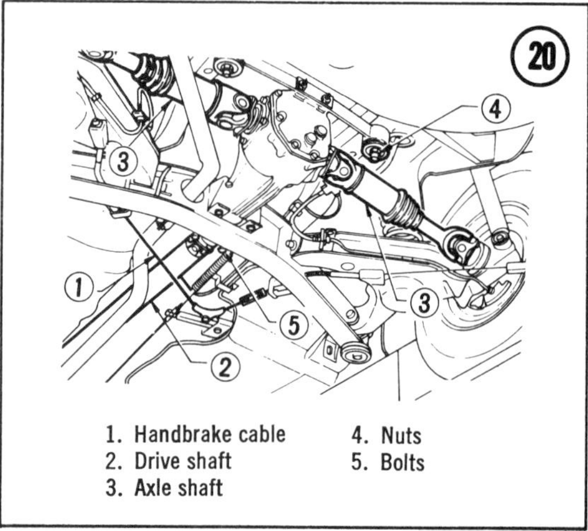

1. Handbrake cable
2. Drive shaft
3. Axle shaft
4. Nuts
5. Bolts

3. Disconnect the axle shafts (3, Figure 20). On 1968-1973 cars, unbolt the inner ends from the differential. On 1974-76 models unbolt the outer ends of the shafts, then the inner ends. Take the shafts out.

4. Place a transmission jack under the differential. Transmission jacks are available from rental dealers.

5. Remove 2 nuts attaching the differential member to the car (4, Figure 20).

6. Remove 4 bolts (5, Figure 20) attaching the front end of the differential to the mounting member.

7. Remove the differential downward and to the rear.

8. Installation is the reverse of these steps. Be sure to insert the front bolt spacers (**Figure 21**). Tighten all nuts and bolts to specifications (end of chapter).

Removal/Installation (Rigid Axles)

1. Securely block both front wheels so the vehicle will not roll in either direction. Jack up the rear end and place it on jackstands.

2. Disconnect the drive shaft from the differential. Mark the drive shaft and differential flanges so they may be reassembled in the same relative positions.

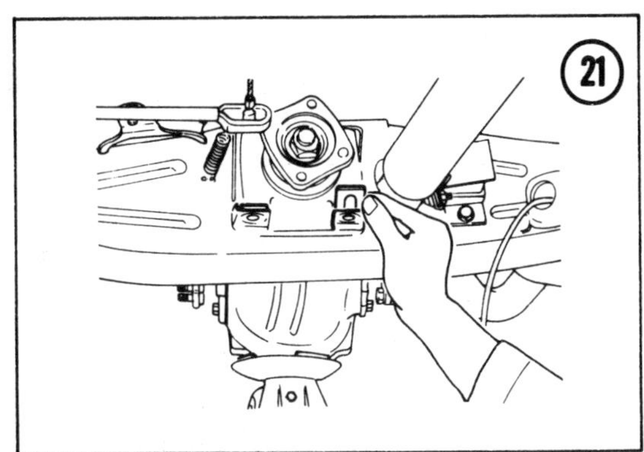

3. Remove the rear axle shafts as described previously.

4. Remove the differential attaching nuts (**Figure 22**). Lift the differential out.

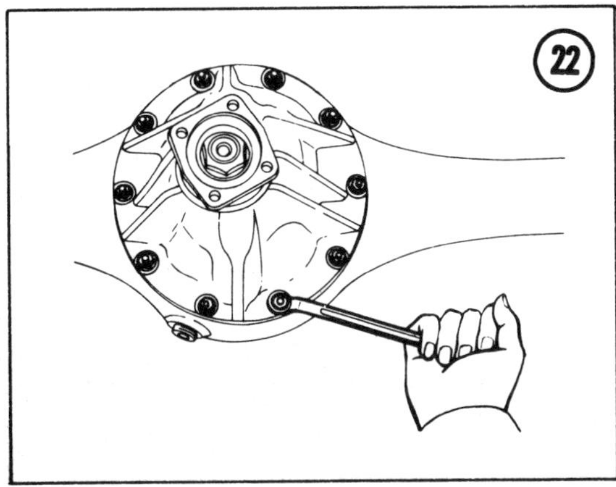

5. Installation is the reverse of these steps. Use a new gasket between differential and axle housing. Tighten all nuts and bolts to specifications at the end of the chapter.

Inspection (All Models)

1. Drain the gear oil from the differential.

2. Place the differential on a workbench. On IRS cars, remove the inspection cover.

3. Look for visible wear or damage and check the gears for chipped or missing teeth.

4. Check the tooth contact pattern of the ring gear. To do this, apply a thin, even coat of red lead oxide to 4 or 5 ring gear teeth at 2 or 3 positions on the gear. Turn the gear several turns in both directions so the contact pattern of the teeth is pressed into the coat of lead oxide. Compare the contact pattern with the following illustrations to determine differential condition.

Figure 23—Correct contact pattern.

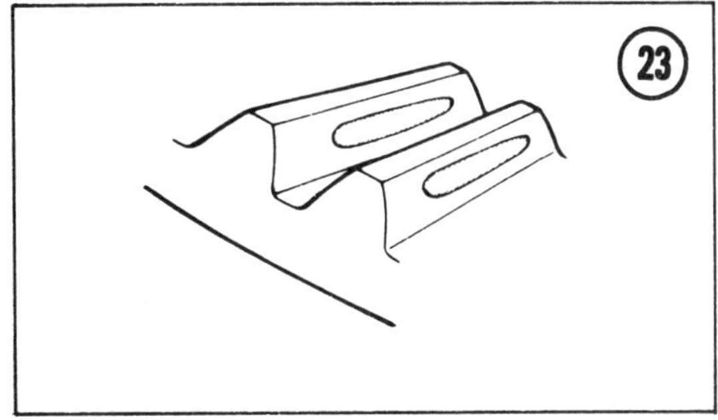

Figure 24—Heel contact. Indicates that the thickness of the pinion adjusting shim and washer should be increased to move the pinion closer to the ring gear.

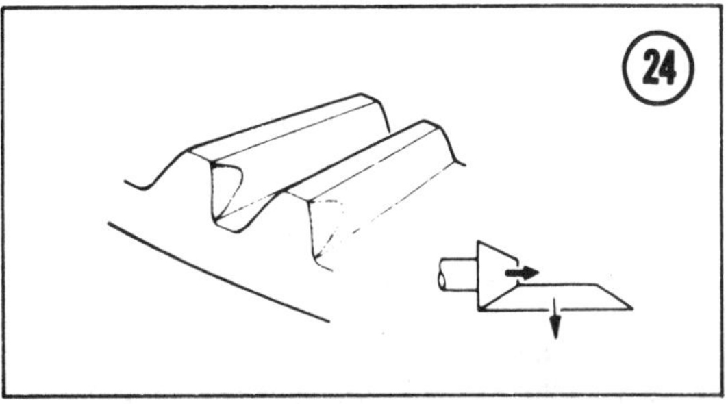

Figure 25—Toe contact. Indicates that thickness of the pinion adjusting shim and washer should be reduced to move the pinion away from the ring gear.

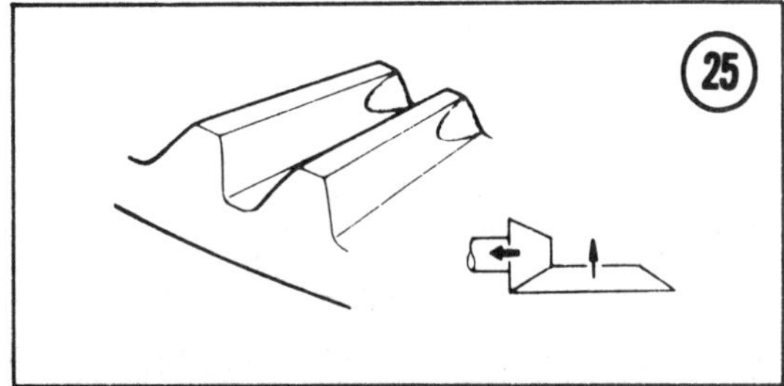

Figure 26—Flank contact. Adjusted in the same manner as toe contact.

Figure 27—Face contact. Adjusted in the same manner as heel contact.

Connect a dial gauge as shown in **Figure 28** and measure backlash of the pinion and ring

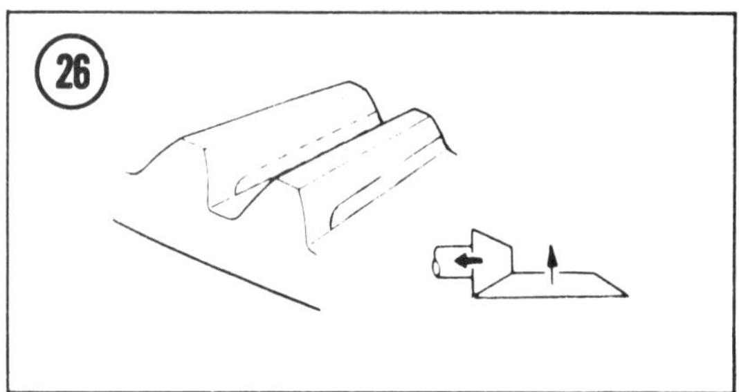

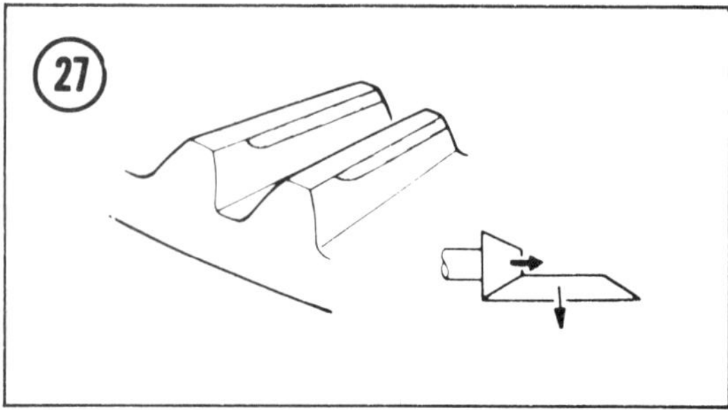

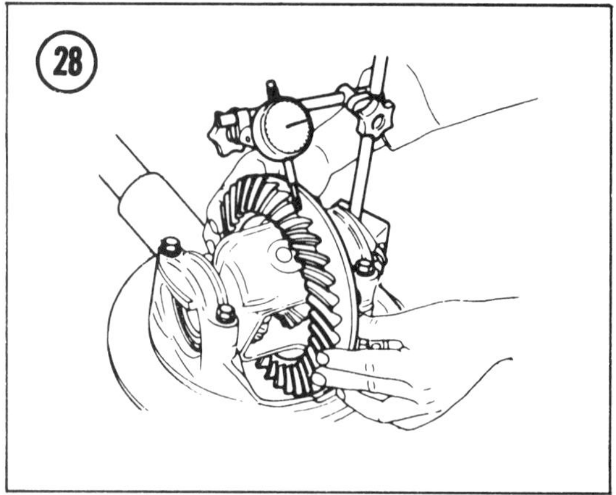

gear. To measure, hold the pinion from turning and move the ring gear while noting the reading on the gauge. Compare this reading with backlash specifications (**Table 2**). Excessive or insufficient backlash requires disassembly and adjustment of the differential.

REAR SUSPENSION

Rear Shock Absorber Replacement

For this procedure, refer to the following illustrations.

510 and 610 sedan and hardtop—**Figure 29 and Figure 30**.

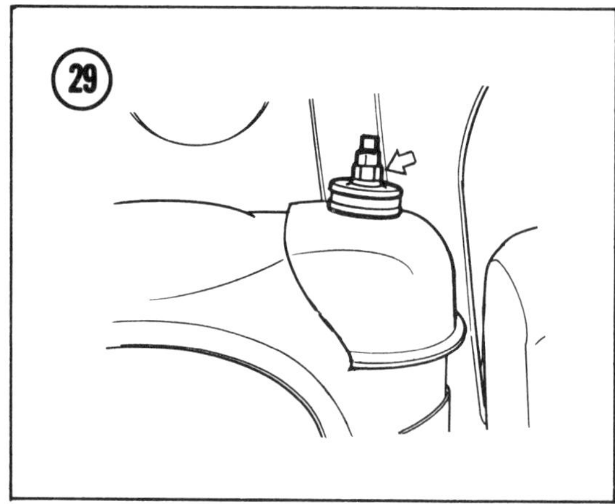

510 station wagon—**Figure 31 and Figure 32**.

610 station wagon—Figure 32 and **Figure 33**.

Table 2 RING GEAR BACKLASH

Model	Inches	mm
510 sedan and hardtop	0.004-0.008	0.10-0.20
510 wagon	0.006-0.008	0.15-0.20
610 sedan and hardtop	0.004-0.008	0.10-0.20
610 wagon		
1973	0.005-0.007	0.13-0.18
1974-76 manual	0.006-0.008	0.15-0.20
1974 automatic	0.004-0.006	0.10-0.15
1975-76 automatic	0.006-0.008	0.15-0.20
710	0.004-0.006	0.10-0.15

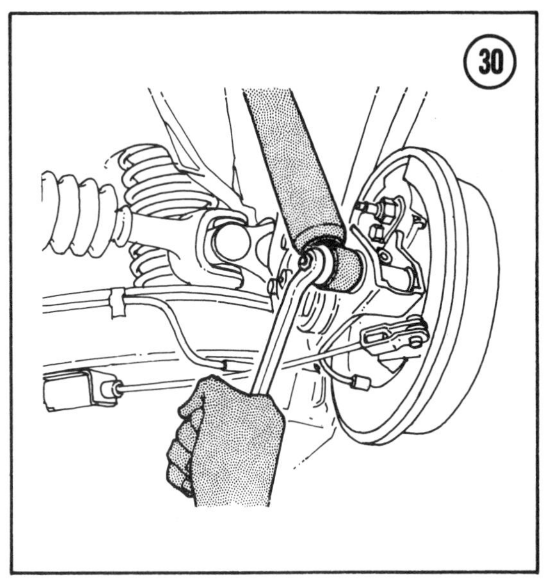

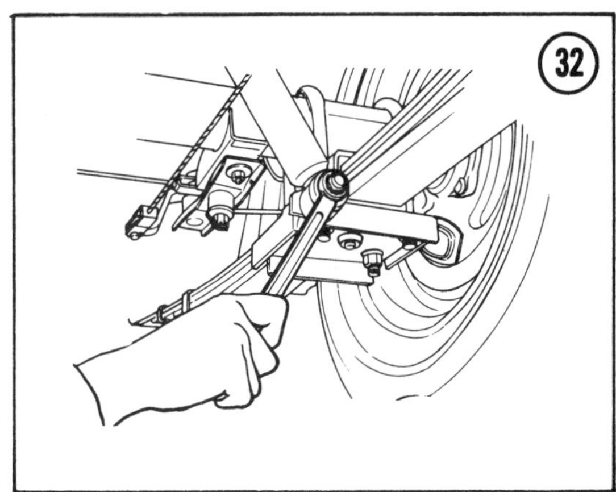

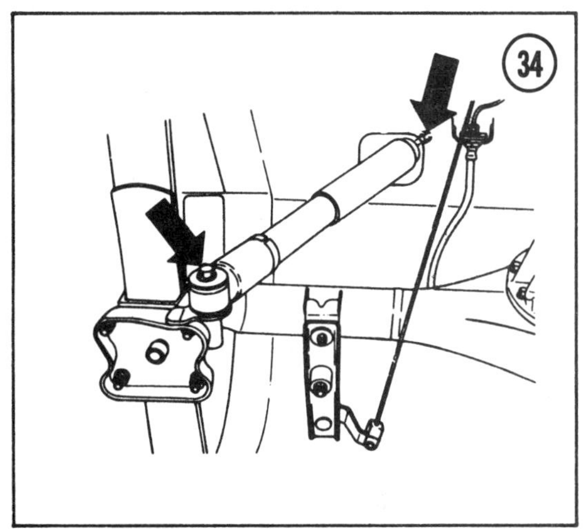

710 sedan and hardtop—**Figure 34**.

710 station wagon—**Figure 35**.

1. Securely block both front wheels so the vehicle will not roll in either direction. Jack up the rear end and place jackstands beneath the frame.

2. Place a jack beneath the axle (wheel bearing housing on IRS cars). The jack is used to raise or lower the axle.

3. Detach the lower end of the shock absorber, then the upper end. Remove it from the vehicle.

4. Installation is the reverse of these steps. Tighten all nuts and bolts to specifications (end of chapter). On 510's and 610's, the car's weight must be on the wheels before the lower end of the shock absorber is tightened. On 710's, the car must be on its wheels before either end is tightened.

Coil Spring Removal/Installation (IRS)

1. Securely block both front wheels so the car will not roll in either direction. Loosen the rear wheel nuts, jack up the rear end of the car, place it on jackstands, and remove rear wheels.

> NOTE: *Place the jackstands beneath the frame, located so they won't obstruct suspension arm movement.*

2. Referring to **Figure 36**, disconnect the handbrake cable turnbuckle (1) and return spring (2).

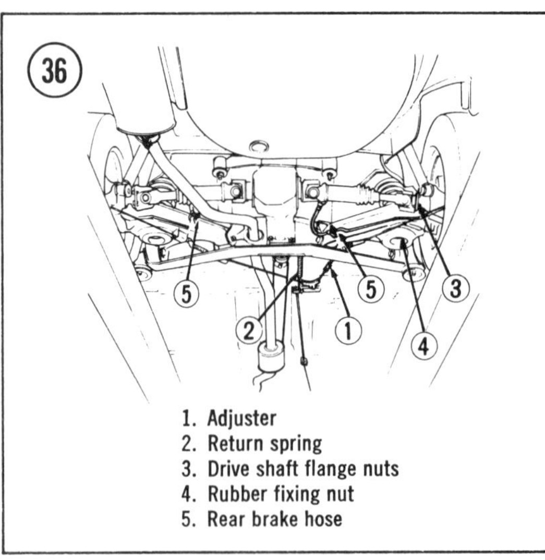

1. Adjuster
2. Return spring
3. Drive shaft flange nuts
4. Rubber fixing nut
5. Rear brake hose

3. Unbolt the outer end of the axle shaft (3) from the wheel bearing spindle.

4. With a container handy to catch dripping brake fluid, disconnect the brake line (5) at the suspension arm.

5. Remove the nut securing the rebound bumper (4).

6. Place a jack beneath the suspension arm. Raise it to relieve pressure on the shock absorber, then disconnect lower end of shock.

7. Slowly lower the jack until the spring is fully extended. Take the spring out (**Figure 37**).

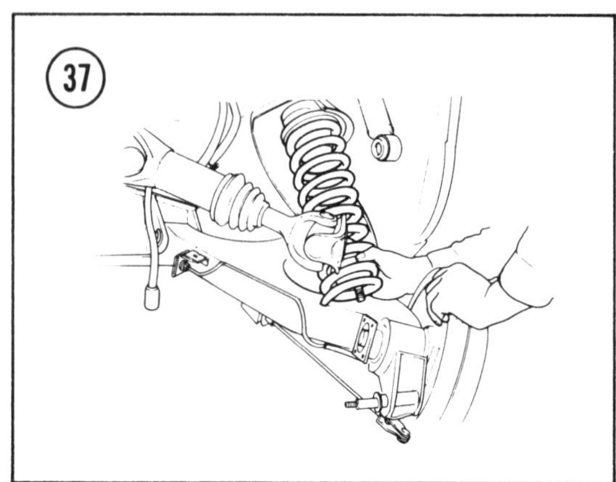

8. Check the spring for cracks, deformation, or damage. Check rubber parts for deterioration. Replace as needed.

9. Install by reversing Steps 1-7. The flat end of the spring goes on top. Tighten the nuts on rebound bumper and shock absorber lower end to 12-16 ft.-lb. (1.6-2.2 mkg). Tighten the axle shaft outer end to 36-43 ft.-lb. (5-6 mkg).

> NOTE: *The car's weight must be on the wheels before tightening the shock absorber lower end.*

Suspension Arm Removal/Installation (IRS)

1. Securely block both front wheels so the car will not roll in either direction. Loosen the rear wheel nuts, jack up the rear end of the car, place it on jackstands, remove the rear wheels.

2. Remove the brake drum. Disconnect the handbrake cable from the wheel cylinder lever.

3. Disconnect the flexible brake hose (5, Figure 36) at the suspension arm. Plug the hose and brake line.

4. Unbolt the outer end of the axle shaft (3, Figure 36).

5. Remove the rear wheel bearings and spindle as described earlier in this chapter.

6. Remove 4 bolts securing the brake backing plate (**Figure 38**). Lift the brake assembly off.

7. Perform Steps 5-7, *Coil Spring Removal/Installation.*

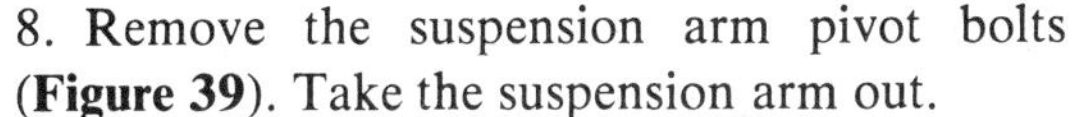

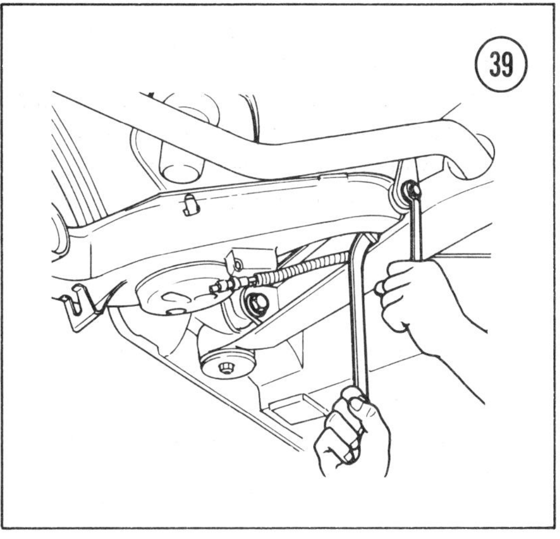

8. Remove the suspension arm pivot bolts (**Figure 39**). Take the suspension arm out.

9. Check the suspension arm for wear, cracks, and deformation. Replace as needed.

10. Check the bushings for wear, looseness, or deterioration. Bushing replacement requires special tools. If replacement is necessary, take the job to a Datsun dealer.

11. Install by reversing Steps 1-8. Use new self-locking nuts on the suspension arm pivot bolts. Tighten the pivot bolts and shock absorber lower nuts with the car's weight resting on the wheels. See Table 3 (end of chapter) for torque specifications.

Suspension Removal/Installation (IRS)

If the suspension is heavily damaged, it can be removed as a unit. Refer to **Figure 40**.

1. Securely block both front wheels so the car will not roll in either direction. Loosen the rear wheel nuts, jack up the rear end of the car, place

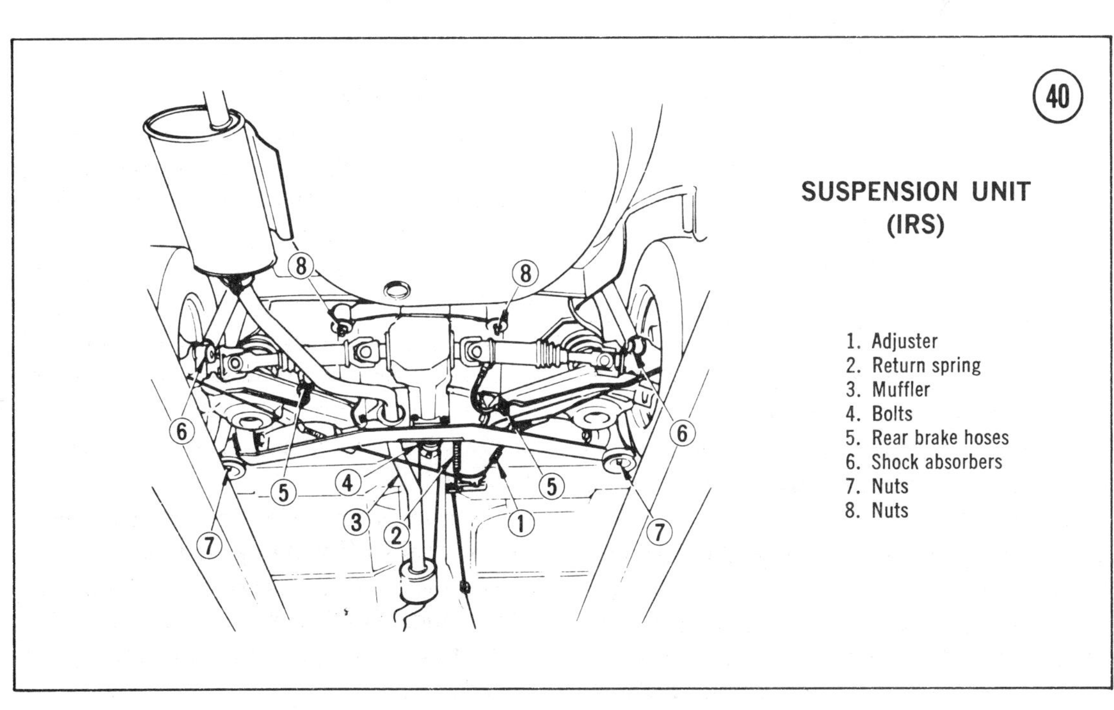

it on jackstands, and remove the rear wheels. Be sure the stands are placed solidly beneath the frame, and located where they will not interfere with suspension removal.

2. Disconnect the handbrake cables at the turnbuckle (1, Figure 40) and return spring (2).

3. Remove the muffler and rear exhaust pipe.

4. Unbolt the drive shaft (4) from the differential. Mark the drive shaft and differential flanges so they may be reassembled in the same relative positions.

5. With a container handy to catch dripping brake fluid, disconnect the flexible brake hoses (5) at the suspension arms. Plug the hoses and metal tubes to keep dirt out.

6. Use a jack to raise one suspension arm, then disconnect the lower end of the shock absorber. Do the same on the other side of the car.

7. Place a transmission jack under the differential. Transmission jacks are available from tool rental dealers.

8. Remove the suspension member nuts (7) and differential member nuts (8). Lower the suspension and pull it out from under the rear of the car.

9. Installation is the reverse of these steps. Tighten all nuts and bolts to specifications (Table 3, end of chapter). Suspension arm pivot bolts and shock absorber lower nuts must be tightened with the car's weight resting on the wheels.

Leaf Spring Removal (Rigid Axles)

1. Securely block both front wheels so the vehicle will not roll in either direction. Jack up the rear end, place it on jackstands, and remove the rear wheels.

2. Place a jack beneath the center of the axle to support it.

3. Remove the nuts from U-bolts and shock absorber lower end. **Figure 41** is typical.

4. Remove the bolts from the rear shackle. **Figure 42** shows the 610 version. All other models are basically the same.

5. Detach the front end of the spring. See **Figure 43** (510), **Figure 44** (610, 710 wagon), or **Figure 45** (710 sedan and hardtop).

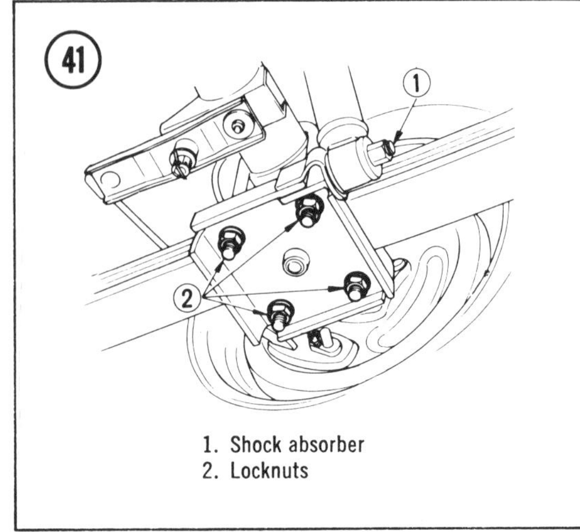

1. Shock absorber
2. Locknuts

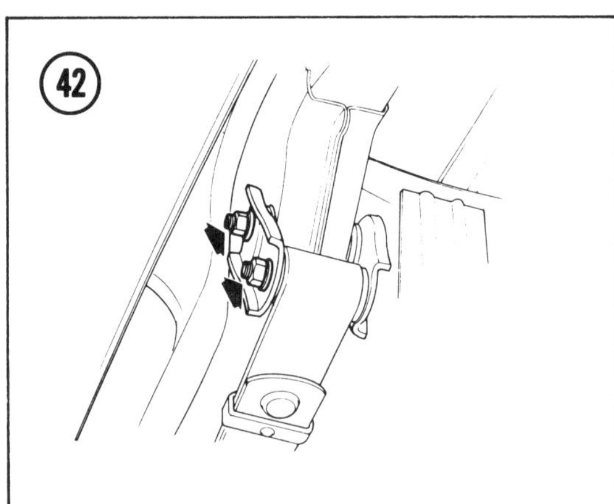

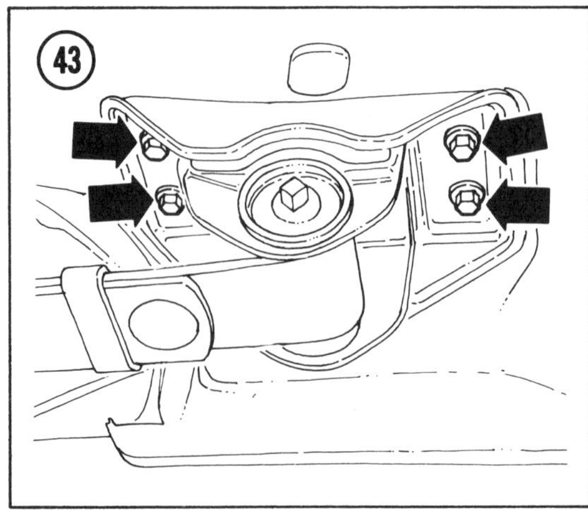

6. Lower the spring away from the car.

7. Check all parts for rust, wear, or damage. Replace as needed.

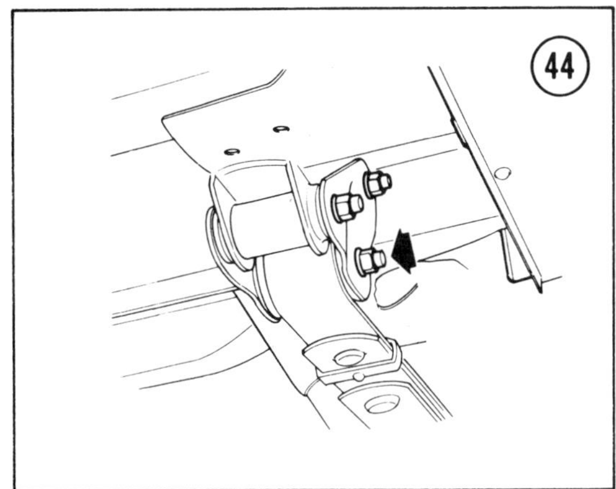

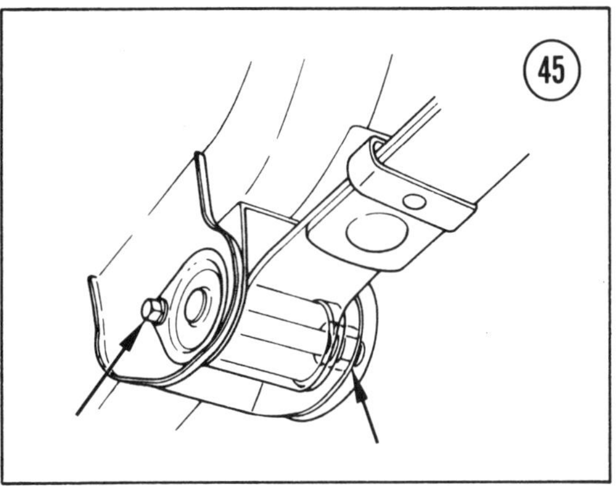

Leaf Spring Installation (Rigid Axles)

Installation is the reverse of the removal procedure, plus the following.

1. Coat rubber bushings with soapy water before installation.
2. Tighten U-bolt nuts evenly in a diagonal pattern. Be sure U-bolts are vertical, not tilted to one side.
3. Nuts and bolts at front and rear ends of springs and lower ends of shock absorbers must be tightened with the vehicle's weight on the rear wheels. Tighten all nuts and bolts to specifications (Table 3).

Table 3 TIGHTENING TORQUES

	Ft.-lb.	Mkg
Drive Shaft		
510 flange bolts	15-20	2.0-2.7
610		
Flange bolts, 1973	15-20	2.0-2.7
Flange bolts, 1974-76	17-24	2.4-3.3
Center bracket nuts, wagon	14-19	1.9-2.6
Center bracket bolts, wagon	26-35	3.6-4.8
710		
Flange bolts, 1974-75	18-23	2.5-3.2
Flange bolts, 1976	17-24	2.4-3.3
Axle Shafts (IRS)		
Through 1973, all bolts	36-43	5-6
1974-76 outer bolts	36-43	5-6
1974-76 inner bolt	23-31	3.2-4.3
Axle Shafts (Rigid Axle)		
510 wagon	21-28	2.8-3.9
610 wagon, 710	16-20	2.2-2.7
Differential (IRS)		
510 sedan and hardtop		
Differential to suspension member	43-51	6-7
Differential to rear member	43-58	6-8
Rear member to car	62	8.5
Inspection cover bolts	14-19	1.9-2.6
610 sedan and hardtop		
Differential to suspension member	36-51	5-7
Differential to rear member	43-58	6-8
Rear member to car	51-72	7-10
Inspection cover bolts	14-19	1.9-2.6
Differential (Rigid Axles)		
Attaching nuts, 510 wagon	14-16	2.0-2.2
Attaching nuts, 610 wagon and 710	14-18	2.0-2.5
Shock Absorbers		
510 sedan and hardtop		
Upper	17	2.3
Lower*	17	2.3

(continued)

Table 3 TIGHTENING TORQUES (continued)

	Ft.-lb.	Mkg
Shock Absorbers (continued)		
510 wagon		
Upper nuts	12-16	1.7-2.2
Mounting plate bolts	11-18	1.5-2.5
Lower nuts*	25-33	3.5-4.5
610 sedan and hardtop		
Upper	12-16	1.6-2.2
Lower*	12.16	1.6-2.2
610 wagon		
Upper	6½-9	0.9-1.2
Lower*	25-33	3.5-4.5
710 sedan and hardtop		
Upper*	Tighten until threads are used up, then secure with locknut	
Lower*	12-16	1.6-2.2
710 wagon		
Upper*	6½-9	0.9-1.2
Lower*	12-16	1.6-2.2
Suspension (IRS)		
Suspension arm pivot bolts*	58-72	8-10
Brake backing plate bolts	20-27	2.7-3.7
Suspension member to car		
510	72	10
610	51-72	7-10
Springs (Rigid Axles)		
510 wagon		
Front pin and rear shackles*	33-36	4.5-5.0
U-bolts*	43-47	6.0-6.5
610 wagon		
Front pin, rear shackle, and U-bolts*	43-47	6.0-6.5
710 sedan and hardtop		
Front pin and rear shackle	37-50	5.1-6.9
Square-head front pin bolt*	6-7	0.8-1.2
U-bolts*	25-35	3.5-4.8
710 wagon (all fasteners)*	43-47	6.0-6.5

*Torque with car weight on wheels (car on ground).

11

CHAPTER TWELVE

FRONT SUSPENSION, WHEEL BEARINGS, AND STEERING

Datsun cars use a McPherson strut front suspension. The shock absorbers and springs are combined into a single unit, with the bearing spindles permanently attached at the bottom. The struts are bolted to the inner wheel wells at the top and through ball-joints to the lower transverse links at the bottom. The front-rear movements of the transverse links are controlled by tension rods. A stabilizer connects the transverse links.

Specifications (**Table 1**) and tightening torques (**Table 2**) are at the end of the chapter.

WHEEL ALIGNMENT

Several front suspension angles affect the running and steering of the front wheels. These angles must be properly aligned to prevent excessive wear, as well as to maintain directional stability and ease of steering. The angles are as follows:

a. Caster
b. Camber
c. Toe-in
d. Steering axis inclination
e. Steering angles

On cars, caster, camber, and steering axis inclination are built in and cannot be adjusted. These angles are measured to check for bent suspension parts. Steering angles should not be adjusted without a front-end rack. Toe-in can be adjusted as described later in this chapter.

Pre-alignment Check

Adjustment of the steering and various suspension angles is affected by several factors. Perform the following steps before any adjustments are attempted.

1. Check tire pressure and wear. See *Tire Wear Analysis*, Chapter Three.
2. Check play in front wheel bearings. Adjust if necessary.
3. Check play in ball-joints. See Chapter Three.
4. Check for broken springs.
5. Remove any excessive load.
6. Check shock absorbers.
7. Check steering gear adjustments.
8. Check play in steering linkage.
9. Check wheel balance.
10. Check rear suspension for looseness.

Front tire wear patterns can indicate several alignment problems. These are covered under *Tire Wear Analysis*, Chapter Three.

Caster and Camber

Caster is the inclination from vertical of the line through the ball-joints or kingpins. Positive caster shifts the wheel forward; negative caster shifts the wheel rearward. Caster causes the wheels to return to the straight ahead position after a turn. It also prevents the wheels from wandering due to wind, potholes, or uneven road surfaces.

Camber is the inclination of the wheel from vertical. With positive camber, the top of the tire leans outward. With negative camber, the top of the tire leans inward.

Toe-in

Since the front wheels tend to point outward when the vehicle is moving forward, the distance between the front edges of the tire (A, **Figure 1**) is slightly less than the distance between the rear edges (B) when the vehicle is at rest.

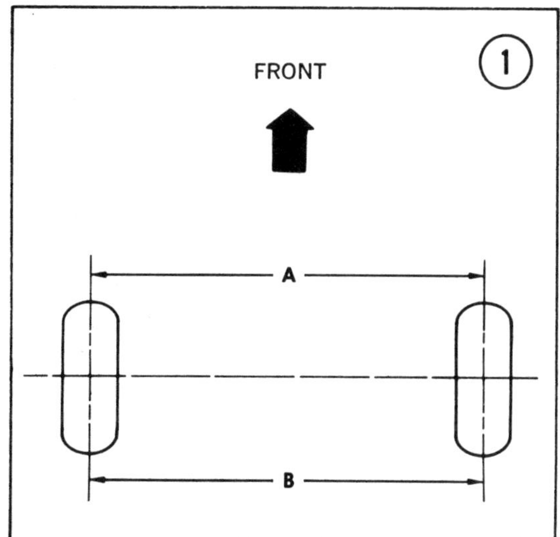

To adjust toe in, loosen the locknuts on the tie rod adjusting bars (**Figure 2**). Rotate the adjusting bars as needed to increase or reduce toe-in.

Steering Axis Inclination

Steering axis inclination is the inward or outward lean of the struts. The angle is not adjustable.

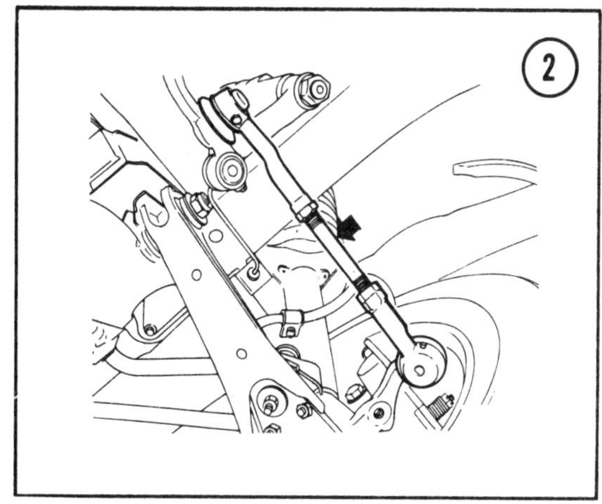

Steering Angles

When a car turns, the inside wheel makes a smaller circle than the outside wheel. Because of this, the inside wheel turns at a greater angle than the outside wheel. These angles are adjustable, but the job should be left to a dealer or front-end specialist.

FRONT SHOCK ABSORBER REPLACEMENT

The front shock absorbers are located inside the suspension struts (**Figure 3**). Replacement requires several special tools. However, much expense can be saved by removing the strut assemblies yourself and taking them to a dealer for shock absorber replacement.

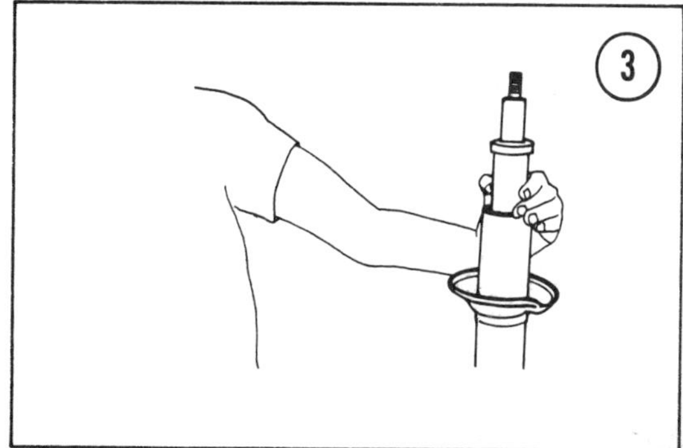

1. Loosen the front wheel nuts, jack up the front end of the car, place it on jackstands, and remove the front wheels.
2. Disconnect the caliper brake hose from the metal brake line. On 610's and 710's, detach

the hose from its bracket on the strut as well. **Figure 4** shows the 610 arrangement; 510's and 710's are similar.

3. Remove caliper attaching bolts (**Figure 5**) and lift the caliper off.

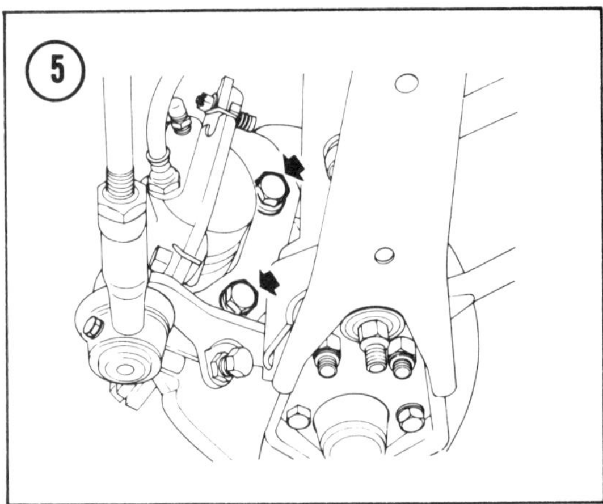

4. Remove 2 bolts attaching the knuckle arm to the strut (**Figure 6**).

5. Pry the transverse link downward with a strong steel bar (**Figure 7**). Pull the strut outward, away from the transverse link.

6. Place a jack beneath the strut to support it. Remove 3 self-locking nuts securing the top of the strut to the fender well (**Figure 8**).

WARNING

Do not remove the center nut from the top of the strut. This could allow the coil spring to fly out and cause serious injury.

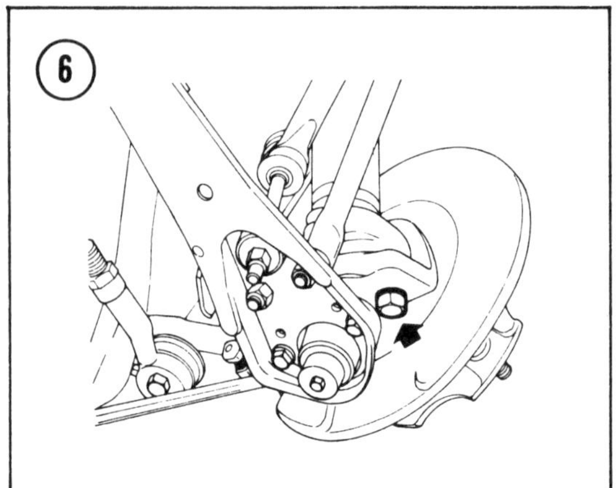

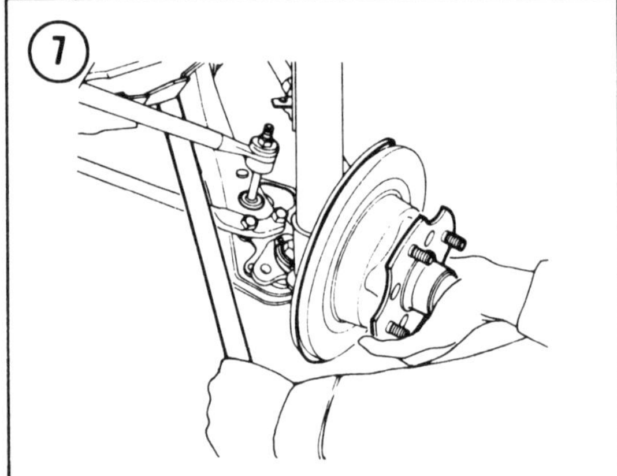

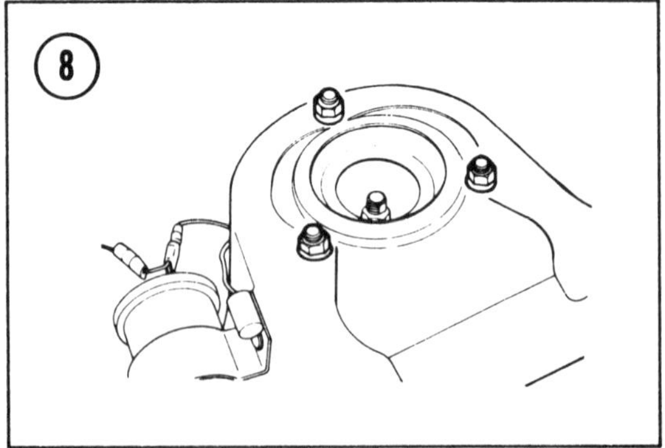

7. Lower the jack beneath the strut and take it out (**Figure 9**).

8. Have new shock absorbers installed in the struts by a Datsun dealer.

9. Installation is the reverse of these steps. Use new self-locking nuts at the top of the strut. Before bolting the knuckle arm to the strut, apply gasket sealer to the strut base as shown

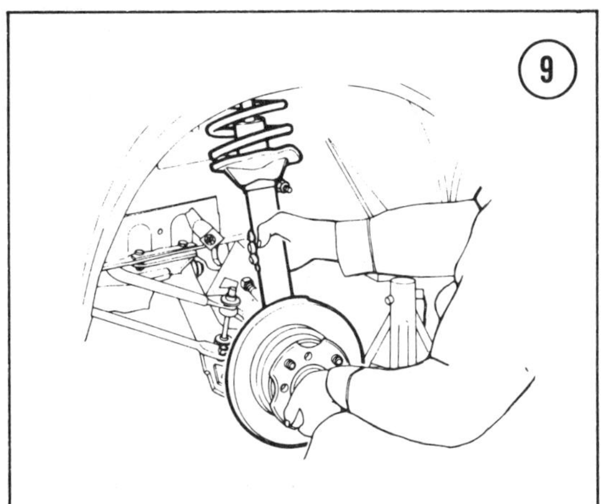

in **Figure 10**. Tighten all fasteners to torque specifications at the end of the chapter. Bleed the brakes after installation.

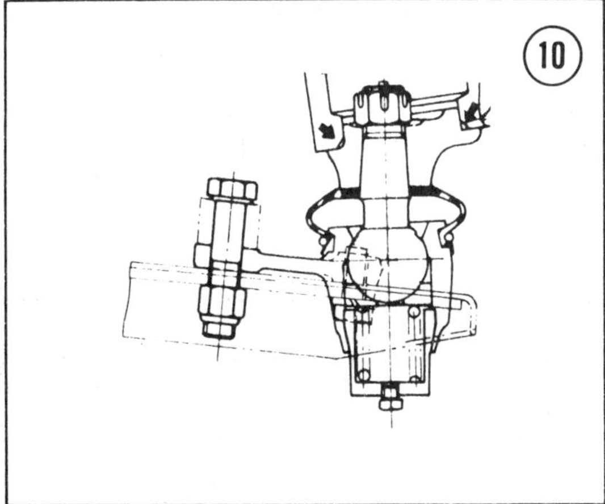

COIL SPRING REPLACEMENT

The coil spring is part of the strut assembly. To replace the spring, follow the shock absorber procedure. Since the procedure requires special tools, it is best to remove the strut assembly yourself and let a dealer install the new spring. Then install the strut using the same procedure.

STABILIZER

Removal/Installation

1. Jack up the front end of the vehicle and place it on jackstands.

2. Detach the stabilizer brackets from the vehicle frame. **Figure 11** shows a typical installation.

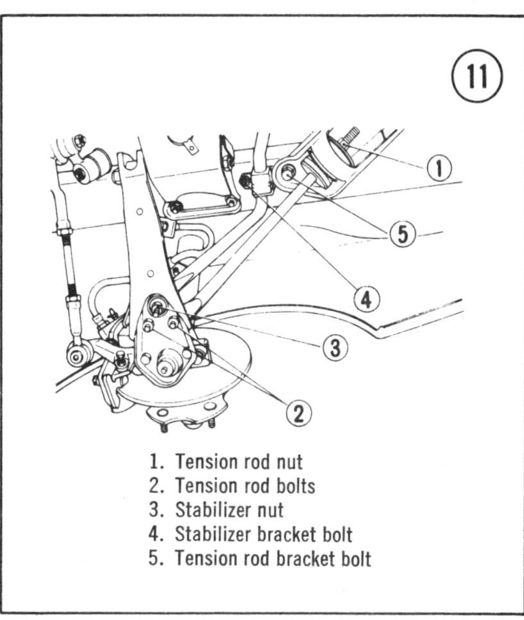

1. Tension rod nut
2. Tension rod bolts
3. Stabilizer nut
4. Stabilizer bracket bolt
5. Tension rod bracket bolt

3. Detach the stabilizer from the transverse links, then take it out.

4. Check the rubber mounting bushings for wear, cracks, or general deterioration. Replace as needed.

5. Installation is the reverse of these steps. Make sure the stabilizer is centered in the brackets. Make sure the clearance between tension rod and stabilizer bar is equal on both sides. See **Figure 12**. Tighten all fasteners to specifications (end of chapter).

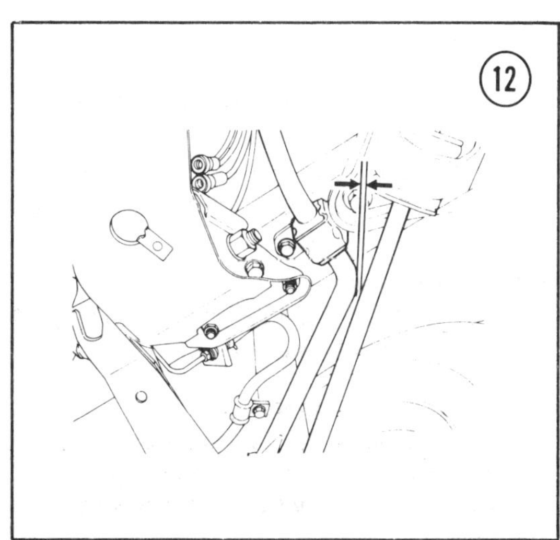

TENSION RODS

Removal/Installation

1. Jack up the front end of the car and place it on jackstands.

2. Remove the tension rod nut and bolts (1 and 2, Figure 11). Take the tension rod out.

3. The 610's and 710's use removable tension rod brackets. If necessary, remove 4 bolts (5, Figure 11) and take the bracket off.

4. Installation is the reverse of these steps. Be sure the tension rod bushings are compressed evenly. Tighten all nuts and bolts to specifications (end of chapter).

TRANSVERSE LINKS AND BALL-JOINTS

Removal

1. Loosen the front wheel nuts, jack up the front end of the car, place it on jackstands, and remove the front wheels.

2. Remove the stabilizer nut and tension rod bolts (**Figure 13**).

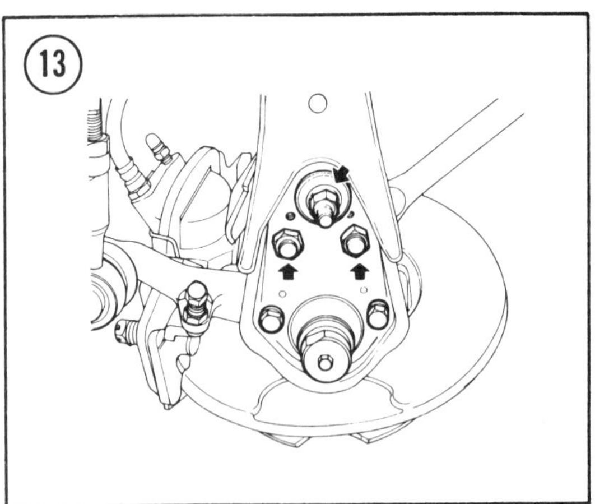

3. Detach the tie rod from the knuckle arm.

4. Remove 2 bolts securing the knuckle arm to the strut (Figure 7). This separates the knuckle arm, ball-joint, and transverse link outer end from the strut assembly.

5. Remove the transverse link nut (**Figure 14**). Take the transverse link out.

6. Place the transverse link in a vise. Remove the cotter pin and nut from the ball-joint stud. Separate the knuckle arm from the ball-joint.

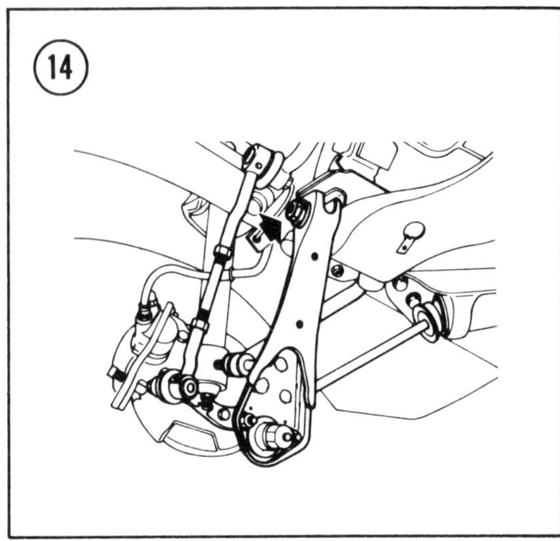

7. Unbolt the ball-joint from the transverse link and take it out.

8. Installation is the reverse of these steps. Tighten the transverse link nut with the car's weight on the wheels.

Inspection

1. Check the knuckle arm for wear, cracks, and other visible defects. Replace if these are found.

2. Check the transverse link bushing for wear and damage. If worn, have it replaced by a Datsun dealer or machine shop. If the rubber is melted or the bushing metal is cracked, replace the transverse link.

3. Check the transverse link for bending, cracks, or other damage. Replace if these are found.

4. Check the ball-joint for a cracked rubber boot or other visible damage. Place the ball-joint in a vise with the stud pointing upward. Set up a dial gauge with its pointer contacting the ball-joint stud. Move the stud up and down and note the movement. If it exceeds 0.004 in. (0.1mm), replace the ball-joint.

CROSSMEMBER

Removal/Installation

1. Loosen the front wheel nuts, jack up the front end of the car, place it on jackstands, and remove the front wheels.

NOTE: *Position the jackstands so they will not obstruct crossmember removal.*

2. Detach the inner ends of the transverse links from the crossmember. See Step 5, *Transverse Link Removal.*
3. Support the engine with a hoist (**Figure 15**).

NOTE: *Use a hoist which can be locked in one position, and which is capable of supporting the engine throughout this procedure. Hydraulic hoists, available from tool rental dealers, are effective and easy to use.*

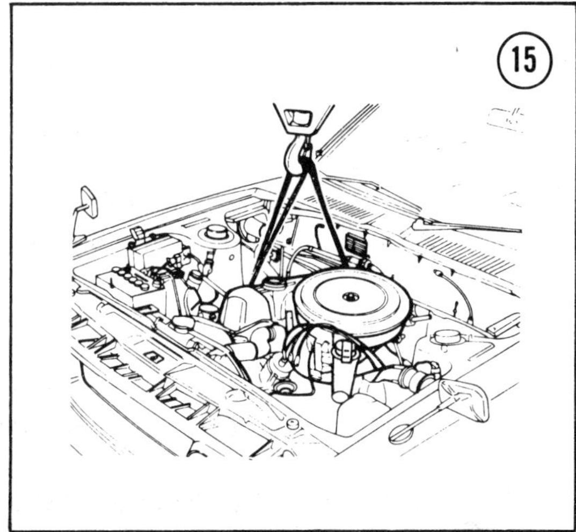

4. Unbolt the motor mounts from the crossmember (**Figure 16**).

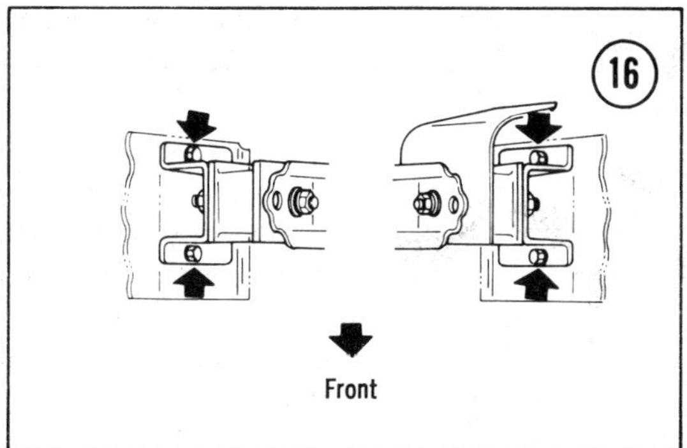

5. Make sure the hoist is supporting the engine fully, then remove the crossmember-to-frame bolts. **Figure 17** shows the bolts for one side.
6. Installation is the reverse of these steps. Tighten bolts to specifications (end of chapter).

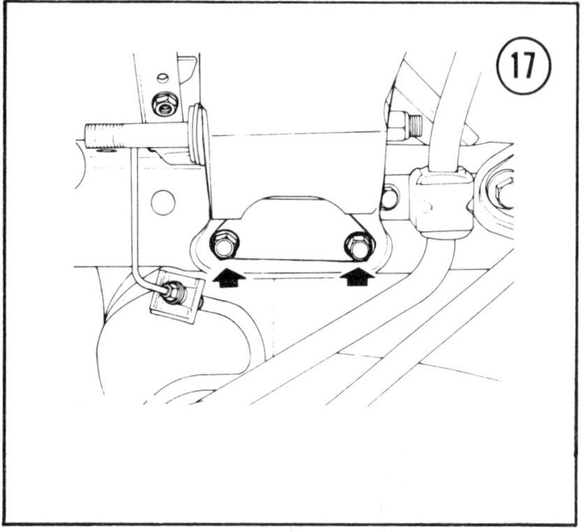

WHEEL BEARINGS

Removal

1. Loosen the front wheel nuts, jack up the front end of the vehicle, place it on jackstands, and remove the front wheels.
2. Remove the brake caliper as described in Chapter Ten.
3. Remove the grease cap from the wheel hub (**Figure 18**).

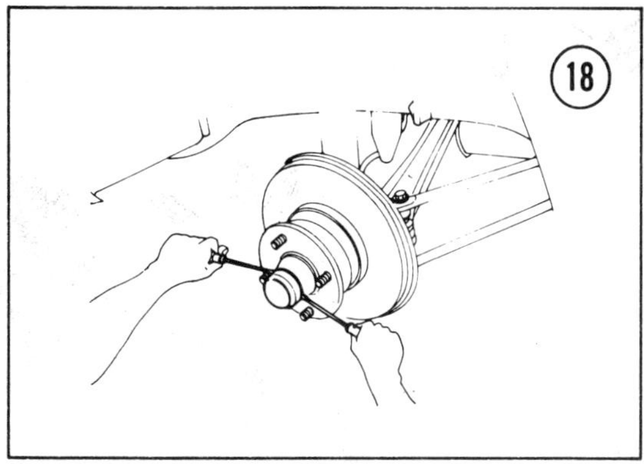

4. Remove the cotter pin from the wheel bearing locknut (early models) or stamped metal nut lock (later models). Remove the wheel bearing nut from the spindle.
5. Pull the hub and brake disc off the spindle (**Figure 19**).
6. Pry the grease seal out of the hub with a screwdriver. Remove the bearing cones.
7. Using a hammer and brass bar, tap the bearing outer races out of the hub (**Figure 20**).

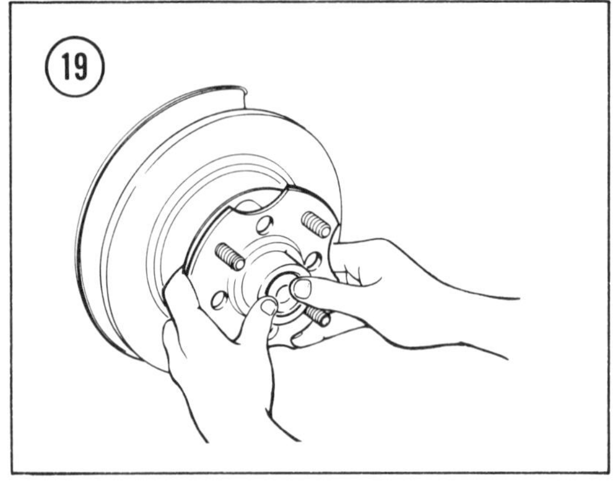

19

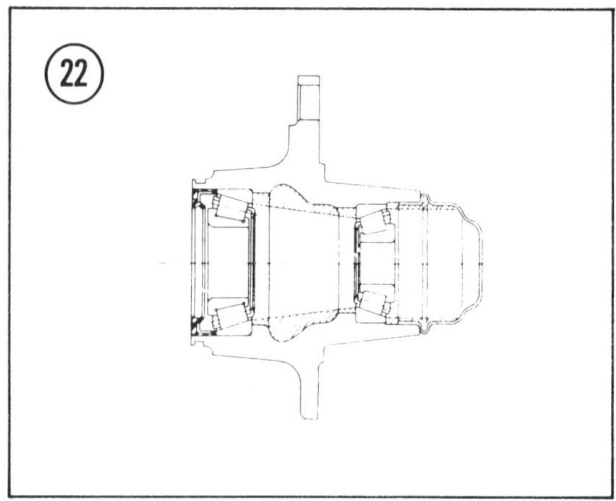

22

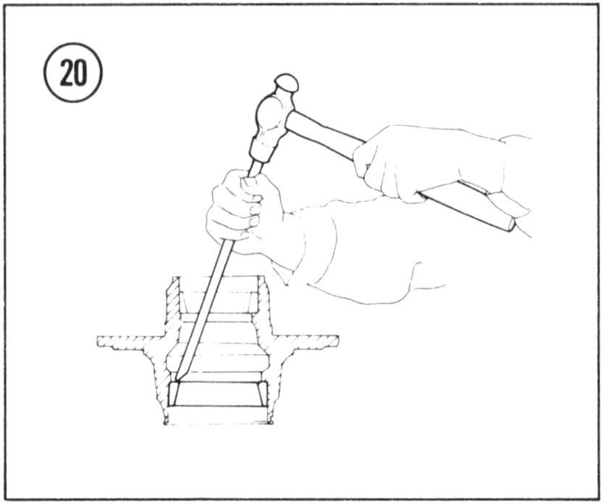

20

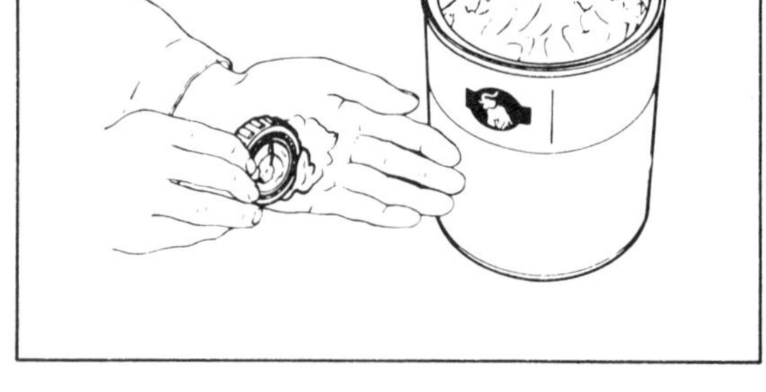

23

Inspection

1. Thoroughly clean the wheel bearings and hub in solvent.

2. Inspect inner and outer races for rust, galling, and the bluish tint that indicates overheating. Rotate the bearings and check for roughness and excessive noise. Compare the races and rollers to the defective bearing parts shown in **Figure 21**. Replace any bearings that have similar defects.

Installation

1. Tap the outer bearing races into place in the hub. Use a drift (such as a piece of pipe) with the same diameter as the outer race.

2. Fill the hub and grease cap (shaded areas in **Figure 22**). Use multipurpose lithium grease.

3. Work as much grease as possible between the wheel bearing rollers (**Figure 23**).

4. Install the inner wheel bearing in the hub, then install the grease seal. Coat the grease seal lips with grease.

5. Apply a light coat of grease to the bearing spindle, including the threaded area. Install the hub (together with the brake disc on cars).

6. Install the outer wheel bearing. Lightly grease the bearing washer and the spindle nut threads. Install the washer and nut.

7. Adjust wheel bearings as described in the following procedure.

Adjustment

1. On 1968-73 cars, tighten the spindle nut to 22-25 ft.-lb. (3.0-3.5 mkg). On 1974-76 cars, tighten spindle nut to 18-22 ft.-lb. (2.5-3.0 mkg).

2. Rotate the hub several turns in both directions, then retighten to specifications.

3. On 1968-73 cars, back off the locknut 90 degrees. On 1974-76 cars, back it off 60 degrees. Tighten the locknut until one of its cotter

21

a) Inner race flaking

b) Roller flaking

c) Chipped inner race

d) Chipped roller

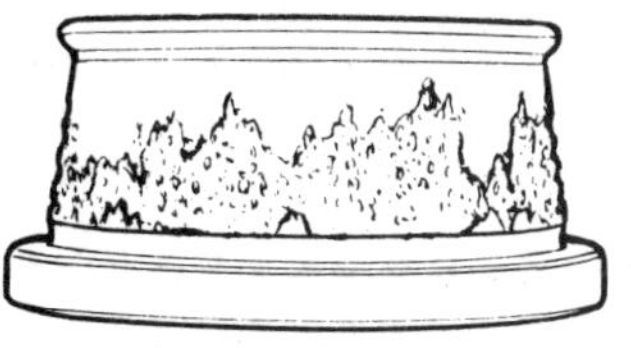

e) Recess on inner race

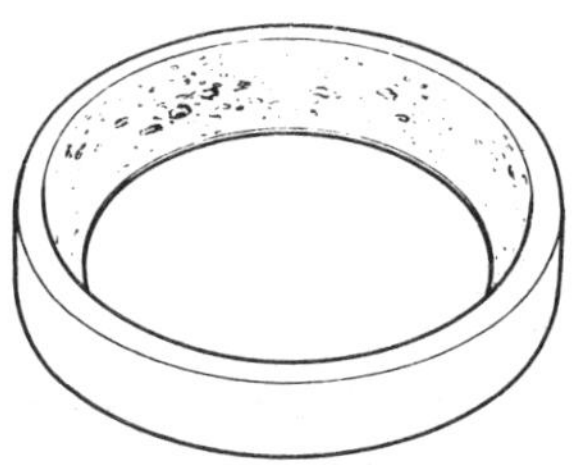

f) Recess on outer race

g) Recess on roller

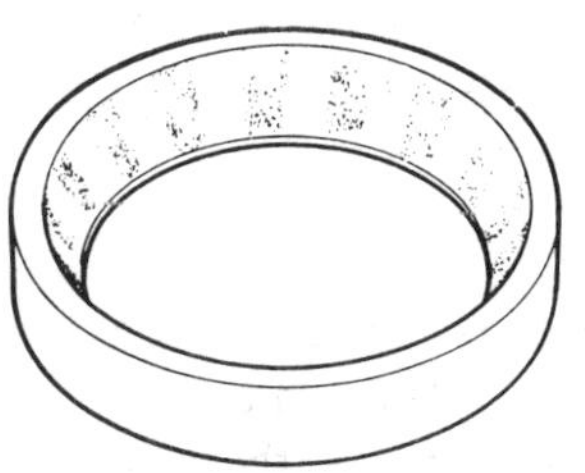

h) Rust on outer race

pin holes aligns with the cotter pin hole in the spindle. The locknut may be tightened as much as 15 degrees.

> NOTE: *Later models use a plain nut and a stamped metal nut lock. The adjustment procedure is the same as for castellated locknuts.*

4. Rotate the hub. Check for noise or rough movement. If these are present, remove the wheel bearings and check for foreign material.
5. If the hub rotates smoothly, attach a spring scale (**Figure 24**) and measure the force necessary to turn the hub. If within specifications (**Table 3**), install a cotter pin and spread it. See **Figure 25**.

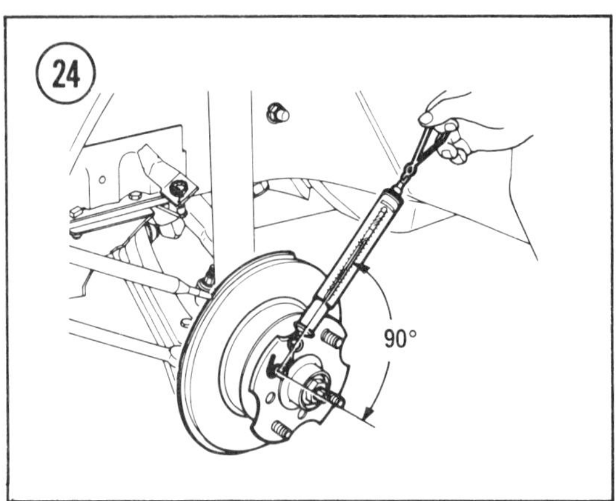

6. Install the grease cap in the hub.
7. Install the brake caliper assembly. See Chapter Ten.
8. Install the wheel(s) and lower the car.

STEERING

Steering Wheel Removal/Installation

1. Disconnect the negative cable from battery.
2. Turn the steering wheel to the straight ahead position.

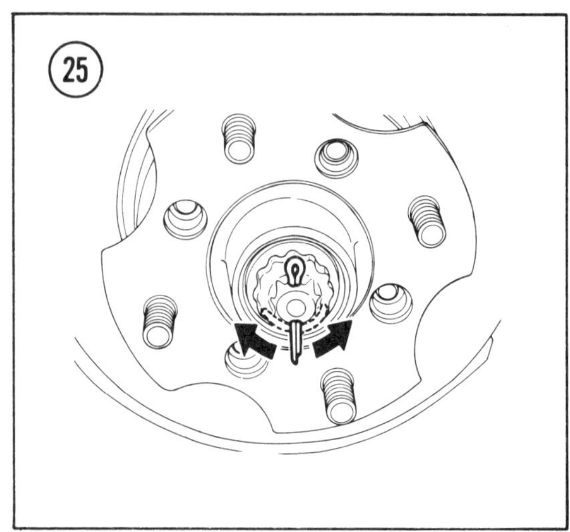

3. Remove the horn pad as follows:

   510—Push down, turn counterclockwise, and pull off.

   1973-74 610, 2-spoke steering wheels and steering wheels stamped NP—Pull horn pad off.

   1973-74 610, horn pad without letters NP—Push down, turn counterclockwise and pull off.

   1975-76 610 and all 710, 2-spoke steering wheels—Slide horn pad up, then pull off. See **Figure 26**.

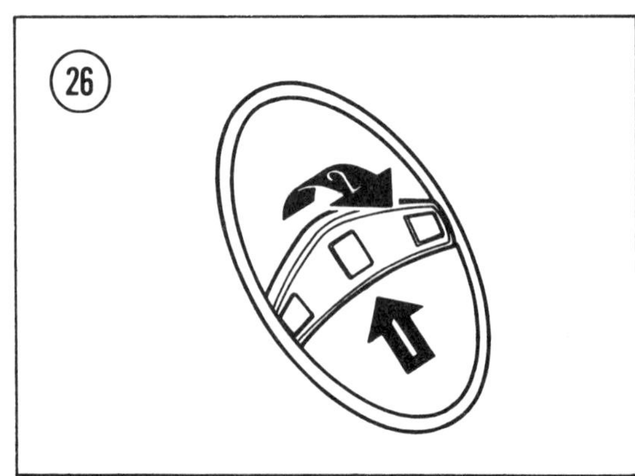

Table 3 WHEEL BEARING ROTATING FORCE

Vehicle	Used Parts	New Parts
510, 1973-74 610	1.5 lb.	2.7 lb. or less
1975-76 610, all 710	1.7 lb.	3.3 lb. or less

1975-76 610 and all 710, 3-spoke steering wheels—Pull horn pad off.

4. Remove the steering wheel nut.
5. Make alignment marks on steering wheel and column, then remove the wheel.
6. Installation is the reverse of these steps. Be sure to align the match marks on steering wheel and column. Tighten the steering wheel nut to specifications (end of chapter).

Steering Column Removal/Installation

Figure 27 shows a typical steering mechanism. Refer to it as needed for this procedure.

1. Remove the steering wheel as described previously.
2. Remove steering column shell (**Figure 28**).

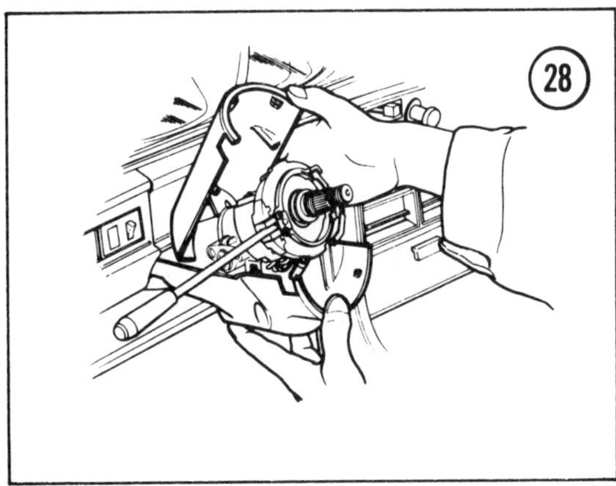

3. Remove 2 screws securing the turn signal switch. Take it off the steering column. See **Figure 29**.

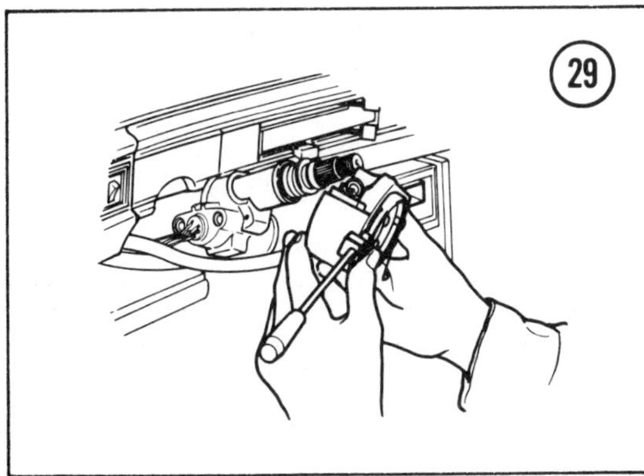

4. Remove 4 screws or bolts securing the steering column seal to the floor (**Figure 30**).

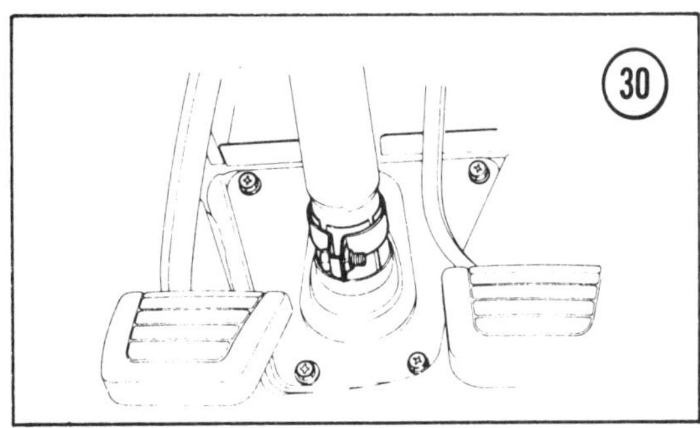

5. Remove 2 bolts or screws from the steering column clamp (**Figure 31**).

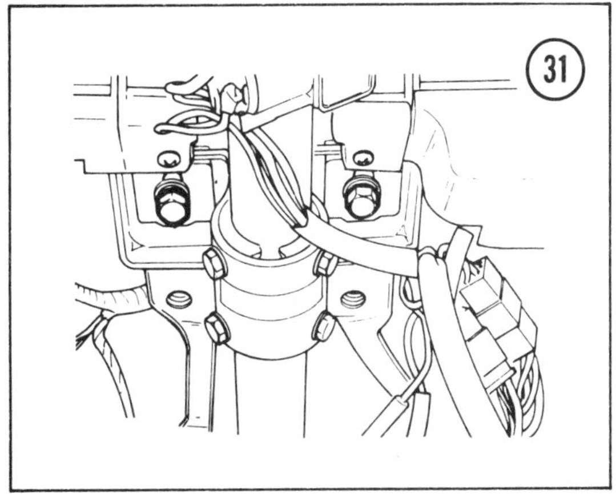

8. Remove the clamp bolt from the universal joint or rubber coupling (**Figure 32**).

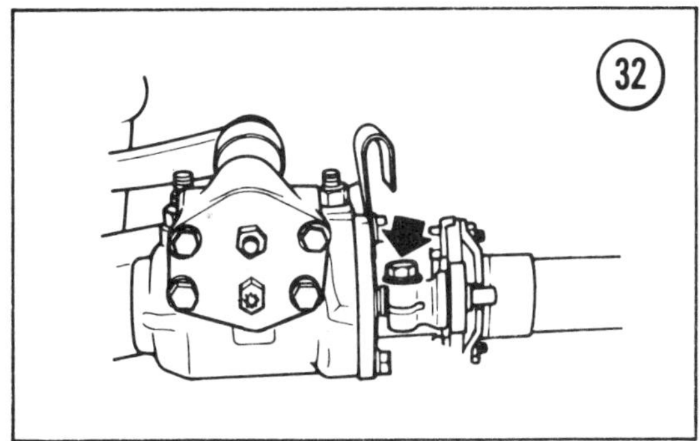

9. Remove the steering column into the passenger compartment.
10. Installation is the reverse of these steps. Tighten all nuts and bolts to specifications (end of chapter).

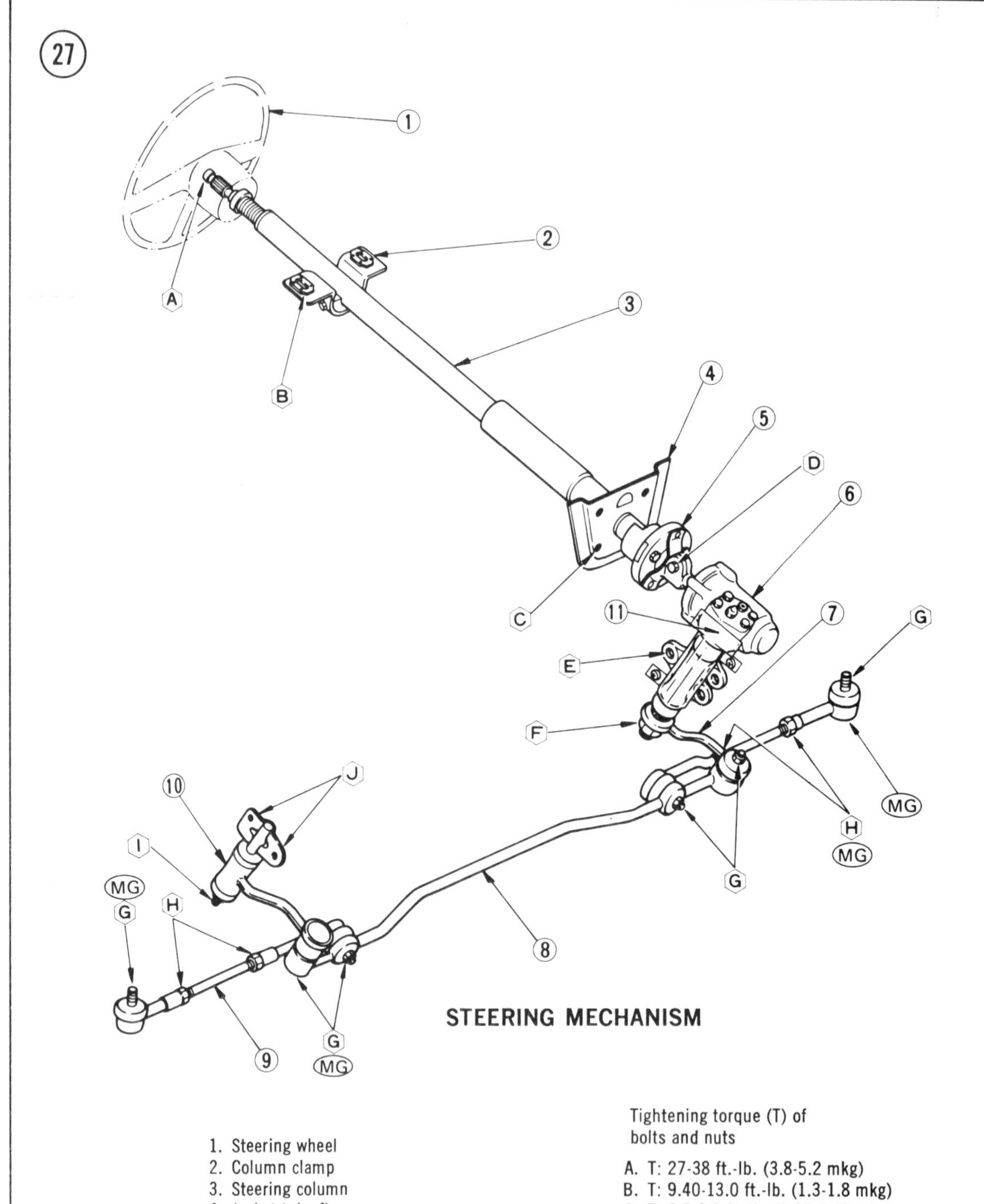

1. Steering wheel
2. Column clamp
3. Steering column
4. Jacket tube flange
5. Rubber coupling
6. Steering gear
7. Gear arm
8. Cross rod
9. Side rod
10. Idler arm
11. Heat shield plate

Tightening torque (T) of bolts and nuts

A. T: 27-38 ft.-lb. (3.8-5.2 mkg)
B. T: 9.40-13.0 ft.-lb. (1.3-1.8 mkg)
C. T: 2.5-3.3 ft.-lb. (0.35-0.45 mkg)
D. T: 29-36 ft.-lb. (4.0-5.0 mkg)
E. T: 51-58 ft.-lb. (7.0-8.0 mkg)
F. T: 101-ft.-lb. (14.0 mkg)
G. T: 40-72 ft.-lb. (5.5-10.0 mkg)
H. T: 40-55 ft.-lb. (5.5-7.6 mkg)
I. T: 29-36 ft.-lb. (4.0-5.0 mkg)
J. T: 32-44 ft.-lb. (4.4-6.1 mkg)

MG : Multi-purpose grease

Steering Gear Removal/Installation

1. If equipped with a heat shield, remove 2 screws and take it off (**Figure 33**).

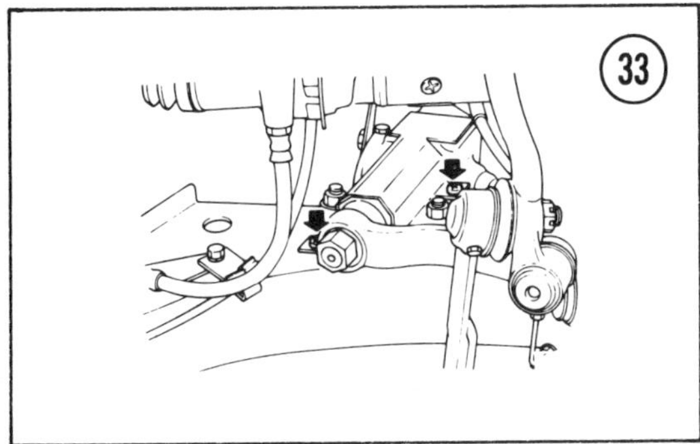

2. Remove the clamp bolt from the rubber coupling or universal joint (Figure 32).

3. Scribe match marks on the steering gear arm and steering gear. Detach the gear arm from the gear. Use a puller such as ST 27200000 (**Figure 34**) or a small gear puller.

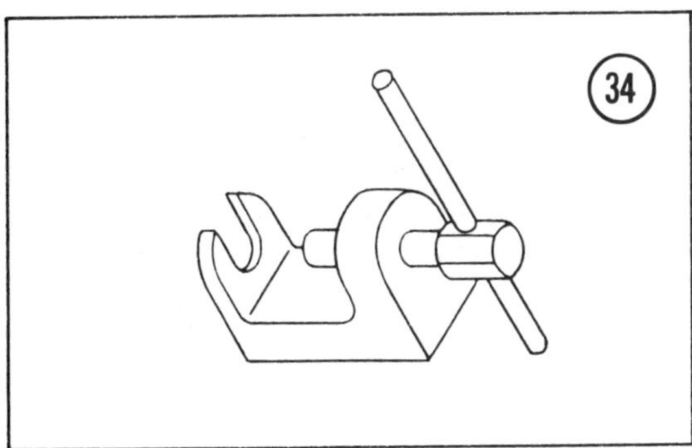

4. Remove 3 nuts and bolts securing the steering gear to the frame (**Figure 35**). The steering gear can then be removed.

5. Installation is the reverse of these steps. Tighten all nuts and bolts to specifications (end of chapter). Check steering gear oil level as described in Chapter Two.

STEERING LINKAGE

Figure 35 shows the steering linkage.

Lubrication

1. Remove the grease filler plugs from the tie rod ball-joints. Remove the plugs from the suspension ball-joints located under knuckle arms.

2. Install a grease nipple in place of each plug. The grease nipple may be transferred from one lubrication point to another.

3. Use a grease gun to inject new grease until the old grease is forced out.

4. Remove grease nipple. Install filler plug.

Overhaul

If the steering linkage shows signs of looseness, it should be overhauled as follows.

1. Loosen the front wheel nuts, jack up the front end of the car, place it on jackstands, and remove the front wheels.

2. Remove the cotter pins and locknuts from the outer tie rod ball-joints.

3. Detach the tie rod ball-joints from the knuckle arms. If available, use a fork-type separator such as ST 27850000 (**Figure 36**). If the special tool is not available, hold a large hammer or heavy steel body tool against the knuckle arm boss (the part the ball-joint stud goes through) and tap the other side of the boss with a hammer. Do not tap the ball-joint stud, ball-joint socket, or tie rod.

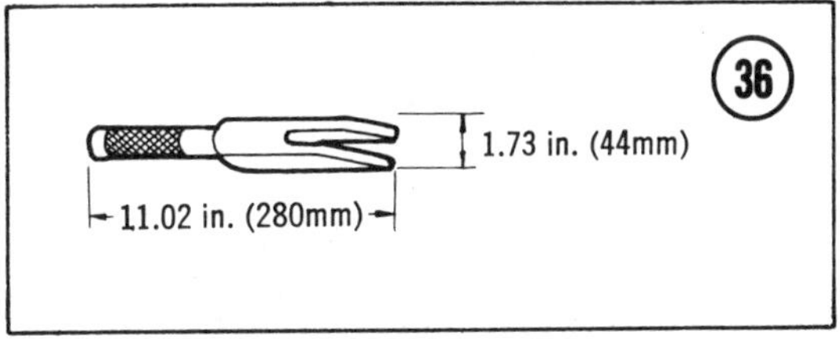

4. Scribe match marks on the steering gear arm and steering gear. Detach the gear arm from the gear with a puller such as ST 27200000 (Figure 34). Use a small gear puller if the special tool is not available.

5. Remove 2 bolts securing the idler arm assembly to the frame.

6. Remove the steering linkage as an assembly.

7. Separate the remaining steering linkage ball-joints as described in Step 3. Remove the nut from the idler arm assembly.

8. Clean metal parts in solvent. Do not immerse ball-joints. Wipe them with a rag dipped in solvent.

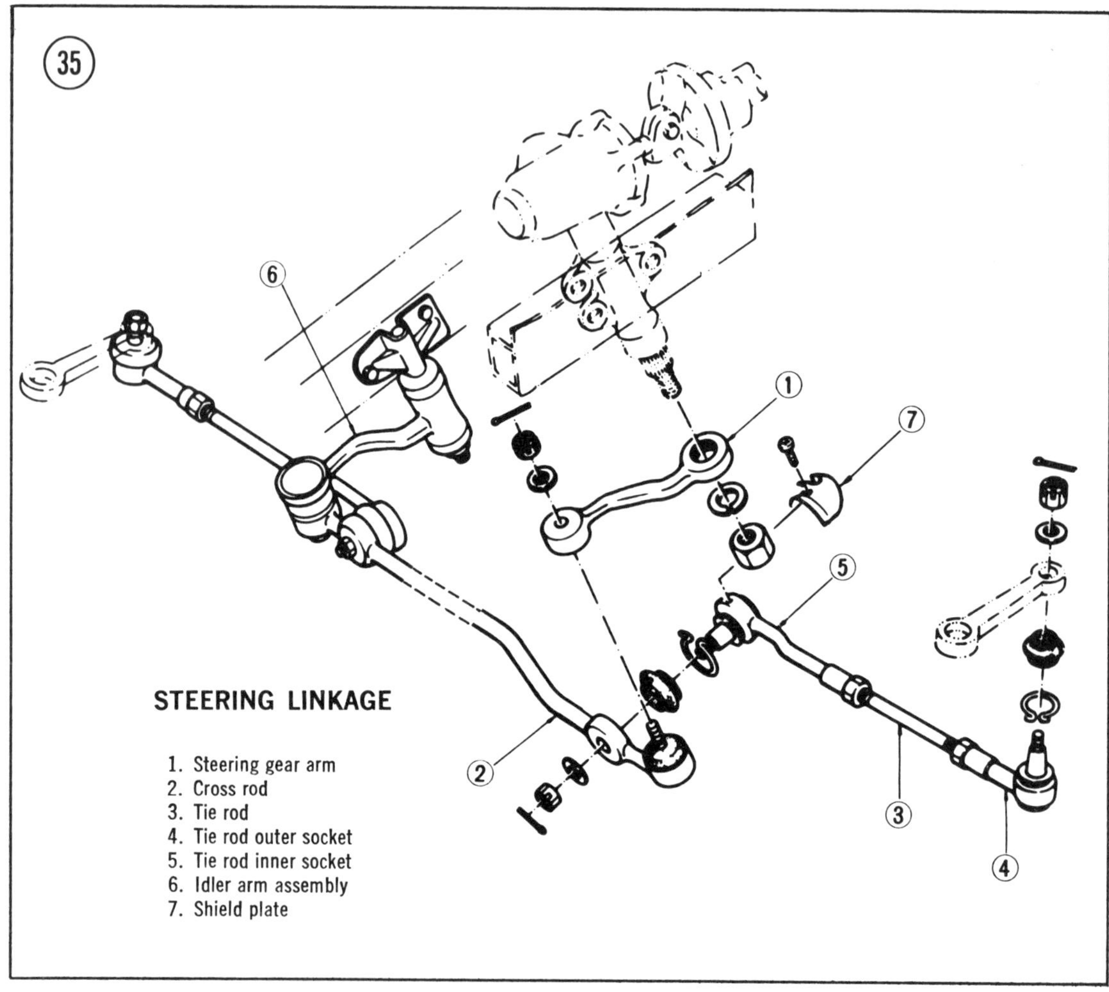

9. Check tie rods and the cross rod for bends, cracks, or damaged threads. Replace if these conditions are found.

10. Check the idler arm bushings for wear or damage. Replace as needed.

11. Place each ball-joint in a vise with the stud upward. Set up a dial gauge with its pointer contacting the end of the stud. Pull the stud up and down and measure the movement. This is axial play. Permissible play is 0.004-0.020 in. (0.1-0.5mm). Replace any ball-joints with play outside this range.

12. Assemble and install by reversing Steps 1-7. Tighten all nuts and bolts to specifications (end of chapter).

Table 1 FRONT SUSPENSION AND STEERING SPECIFICATIONS

Steering	
Type	Recirculating ball
Gear ratio	
510 and 1973 610	15.0:1
1974-76 610 and 710	16.48:1
Caster	
510	
Sedans	1° 35′
Wagons through 1972	1° 05′
1973 wagon	1° 40′
610	
1973 sedan, hardtop	45′ to 2° 15′
1973 wagon	55′ to 2° 25′
1974-75, all	1° 15′ to 2° 45′
1976, all	1° 05′ to 2° 35′
710	
1974-75	1° 10′ to 2° 40′
1976	1° 05′ to 2° 35′
Camber	
510	
Sedans	25′
Wagons through 1972	10′
1973 wagon	35′
610	
1973 sedan, hardtop	1° 00′ to 2° 30′
1973 wagon	1° 10′ to 2° 40′
1974-75 sedan, hardtop	1° 15′ to 2° 45′
1974-75 wagon	1° 30′ to 3° 00′
1976, all	1° 15′ to 2° 45′
710	
1974-75	1° 25′ to 2° 55′
1976	1° 15′ to 2° 45′
Toe-In	
510	
Sedans	0.118-0.236 in. (3-6mm)
Wagons through 1972	0.079-0.197 in. (2-5mm)
1973 wagon	0.158-0.276 in. (4-7mm)

(continued)

Table 1 **FRONT SUSPENSION AND STEERING SPECIFICATIONS** (continued)

Toe-in (continued)	
610	
1973 sedan, hardtop	0.236-0.254 in. (6-9mm)
1973 wagon	0.315-0.433 in. (8-11mm)
1974-75, all	0.433-0.551 in. (11-14mm)
1976, radial ply tires	0.16-0.24 in. (4-6mm)
1976, bias ply tires	0.24-0.31 in. (6-8mm)
710	
1974	0.5551-0.669 in. (14-17mm)
1975	0.315-0.433 in. (8-11mm)
1976, radial ply tires	0.16-0.24 in. (4-6mm)
1976, bias ply tires	0.24-0.31 in. (6-8mm)
Steering Axis Inclination	
610	
1973 sedan, hardtop	6° 21′ to 7° 50′
1973 wagon	6° 10′ to 7° 40′
1974-75 sedan, hardtop	5° 55′ to 7° 25′
1974-75 wagon	5° 45′ to 7° 15′
1976, all	6° 15′ to 7° 45′
710	
1974-75	6° 25′
1976	6° 15′ to 7° 45′
Steering Lock Angles	
510	
Inside wheel	38°
Outside wheel	31° 40′
610 and 710, 1973-74	
Inside wheel	37-38°
Outside wheel	30° 42′ to 32° 42′
610 and 710, 1975-76	
Inside wheel	32-33°
Outside wheel	20° 30′ to 31° 30′

Table 2 TIGHTENING TORQUES

	ft.-lb.	mkg
Stabilizer to transverse link	9-12	1.2-1.7
Stabilizer to frame	10-13	1.4-1.8
Tension rod to bracket		
All except 1976 610	33-40	4.5-5.5
1976 610	36-40	5.0-5.5
Tension rod to transverse link	35-46	4.9-6.3
Tension rod bracket to frame*	37-50	5.1-6.9
Transverse link to crossmember	65-72	9-10
Crossmember to frame		
510	14-18	1.9-2.5
610, 710	29-36	4-5
Ball-joint to transverse link**	14-18	1.9-2.5
Ball-joint to knuckle arm	40-55	5.5-7.6
Strut to knuckle arm		
510	44-58	6-8
610 and 710	53-72	7.3-9.9
Strut to body		
510	28-38	3.9-5.2
610 and 710	18-25	2.5-3.5
Steering gear arm nut		
510	90-101	12.5-14.0
610 and 710	101	14
Gear housing to body		
510	72	10
1973 610	44-58	6-8
1974-76 610, 710	51-58	7-8
Idler arm nut		
510	40-55	5.5-7.6
610 and 710	32-44	4.4-6.1
Idler arm to body	32-44	4.4-6.1
Steering linkage ball-joint nuts		
510 and 1973 610	40-55	5.5-7.6
1974-76 610 and 710	40-72	5.5-10.0
Steering column clamp bolts		
All except 1976 610	10-13	1.4-1.8
1976 610	6-8	0.8-1.1
Column to gear housing U-joint clamp bolt (510 only)	22	3
Column to gear housing rubber coupling clamp bolt (610 and 710)	29-36	4-5
Rubber coupling securing bolts or nuts (610 and 710 only)	11-16	1.5-2.2
Steering wheel nut	29-36	4-5

*Does not apply to 510.

**On 710's, bolt shared with tension rod is tightened to 35-46 ft.-lb.

12

SUPPLEMENT

1977 SERVICE INFORMATION

The following supplement covers 1977 model changes. Use it together with the main body of the book to service 1977 models.

CHAPTER TWO

LUBRICATION, MAINTENANCE, AND TUNE-UP

VACUUM LINES

Check vacuum lines for cracks or deterioration. **Figure 1** shows the lines used on California models; **Figure 2** shows the non-California arrangement.

CARBURETOR ADJUSTMENT

Datsun recommends use of a CO meter to set idle mixture, especially on California models. While mixture can be set without a CO meter, the instrument is necessary to ensure that exhaust emissions are within legal limits.

1. Disconnect the air hose from the check valve. See **Figure 3**.

2. Warm the engine to normal operating temperature, then connect a tune-up tachometer.

3. Race the engine 2 or 3 times at 1,500-2,000 rpm, then let it idle for one minute.

4. On automatic transmissions, block the wheels so the car will not roll forward; then shift to DRIVE.

5. If a CO meter is available, set idle speed at 600 rpm. **Figure 4** shows the adjusting screws. Set CO percentages at 0.3-2.0 percent with the mixture screw. If this changes idle speed, reset it with the idle speed screw.

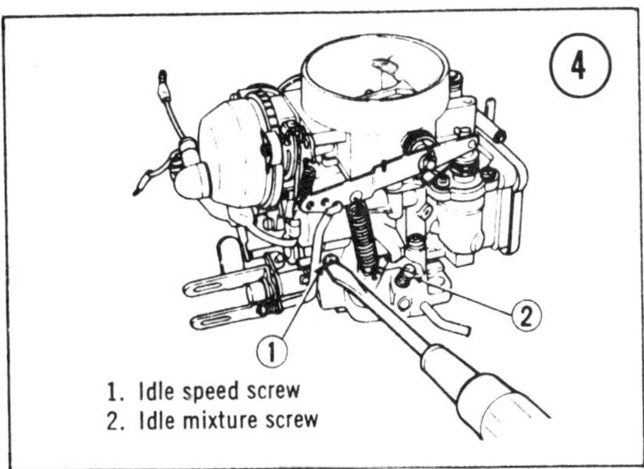

1. Idle speed screw
2. Idle mixture screw

6. If a CO meter is not available, set idle speed at 650 rpm. Turn the mixture screw to obtain the fastest smooth idle. If this changes idle speed, reset it to 650 rpm with the idle speed screw. Then turn the *mixture* screw clockwise (for a leaner mixture) until idle speed drops 45-55 rpm's.

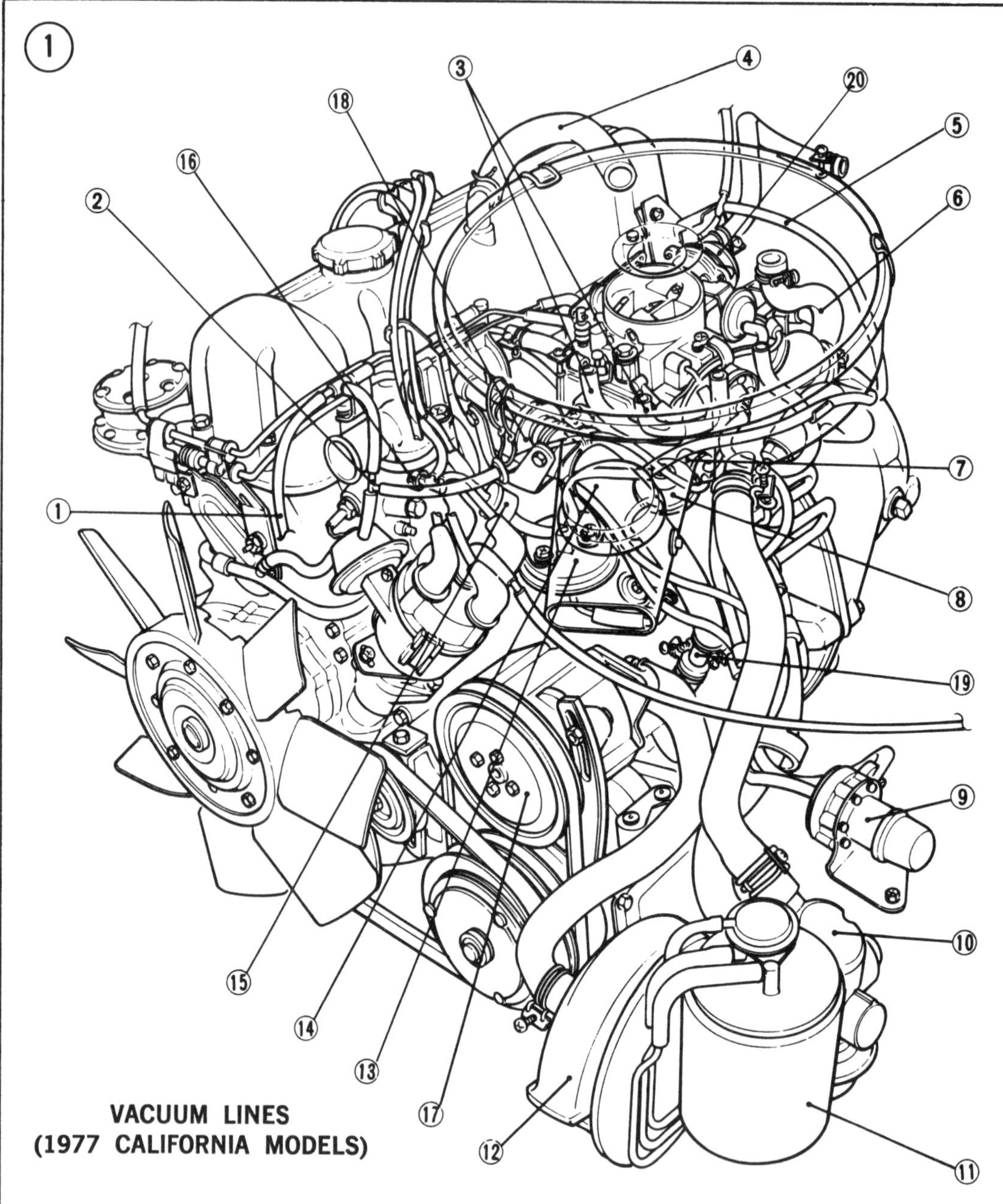

VACUUM LINES
(1977 CALIFORNIA MODELS)

1. Vacuum tube for carbon canister
2. 3-way connector
3. Hose for altitude compensator
4. PCV gas hose
5. Vacuum tube for AB valve
6. AB valve
7. Vacuum switching valve (M/T only)
8. EGR control valve
9. BCDD vacuum control valve
10. CAC valve
11. Carbon canister
12. Air pump air cleaner
13. BPT valve
14. ATC air cleaner
15. Vacuum delay valve
16. Thermal vacuum valve
17. Air pump for AIS
18. Check valve for AIS
19. 3-way connector for AIS
20. Automatic choke

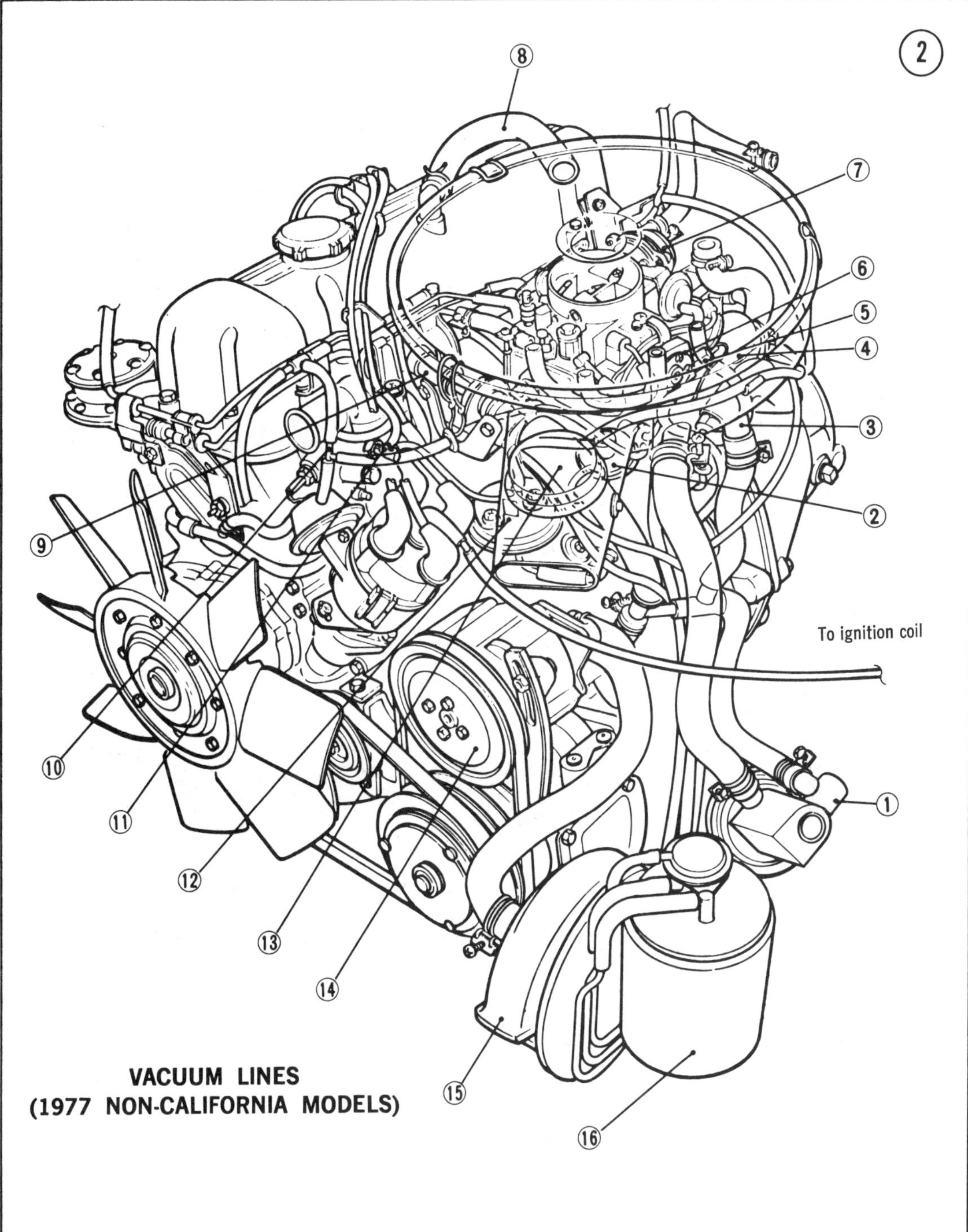

VACUUM LINES
(1977 NON-CALIFORNIA MODELS)

1. Air control valve
2. EGR control valve
3. Air relief valve
4. AB valve
5. BCDD solenoid valve
6. BCDD
7. Automatic choke
8. PCV hose
9. Check valve for AIS
10. 3-way connector (M/T)
11. Thermal vacuum valve
12. BPT valve
13. ATC air cleaner
14. Air pump for AIS
15. Air pump air cleaner
16. Canister

CHAPTER FIVE

FUEL AND EXHAUST SYSTEMS

ALTITUDE COMPENSATOR

The 1977 altitude compensator (**Figure 5**) is controlled manually. At 4,000 ft. (1,219 m) above sea level, the lever should be set to the "H" position. This admits more air to the carburetor, compensating for the air's thinness. At lower altitudes, the lever should be set to the "L" position.

To test the altitude compensator, disconnect the air lines from the carburetor. With the lever in the "L" position, it should not be possible to suck air into the lines. With the lever in the "H" position, this should be possible. If the altitude compensator does not perform properly, replace it.

CARBURETOR

Fast Idle Adjustment

1. Place the fast idle screw on the first step of the fast idle cam. See **Figures 6 and 7**.

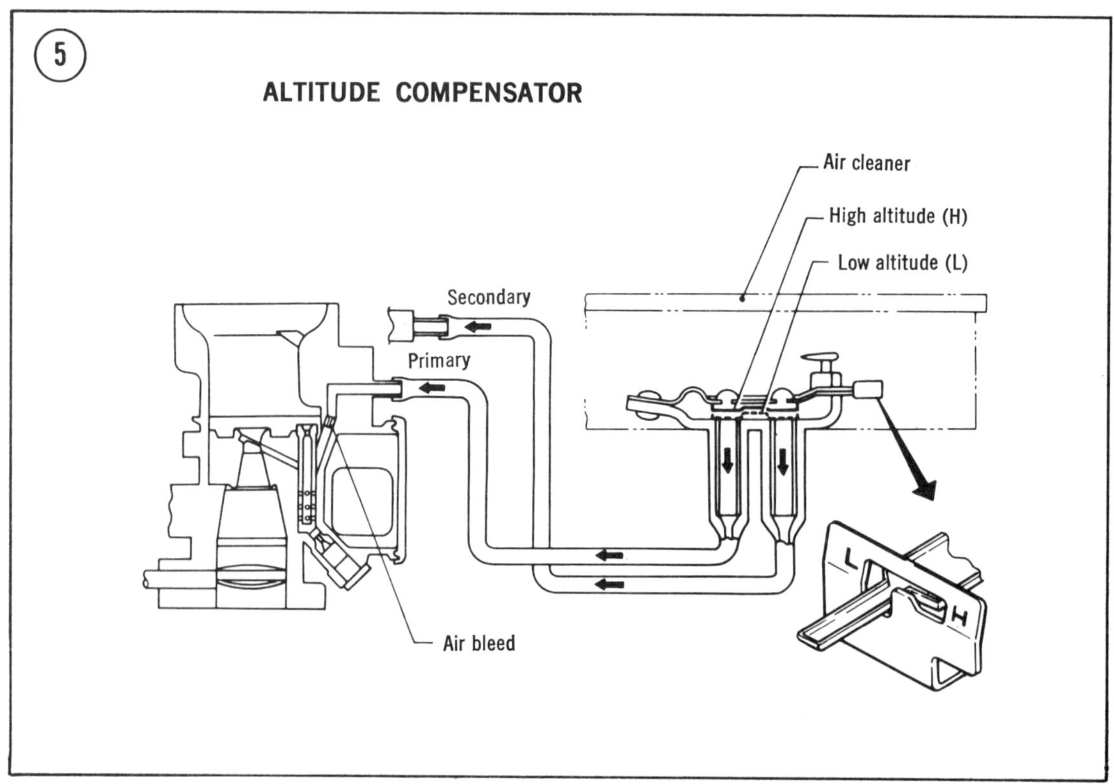

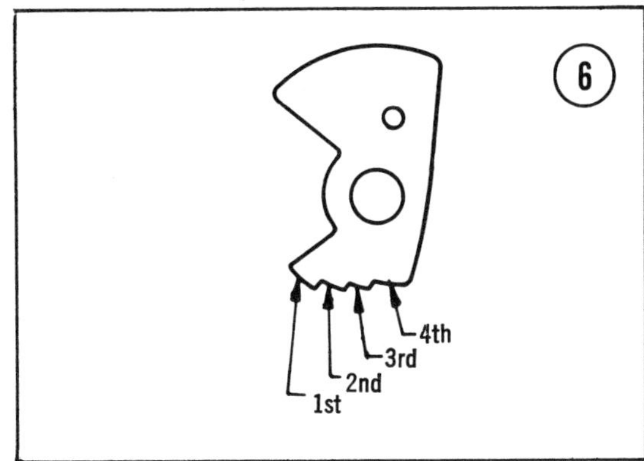

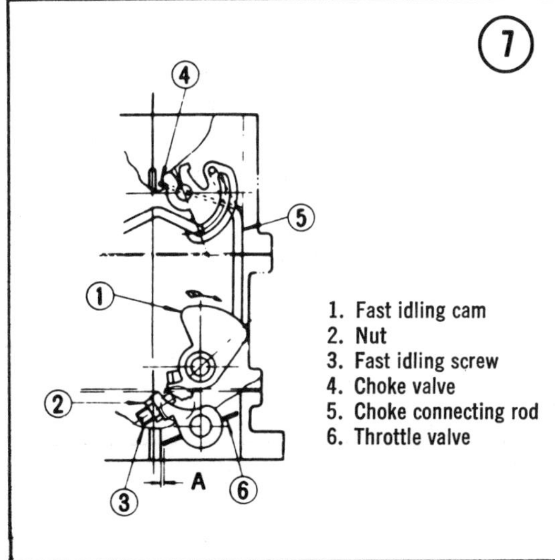

2. Measure the gap between primary throttle valve and carburetor bore (dimension "A", **Figure 8**). It should be 0.052-0.058 in. (1.33-1.47mm) on manual transmission models or 0.062-0.068 in. (1.58-1.72mm) on automatics.

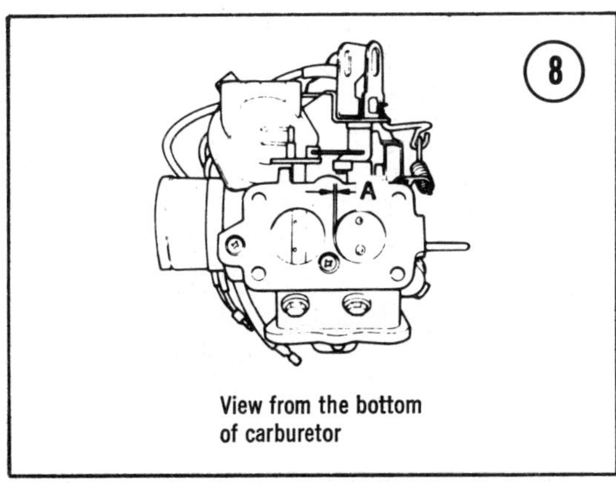

View from the bottom of carburetor

3. If the gap is incorrect, loosen the locknut on the fast idle screw (**Figure 7**). Turn the screw to change the gap, then tighten the locknut.

AIR INJECTION SYSTEM

The California version (**Figure 9**) uses a combined air control valve in place of the air relief and emergency air relief valves used on 1976 models. The non-California version (**Figure 10**) uses the air relief valve. These valves vent excess pump air to the air cleaner or the atmosphere.

Combined Air Control Valve Test

1. Make sure the valve hoses are in good condition.

2. Warm the engine to normal operating temperature.

3. Disconnect and plug the combined air control (CAC) valve vacuum hose (**Figure 11**). Make sure air blows from the CAC valve when the engine idles.

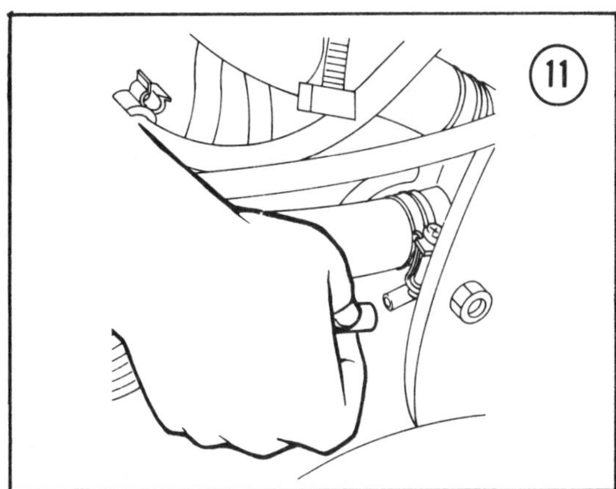

4. Connect a vacuum pump to the vacuum hose fitting (**Figure 12**). Vacuum pumps are available at auto parts stores.

5. With the engine idling, raise vacuum to 8-10 in. (200-250mm). Increase engine speed to 3,000 rpm. There should not be any air flowing from the CAC valve.

6. Disconnect and plug the check valve air hose (**Figure 13**). With vacuum at 8-10 in. (200-250mm), and engine speed at 3,000 rpm, air should again flow from the CAC valve.

9

AIR INJECTION SYSTEM (CALIFORNIA MODELS)

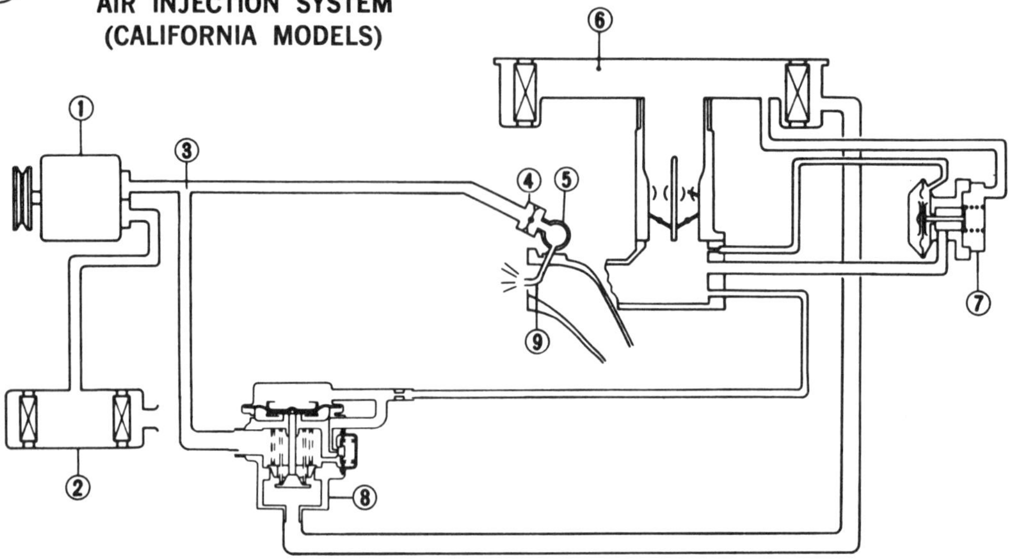

1. Air pump
2. Air pump air cleaner
3. 3-way connector
4. Check valve
5. Air gallery pipe
6. Air cleaner
7. Anti-backfire valve
8. CAC valve
9. Injection nozzle

10

AIR INJECTION SYSTEM (NON-CALIFORNIA MODELS)

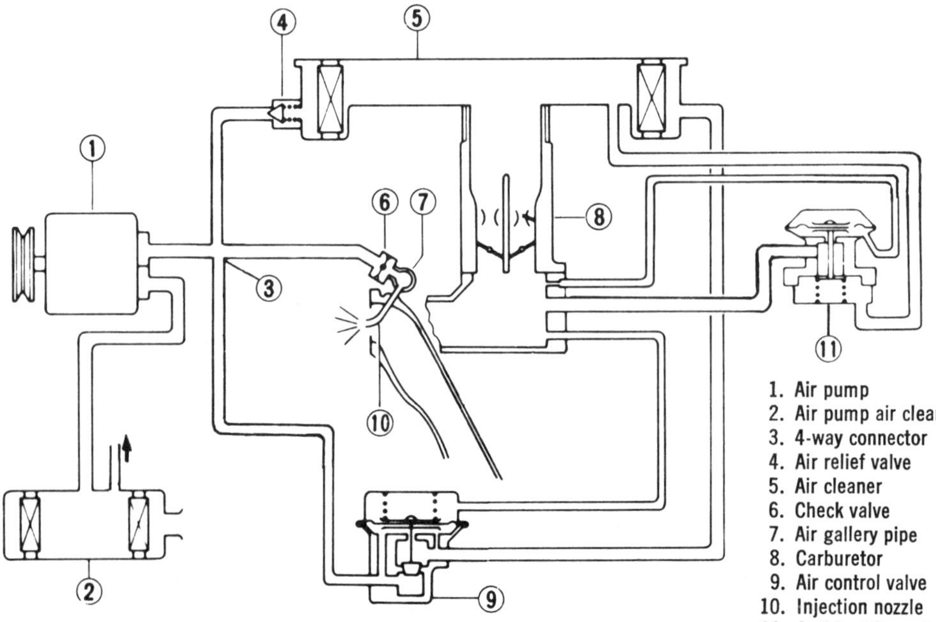

1. Air pump
2. Air pump air cleaner
3. 4-way connector
4. Air relief valve
5. Air cleaner
6. Check valve
7. Air gallery pipe
8. Carburetor
9. Air control valve
10. Injection nozzle
11. Anti-backfire valve

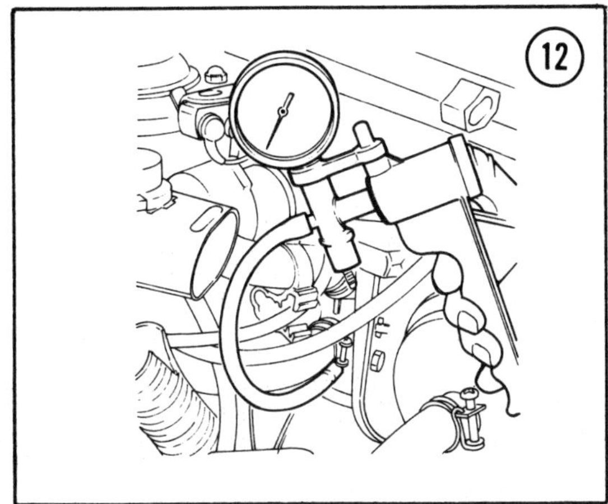

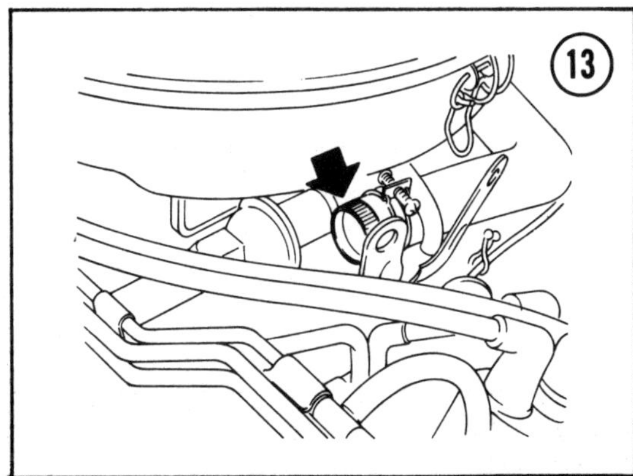

Air Relief Valve Test

1. Warm the engine to normal operating temperature.
2. Disconnect the check valve hose and the air control valve hose from the 4-way connector (**Figure 10**). Plug the connector openings.
3. Run the engine at approximately 3,000 rpm. Check for air flow from the relief valve (**Figure 14**). If air does not flow, replace relief valve.

EGR SYSTEM

The exhaust gas recirculation system (**Figure 15**) for the 1977 model includes a back pressure transducer (BPT) and a vacuum delay valve. The back pressure transducer regulates exhaust gas flow according to exhaust system back pressure. The vacuum delay valve prevents any rapid drop on EGR control line vacuum.

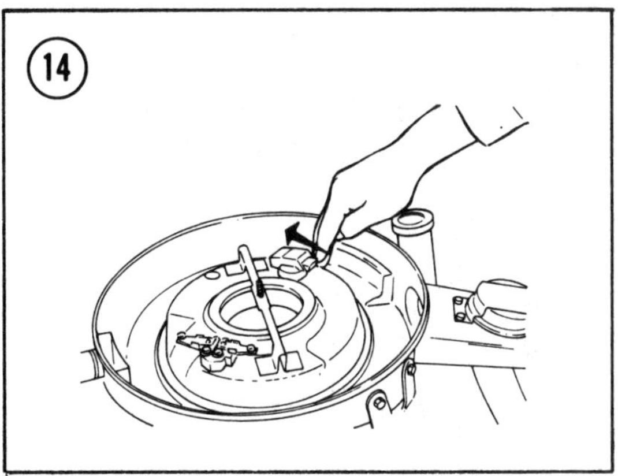

BPT Test

1. Disconnect the BPT hoses.
2. Plug one of the upper ports of the BPT. Attach a hose to the other. See **Figure 16**.

The system test is the same as for earlier models, with the addition of the following tests for the BPT and vacuum delay valve.

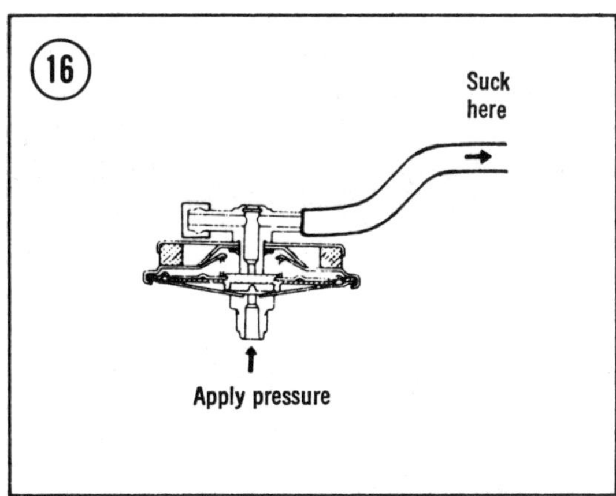

3. Apply a slight air pressure to the bottom of the BPT, and try to suck air through the hose. This should not be possible. If it is, replace the BPT.

Vacuum Delay Valve Test

Disconnect the hoses from the vacuum delay valve. It should be possible to blow air through the valve from the back pressure transducer side, but not from the thermal vacuum valve side (colored brown). If the valve does not perform properly, replace it.

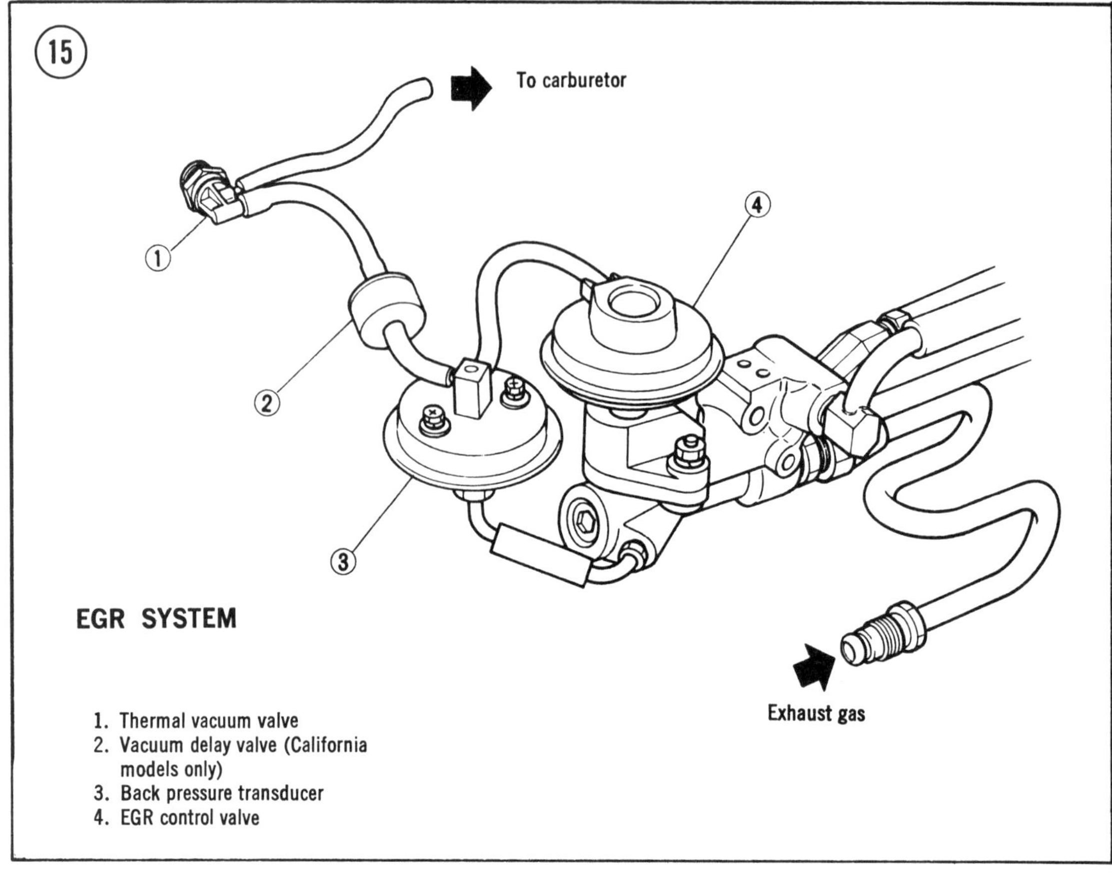

EGR SYSTEM

1. Thermal vacuum valve
2. Vacuum delay valve (California models only)
3. Back pressure transducer
4. EGR control valve

CHAPTER SIX

COOLING SYSTEM AND HEATER

Cooling system capacity for the 1977 model is 8⅛ qt. (7.7 liters).

CHAPTER SEVEN

ELECTRICAL SYSTEM

SPARK TIMING CONTROL SYSTEM

This system (**Figure 17**) is used on manual transmission models only. It consists of a transmission switch, vacuum switching valve, and related tubing. In any gear but fourth, the system opens the distributor vacuum line to air, eliminating vacuum advance. In fourth gear, the vacuum switching valve closes and ignition timing advances.

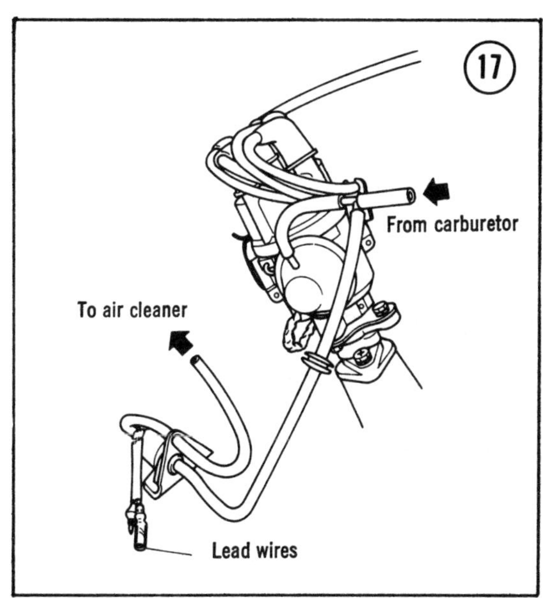

System Test

1. Make sure the system's wires and hoses are in good condition and properly connected.
2. Connect a timing light and tune-up tachometer to the engine.
3. Have an assistant run the engine at about 2,000 rpm while moving the shift lever through the gears. Note ignition timing. It should be more advanced in fourth gear than in any other.

WARNING
Make sure that your assistant does not release the clutch pedal while shifting, or the car will jump forward.

If timing advances in fourth gear, the system is working properly.

4. If timing does not change, disconnect the vacuum switching valve green wire. Connect the wire directly to the positive battery terminal with a jumper wire. See **Figure 18**.

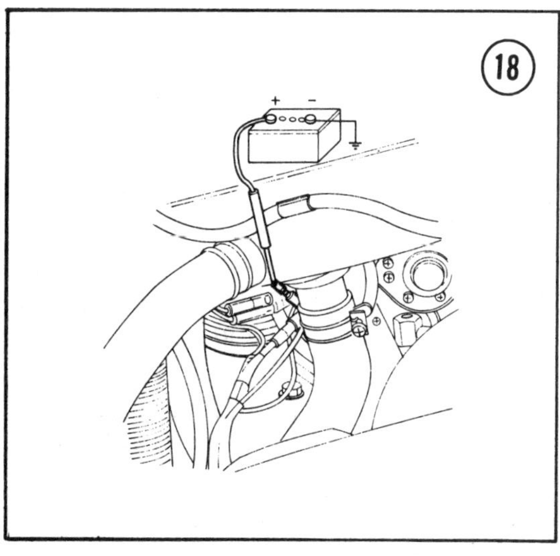

5. Have an assistant run the engine at 2,000 rpm. Ignition timing should advance and retard as the jumper wire is connected and disconnected. If it does not, replace the vacuum switching valve.

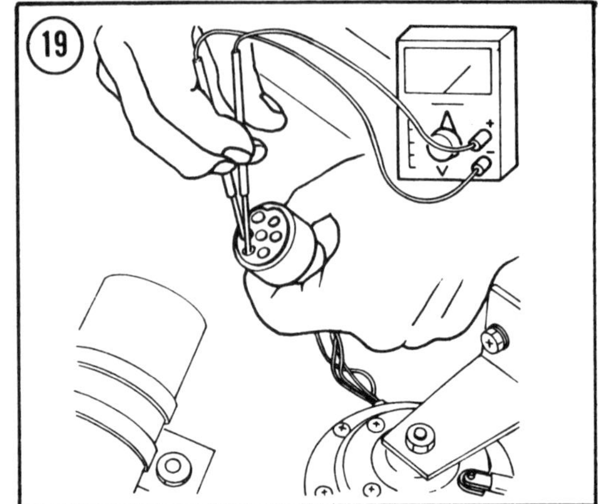
19

6. If the vacuum switching valve is good, test the wiring. Switch the ignition on (but do not start the engine) and connect a voltmeter between test connector terminals "A" and "B". See **Figure 19**. The voltmeter should indicate 12 volts in fourth gear, and zero volts in all other gears. If it does not, check for a blown fuse or bad wiring.

INDEX

V

W

NOTES

NOTES